CW01262544

The Mathematics of Options Trading

C. B. Reehl

McGraw-Hill
New York   Chicago   San Francisco   Lisbon   London   Madrid
Mexico City   Milan   New Delhi   San Juan   Seoul
Singapore   Sydney   Toronto

The McGraw·Hill Companies

Copyright © 2005 by The McGraw-Hill Companies, Inc. All rights reserved. Printed in the United States of America. Except as permitted under the United States Copyright Act of 1976, no part of this publication may be reproduced or distributed in any form or by any means, or stored in a data base or retrieval system, without the prior written permission of the publisher.

1 2 3 4 5 6 7 8 9 0   DOC/DOC   0 9 8 7 6 5

P/N 144529-3
PART OF
ISBN 0-07-144528-5

McGraw-Hill books are available at special quantity discounts to use as premiums and sales promotions, or for use in corporate training programs. For more information, please write to the Director of Special Sales, Professional Publishing, McGraw-Hill, Two Penn Plaza, New York, NY 10121-2298. Or contact your local bookstore.

This publication is designed to provide accurate and authoritative information in regard to the subject matter covered. It is sold with the understanding that neither the author nor the publisher is engaged in rendering legal, accounting, futures/securities trading, or other professional service. If legal advice or other expert assistance is required, the services of a competent professional person should be sought.

—From a Declaration of Principles jointly adopted
by a Committee of the American Bar Association
and a Committee of Publishers

This book is printed on recycled, acid-free paper containing a minimum of 50% recycled, de-inked fiber.

Library of Congress Cataloging-in-Publication Data

Reehl, C. B.
    The mathematics of options trading / by C. B. Reehl.
      p. cm.
    Includes index.
    ISBN 0-07-144528-5 (hardcover : alk. paper)
  1. Options (Finance)—Mathematical models. 2. Portfolio management—Mathematical models. I. Title.

    HG6024.A3.R44   2004
    332.64'53'015195—dc22

2004016634

To my wife and partner, Kathryn, without whose encouragement and assistance, this book would not have been possible

CONTENTS

PREFACE   vii

Chapter 1
The Wall Street Casinos: A Typology of Financial Products   1

Chapter 2
Statistics, Probability, and Other Wonders   29

Chapter 3
Visualizing Option Structures and Strategies   69

Chapter 4
Mathematical Expectation and Optimal Position Size   123

Chapter 5
Volatility and Sensitivity to Change   153

Chapter 6
Determining Expected Results of Options Trades: Naked Options and Basic Spreads   185

Chapter 7

Determining Expected Results of Options Trades: Straddles and Other Strategies   225

Chapter 8

Other Useful Techniques   253

Chapter 9

Putting It All Together   289

Appendix A: Sample Output from *Expectation.exe*   321

Appendix B: Sample Output from *DailyCheck.exe*   341

Appendix C: Details of Test Period Trades   355

INDEX   365

PREFACE

Why a book on options math? Trading options is quite different from buying and selling other financial instruments. For analytical purposes, options have the properties of a "closed system." There is a beginning (inception or trade date) and an end (expiration date), and all possible results of an options trade may be modeled mathematically. Options trades imply a forecast of the *magnitude* of a price change in the underlying instrument—whether or not the trader consciously thinks about it. Depending on the strategy employed, a forecast of price *direction* may or may not be implied. Contrast this with trading stocks, which is simply an open-ended exercise—success being entirely dependent on correctly forecasting the direction of price moves in a never-ending time series.

Almost anyone can trade anything with little or no knowledge of the thing being traded or how best to trade it. Notice I did not say "trade profitably." Absent clairvoyance, one simply cannot trade options profitably on a consistent basis without having some basic math skills. The study of options necessarily involves some mathematical sophistication despite the claims of hucksters selling strategies requiring only "10 minutes of your time per day—and I'll make you rich." The available literature falls generally into three groups—books exhibiting mathematical illiteracy but sometimes entertaining (and occasionally dangerous), worthwhile books favoring a nonnumerical approach, and otherwise excellent texts containing mathematical treatments far beyond the average reader's ability to comprehend. This book is designed to blur these distinctions by actually teaching you all the math you need to understand options.

This book is also a reference work—enabling you to customize your own programs or spreadsheets from the numerous solved examples presented. On completion, you will have learned how to determine the expected results of an options trade *before* committing capital. Moreover, should you wish to enter the trade, you will have learned how to determine the optimal position size. The coverage of these two concepts, expected results and optimal position size, is based on original, never-before-published work. A CD accompanying this book contains two computer programs for analyzing opportunities for trading options using numerous different strategies.

Along the way, many references will be made to other forms of financial adventuring (e.g., casino gambling, sports betting, etc.) not only because they are excellent teaching devices but also because they represent near perfect analogs of financial market participation. Whether one seeks to gain an "edge" in gambling situations or attempts to maximize "excess risk-adjusted returns" on Wall Street, the motives are identical. The difference between paying *vigorish* to a sports book and paying commissions to a stock broker is not worthy of mention.

After many years of observing the methods by which individuals and institutions risk their money, I remain convinced that random chance plays the single most significant role in the majority of outcomes. Whether these risks take the form of investment in equities, speculation in commodity futures, capitalization of new businesses, or simply wagering on a sporting event, it appears to make little difference. This thesis differs markedly from widely held beliefs that success is a function of some identifiable combination of art and science that may be applied consistently while ignoring the influence of random events. The fundamentalists cling tenaciously to their cause-and-effect relationships; the technicians embrace pattern-generating time series of past performance data; the entrepreneurs boast of their ability to understand certain markets, thus enabling them to outpace the competition; and the gamblers believe in runs of luck. To be sure, from time to time a popular guru appears on the scene, demonstrates some successes, amasses a following, and eventually departs with a whimper. No successful approach to risk-taking that mindlessly ignores probability theory has stood the test of time. The cancer of random chance devours consistency. While risk can be managed, it cannot be eliminated.

All forms of financial risk-taking depend for their existence on *devices of decision*. Although I did not coin this term, I believe it to be especially apt. A particular device of decision might be the price movement of a security, the market appeal of a new product, or simply a pair of dice. All risk-taking eventually reduces to wagering on the behavior of the chosen device of decision. Intuitively, examination of cause and effect and studies of past performance data relative to a given device of decision appear to be rational approaches to making an appropriate wager. Indeed, studies of this type are quite relevant insofar as they are undertaken to determine the *probabilities* associated with the game.

Many popular approaches or strategies are developed in total ignorance of the probabilities surrounding the behavior of the chosen device of decision. This is so because of the mathematical sophistication required to describe the behavior of the variables involved. Nonetheless, a strategy bereft of the knowledge of its probabilistic outcomes always will be subject to the adverse elements of random chance and cannot be expected to pass the consistency test in the long run. Conversely, once the probabilities are known or can be estimated reliably, risk-taking reduces to a series of relatively simple choices.

Consider, for example, the game of roulette. The probabilities associated with this device of decision can be calculated easily and may be verified by experiment. In other words, the dynamics of the game are understood completely, and no amount of additional study will contribute to the body of knowledge surrounding roulette. It can be shown that a player has a 5.26 percent *disadvantage* when wagering on a single number and, therefore, should expect to lose $5.26 per $100 wagered in the long run. These figures are immutable (assuming an unbiased American roulette wheel), and no strategy exists that will alter the probabilities. Why, then, would anyone play roulette? A player might be totally ignorant of the probabilities. A player might consider the game to be a form of entertainment and the $5.26 simply the price of admission. I suspect the real reason is much different. Probability is a long-run concept sometimes referred to as the *law of large numbers*. Casinos are certainly subject to this law because they operate 24/7 seemingly forever. However, an individual player only operates in the short run—making relatively few wagers in the overall betting scheme. Although such a player may know the long-run odds are against him, he somehow believes his short-run experience will be a favorable departure from the long-run expectation. Occasionally, the player's belief is actually justified and, as we shall learn, should be expected.

To some, it might seem trivial to employ games of chance in serious studies of financial markets. I assure you that this is not so. Indeed, in 1944, John Von Neumann, a Princeton mathematics professor, elevated game theory to a reputable scientific endeavor in his classic treatise, *The Theory of Games and Economic Behavior*. Simple games of chance remain the best introduction to probability theory. From there, one may embark on studies of more complex behaviors in financial markets—hopefully to reduce risk-taking to the simple choices mentioned earlier. In the roulette example, what are the rational choices? One choice is simply to have fun and pay the price. Another is to eliminate roulette from the list of potential devices of decision (don't be a player). Finally, one could elect to purchase a roulette wheel and attempt to attract other players.

Most risk-takers employ devices of decision that do not have known probabilities. Interestingly, one economist (whose name I have long since forgotten) believed the difference between a gambler and a speculator could be explained in terms of whether the probabilities were known or not known (the uncertain case). In that economist's definition, a gambler wagers on probabilistic events, whereas the speculator wagers on uncertain ones. This economist would view attempts to profit in the financial markets as speculative exercises.

Fortunately, almost every popular form of speculation has been studied and widely published in books and technical journals. A body of knowledge has developed over time such that a researcher today has a credible base of information from which to launch her particular set of inquiries. This knowledge base is almost instantaneously available on the Internet. In certain cases, however, experimentation is still required to provide some notion of the probabilities involved with a device of decision. Many researchers tend to overlook (or ignore) the fact that experimental results that are valid for the time frame of the experiment may not be valid in the future. Some provision must be made for feedback, recalculation, and continuous updating of the experiment. Financial markets, for example, have time-dependent parameters that may not be constant for different time periods.

Another problem with devices of decision is that certain *overhead* costs typically are involved and occur irrespective of the results or dynamics of the game. The owner of a roulette wheel might incur costs associated with (1) advertising for players, (2) renting a facility to house the game, (3) furnishing the facility, (4) depreciation of the wheel, etc. Another risk taker, having chosen the stock market as his device of decision, would be subject to commissions, slippage, taxes, cost of advisory services, and deposit requirements. It is important to note that even though a positive advantage might accrue to a player from the game dynamics, the bottom-line results ultimately depend on the overhead costs as well.

I stated early on my belief that the outcomes of most risk-taking are influenced largely by the vagaries of chance. This is certainly true for options trading. More important, because most options traders operate in the range of 500 to 2,000 trades per year, they are subject to the *law of small numbers,* which may result in substantial differences from expectations based solely on long-run probabilities. Studying options in this light should provide significant opportunities for reducing risk and taking advantage of favorable odds in certain situations. Join with me now in an adventure into the fascinating world of Puts, Calls, and probabilities.

C. B. Reehl

CHAPTER 1

The Wall Street Casinos: A Typology of Financial Products

> *Fait vos jeux, mesdames et messeiurs. Fait vos jeux!. Les jeux sont fait. Rien ne va plus!* (Place your bets, ladies and gentlemen. Place your bets! The bets are placed. No more bets!)
>
> —Cry of the roulette croupier in Monte Carlo

Use of the term *casino* is not intended to insult the serious long-term investor or in any way suggest that all activity carried out in worldwide financial markets is tantamount to gambling. It is, however, intended to convey the notion that much of the short-term action has a lot in common with games of chance—without the knowledge of how probable the various outcomes are. Motivations of an individual participant generally determine whether his activity is long-term investing, hedging an existing position, or simply wagering. Most pure speculators in financial products are engaging in a zero-sum game—a game in which the winnings of the winners are equal to the losses of the losers. This book is devoted to the options traders who, more often than not, are motivated by short-term gains and are likely to view Wall Street as a place to make wagers.

Games of chance are, for the most part, easy to understand but rarely result in consistent gains. Investing and trading on Wall Street are more difficult to understand but, given the right strategies (and a bit of luck), sometimes can be quite profitable. Likewise, while there are limited varieties of games in Las Vegas, there are numerous opportunities for wagering on financial products. *Financial products* refer to financial instruments (or derivatives thereof) available to the public for investment or trading (exclusive of insurance contracts, precious metals, coins, and other collectibles).

From the penny stock hustlers in Denver and Salt Lake City and the boiler rooms in Newport Beach to the massive financial enclaves on Wall Street, not a day goes by that we are not inundated with a mind-boggling array of offers. Schemes to make us wealthy and tips on individual financial products arrive in the mail, over the Internet, by telephone, and on our FAX machines. In addition, we are also subject to offers for newly minted and sometimes sophisticated computer software to aid in selecting appropriate investment instruments. Is it any wonder that confusion reigns? This chapter is devoted to sorting out and explaining most of the available types of financial products offered as of the date of this writing.

Any investor (or potential investor) should be aware of the risks, rewards, and basics of all the financial products covered in this chapter. Each product may be an *alternative* to options trading. While they also may be alternatives to one another, they need not be mutually exclusive. For example, an investor may have significant real estate holdings while speculating in stock options.

Just as all Thoroughbreds are descended from three specific horses,[1] all financial products belong to or are descended from the four basic financial asset groups: equities (stocks), fixed-income debt securities (bonds), commodities (wheat and corn), and real estate (properties and mortgages). We call the descendants of the basic four *derivatives*. No matter what financial asset group is chosen for investment or trading, the criteria for selection are almost always the same:

- Safety of principal
- Return (income)
- Return (capital growth)
- Liquidity (marketability)

THE INFRASTRUCTURE OF INVESTING AND TRADING

Investments (trades) are placed with brokers who are members of or otherwise affiliated with one or more *exchanges,* where the actual trans-

---

[1] The Darley Arabian, the Godolphin Barb, and the Byerly Turk.

actions take place. A *securities exchange* may be defined as a physical facility in which buyers and sellers of securities, or their agents, meet to effect transactions. Exchanges such as the New York Stock Exchange (NYSE) and the American Stock Exchange (AMEX) have a physical presence in New York City, with *specialists* providing an orderly and liquid market for each listed stock and floor traders to make the actual trades by open outcry. The Nasdaq (an exchange heavily weighted toward technology companies), however, is an electronic exchange using computers to connect one or more *market makers* for each security traded who provide liquidity to the system.

The OTC Bulletin Board (OTCBB) is a regulated quotation service displaying real-time quotes for over-the-counter (OTC) equity securities. An OTC equity security is any equity security not listed or traded on the Nasdaq or any national securities exchange. Beginning operation in June 1990, the OTCBB became permanent in April 1997. It provides access to more than 3,600 securities and includes more than 330 participating market makers.[2]

Certain quasi-exchanges have come to exist recently and are called *electronic communications networks* (ECNs). An ECN is an electronic system that attempts to facilitate (for market makers) and eliminate (for individual investors) third-party orders entered by a client's brokerage firm to be executed in whole or in part. ECNs network major brokerages and traders so they can trade between themselves without having to go through a middleman. One advantage of an ECN is that it displays all order information, including the number of shares offered at each price, whereas on the NYSE, most investors are limited to viewing only the *best* bid and ask prices.[3] Another advantage of ECNs is the extended trading time—typically 6:00 A.M. to 8:00 P.M. EST.

Regional exchanges such as the Boston, Chicago, Cincinnati, Pacific, and Philadelphia stock exchanges concentrate on listing stocks of corporations in their geographic locations. Many stocks listed on regional exchanges are not listed on the national exchanges; however, certain stocks are listed on both regional and national exchanges.

Although referred to as *stock* exchanges, many major exchanges also accept trading in futures, options, and other derivatives. Alternatively, certain exchanges trade only options, metals, futures, or curren-

---

[2] "Overview and History of the OTCBB," OTC Bulletin Board, © 2004, The Nasdaq Stock Market, Inc.; reprinted with permission, available at www.otcbb.com/aboutOTCBB/overview.stm.

[3] "Electronic Trading Tutorial," Investopedia.com, February 2004; available at www.investopedia.com/university/electronic trading/, p. 4 of 7.

cies. In the last decade, many of the traditional "bricks and mortar" exchange member brokers have acquired a Web presence, resulting in faster executions and lower commissions. Some brokers such as E*Trade are entirely Web based.

FIXED-INCOME (DEBT) SECURITIES

For individual investors, the most common parking place for idle funds is a savings (passbook) account at a commercial bank. Called *time deposits,* these funds earn interest at varying rates determined periodically by the bank. Generally speaking, savings deposits are quite safe because they are insured by the Federal Deposit Insurance Corporation (FDIC) up to $100,000. The income return will be low (commensurate with the limited risk), and the investment is very liquid. There is no capital appreciation. Interest income typically is deposited (reinvested) in the savings account.

As with all debt securities, an investor therein is actually a *lender.* A savings deposit is simply a loan by the investor to the bank, which, in turn, lends the funds out to all types of borrowers at higher interest rates. The one feature of most debt instruments that is lacking in savings deposits is *maturity,* or the length of time for which the investment is made. The savings depositor simply may withdraw funds at any time without penalty. To lock in funds for a specific rate of interest and for a specific time period, a bank will offer *certificates of deposit* (CDs). To cash in a CD prior to its maturity date, an investor will pay a penalty (usually one month's interest). CDs pay a higher interest rate than passbook accounts because of the imposition of a fixed maturity—the further out the maturity date, the higher is the interest rate.

Debts may be formalized by instruments such as a promissory note that specifies the face amount of the debt, the payee, the rate of interest, and the time and place of repayment. To make repayment more likely, a lender may require *collateral* in the form of a security interest in certain of the borrower's other assets (automobiles, boats, etc.). Such collateral would be forfeited in the event of the borrower's default. Promissory notes are usually agreements between individuals or borrowers and lending institutions and are not traded on any secondary markets. Certain kinds of promissory notes such as real estate mortgages, are pooled, securitized, and made available to investors (see section below entitled, "Investing in Real Estate as a Lender").

Like a promissory note, a *bond* is also formal evidence of a debt. The issuer of a bond promises to pay the investor a specified amount of interest at specified times and to repay the principal (face amount of the bond) at some fixed date in the future. Most bonds are issued by the U.S. government, state agencies, municipalities, and publicly traded corporations.

TREASURY SECURITIES[4]

Obligations of the U.S. government generally are held to be the safest of all investments. Indeed, the "risk free" interest rate (called for in many financial calculations) is usually the rate on Treasury obligations of comparable maturity. If held to maturity, the income return is fixed. If sold prior to maturity, some capital gain or loss is possible. Treasury securities are highly liquid.

Treasury bills (T-bills) are short-term securities that mature in one year or less from their issue date and are sold at a price less than their face (par) value—i.e., discounted. At maturity, the investor receives par value, and his interest amount is the difference between the purchase price and par. If the T-bill is sold prior to maturity, the investor's interest amount is the difference between the sales and purchase prices.

Treasury notes and bonds are securities that pay a fixed rate of interest every six months until maturity, at which time the par value is paid. The only difference among them is the length of their maturity. Treasury notes mature in more than one year but no more than 10 years, whereas Treasury bonds have maturity dates in excess of 10 years. The Treasury Department has not offered a Treasury bond since it suspended issuance of the 30-year bond in October 2001. Treasury bonds issued prior to October 2001 still trade in the secondary market.

FEDERAL AGENCY ISSUES

Agency securities (or simply *agencies*) are obligations of certain organizations either *owned* or *sponsored* by the federal government. Because these issues are slightly less liquid than Treasuries, they command a marginally higher yield. Most securities offered by government-*owned* agencies have the same "full faith and credit of the United States" guarantee that underlies Treasury securities. While lacking this guarantee, issues of government-*sponsored* agencies are considered by most money

---

[4] "The Basics of Treasury Securities," Bureau of Public Debt Online, February 10, 2004; available at www.publicdebt.treas.gov/of/ofbasics.htm, p. 1 of 5.

market experts to carry an implicit guarantee of repayment. Agency securities may not be purchased directly—they are obtained through a bank or broker.

The Government National Mortgage Association ("Ginnie Mae") and the Tennessee Valley Authority (TVA) are examples of government-owned agencies. The Federal Home Loan Mortgage Corporation ("Freddie Mac") and the Small Business Association (SBA) are examples of government-sponsored agencies.

MUNICIPAL BONDS

Municipal bonds are fixed-rate, fixed-term debt obligations of state and local government agencies. Because certain municipal bonds are exempt from federal taxation, the investor's tax profile dictates whether these instruments are suitable. For example, for an investor in the 28 percent tax bracket, a 6 percent fully-tax-exempt municipal bond yields the taxable equivalent of 8.3 percent.

Municipal bonds are rated by Moody's, Standard & Poor's, and Fitch. It is no longer true that municipal bonds are automatically safe. State and local government agencies can and do default on both interest and principal payments—witness the bankruptcy of Orange County, California, in the mid-1990s.

CORPORATE BONDS

In general, corporate bonds are obligations of publicly traded corporations using debt to finance their ongoing activities. Corporate bonds backed only by the corporation's general credit are called *debentures*. Occasionally, a security interest in specific corporate assets is offered as added incentive to purchasers. Moody's and Standard & Poor's rate corporate bonds on the issuer's willingness and ability to repay debt from the highest rated (investment-grade bonds) to the lowest rated (junk bonds). Interest rates will reflect a bond's inherent risk—with junk bonds providing the highest yields. In a corporate liquidation, the bondholder shares in recovery with the other unsecured creditors, ahead of the equity interests.

Bond prices fluctuate inversely with market interest rates—interest rates up, bond prices down, and vice versa. This phenomenon gives rise to potential capital gains and losses in the bond market because bonds may be purchased at a premium or discount to par. It also gives rise to different yields on bonds. The *coupon rate* or *yield* is the stated rate of interest to be applied to par. The *current yield* on a bond is the annual interest amount divided by the bond's actual cost. The *yield to maturity* for a bond is the composite rate of return of all payouts, interest as well as capital gains or losses. Since many issuers make their bonds *callable* at a certain future date prior to maturity, the *yield to call* is also an important measure of potential bond income.

While investment-grade bonds generally are safe and liquid, they do not permit the investor to participate in the fortunes of the company (good or bad). As an alternative, an investor might wish to consider *convertible debentures*—bonds that may be exchanged for shares of stock of the company at a specified price. If the stock price rises, the bond may be converted into stock or sold for a capital gain.

EQUITIES

Unlike lending money by purchasing debt securities, investment in an equity means the investor actually *owns* all or a part of the investment asset. Although we might have *equity* in a piece of real estate, be a sole proprietor of a small business, or own a portion of a business as a partner, the term *equities* generally refers to shares of stock held in public corporations that trade on one or more exchanges in the United States or abroad. Equities are considered to be highly liquid investments.

Outright ownership of equities permits the holder to participate in both the good and bad fortunes of the enterprise. In good times, a portion of the corporation's earnings may be paid to the shareholder as dividends (income return), and the price of the stock may increase (capital growth return). In bad times, the dividend may be reduced or eliminated, and the price of the stock may fall. In a corporate liquidation, the equity holder is last in line for any recovery.

Equities come in two flavors—common and preferred. There may be several *classes* of common stock, but the holders' rights therein are generally similar. Preferred stock, on the other hand, is somewhat of a hybrid between ownership and a fixed-income security. Preferred shareholders will have a *liquidation preference* of some kind that puts them ahead of the common shareholders in a liquidation. Also, the preferred shareholder will be entitled to a *fixed dividend* limited to the amount specified when the stock was issued. Preferred stock may be participating, cumulative, redeemable, and/or convertible. A preferred shareholder is an owner rather than a creditor (who might hold convertible debentures) and, while being preferred over the common shareholder, is behind the creditors (including bondholders) in a liquidation.

Many listed securities may be purchased on *margin,* that is, for a cash down payment of less than 100 percent of the purchase price, with the balance being borrowed from the broker. Based on subsequent fluctuations in the price, additional (maintenance) margin may be required (*margin call*). If the margin call is not met, the securities may be sold by the broker. Currently, the margin requirement is 50 percent—set by the Federal Open Market Committee of the Federal Reserve. Margin is an extremely important consideration in investing and trading because margin requirements vary considerably among different kind of financial activities, thereby affecting yields. Trading on margin introduces the concept of *leverage.* Generally, leverage refers to the ratio of debt on a purchased asset to the asset's value. For example, if IBM is selling for $95 per share, 200 shares (worth $19,000) can be purchased on 50 percent margin for a cash outlay of only $9,500. The other $9,500 is borrowed from a broker. With 50 percent margin, any future gains or losses are doubled (plus or minus the interest paid on the margin account) over those obtained without the margin.

INVESTMENT COMPANIES (THE FUNDS)[5]

Generally, an *investment company* is a corporation, business trust, partnership, or limited-liability company that pools investor funds, issues its own securities, and is engaged primarily in the business of investing in other marketable securities. Investment companies fall into three basic types:

- Mutual funds (open-end companies)
- Closed-end funds (closed-end companies)
- Unit investment trusts (UITs)

A *mutual fund* is a company that pools money from investors and invests in stocks, bonds, money-market instruments, or other securities. Investors purchase and redeem mutual fund shares directly from the fund itself or through a broker acting for the fund but *not* from other investors in a secondary market or exchange. Mutual fund shares are valued at the end of each day at the net asset value of the fund, which value generally

---

[5] "Investment Companies," Securities and Exchange Commission Web site, February 11, 2004; available at www.sec.gov/answers/mfinvco.htm, p. 1 of 2.

is based on the closing price of the included securities as determined by the primary exchange for each stock. Mutual funds usually sell their shares on a continuous basis, hence the term *open-end*. If a fund becomes too large, sales may be discontinued. Mutual funds may be *load* or *no load* depending on whether they charge a sales fee.[6]

Closed-end funds generally do not offer their shares for sale continuously, hence the term *closed-end*. They typically sell a fixed number of shares at one time in an initial public offering (IPO), after which the shares trade in a secondary market such as the NYSE or Nasdaq. The price of shares in a closed-end fund are determined by the market and may be greater or less than their net asset value. Such shares trade continuously throughout the day.[7]

A *unit investment trust* (UIT) typically issues redeemable securities or "units" like a mutual fund. However, some exchange-traded funds (ETFs) are structured as UITs and are traded on a secondary market just like stocks (see section entitled, "Exchange-Traded Funds," below). A UIT generally will make a one-time public offering of a specific, fixed number of units like a closed-end fund. Many UIT sponsors, however, will maintain a secondary market that allows owners of UITs to sell them back to the sponsors and allows other investors to buy UIT units from the sponsors. A UIT will have a termination date (which could be 50 years or more from inception), at which time all investments will be sold and the proceeds distributed to the investors. UITs do not actively trade their investment portfolios. Most investments are held with little or no change for the duration of the UIT.[8]

The two stated reasons for investing in investment companies (generally suitable for long-term investors only) are diversification and professional management. An investor with limited funds can own a selection of more companies than otherwise possible. A busy individual need not spend the time managing her own investments.

EQUITY MARKET INDICES

Although usually not financial products themselves, market indices are compilations of individual financial instruments that can be used as

---

[6] "Mutual Funds," Securities and Exchange Commission Web site, February 11, 2004; avaliable at www.sec.gov/answers/mutfund.htm, p. 1 of 2.

[7] "Closed-End Funds," Securities and Exchange Commission Web site, February 11, 2004; available at www.sec.gov/answers/mfclose.htm, p. 1 of 2.

[8] "Unit Investment Trusts," Securities and Exchange Commission Web site, February 11, 2004; available at www.sec.gov/answers/uit.htm, p. 1 of 2.

benchmarks against which to measure the performance of individual securities. Certain indices are replicated by other stocks or funds such that one actually may *trade an index*. The best known of all the equity indices is the Dow Jones Industrial Average (DJIA), which is composed of 30 frequently traded, price-weighted stocks of the largest, most influential companies in a diverse sampling of industries. Daily publication of this average began in 1896 in the *Wall Street Journal*. At the end of 2002, the DJIA accounted for more than 28 percent of the investable U.S. market. Even today, the market being "up or down" generally refers to the position of the DJIA relative to yesterday's close.

The next best known equity index is the Standard & Poor's 500 Index (S&P 500). Its ticker symbol is $INX (formerly SPX). Dating back to 1923, the S&P 500 is considered a proxy for a major segment of the U.S. equities market. The S&P 500 includes a representative sample of 500 leading companies in leading industries in the U.S. economy. The main focus of the S&P 500 is on the large-cap segment of the market with over 80 percent coverage.

A subset of the S&P 500 is the S&P 100—often known by its ticker symbol, OEX. Since its introduction in 1983, the OEX measures the performance of the largest (by market capitalization) 100 companies in the S&P 500 group. Another criterion for inclusion in the OEX is the availability of tradable stock options. The OEX is a favorite among options traders.

The Nasdaq Composite Index (COMPX) includes stocks in industrial, insurance, and banking sectors. It is an index of all domestic and non-U.S. common stocks listed on the Nasdaq. The Nasdaq-100 Index (NDX) is an index of the top 100 Nasdaq companies. One actually may trade a stock called the *Nasdaq-100 Tracking Stock* (QQQ) that is invested in each of the NDX stocks.

EXCHANGE-TRADED FUNDS

Exchange traded funds (ETFs) are *closed-end* investment companies or UITs holding a basket of securities (stocks or bonds) that attempt to replicate an established market index or track certain industry segments. Unlike index mutual funds, which are priced only once a day, ETFs trade like a single stock.

Certain ETFs are also UITs that have been established to track a specific index. A spider, or Standard and Poor's Depository Receipt (SPDR), represents ownership in the SPDR, Trust Series 1, a UIT established to hold a portfolio of the equity securities consisting the S&P 500 Index.[9] Unlike index mutual funds that can be bought or sold at the end of each trading day, SPDRs trade throughout the trading day.

INVESTING IN REAL ESTATE AS AN *OWNER*

Owning real estate is part of the American Dream—particularly with regard to one's personal residence. Although developers of raw land might want to turn a profit more quickly, real estate investments generally are made for the longer term. Although such investments are less volatile than stocks and bonds in the short term, they are illiquid and subject to longer cycles of boom and bust. While many people have become multimillionaires by investing in real estate, an investor must have other liquid assets and the patience to weather the cycle bottoms.

Basically, there are two types of real estate—improved (developed) and unimproved (raw) land. Developed land includes land improved with the installation of services (roads, sewers, water, etc.) and/or with construction of any type of building thereon. When we speak of developed land we generally mean single-family dwellings, multifamily dwellings (condominiums, town homes, apartment complexes, etc.), manufacturing facilities, shopping centers, and other specific uses such as entertainment, transportation, and storage facilities.

Purchasing real estate generally involves borrowing. Two types of instruments generally are required to borrow money on real estate: a promissory note and a document evidencing the security given for the loan—usually either a mortgage or a trust deed. In about two-thirds of the states, real estate loans are secured by *mortgages* (a term derived from the French literally translated as "death grip"). In the remaining states, *trust deeds* are used to secure real estate loans. While there are certain legal differences between mortgages and trust deeds, they both evidence a loan between a borrower and a lender and a security interest in real property given by the borrower to the lender. Differences in the two instruments generally relate to the respective legal rights of the parties in the event the borrower defaults and the lender forecloses on the property.

A mortgage or trust deed generally contains many restrictions and conditions affecting other rights of both the lender and borrower. Chief

---

[9] American Stock Exchange LLC, "SPDRS—SPY," February 11, 2004; available at www.amex.com/etf/prodInf/EtPiOverview.JSP?Product_Symbol=SPY.

among these are the *prepayment* and *assumability* clauses. The typical prepayment clause allows the borrower to pay off the loan early in exchange for a monetary penalty—usually three to six months' interest. The assumability clause dictates the terms and conditions under which the loan may be assumed by another borrower, if at all.

INVESTING IN REAL ESTATE AS A *LENDER*

Private investing in real estate as a lender is somewhat the inverse of investing as an owner. Owners will want the lowest interest rates, the most favorable borrowing terms, and the most flexible treatment in the event of a default. Lenders want just the opposite. While the owner looks to periodic rents and capital gains as his potential reward, the lender looks to fixed interest payments together with the timely repayment of the loan. Among other things, any real property lender, private or institutional, must be concerned with

- The property's market value
- The debt-service coverage
- Creditworthiness of the borrower
- The loan-to-value (LTV) ratio

The market value of real property generally is determined by an appraisal that usually considers three approaches to measuring such value. The *market approach* looks at comparable properties sold in the same geographic location. The *cost approach* looks at what the probable replacement cost would be in today's dollars. The *income method* is based on the theory that any asset is worth its future benefits (income or cash flows) discounted to the present. Appraisers today mostly rely on the market and income approaches.

A potential lender on commercial property (apartment complex or shopping center) might require a debt service coverage (DSC) of 1.3. This means the property must throw off operating income of at least 1.3 times the monthly mortgage payment. DSC provides the lender with a "cushion" to ensure that the cash flow will be there to make the required loan payments.

Creditworthiness of a borrower is the cornerstone of lending. It is the best indicator of a borrower's ability and willingness to repay debt. Without it, no loan is safe—no matter what the property's value or DSC is. A thorough check on a borrower's credit history is always necessary.

The loan-to-value (LTV) ratio of a mortgaged property measures the lender's exposure, whereas its complement (1 − LTV) indicates the borrower's equity in such property. Borrower's equity is the lender's cushion should the property's market value fall.

Instead of lending directly to a borrower as a private party, an investor simply could purchase mortgages or trust deeds through a mortgage loan broker. If an investor does not want the hassle of trying to service mortgages or trust deeds herself, she may invest in pools of loans that are secured by mortgages on real estate:

- Mortgage-backed securities (MBS)
- Real estate limited partnerships
- Real estate investment trusts (REITs)

Mortgage-backed securities from Ginnie Mae, Fannie Mae, and Freddie Mac (*agencies*) are quite liquid, and their yields are generally at least one percentage point higher than for other bonds of comparable maturity.

Real estate limited partnerships raise cash (typically $1,000 to $5,000 minimum) from investors to purchase or build a diversified portfolio of income-producing real property or to make loans to other real estate investors. Investments in real estate limited partnerships are highly *illiquid*.

Real estate investment trusts (REITs) are publicly traded on a stock exchange; thus investments therein are highly liquid. Prices per share are usually much lower than for equity in a limited partnership. *Equity* REITs invest in income properties with the expectation of a later sale and capital gain while collecting rents in the interim. *Mortgage* REITs lend money to buyers or builders of various kinds of real property. Investing in REITs permits the investor to speculate in real estate simply by dealing with a broker or a mutual fund.

COMMODITY FUTURES

Thought to be the riskiest of all financial adventures, trading commodity futures involves predicting the future course of commodity prices, interest rates, and even stock indices. Ironically, futures contracts existed initially as a means of *reducing risk* for producers and sellers, thereby smoothing price fluctuations to the end user of a product at the retail level. For example, a farmer may wish to sell his wheat crop before it is even planted owing to a favorable futures price at or about the anticipated harvest time. Assuming he can make the promised delivery, he will have locked in his profit. He will not suffer a loss, nor will he experience any windfall profits. He is said to be *hedged* and now likely will be eligible for a bank loan to purchase seed and other necessary items. On the other side of the contract is the miller who wants an inventory of wheat (at or about the farmer's harvest date) to grind into flour to fulfill her obligations to many large bakers. By purchasing the wheat future now, the miller knows the cost of her raw materials in advance and can plan accordingly. The farmer and miller are called *hedgers*.

If the risk of changing supply and demand and widely fluctuating prices is removed from the hedgers, where does it go? Enter the *speculator*. Speculators gladly accept these risks because of the potentially high rewards available. They attempt to forecast the direction of prices between the contract inception date and the contract delivery date in anticipation of large profits. If a speculator buys or sells a futures contract and later wishes to take his profits (or losses), he simply buys or sells an *offsetting* contract. There is no uptick rule for selling futures contracts as there is with selling a stock short.

Commodity futures contracts have been around since ancient times, when merchants bargained directly with producers and each other. Today, rather than face-to-face negotiations between the parties (hedgers), futures contracts are purchased and sold on large futures exchanges such as the Chicago Board of Trade (CBOT)—the oldest derivatives exchange in the United States, established in 1848. Technically, the *commodities clearinghouse* is the other party in every trade and sorts out contract obligations every day.

The basic commodities traded include agricultural products, livestock, petroleum, fiber, food, wood, and metals. Other futures consist of bonds, foreign currencies, and stock indices. A relatively recent addition (November 2002) is the single-stock future (SSF). A speculator now may wager on what IBM's price will be at certain specified dates in the future. Currently, SSFs are traded on only two exchanges: One Chicago and Nasdaq-LIFFE Markets (NQLX). Although there are many exchanges all over the world trading commodity futures, the five most active are

- New York Board of Trade (NYBT)
- International Monetary Market (IMM)
- New York Mercantile Exchange (NYMX)

- Chicago Mercantile Exchange (CME)
- Chicago Board of Trade (CBOT)

Commodity futures contracts call for either physical delivery or cash settlement on a certain date specified in the contract. Physical delivery is made by furnishing the holder with a negotiable instrument indicating ownership of the commodity stored at a specified location. Actual physical delivery, however, is rare. Not many speculators want to make or take delivery of 5,000 bushels of wheat. They simply will liquidate their positions with offsetting contracts prior to the expiration date. Likewise, even hedgers do not often make or take delivery—they, like the speculators, usually liquidate their futures positions and then buy or sell the particular commodity in the cash market at contract expiration time. Because delivery *can* occur, the futures price and the cash price will converge and be the same at expiration of the futures contract. Cash settlement contracts automatically converge and settle in cash on the expiration date. An example of a cash settlement contract is a stock index future. Obviously, it would be impractical to actually deliver all the stocks making up the index.

The lure of futures trading exists because of the potential leverage arising out of the relatively low *margin requirements*. With common stocks, margin represents a cash down payment and interest paid on the balance owed to the broker. The margin required for the purchase or sale a futures contract represents a deposit of good faith money that can be drawn on by a broker in the event of losses in the account. No interest is paid, although margin calls are possible. The exchange on which the contract is traded sets the minimum margin requirements, which typically are about 5 to 10 percent of the current value of the futures contract. Margin requirements for SSFs are currently 20 percent. As an example of the high leverage available, consider the contract size for wheat, which is 5,000 bushels. If the current price of wheat to be delivered in 90 days were, say, $4.00 a bushel, a speculator could control $20,000 worth of wheat with a deposit of only $1,000 (.05 × 20,000). If the price increased to $4.50 in 30 days, his yield on the investment would be 250 percent (.5 × 5,000/1,000), and his annual rate of return would be 625 percent (2.5/.4).

The margin deposited with a broker at the time a futures trade is initiated is called the *initial margin*. The exchange also will specify another margin amount (lower than the initial margin) called the *maintenance margin*. Margin accounts at a brokerage are *marked to market* daily based on the activity in the underlying asset or index. If the margin account dips below the maintenance margin amount, a *margin call* is issued to top off the margin account, thereby bringing its balance back to the initial margin level. If the owner of the futures contract fails to deposit the required funds, the position will be sold by the broker.

With such high leverage, it is possible to garner enormous profits from futures trading. However, leverage is a two-way street—enormous losses are also possible. It is said that about 80 percent of all futures transactions by small speculators result in losses. The large risks are partially offset by daily trading limits on price changes imposed by the exchanges.

Futures contracts are traded in "pits" sunk into the floors of an exchange. Each commodity has its own pit where hedgers and speculators gather and place orders through floor traders who execute them by open outcry. The small speculator places orders through a brokerage having a representative at the exchange. Brokerages are registered with the Commodity Futures Trading Commission (CTFC), which regulates futures in a manner similar to the Securities and Exchange Commission (SEC), which regulates stocks.

EQUITY OPTIONS

Most of the foregoing was covered before introducing options because options are *derivatives* of equity, index, futures, and real estate instruments. An *option* is simply the *right* but not the obligation to buy or sell something at a specified price (*strike price*) for a specified time. An option to buy something is called a *Call,* whereas an option to sell something is called a *Put*. One of the best understood and popular options is an option to purchase residential real property. For example, a potential home buyer, unsure of the direction of residential real estate prices, offers $2,000 to a home owner for the *right* to buy the real property anytime during the next year at today's price of $475,000.

In the preceding example, all the elements of an options contract are in place. The option *premium* is the $2,000 offered by the potential real estate buyer (*option buyer*), the *strike price* is $475,000, and the *expiration date* is one year hence. If the potential real property buyer actually buys the property on or before the expiration date, she has *exercised* her option. If she fails to exercise her option on or before the expiration date, the option expires, and the premium is kept by the home owner (*option writer*). Whether to exercise the option or let it expire depends on its value on the expiration date. Suppose that the value of the real property were $500,000 on the expiration date—a 5 percent increase over the year. The option's value is $25,000 ($500,000 − $475,000). Obviously, the option buyer would exercise the option because of the approximate $23,000 ($25,000 − $2,000) gain (either as equity in an owner-occupied residence or as an amount realized on a potential sale of the property). If, on the other hand, the property value had declined to $470,000 by the expiration date, the option would expire worthless; the option buyer would lose $2,000 instead of a potential $5,000 (had she purchased the property one year before), and the option writer recoups $2,000 of a potential $5,000 loss.

In the real estate example, there was no ready market into which the option buyer could sell her option during the year—if she wanted to profit from the property's increasing value, she had to exercise the option and then sell the property, thus incurring additional transaction costs. With *equity* options (options on publicly traded stocks), there is a highly liquid market for the options themselves, virtually eliminating the need for exercise. Most equity options are traded on the Chicago Board Options Exchange (CBOE), NYSE, AMEX, Philadelphia Stock Exchange, and Pacific Stock Exchange. A *Call* option confers on the buyer the right but not the obligation to *purchase* 100 shares of stock at a specified price (strike price) for a fee (premium) on or before a certain date in the future (expiration date). Likewise, a *Put* option confers on the buyer the right but not the obligation to *sell* 100 shares of stock under the same conditions. Although the *requirement* for exercise has been substantially eliminated, certain option holders may still wish to take possession of or deliver the actual shares and will elect to exercise their options rather than buying or selling to cover their original transaction.

Price (premium) quotes for equity options are set forth by strike price within expiration month. All equity option contracts expire at the close of business on the third Friday of a specified expiration month. Generally, strike prices are shown in $5.00 increments except for lower-priced stocks, for which the increments are $2.50. Table 1–1 shows the premium quotes for IBM on February 19, 2004, at 12:40 P.M. EST when the stock was selling for $98.59 per share. Quotes are for the March, April, and July expirations.

Table 1–1 conveys an enormous amount of information. Premiums for Calls decrease as strike prices increase. If an options trader purchases the right to purchase IBM stock for $95 when it is currently selling for $98.59, he can expect to pay, at least, $3.59 ($98.59 − $95) plus some additional amount relating to the option's remaining time. The 95 Call

TABLE 1-1

IBM option quotes, February 19, 2004

	March 3/19/04 (30 days)		April 4/16/04 (58 days)		July 7/16/04 (149 days)	
Strike	Bid	Ask	Bid	Ask	Bid	Ask
Calls						
90	8.90	9.00	9.40	9.60	10.80	11.00
95	4.40	4.60	5.40	5.60	7.30	7.40
100	1.40	1.50	2.45	2.55	4.40	4.60
105	0.25	0.35	0.85	0.95	2.45	2.55
110	0.05	0.10	0.25	0.30	1.20	1.30
Puts						
90	0.20	0.25	0.75	0.80	2.10	2.15
95	0.80	0.90	1.70	1.75	3.50	3.60
100	2.75	2.85	3.70	3.80	5.60	5.80
105	6.60	6.70	7.10	7.20	8.60	8.80
110	11.40	11.50	11.50	11.60	12.40	12.60

Source (data): E*Trade.

(at $4.60 ask) is said to be *in the money* and has an *intrinsic value* of $3.59 and a *time value* of $1.01 ($4.60 − $3.59). By contrast, the 100 Call (at $1.50 ask) is *out of the money*, has no intrinsic value, and the premium of $1.50 consists entirely of time value.

Premiums for Puts vary directly with strike prices. If an options trader purchases the right to sell IBM stock for $100 when it is currently selling for $98.59, she can expect to pay, at least, $1.41 ($100 − $98.59) plus an additional amount for time value. The 100 Put (at $2.85 ask) is in the money and has an intrinsic value of $1.41 and a time value of $1.44 ($2.85 − $1.41). By contrast, the 95 Put is out of the money, has no intrinsic value, and its $.90 premium consists entirely of time value. In later chapters we shall see that the time-value portion of an option is related to the number of days remaining, the volatility of the stock price, and the level of interest rates.

As with futures, tremendous leverage may exist with options trades. Suppose an investor purchases 1,000 shares of IBM on February 19, 2004, for $98.59 per share. He gives his broker $49,295 in cash and borrows the remaining $49,295 from the broker at 7 percent. Thirty days later when IBM is selling for $105.59, the investor sells all 1,000 shares.

Table 1-2 illustrates how the investor fared versus an options trader controlling the same 1,000 shares of IBM stock.

The returns tell the story. In terms of rate of return, the options trader is nearly 19 times better off. While Table 1-2 paints a somewhat rosy picture of what happens to the options trader when the underlying asset behaves in the desired manner, purchasing options instead of the underlying stock has another advantage. When an options trader *purchases* a Call or Put, her overall loss is limited to the cost of the premiums plus commissions. Suppose the IBM stock price had *declined* $7 to $91.59. The stock investor would have lost $7,000 plus the cost of commissions and interest. The options trader would have lost $1,500 plus commissions. Clearly, it is less risky to purchase options than to purchase stock outright. What about selling options?

In any options transaction, there is an open and a close. There are two kinds of options traders. An options buyer *buys to open* a position and later *sells to close out* the position (or lets the options expire worthless). Selling options to close a position is the province of the *options buyer*. Other traders will sell (write) options to *open* a position and later buy them back or simply let them expire worthless. Selling options to open a position is the province of the *options writer*. As described earlier,

TABLE 1-2

Stock investor versus options trader
1,000 shares of IBM stock

	Stock investor	Options trader
Cash down payment on 1,000 shares IBM stock	$49,295.00	
Premium on 10 contracts IBM 100 Call at $1.50		$1,500.00
Commissions	19.90	30.00
Interest	287.55	
Total cash outlay	49,602.45	1,530.00
Proceeds of sale:		
1,000 share of IBM at $105.59	105,590.00	
10 contracts IBM 100 Call at $5.59		5,590.00
Original cost	(98,590.00)	(1,500.00)
Profit	7,000.00	4,090.00
Return on cash	14.11%	267.32%
Annualized return on cash	169.35%	3207.84%

the options buyer has limited exposure to losses. This is not true for the options writer. Since the potential for a stock price to increase is theoretically unlimited, the writer of a Call (who expects the price to remain stable or decline) is exposed to unlimited losses. Also, the maximum gain for such a Call writer is limited to the options premium received. Since a stock's price cannot fall below zero, the writer of a Put (who expects the price to remain stable or increase) is exposed to a maximum loss of an amount equal to the difference between the strike price and the premium received (stock becomes worthless). Like the Call options writer, the Put options writer's maximum gain is limited to the premium received.

Options writers make most of their money when the options they write expire worthless and they keep the premium. Lest the foregoing paragraph scare off any would-be options writers, it should be noted than many, many more options expire worthless than finish in the money. Premium income from expiring options is one of the major reasons speculators write options—called *naked* options writing. Another reason is to protect an existing stock position by writing Calls against it—called *covered Call writing*. If the stock price declines temporarily, the Call value will increase, thus eliminating the need for selling the stock.

A third reason to write options is to acquire stock at a better price. If an investor likes a certain stock but believes it is overpriced, he can write a naked Put at a lower-than-market strike price, anticipating a price drop and assignment (buyer of the Put exercises). The stock would be delivered at a price favorable to the Put writer, and the premium would be retained, reducing the basis in the stock even further. If the stock price at expiration were unchanged, the acquisition cost to the Put writer would be the market price less the premium. If the stock price began to increase, the Put writer simply would buy to close, thereby limiting his losses. Many of the strategies covered in later chapters are based on writing options.

Since an options buyer has the right to require delivery (exercise her option), the options writer must be prepared to deliver the shares from his own inventory or purchase them in the market if called on to do so. If an options buyer gives notice of exercise, the Options Clearing Corporation (OCC) randomly selects clearing members (brokers) to be assigned the exercises. The clearing member then selects individual accounts that are short the options for allocation of the exercises on a "first in, first out" basis. Only about 10 percent of all options are exercised.

Expiration months for equity options will vary. An equity option may or may not trade each month of the year. Technically, equity options expire on the Saturday following the third Friday of an expiration month, making that Friday the last trading day. Settlement prices are based on Friday's closing prices.

Regular equity options have a maximum life of nine months. *Long-term equity options* (LEAPS) have at least one year of life remaining. LEAPS expire in January of a specified year. Generally, when LEAPS are issued, they have expiration dates of between two and three years out. As time passes, these LEAPS become regular options once the expiration date is less than one year out.[10]

Ticker symbols for options are a combination of a *base symbol,* an *expiration code,* and a *strike price code.* Expiration codes are standardized, as shown in Table 1–3.[11]

Strike price codes are also standardized, as shown in Table 1–4.[12] For example, the ticker symbol for International Business Machines Corp. is IBM. For the May 80 IBM options, the base symbol is also IBM. From Tables 1–3 and 1–4 we get

    IBMEP for the Call

    IBMQP for the Put

If the underlying asset or index is trading at more than $100, the strike price codes refer to the last two digits of the strike price. For options

TABLE 1-3

Standardized expiration codes

Month	Call code	Put code	Month	Call code	Put code
Jan	A	M	Jul	G	S
Feb	B	N	Aug	H	T
Mar	C	O	Sep	I	U
Apr	D	P	Oct	J	V
May	E	Q	Nov	K	W
Jun	F	R	Dec	L	X

Source (data): McMillan, *Profit with Options.*

---

[10] Lawrence G. McMillan, *Profit with Options* (New York: Wiley, 2002), pp. 10–13; used by permission of John Wiley & Sons, Inc.
[11] *Ibid.*, p. 11.
[12] *Ibid.*, p. 12.

TABLE 1-4

Standardized strike price codes

Code	Strike price	Code	Strike price
A	5	K	55
B	10	L	60
C	15	M	65
D	20	N	70
E	25	O	75
F	30	P	80
G	35	Q	85
H	40	R	90
I	45	S	95
J	50	T	100

Source (data): McMillian, *Profit with Options*.

with strike price increments of 2.5 points, use Table 1–5 to obtain the strike price codes.[13]

With LEAPS, the symbol situation becomes more complicated. To differentiate among expiration years, a different *base symbol* is used. For example, the symbols for the January 2005 IBM 80 LEAP options are

TABLE 1-5

Other strike price codes

Code	Strike prices		
	1	2	3
U	7.50	37.50	67.50
V	12.50	42.50	72.50
W	17.50	47.50	77.50
X	22.50	52.50	82.50
Y	27.50	57.50	87.50
Z	32.50	62.50	92.50

Source (data): McMillian, *Profit with Options*.

---

[13] *Ibid.*, p. 12.

ZIBAP for the Call
ZIBMP for the Put

The symbols for the January 2006 IBM 80 LEAP options are

WIBAP for the Call
WIBMP for the Put

Stock rights and warrants also evidence the right to purchase stock at a specified price for a specified time. Typically, *warrants* are issued in connection with a company's IPO and may be detachable from the stock certificates themselves. Detachable warrants may trade by themselves in the secondary market. Although warrants and rights have some similarities to Call options, there are major differences. A warrant's lifetime is usually measured in years, whereas an option's expiration generally is only months away. An option is written by a third party, whereas warrants and rights are issued by the company whose stock is being traded. Stock *rights* usually are issued in lieu of stock and can trade in the secondary market until expiration or exercise. Such rights and warrants should not be confused with equity options.

INDEX OPTIONS

Index options exist because many traders prefer to "trade a market" rather than trade an individual security. It is said that 70 percent of a stock's performance is due to the overall market's performance, whereas 20 percent is due to the performance of the industry or sector within which the stock is positioned. This theory leaves only 10 percent of the stock's performance accounted for by an individual company's fundamentals.[14]

Index options also were born out of the enormous growth and concentration of institutionally managed funds numbering in the hundreds of billions of dollars. For these fund managers to trade in individual stocks for that level of investment would mean excess volatility and exaggerated price moves. It is much less disruptive to be able to trade a market or industry segment of the market.[15]

---

[14] James B. Bittman, *Trading Index Options* (New York: McGraw-Hill, 1998), pp. xiii–xvii.
[15] *Ibid.*, pp. xiii–xiv.

Index options began trading in 1983 on the CBOE for OEX (S&P 100 Index) options as a way to let investors hedge or speculate on a broad market index. Subsequently, the CBOE and other exchanges have added dozens of other index options. Generally, index options work the same as equity options; however, there are a few differences. Most index options (with the exception of the QQQ) are *cash-settled,* meaning that on exercise, the exerciser receives cash rather than the assets in the underlying index. The amount of cash settlement is the difference between the *settlement price* and the *strike price*. Like equity options, index options expire on the third Saturday of an expiration month. Like equity options, the settlement price for certain index options is calculated based on Friday's *closing prices*—called a P.M. *settlement.* The settlement prices for certain other index options are calculated based on Friday's opening prices—called an A.M. *settlement.* Effectively, the last day of trading index options with an A.M. settlement is the prior Thursday. Also, if stocks in an index option with an A.M. settlement open late, the settlement price for that index option might not be known until late on Friday.[16] Many index options also have a different symbol for their settlement prices.

There are two basic kinds of options—*European* style and *American* style. The most common exercise style for index options is the European style, which provides that exercise may take place *only* on the expiration date. By contrast, all equity options employ the American-style exercise, which provides for exercise at any time up to and including the expiration date. Traders may trade in and out of European-style index options at any time prior to expiration—they just can't exercise them. The less common American-style index option is exercisable at any time prior to expiration—just like the equity options. The most notable example of the American-style index option is the OEX. When index options are exercised, the difference between the strike price and the index closing value is multiplied by a multiplier, and that product is paid by the option writer to the option buyer.

Generally, the minimum tick value for index options is $5 for options trading for less than $3 and $10 for all other series. Table 1–6 shows an example of certain index options and some of their attributes. American-style index options are designated with an *A*, whereas European-style options are denoted with an *E*.

---

[16] "Index Options," *Mr. Stock Web site,* February 20, 2004; available at www.mrstock.com/resourceCenter/indexOptions.msp?Member=false.

TABLE 1-6
Attributes of certain index options

Index	Sym	Exercise style	Point value	Strike price interval (points)	Multiplier	Settlement Type	Sym
DJIA	DJX	E	$100	1	$100	A.M.	DJS
NASDAQ 100	NDX	E	$100	5	$100	A.M.	NDX
Russell 1000	RUI	E	$100	5-10	$100	A.M.	RHJ
Russell 2000	RUT	E	$100	5-10	$100	A.M.	RUU
Russell 3000	RUA	E	$100	5-10	$100	A.M.	RAS
S&P 100	OEX	A	$100	5-10	$100	P.M.	OEX
S&P 100	XEO	E	$100	5-20	$100	P.M.	XEO

Source (data): cboe.com.

FUTURES OPTIONS

Many people become confused when it comes to the differences between options and futures contracts. While options contracts create rights, futures contracts create obligations, e.g., the obligation to make or take delivery at some future date. Futures options, therefore, create the *right* to take on an obligation. Another difference relates to *time*. While a futures contract *must* be fulfilled *on* a specific date, an options contract *may* be fulfilled any time *prior to* a specific date. A futures contract expiring in a given month may have options expiring in the same or prior months.

Assume a trader believes the September T-bond futures are going to decrease due to rising interest rates. He buys a September 104 T-Bond Put for a $2,234 premium ($2^{15}/_{64}$ × $1,000). If, at expiration of the option, the September T-bond futures price has fallen to $98, the trader can realize a six-point increase ($6,000) by selling or exercising the option. Since the premium paid was $2,234, the trader's profit is $3,766 less transaction costs. If the trader had been wrong about the direction of T-bond futures prices, *no matter how wrong he was,* the maximum he could have lost was $2,234 plus transaction costs.

Assume a trader believes an increase in the price of corn is destined to take place over the next six months. She pays a premium of $1,600 ($0.32 × 5,000 bushels) for a December 310 corn Call option giving her the right to buy 5,000 bushels of corn at $3.10 per bushel ($15,500). Assume at option expiration, the December corn future is selling for

$3.70 per bushel. This is a $0.60 increase on 5,000 bushels, or $3,000. The trader's profit is $1,400 ($3,000 − $1,600 premium) less transaction costs. Like the Put option buyer earlier, the Call option buyer's maximum exposure to the trade is the $1,600 premium.

In addition to the *spot,* or cash price, prices are quoted for both the future and options on that future. Table 1–7 shows the futures quote series for the S&P 500 Index, whose symbol is now $INX (formerly SPX).

Price quotes together with volume and open interest data for the Call and Put options available for the March 2004 $INX future (SPH04) are given in Table 1–8. The option closest to being at the money is highlighted in boldface.

While owners of stocks or futures contracts are exposed to large losses (as much as the purchase price or contract value), purchasers of options on stocks or futures contracts have a loss exposure limited to the premiums paid. Additionally, there is more leverage associated with futures and options. Suppose there are three traders interested in trading the broad market represented by the S&P 500 Index. Each trader goes about trading a little differently.

Trader A buys $285,025 worth of stocks that comprise the S&P 500 Index on 50 percent margin. Trader A's margin deposit is $142,512.50 Maximum possible loss is $285,025 plus transaction costs.

Trader B buys one contract of the March 2004 S&P 500 Index futures (SPH04) at 1140.1 (see Table 1–7) for a total contract value

TABLE 1-7

S&P 500 ($INX) futures quotes
Settlement on February 23, 2004
($INX closed at 1140.99)

Symbol	Expire	Price
SPH04	Mar-04	1140.10
SPM04	Jun-04	1139.10
SPU04	Sep-04	1138.10
SPZ04	Dec-04	1137.50
SPH05	Mar-05	1139.00
SPM05	Jun-05	1142.50
SPU05	Sep-05	1146.50
SPZ05	Dec-05	1150.50

Source (data): futuresource.com.

TABLE 1-8

Options on $INX future SPH04
Settlement on February 23, 2004
($INX Closed at 1140.99)

		Calls				Puts		
Strike price	Price	Vol.	Open int.	Value	Price	Vol.	Open int.	Value
1120	29.60		386	7400	9.50	208	491	2375
1125	26.00	1	1616	6500	10.90	592	1540	2725
1130	22.60	2	278	5650	12.50	21	187	3125
1135	19.50		333	4875	14.40	6	27	3600
1140	**16.50**	**74**	**404**	**4125**	**16.40**	**253**	**449**	**4100**
1145	13.90	71	271	3475	18.80	13	225	4700
1150	11.50	105	3436	2875	21.40	147	698	5350
1155	9.50	37	92	2375	24.40	14	224	6100
1160	7.80	67	3961	1950	27.70	65	495	6925

Source (data): futuresource.com.

of $285,025 (1140.1 × $250). Trader B's initial margin is $20,000 (approximately 7 percent), with maintenance margin of $16,000. Maximum possible loss is $285,025 plus transaction costs.

Trader C buys one March 2004 1140 Call option on the March 2004 S&P 500 Index future. The premium for the Call option is $16.50 (see Table 1–8), making the total purchase price of the Call option contract $4,125 ($16.50 × 250). Since the entire purchase-price of a Call option must be deposited as margin, Trader C's margin is $4,125. Maximum possible loss is $4,125.

If the S&P 500 Index increases by 30 points by the expiration date (a European-style expiration), the dollar value of the gain for Trader A and Trader B will be $7,500 (30 × $250). Trader C's gain will be $3,375 ($7,500 − $4,125 premium). Here's how the traders would have fared based on return on invested capital (margin) excluding transaction costs:

$$\text{Trader A: Return} = \frac{7,500}{142,512.5} = 5.3\%$$

$$\text{Trader B: Return} = \frac{7,500}{20,000} = 37.5\%$$

$$\text{Trader C: Return} = \frac{3,375}{4,125} = 81.8\%$$

If the S&P 500 Index decreases by 30 points by the expiration date, Traders A and B would have lost $7,500. Trader C would have lost $4,125.

THE MATHEMATICS OF OPTIONS TRADING

We have introduced the major financial products, some of their derivatives, and the role of options thereon. To be sure, there are many other specific investment, speculative, and trading opportunities not covered here. New opportunities arise almost daily. The discussion of financial products has been limited to the major trading instruments that not only are optionable but for which there is also a liquid secondary market for such options. For the remainder of this book we will concentrate on *equity and index options*. We will now investigate some basic math techniques in Chapter 2 before introducing the basic option strategies in Chapter 3.

CHAPTER 2

Statistics, Probability, and Other Wonders

He uses statistics as a drunken man uses lamp-posts—for support rather than illumination.

—Andrew Lang (1844–1912)

To understand how options really work and how strategies for profit may be developed in a practical manner, an elementary knowledge of statistics and probability is essential not only for this text but also for the myriad of other published books and papers about options. Some people gravitate toward options trading primarily because of the ability to create and manipulate mathematical models. To others, the use of mathematical techniques is the ultimate turn-off. While certain basic calculus operations will be introduced (e.g., area under the curve, rates of change, etc.), the *C* word need not send anyone to the showers. Every effort has been made to render the examples as interesting and painless as possible in order to bring all readers to the same level of understanding. The subject matter is limited to the topics necessary for grasping the essentials of options trading strategies.

At a basic level, however, some of the concepts presented may appear as confusing to the novice as they are boring to the learned. The learned should page through the material until they find something more interesting, whereas the novice should attempt to understand each of the explanations presented herein. With today's modern electronic computers, calculators, and spreadsheet programs, such as Microsoft Excel, the mathematical operations should not prove especially challenging.

SOME ALGEBRAIC NOTATION

Algebraic notation refers to allowing *letters* to stand for numbers we might wish to substitute for them according to the problem at hand. A *formula (equation)* is simply the collection of the letters and the operations to be performed on them that, in turn, forms the rules for solving a particular problem. Suppose, for example, we observed four numbers and wished to obtain their average. We let x stand for any one of the numbers, and denote each individual number with a *subscript:*

$$x_1 = 6 \quad x_2 = 5 \quad x_3 = 2 \quad x_4 = 3$$

Letting n be the total number of observations, the equation becomes

$$\text{Average} = \frac{x_1 + x_2 + x_3 + x_4}{n}$$

Mathematicians use a shorthand notation for many arithmetic operations. For summing up a series of numbers, the shorthand notation is the capital Greek letter Σ, which is called *sigma*. Thus, by letting i be the general subscript for any x, we have

$$\text{Average} = \frac{\sum_{i=1}^{n} x_i}{n}$$

which is read, "the sum of all x_i (for i equal 1 to n) divided by n." For our four observed numbers, we have

$$\text{Average} = \frac{6 + 5 + 2 + 3}{4} = \frac{16}{4} = 4$$

Two important mathematical concepts used widely in science and economics are exponents and logarithms. An *exponent* (or *power*) indicates the number of times a quantity must be multiplied by itself. If $y = 2^4$, then $y = 2 \times 2 \times 2 \times 2 = 16$ (where 4 is the exponent). If we have

$$x = a^p \quad \text{and} \quad y = a^q$$

the three common laws of exponents are

Multiplication

$$xy = a^{p+q}$$

Division

$$\frac{x}{y} = a^{p-q}$$

Power

$$x^n = (a^p)^n = a^{pn}$$

Equations of the form $y = a^x$ are called *exponential functions* (where a constant, or *base,* is raised to some power).

Conversely, a *logarithm* of a number is the exponent to which some base must be raised to yield that number. For the exponential function $y = a^x$, its logarithmic equivalent (abbreviated *log*) is $\log_a y = x$ read "log base *a* of *y* equals *x*").

The invention of logarithms (as we know them) is generally credited to Henry Briggs (*circa* 1617), who modified the work of John Napier to produce tables of logarithms to the base 10 (called *common logs* today). Napier originally had developed a set of logarithms to reduce the then-tedious arithmetic operations of multiplying and dividing to the simpler level of adding and subtracting.

If we have the following:

$$x = a^p \quad \text{and} \quad y = a^q$$

then

$$p = \log_a x \quad \text{and} \quad q = \log_a y$$

From the law of exponents indicated earlier, we may derive the three laws of logarithms.

Multiplication

Since, from the law of exponents, $xy = a^{p+q}$, then

$$\log_a(xy) = p + q$$

$$\log_a(xy) = \log_a x + \log_a y$$

The log of a product of two numbers is simply the sum of the individual logs.

Division

Since, from the law of exponents, $x/y = a^{p-q}$, then

$$\log_a\left(\frac{x}{y}\right) = p - q$$

$$\log_a\left(\frac{x}{y}\right) = \log_a x - \log_a y$$

The log of a quotient of two numbers is simply the log of the numerator less the log of the denominator.

Power

Since, from the law of exponents, $x^n = (a^p)^n = a^{pn}$, then

$$\log_a(x^n) = np$$

$$\log_a(x^n) = n \log_a x$$

The log of a number raised to a power is simply the log of the number multiplied by the power.

To understand the monumental breakthrough that logarithms represented to early mathematicians and astronomers, imagine a world without computers, calculators, or even slide rules (remember those?). Hundreds and hundreds of tedious multiplications and divisions of large, complex numbers were made by hand daily. The somewhat arduous task of dividing 9,427.84 by 5,476.8921 is child's play with a table of common logs. We simply subtract the log of the denominator (3.73853) from the log of the numerator (3.97441), which yields .23588. To obtain the answer, we interpolate from the tables and find the *antilog* of .23588 ($10^{.23588}$), which is 1.72134—the same answer as obtained by dividing the two numbers longhand. Incidentally, as late as the 1950s, most repetitive multiplication and division were performed on clunky mechanical or electromechanical machines consuming vast amounts of time. As a shortcut, slide rules (which are logarithmic devices) could be used for multiplying and dividing if great precision was not required.

Although any number may be used as a base for logarithms, only two are in general use today—the *common log system* (base 10) and the *natural log system,* based on the constant e, which, to five decimal places, is 2.71828. Like the constant π, which represents the ratio of a circle's circumference to its diameter, the Euler number e (named for Leonhard

Euler, an eighteenth-century Swiss mathematician) has important mathematical properties, particularly in the study of rates of growth or decay. It represents the limit of

$$e = \lim_{n \to \infty} \left(1 + \frac{1}{n}\right)^n$$

where the right side of the equation is read "the limit of the expression in parentheses as n becomes infinitely large." It also may be defined as the sum of the infinite series

$$e = \sum_{k=0}^{\infty} \frac{1}{k!}$$

where $k!$ is read "k factorial." A factorial indicates a product of successively smaller integers until zero is reached. 0! equals 1. If $k = 4$, then $k!$ would be calculated by

$$k(k-1)(k-2)(k-3) = (4)(3)(2)(1) = 24$$

A factorial also indicates the number of ways things can be arranged without regard to their order (permutations). For example, three letters of the alphabet can be arranged in six different ways—from

$$3! = 3(3-1)(3-2) = 6$$

For the remainder of this book, whenever logarithms are called for, natural logs will be used—designated by *ln*. In Excel, this is the LN function. Also in Excel, e is represented by the EXP function. These two functions also appear on most modern electronic calculators. Note the inverse relationships between *ln* and *e*:

$$\ln(e^x) = x = e^{\ln(x)}$$

Therefore, if:

$$\ln(x) = 2,$$

then

$$x = e^2 = 7.389$$

And if

$$e^x = 2,$$

then

$$x = \ln(2) = .693$$

If $z = x^a y^b$, then

$$\ln(z) = aLn(x) + bLn(y)$$

We use the following operator to specify the *greater* of x or y:

$$\max(x, y)$$

And, for the *lesser* of x or y,

$$\min(x, y)$$

Finally, we use Δ to mean "a change in." A change in y is denoted

$$\Delta y$$

More special notations and operations will be introduced as required.

ON THE AVERAGE

Statistics refers to the collection, analysis, interpretation, and presentation of numerical data and is typically classified as either *descriptive* or *inductive*. By descriptive statistics, we mean any treatment of numerical data not involving generalizations—only those measures which *describe* a given set of data. Inductive statistics, on the other hand, involves generalizations, predictions, or estimates.

Averages are a major component of descriptive statistics. They are measures of location or central tendency. Called the *mean* of a data set, they attempt to describe something about an entire collection of numerical data with a single measure. When we refer to the mean of all the elements of a given data set, it is a *population mean,* denoted by the Greek letter μ pronounced "mu." If we are referring to a subset or sample of the elements contained in a population, its mean is a *sample mean,* denoted by the letter $\bar{x}$ (pronounced "x bar").

There are several categories of means available to describe a set of numerical data. The simple average of the four numbers calculated earlier is called the *arithmetic mean*. If the four observations comprised the entire data set, we would write

$$\mu = \frac{\sum_{i=1}^{n} x_i}{n} \tag{2.1}$$

If the four observations were only a sample of a larger population, we would replace the μ in Equation (2.1) with $\bar{x}$.

With truly large masses of data it is sometimes preferable to reduce the work load and settle for an approximation by grouping the data into *classes* (or *ranges*) and finding the *class marks*, which then become the new x_i. For example, suppose there were over 3,000 people attending various business conferences at a large resort hotel. For one reason or another (probably marketing), we wish to estimate the arithmetic mean of their heights. One of the conference chairpersons gives us permission to measure the heights of the 50 people in her room. We decide on four classes (denoted by k) for our sample. On measuring their heights, we group the measurements into the $k = 4$ classes and complete Table 2–1. This practice will yield slightly less accurate results than accounting for each and every individual measurement; however, deviations above and below the class mark are expected to "average out" and yield reasonably accurate results.

Here, we use the class marks as the x_i representing the midpoint of each class. The equation for the arithmetic mean of grouped data is

$$\bar{x} = \frac{\sum_{i=1}^{k} x_i f_i}{\sum_{i=1}^{k} f_i} \tag{2.2}$$

For the observations in Table 2–1

TABLE 2-1

Observation of heights of conference attendees

Height range in inches (classes)	Class mark x_i	No. of persons (frequency) f_i	$x_i f_i$
65–67.99	66.495	5	332.475
68–70.99	69.495	31	2,154.345
71–73.99	72.495	10	724.95
74–76.99	75.495	4	301.98
		50	3,513.75

$$\bar{x} = \frac{3513.75}{50} = 70.275 \text{ in}$$

Note that we are still dealing with descriptive statistics because we have not yet attempted to generalize or estimate anything. We simply have calculated the mean of a sample. We shall return later to solve the estimation problem after learning more about means and other descriptive statistical measures.

At this point we introduce the notion of frequency distributions. Until now, we have referred to numerical data sets. A *frequency distribution* is just another way of describing a population or sample of data. It defines the distribution of the data elements over the entire range of such elements. For raw data, such as the earlier four-number example, the frequency distribution would look like Figure 2–1.

Each of the numbers occurred only once; hence the series of four bars each with heights equal to 1 on the "Frequency" axis.

When data include more than one element of the same value or have been grouped into classes as in Table 2–1, the frequency distribution looks a little different. Figure 2–2 shows the distribution of the elements in Table 2–1. Figures 2–1 and 2–2 are called *histograms*—graphic representations of frequency distributions. Dropping the adjective *frequency* (which is implied), numerical data sets simply will be referred to as *distributions* from this point forward.

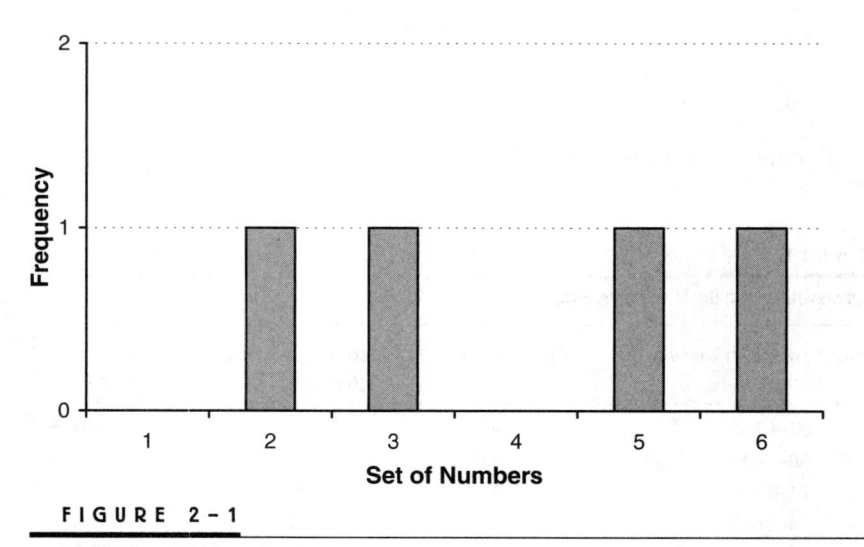

FIGURE 2–1

Distribution of four numbers

FIGURE 2-2

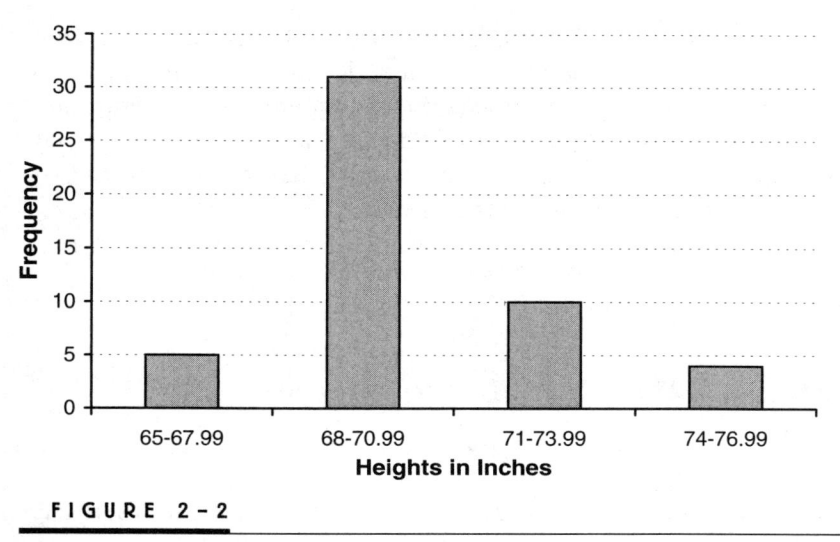

Distribution of heights of conference attendees

Depending on what the particular data represent, there are different ways to calculate the mean. If the data consist of quantities that follow a geometric or exponential progression, such as population growth, the *geometric mean* is a better measure of central tendency. For n observations, the geometric mean (denoted by G) is the nth root of the products of the individual observations. Letting Π be the shorthand notation for multiplying a series of numbers together, we have

$$G = \sqrt[n]{\prod_{i=1}^{n} x_i} \qquad (2.3)$$

Because of the amount of work involved, Equation (2.3) is seldom used. Changing Equation (2.3) into its logarithmic form gives

$$\ln(G) = \frac{\sum_{i=1}^{n} \ln(x_i)}{n}$$

Therefore,

$$G = e^{\sum_{i=1}^{n} \ln(x_i)/n} \qquad (2.4)$$

Consider a city in which the 1990 Census indicated a population of 275,000, and the 2000 Census placed the number at 525,000. How would we estimate the 1995 population? We could take a simple arithmetic mean using Equation (2.1), which yields 400,000. This would be a reasonable answer *only* if the city's population grew by the same number each year. However, populations typically don't grow in this way. As cities grow in size, populations tend to grow at ever increasing rates—a prime candidate for the geometric mean.

$$\ln(275,000) = 12.525$$

$$\ln(525,000) = 13.171$$

The total of 12.525 and 13.171 is 25.696. Therefore,

$$G = e^{25.696/2} = 380,028$$

Use of the arithmetic mean produces more than a 5 percent difference.

In a similar fashion, *rates* (e.g., miles per hour, dollars per dozen, etc.) are not amenable to arithmetic averaging. The *harmonic mean* is a much better descriptor of central tendency for a series of rate observations. The harmonic mean (denoted by H) of n observations is n divided by the sum of the reciprocals of the x_i.

$$H = \frac{n}{\sum_{i=1}^{n}(1/x_i)} \qquad (2.5)$$

One of the best examples of the mistakes encountered when attempting to arithmetically average rates is shown by an airplane flying around a 100-mile square. It flies the first side at 100 mi/h, the second side at 200 mi/h, the third side at 300 mi/h, and the fourth side at 400 mi/h. What is the average speed of the plane during its flight around the square? Equation (2.1) would show the average speed to be 250 mi/h. But this cannot be so.

Table 2–2 shows the total time the plane takes to traverse the 400 miles. The plane has flown 400 miles in 125 minutes, or 2.0833 hours. This equates to an average speed of 192 mi/h—a far cry from the 250 mi/h obtained by arithmetic averaging. Here, the harmonic mean saves the day. From Equation (2.5),

$$H = \frac{4}{\frac{1}{100} + \frac{1}{200} + \frac{1}{300} + \frac{1}{400}} = \frac{4}{\frac{25}{1200}} = \frac{4800}{25} = 192 \text{ mi/h}$$

TABLE 2-2

Total time to fly the square

Side	Minutes
1	60
2	30
3	20
4	15
Total	125

OTHER MEASURES OF CENTRAL TENDENCY

Means are not the only measure of central tendency in a data set. A second measure used to describe the "middle" of a data set is called the *median*. When the elements of a data set are arranged in ascending or descending order, the *median* is the value of the middle item (or the mean of the values of the two middle items).

A measure of central tendency should be representative of a homogeneous group. Many distributions, while being homogeneous in the sense that their elements are similar, have great discrepancies between the largest and smallest members and exhibit a marked lack of symmetry. Suppose among a city's 250,000 inhabitants, the income per capita were distributed as shown in Figure 2-3.

If we wished to describe this distribution with a single measure, would it be reasonable to use the arithmetic mean? Equation (2.2) produces a value of $43,875 (if we cap the last range at $500,000). Does this value accurately describe the per-capita income distribution for this city? Certainly not very well. Intuitively, a much better description is the median. Since half the inhabitants (125,000) have incomes under $25,000 and half have incomes over that amount, the *median* income is $25,000—a marked difference from the arithmetic mean. Notice that the median is not affected by the extreme values in the "tail" of the distribution.

Another measure of central tendency also unaffected by extreme values is called the *mode,* which is simply the most commonly occurring value. The mode in Figure 2-3 is also $25,000. Generally, the mode's principal value is to describe qualitative data. It is not well suited to further mathematical manipulation.

If we were to think of a distribution as a continuous curve that included all our data, the median would divide the *area under the curve* into two equal parts, whereas the mode would pass through the highest

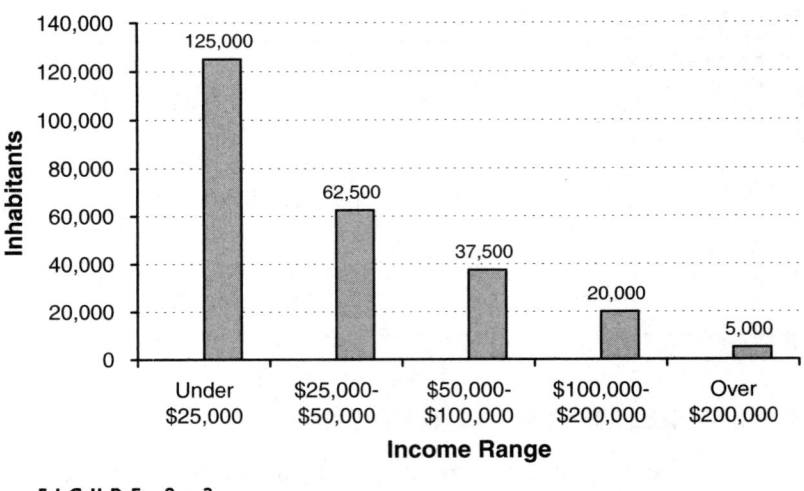

FIGURE 2-3

Distribution of per capita income

point on the curve. By contrast, the mean could appear anywhere along the curve depending on the individual data values. For solving problems of sampling and estimation (the kinds of problems associated with the stock market and options), the arithmetic mean will be used extensively as the measure of central tendency owing to its favorable mathematical properties.

VARIABILITY

The second major component of descriptive statistics is a measure of variability. In a general sense, measures of variation tend to provide guidance as to just how good the mean is as a descriptor of a distribution. Take the old saw:

> *If a man sleeps with his head in the oven and his feet in the refrigerator— he will be comfortable on the average.*

Obviously, being comfortable on the average does not quite cut it as a description of a person's physical well-being in the preceding circumstance. We need to know something about the *differences* from the average to be able to discuss the range of the person's various physical states. Indeed, the *range* of a distribution is the first measure of variation to be considered.

The *range,* or the difference between the largest and smallest elements of a distribution, is the easiest measure to come by and provides a quick but not particularly accurate measure of variation. Its usefulness is limited because it accounts for only the extreme values and says nothing about the dispersion of the remaining elements in a given distribution.

A better way to measure variability is to look at the deviations of the individual elements from their mean. These positive and negative differences simply could be averaged, but since their *size* is of more interest than their signs, we get a better measure by squaring the deviations, dividing by the number of observations, and taking the square root of the resulting quotient (the *root-mean-square method*). Thus we get a measure of variation called the *standard deviation,* denoted by the lowercase Greek letter σ (sigma), where

$$\sigma = \sqrt{\frac{\sum_{i=1}^{n}(x_i - \mu)^2}{n}} \qquad (2.6)$$

If the observations were a *sample* of a larger population, the standard deviation would be denoted by s, and $n - 1$ would be substituted for n in the divisor.

$$s = \sqrt{\frac{\sum_{i=1}^{n}(x_i - \bar{x})^2}{n - 1}} \qquad (2.7)$$

Substituting $n - 1$ for n in Equation (2.7) is particularly useful when dealing with small samples. If the sample size is greater than, say, 100, the difference between using $n - 1$ and n is negligible.

While Equations (2.6) and (2.7) reveal what is truly meant by a standard deviation, they are seldom used in actual practice because there are shortcut formulas available.

$$\sigma = \frac{1}{n}\sqrt{n\sum_{i=1}^{n}x_i^2 - \left(\sum_{i=1}^{n}x_i\right)^2} \qquad (2.8)$$

$$s = \sqrt{\frac{n\sum_{i=1}^{n}x_i^2 - \left(\sum_{i=1}^{n}x_i\right)^2}{n(n - 1)}} \qquad (2.9)$$

Just as means may be calculated using classes or ranges to reduce the work load, standard deviations likewise may be calculated for n observations grouped into k classes.

$$\sigma = \sqrt{\frac{\sum_{i=1}^{k}(x_i - \mu)^2 f_i}{n}} \qquad (2.10)$$

$$s = \sqrt{\frac{\sum_{i=1}^{k}(x_i - \bar{x})^2 f_i}{n - 1}} \qquad (2.11)$$

Absent the radical sign in Equations (2.10) and (2.11), we have the sample *variance* s^2 and the population *variance* σ^2. The variance is a measure of variability used extensively in statistical analysis. However, for our purposes in analyzing options, we will concentrate on the standard deviation.

Recall the problem of estimating the heights of over 3,000 conference attendees based on a sample of 50 measurements subdivided into four classes, as shown in Table 2–1. Previously, we calculated the sample mean at 70.28 inches. Now we are ready to calculate the second parameter of the height distribution for the sample—the standard deviation. We expand Table 2–1 to include the data for determining s and complete Table 2–3.

Table 2-3 contains the necessary tabulations for solving Equation (2.11) (remember, this is a sample distribution).

$$s = \sqrt{\frac{248.58}{49}} = 2.25$$

We are now able to describe the sample distribution of 50 heights as having a mean of 70.28 inches with a standard deviation of 2.25 inches.

What can we do with our new-found knowledge? The mean and standard deviation are important parameters to know because there are certain population distributions in which

- 68.3 percent of the values will differ from the mean by less than 1 standard deviation.

TABLE 2-3

Observation of heights of conference attendees

Height range in inches k_i	Class mark x_i	$x_i - \bar{x}$	$(x_i - \bar{x})^2$	No. of persons (frequency) f_i	$f_i(x_i - \bar{x})^2$
65–67.99	66.495	−3.78	14.2884	5	71.4420
68–70.99	69.495	−0.78	0.6084	31	18.8604
71–73.99	72.495	2.22	4.9284	10	49.2840
74–76.99	75.495	5.22	27.2484	4	108.9936
				50	248.5800

Mean = 70.275

- 95.4 percent of the values will differ from the mean by less than 2 standard deviations.
- 99.7 percent of the values will differ from the mean by less than 3 standard deviations.

Stated another way, based on our sample and selecting one person at random from *all* the conference attendees, we can be 68.3 percent sure that his height will be between 68.03 and 72.53 inches. We may assert with a probability of 95.4 percent that the person's height will be between 65.78 and 74.78 inches. Also, 99.7 percent of the time, the selected individual's height will fall between 63.53 and 77.03 inches. *Now* we are into inductive statistics! We have moved from the specific (sample) to the general (population).

It appears that knowing the mean and standard deviation enables us to make *probability* statements about the elements in a distribution.

THE CONCEPT OF PROBABILITY

If you ask 10 people their definition of probability, you likely would get 10 different answers—from the philosophical to the mathematical. We deal here only with *statistical probability,* which refers to the relative frequency of an event. The proportion of time an event takes place is called its *relative frequency;* the relative frequency with which it takes place *in the long run* is its *probability.* Thus, if an event occurs x times in n trials, its relative frequency is x/n, and its probability is the x/n we would expect as n becomes infinitely large. For example, if we flipped a perfectly balanced coin 10 times, we *might* get 6 heads. Thus the relative frequency of heads in the sample is 60 percent. If we flipped the coin 10 million times, we would expect to get close to 50 percent heads—the probability.

The first rule of probability is that it must have a value between 0 (impossible) and 1 (certain). We write

$$0 \leq P(A) \leq 1$$

where $P(\ )$ stands for "the probability of," and A represents an event. It follows, then, that the probability of A *not* occurring is

$$1 - P(A)$$

THE THEORY OF PROBABILITY

Probability theory was born in seventeenth-century France amid the gambling parlors of Paris. The Chevalier de Mere, a French nobleman and inveterate gambler, had been playing a simple game in which he would bet even money that he could throw *at least* one six in four rolls of a single die. He was moderately successful at this game, believing his favorable odds could be calculated by

$P(\text{one six}) = 4 \times 1/6 = 2/3$, or a probability of 67%

Soon tiring of this game, he turned to another—this time involving two dice. He began to make even-money bets that he could throw at least one double six in 24 rolls of the dice. He reasoned as before that

$P(\text{double six}) = 24 \times 1/36 = 2/3$, or 67%

After beginning to lose steadily on his second game, de Mere sought the advice of Blaise Pascal (1623–1662), who, in turn, collaborated with Pierre de Fermat (1601–1665) to solve the problem and correctly calculate the probabilities. Pascal and Fermat were two of France's mathematical giants. Pascal determined the correct method for calculating probability for the first game was to first calculate the probability of *not getting a six* in four rolls of the single die and subtracting that result from 1:

$$P(\text{one six}) = 1 - \left(\frac{5}{6}\right)^4 = 51.8\%$$

This slight edge over the other players gave de Mere his modest winnings in the first game (a 50 percent probability would have been a *fair* game with no advantage either way). Likewise, Pascal determined the probability of tossing at least one double six in 24 rolls of two dice:

$$P(\text{one double six}) = 1 - \left(\frac{35}{36}\right)^{24} = 49.1\%$$

which explained why de Mere lost on the second game. De Mere's mistake in both games was that he considered the probabilities to be *additive* rather than *multiplicative*. We shall investigate the details of Pascal's solution later. This exercise (which appears trivial by today's standards) led to Pascal's discovery of the binomial distribution, which is the cornerstone of modern probability theory.

THE RULES OF PROBABILITY

Two events are said to be *mutually exclusive* if they cannot occur together. Two events are said to be *independent* if the occurrence (or nonoccurrence) of either in no way affects the occurrence of the other. We consider the rules of *multiplication* first.

Special rule of multiplication (when A and B are independent):

$$P(A \text{ and } B) = P(A) \times P(B) \qquad (2.12)$$

General rule of multiplication (where $P(A|B)$ is read "the conditional probability of A given that B has taken place"):

$$P(A \text{ and } B) = P(B) \times P(A|B) \qquad \text{or}$$

$$P(A \text{ and } B) = P(A) \times P(B|A) \qquad (2.13)$$

To illustrate the rules of multiplication, first consider the probability of getting two heads in two successive flips of a coin. A represents getting a head the first time, and B represents getting a head on the second toss. A and B clearly are independent because the outcome of one toss in no way affects the outcome of the other. Therefore, Equation (2.12) applies.

$$P(A \text{ and } B) = .5 \times .5 = 25\%$$

Suppose, however, the probability of one's committing a crime is 50 percent [$P(A)$] and the probability of one's going to jail is 25 percent [$P(B)$]. Since these two events are not necessarily independent, we need to know the probability of one's going to jail *given that one has committed a crime* [$P(B|A)$]. If this conditional probability is 40 percent, we have from Equation (2.13)

$$P(A \text{ and } B) = .5 \times .4 = 20\%$$

An old joke goes something like this: Suppose the odds of there being a bomb aboard the plane in which you are a passenger are 10 million to 1. From Equation (2.12), we know the probability of there being *two* bombs aboard is an infinitesimally small number:

$$\left(\frac{1}{10,000,000}\right)\left(\frac{1}{10,000,000}\right) = \frac{1}{(10,000,000)^2}$$

Therefore, to assure yourself of being subject to the smaller odds, you simply carry a bomb aboard yourself, right? We now know how to deal with this fallacy. If A represents a bomb being aboard and B represents the bomb you brought aboard, Equation (2.13) provides

$$P(A \text{ and } B) = P(A) \times P(B|A)$$

But

$$P(B|A) = 1$$

because the probability of your bomb being aboard given there is already one other bomb aboard is 100 percent. Therefore, $P(A \text{ and } B) = P(A)(1)$ = the original odds.

When we are interested in the probability that one or the other of two events will occur, the rules of addition apply.

Special rule of addition (when A and B are mutually exclusive):

$$P(A \text{ or } B) = P(A) + P(B) \qquad (2.14)$$

General rule of addition (where A and B can *both* occur):

$$P(A \text{ or } B) = P(A) + P(B) - P(A \text{ and } B) \qquad (2.15)$$

Thus, if the probabilities that a person will someday die of heart disease or cancer are 53 and 15 percent, respectively, the probability that the person will die of one of the two diseases is calculated from Equation (2.14).

$$P(A \text{ or } B) = .58 + .15 = 68\%$$

Suppose that in a certain place and at a certain time there was a 70 percent chance of clouds and a 50 percent chance of sunshine. What is the probability that there will be *either* clouds *or* sunshine? Since these two events can both occur, we have to subtract the cases in which they occur together (assume that 40 percent of the time there are both clouds and sunshine). Equation (2.15) yields

$$P(A \text{ or } B) = .7 + .5 - .4 = 80\%$$

Also, there are special cases such as wishing to know the probability of which of two events will occur first.

$$P(A \text{ before } B) = \frac{P(A)}{P(A \text{ or } B)} \qquad (2.16)$$

Sometimes probabilities are expressed as *odds,* meaning the odds to 1 that an event will or will not occur. For example, the collective wisdom of the bettors at a race track results in a certain horse x having 3 to 2 odds against winning. What is their estimate of the probability this horse will win?

Let

Q_x = odds to 1 against (payoff odds to 1) horse x winning expressed as a fraction.

$P(x)$ = the probability the horse will win

Then

$$P(x) = \frac{1}{1 + Q_x} \qquad (2.17)$$

For the horse example:

$$P(x) = \frac{1}{1 + \frac{3}{2}} = \frac{1}{2.5} = 40\%$$

If we want to convert probability to odds, that is, the odds to 1 associated with a 40 percent probability that horse x will win, we write

$$Q_x = \frac{1}{P(x)} - 1 \qquad (2.18)$$

For 40 percent probability:

$$Q_x = \frac{1}{.4} - 1 = 1.5 = 1.5 \text{ to } 1, \text{ or } 3 \text{ to } 2$$

DISCRETE PROBABILITY DISTRIBUTIONS

A distribution is said to be *discrete* if its elements can take on only isolated values. A distribution is said to be *continuous* if its elements may take on any value of a continuous scale. An example of a discrete distribution is the tossing of two dice where the sum on any one toss is limited to the integers 2 through 12. Table 2–4 shows the probabilities for each of the outcomes.

Perhaps the best-known game played with a pair of dice is craps—probably introduced to Europe from the East during the time of the Crusades. Craps is played between two players, one of whom, the shooter, throws the dice. If the first toss is a 7 or 11 (a natural), the shooter wins immediately. If the shooter tosses a 2, 3, or 12 (craps), he loses

TABLE 2-4

Probabilities associated with tossing a pair of dice

Sum	Number of ways to make	Probability Fraction	Probability Decimal
2	1	1/36	.028
3	2	2/36	.056
4	3	3/36	.083
5	4	4/36	.111
6	5	5/36	.139
7	6	6/36	.167
8	5	5/36	.139
9	4	4/36	.111
10	3	3/36	.083
11	2	2/36	.056
12	1	1/36	.028
Total probability			1.000

immediately. If the first toss is any other number (the point), the shooter goes on throwing the dice until he either makes his point again and wins or throws a 7 and loses.

In the casino version of the game, the preceding rules apply to the "pass line" on the crap table. There are many other bets available to the shooter and the other players betting with or against the house. The pass line is where the most action occurs and provides only a small disadvantage for the player. To calculate the probability of winning on the pass line, we set up the following three independent probability statements:

$P(A)$ = probability of tossing a point on the first roll
$P(B)$ = probability of tossing a 7 on the second roll
$P(C)$ = probability of tossing the point before a 7 on the second roll

Note that the probabilities of winning on the first toss can be written down immediately from Table 2–4. We want the probability that A and C will occur because, for any other outcome, the game is decided on the first toss. Suppose that a 4 or 10 is thrown on the first toss (referencing Table 2–4). Then

$$P(A) = .083$$

$$P(B) = .167$$

From Equation (2.16),

$$P(C) = \frac{P(A)}{P(A \text{ or } B)} = \frac{.083}{.083 + .167} = .332$$

From Equation (2.12),

$$P(A \text{ and } C) = .083 \times .332 = .028$$

In a similar manner, the probabilities for winning on any point may be calculated, and Table 2–5 may be completed.

Thus the player has a 49.3 percent chance of winning on the pass line—a slight disadvantage relative to the house's win probability of 50.7 percent.

We will now investigate the more general problem of finding the probability that a given event will take place *exactly* x times in n trials. This exercise involves the most commonly used discrete probability distribution—the *binomial distribution*. It is a distribution of probabilities

TABLE 2-5

Probability of winning at craps (pass line)

	Probability of winning		
Sum	First roll	Successive rolls	Total
2	0	0	0
3	0	0	0
4	0	.028	.028
5	0	.044	.044
6	0	.063	.063
7	.167	0	.167
8	0	.063	.063
9	0	.044	.044
10	0	.028	.028
11	.056	0	.056
12	0	0	0
			.493

describing the outcomes of *Bernoulli trials,* which refer to a sequence of trials involving only two possible outcomes (e.g., success or failure). Bernoulli trials also require that each trial be independent and that the probability (of success) is constant from one trial to another. Bernoulli trials were so named after Jacob (Jacques) Bernoulli (1654–1705), the first in a long line of Swiss mathematicians and whose brother, Johan, actually tutored Leonhard Euler. The Bernoulli brothers made many important contributions to the study of calculus and probability theory.

Calculating binomial probabilities involves the use of the *binomial coefficients,* which come from expansion of the binomial expression

$$(a + b)^n$$

The binomial coefficients also appear in the famous Pascal's triangle—yes, the same fellow who helped de Mere solve his dice problem. The coefficients can be denoted by $_nC_x$, which is read, "the number of ways x successes can occur in n trials" or, in modern parlance, "n choose x." Thus

$$_nC_x = \frac{n!}{x!(n-x)!} \qquad (2.19)$$

The probability of exactly x successes in n trials is given by

$$P(x:n) = {}_nC_x \, p^x(1-p)^{n-x} \tag{2.20}$$

Returning to de Mere's first game, in which we want the probability of *at least one six* in four tosses, we start by calculating the probability of *exactly* one six in four tosses.

$$_4C_1 = \frac{4!}{1!(3!)} = \frac{24}{6} = 4$$

$$P(1:4) = 4\left(\frac{1}{6}\right)^1\left(\frac{5}{6}\right)^3 = \frac{2}{3}\left(\frac{125}{216}\right) = .3858$$

Since the probabilities of tossing exactly two sixes, exactly three sixes, and exactly four sixes in four rolls of a single die also qualify as tossing at least one six, they must be calculated as well.

$$P(2:4) = 6\left(\frac{1}{6}\right)^2\left(\frac{5}{6}\right)^2 = \frac{1}{6}\left(\frac{25}{36}\right) = .1157$$

$$P(3:4) = 4\left(\frac{1}{6}\right)^3\left(\frac{5}{6}\right)^1 = \frac{5}{6}\left(\frac{4}{216}\right) = .0154$$

$$P(4:4) = 1\left(\frac{1}{6}\right)^4 = \frac{1}{1296} = .0008$$

Since the events are mutually exclusive, we sum up the four probabilities according to Equation (2.14) and find the probability of getting at least one six in four rolls is 51.8 percent, which agrees with Pascal's result.

The preceding calculations were presented to show how to calculate exactly x success in n trials. There is a much shorter method for calculating the probabilities in de Mere's first game. The probability of a failure (no six) is 5/6. Therefore, according to Equation (2.20),

$$P(0:4) = 1\left(\frac{1}{6}\right)^0\left(\frac{5}{6}\right)^4 = \frac{625}{1296} = .482$$

Subtracting the probability of a failure (48.2 percent) from 1, we obtain the probability of success (51.8 percent).

Similarly, in de Mere's second game, the probability of tossing no double six in 24 rolls is 35/36 (1 − 1/36). By reference to Equation (2.20),

$$P(0:24) = 1\left(\frac{1}{36}\right)^0\left(\frac{25}{36}\right)^{24} = .509$$

Since the probability of failure is .509, the probability of success (getting at least one double six in 24 rolls) is 49.1 percent.

THE BINOMIAL DISTRIBUTION

The binomial probability distribution also may be described in terms of its mean and standard deviation, where

$$\mu = np \tag{2.21}$$

where p = probability of success

Note: To avoid confusion with the parentheses, whenever the symbol for *probability* is shown as a multiplier or an exponent, the lowercase p (with or without a subscript) will be used. Thus

$$p_A = P(A)$$

$$\sigma = \sqrt{np(1-p)} \tag{2.22}$$

Because it is a distribution of *proportions* rather than absolute values, the calculation of μ and σ for binomial distributions looks different from the calculation of means and standard deviations previously encountered. Both measures are very much dependent on the size of n (the number of trials in the experiment). Earlier we said that for certain distributions, 95.4 percent of the cases differ from the mean by less than 2 standard deviations. If we now consider the distribution of 500 flips of a perfectly balanced coin, we find that

$$\mu = 500\left(\frac{1}{2}\right) = 250$$

$$\sigma = \sqrt{500\left(\frac{1}{2}\right)\left(1 - \frac{1}{2}\right)} = \sqrt{125} = 11.18$$

We can be 95.4 percent certain that the number of heads obtained in 500 flips will fall between 228 [250 − 2(11.18)] and 272 [250 + 2(11.18)]. The expected number of heads would, of course, be 250.

FIGURE 2-4

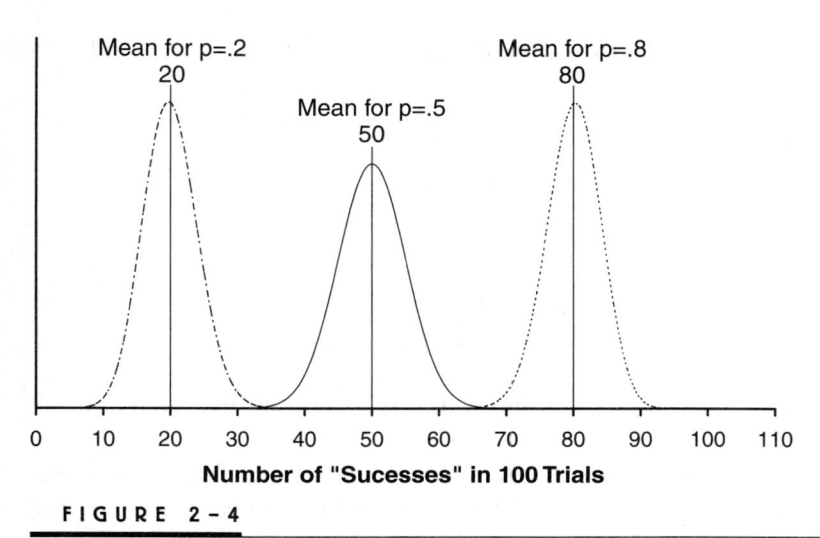

Binomial distributions for $p = .2$, $.5$, and $.8$

Graphically, the binomial distribution appears as a symmetric curve about its mean. Figure 2–4 shows the distributions for three cases ($p = .2, .5,$ and $.8$)—all for $n = 100$. As n increases, σ likewise increases, and the curves will flatten out with a wider base.

INTRODUCTION TO DIFFERENTIATION

Before going on to continuous probability distributions, it is appropriate to introduce the concept of *differentiation*—the process of taking the derivative of an expression with respect to one of its variables. The *derivative* may be interpreted as the instantaneous rate of change in one variable with respect to another. If

$$y = x^2$$

then the expression's derivative is denoted as dy/dx and is read "the derivative of y with respect to x." The dy and dx are called *differentials*. The notation dy/dx means the *instantaneous rate of change* in y (its slope) for a *given change* in x.

The instantaneous rate of change is derived from the *average rate of change* $\Delta y/\Delta x$, where the change in y is measured between any two values of x (the x interval). For example, in the preceding expression

$y = x^2$, what is the *average rate of change* in y between $x = 2$ and $x = 3$? We have

At $x = 2$, $y = 4$
At $x = 3$, $y = 9$

Therefore,

$$\frac{\Delta y}{\Delta x} = \frac{9-4}{3-2} = 5$$

which means, in the specified interval, y is increasing five times as fast as x.

If we let the x interval become smaller and smaller until it approaches zero, we would wind up with the *instantaneous rate of change* in y for any given *value of x*—which is the derivative. Therefore,

$$\frac{dy}{dx} = \lim_{\Delta x \to 0} \frac{\Delta y}{\Delta x}$$

The right-hand side of this equation is read "the limit of the change in y relative to the change in x as the change in x approaches zero."

A familiar example also may help in understanding what we mean by a derivative. Suppose a car travels 100 miles in two hours. What is the car's velocity (speed)? Obviously, the velocity is 50 mi/h. It is the rate of change of distance with respect to time. If distance and time are denoted by D and t, respectively, the formula for velocity V is given by

$$V = \frac{D}{t} = \frac{100 \text{ miles}}{2 \text{ hours}} = 50 \text{ mi/h}$$

or as a derivative,

$$V = \frac{dD}{dt}$$

or in *differential equation* form,

$$dD = Vdt$$

Therefore, the first derivative of distance with respect to time is *velocity*. If we take the derivative of velocity with respect to time, we get *acceleration* (the instantaneous change in speed relative to time).

Letting A = acceleration,

$$A = \frac{dV}{dt}$$

In order to study continuous functions of a random variable, we will use *functional notation*, where the left-hand side of an equation is represented by a function of the variable(s) on the right-hand side. If y is some function of x, we write

$$y = f(x)$$

If $y = x^2$, then $f(x) = x^2$.

In functional notation, derivatives are denoted with f'. Thus

$$f'(x) = \frac{dy}{dx}$$

Higher-order derivatives also may exist. Thus far we have discussed the *first derivative* only. The *second derivative* is denoted by

$$\frac{d^2y}{dx^2} \quad \text{or} \quad f''(x)$$

An example of a second derivative is acceleration A. A is the second derivative of distance with respect to time and is denoted by

$$\frac{d^2D}{dt^2} = A \quad \text{or} \quad A = f''(t)$$

Derivatives have many applications in higher mathematics. They are useful in determining the maximum or minimum points on a curve (assuming the function has a maximum or minimum). Typically, the maximum or minimum values can be found by setting the curve's first derivative equal to zero and solving the resulting equation. A curve's second derivative is useful in determining whether a maximum or minimum exists.

There are basic rules for finding the derivative of various types of mathematical expressions. The basic rule for differentiating an expression in which a variable x is raised to a power n, multiplied by a constant a, and added to a constant C is given below:

If $y = ax^n + C$, since the derivative of a constant by itself is zero,

$$\frac{dy}{dx} = nax^{n-1} \qquad (2.23)$$

And for the expression $y = x^2$ noted earlier,

$$\frac{dy}{dx} = (2)(1)x^{2-1} = 2x$$

For the velocity example, we rearrange the terms to solve for D:

$$D = Vt$$

Therefore,

$$\frac{dD}{dt} = (1)Vt^{1-1} = V$$

PARTIAL DERIVATIVES

Sometimes we will be interested in the rate of change of a quantity that is dependent on more than one variable. Here we may take the *partial derivative* (designated by ∂) of such quantity with respect to a single variable while holding all the other variables constant. For example, suppose we have the following relationship:

$$z = 12xy - 5x^2 - 4y^2$$

The partial derivative of z with respect to x is

$$\frac{\partial z}{\partial x} = 12y - 10x$$

The partial derivative of z with respect to y is

$$\frac{\partial z}{\partial y} = 12x - 8y$$

As with regular derivatives, there can be higher-order partial derivatives. In the preceding relationship, the *second* partial derivative of z with respect to x is

$$\frac{\partial^2 z}{\partial x^2} = -10$$

In the study of options, partial derivatives play an important role. The relationships among the variables in the leading options pricing model are all explained in terms of partial derivatives.

INTRODUCTION TO INTEGRATION

At a basic level, integration can be thought of as the inverse of differentiation. More important, however, the process of integration results in determining the area under a curve. In a histogram (see Figure 2–2), probabilities are represented by the *areas of the rectangles*. The leftmost rectangle in Figure 2–2 has an area of 2.99 inches times 5 inches = 14.95 square inches. The proportion of that area to the total area of the four rectangles is 14.95/149.5, or .1. Therefore, the probability that the height of a conference attendee chosen at random would be between 65 and 67.99 inches is 10 percent. If we approximated the distribution of the heights in the histogram with a smooth curve, the area under the curve would represent the total probability.

The Δxs representing changes in x along the x axis in Figure 2–2 are 2.99 inches for each of the four rectangles. Using functional notation for the y values, we have

$$y_1 = f_1(x) = 5 \qquad y_2 = f_2(x) = 31$$
$$y_3 = f_3(x) = 10 \qquad y_4 = f_4(x) = 4$$

To find the total area for the histogram, we need only to sum up the products of the $f(x)$'s and the Δx's:

$$\text{Area} = \sum_{i=1}^{n} f_i(x)\Delta x \qquad (2.24)$$

$$\text{Area} = 2.99(5 + 31 + 10 + 4) = 149.5$$

Finding the area under a curve is not as simple as summing up the areas of rectangles in a histogram. First, we are no longer dealing with rectangles whose areas are easy to determine. The process called *integration* means to sum up all possible products of $f(x)$ and Δx by letting Δx become increasingly smaller and smaller, where it approaches zero as a limit. The limit of Δx is denoted by dx as before. The n rectangles are replaced by an interval of x values, with a being the lower bound of the interval and b being the upper bound.

The symbol for integration is the elongated S ($\int$), and Equation (2.24) is replaced by

$$\int_a^b f(x)\, dx \tag{2.25}$$

where

$$\int_a^b f(x)\, dx = \lim_{\Delta x \to 0} \sum_1^n f(x_i) \Delta x \tag{2.26}$$

The left member is read "the integral from a to b of $f(x)\, dx$." And the right member is the *limit* of Equation (2.24). In addition, a and b are the boundaries of the interval for which the integral is to be evaluated.

Fortunately, like differentiation, there are basic rules for integrating simple functions and vast tables for evaluating the more complex functions. Because differentiation is basically the inverse of integration, the basic rule for integration is as follows:

If $dy/dx = ax^n$ or, in its *differential equation* form, $dy = ax^n\, dx$, then:

$$y = a \int x^n\, dx = a\left(\frac{x^{n+1}}{n+1}\right) + C \tag{2.27}$$

where C is the *constant of integration*.

The integral in Equation (2.27) is called an *indefinite integral* because numerous functions can have the differential $ax^n\, dx$ depending on the value of C. The constant C is undefined unless we have more information.

In the example in the section on differentiation, we found the derivative of $y = x^2$ to be $2x$. Working backwards, we can find the value of y:

If $dy/dx = 2x$ or $dy = 2x\, dx$, then from Equation (2.27),

$$y = 2 \int x^1\, dx = 2\left(\frac{x^{1+1}}{1+1}\right) + C = 2\frac{x^2}{2} + C = x^2 + C$$

And for the $C = 0$ case,

$$y = x^2$$

which is what we started with.

There is one unique function e (base of the natural logarithm system) that when raised to a power remains unchanged in its derivative and integral:

If $y = e^x$,

$$\frac{dy}{dx} = e^x$$

And

$$\int e^x \, dx = e^x \text{ (ignoring the constant)} \qquad (2.28)$$

Suppose, for example, we wished to find the area under the simple curve represented by $y = x^2$ in the interval from $x = 20$ to $x = 30$. Then

$$y = f(x) = x^2$$

$$\int_a^b f(x) \, dx = \int_{20}^{30} x^2 \, dx$$

From the rules of integration (Equation 2.27),

$$\int x^2 \, dx = \frac{x^3}{3}$$

For $x = 30$,

$$\frac{x^3}{3} = \frac{30^3}{3} = 9{,}000$$

For $x = 20$,

$$\frac{x^3}{3} = \frac{20^3}{3} = 2{,}667$$

FIGURE 2-5

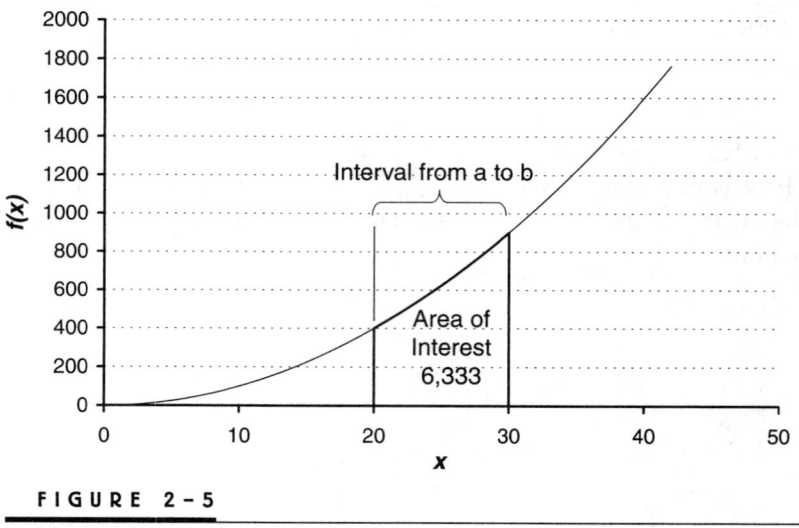

Graph of $f(x) = x^2$

Therefore, in the x interval from 20 to 30, the area under $f(x) = x^2$ is equal to $(9{,}000 - 2{,}667)$, or 6,333. Figure 2-5 shows the graphic representation of the area under the curve.

The preceding exercise explained how to find the *area* under a curve. For the area to represent probability, the function $f(x)$ must be a *probability density function;* that is, the total area under the curve represented by the function must be equal to 1.

$$\int f(x)\, dx = 1$$

Then the probability that a random variable X lies in the interval between a (lower bound) and b (upper bound) is given by

$$P(a \le X \le b) = \int_a^b f(x)\, dx \qquad (2.29)$$

CONTINUOUS PROBABILITY DISTRIBUTIONS: THE NORMAL CURVE

In contrast to the discrete distributions that generally take on only integer values (there being no 4.5 on a single die) are the continuous distributions whose elements can assume all values over a continuous scale. Measures of length, time, and temperature are examples of continuous variables.

There is one theoretical continuous distribution, the *normal curve,* that in many ways is the cornerstone of modern probability theory. Its mathematical properties and theoretical basis were first investigated by eighteenth-century scientists. Also known as the *Gaussian distribution* in honor of one of the discovering scientists, Carl Gauss (1777–1855), this distribution is the well-known *bell-shaped curve* familiar to many. In a normal distribution, the mean, median, and mode are all identical.

The normal distribution is symmetric about its mean, and even though it comes closer and closer to the horizontal axis at the extremes, it never touches. This is not a problem because the area under the curve (probability) becomes negligible at 4 or 5 standard deviations from the mean in either direction. The formula (probability *distribution* function) for a normal curve having the mean μ and standard deviation σ is

$$f(x) = \frac{1}{\sigma\sqrt{2\pi}} e^{-1/2(x-\mu/\sigma)^2} \tag{2.30}$$

And the probability that a random variable X is less than some particular x (the probability *density* function) is

$$P(X \leq x) = \frac{1}{\sigma\sqrt{2\pi}} \int_{-\infty}^{x} e^{-1/2(x-\mu/\sigma)^2} \, dx \tag{2.31}$$

In practice, since we do not want to deal with all possible curves having different means and standard deviations, the x's are transformed into a z scale wherein the distribution of the z's has $\mu = 0$ and $\sigma = 1$. The new function $f(z)$ represents the *standard normal curve* and is given by

$$f(z) = \frac{1}{\sqrt{2\pi}} e^{-z^2/2} \tag{2.32}$$

where

$$z = \frac{x - \mu}{\sigma} \tag{2.33}$$

And

$$P(Z \le z) = \frac{1}{\sqrt{2\pi}} \int_{-\infty}^{z} e^{-z^2/2} \, dz \qquad (2.34)$$

The right side of Equation (2.34) is called the *standard normal density function*. Now we have one standard normal curve for which the cumulative probability (area under the curve) has been published widely in tables for $-\infty \le z$ (values of z greater than negative infinity). In addition, Chapter 8 contains a polynomial approximation for the solution of the normal distribution function for the same interval. Lastly, and most important for today's investigators, Equation (2.34) has been incorporated into Microsoft Excel's NORMSDIST function.

In order to simplify notation, whenever Equation (2.34) is used in a problem solution, it will appear as

$$N(b) - N(a)$$

which is the probability that z will lie between a and b.

The N in the preceding notation is an operator calling for the area under the normal curve between $-\infty$ and z, where z is either a or b (the upper and lower boundaries of the interval of interest). In Excel, simply substitute NORMSDIST for the N.

Sometimes we will want to know the *height* of the standard normal curve for a given probability distribution. Such height for any value of z is calculated from Equation (2.32). Since Equation (2.32) is the *derivative* of Equation (2.34), which calculates $N(z)$, Equation (2.32) is denoted as $N'(z)$.

See Chapter 8 for additional material on normal distributions, including

- The importance of the central limit theorem
- Skewness and kurtosis
- The consequences of taking samples

AN APPLICATION OF THE NORMAL CURVE

To illustrate how the normal distribution can be used, assume there is a huge pile of scrap wood located in one corner of a lumber yard. There are over 5,000 pieces of varying lengths. We want to be able to make some probability statements about the lengths of the scrap wood. Taking great care to ensure randomness by having a back hoe shuffle the pile before each selection, we take a random sample of 40 pieces from the pile, measure their lengths (to the nearest inch), and calculate the mean and standard deviation of the sample. Table 2–6 shows the results of our endeavors.

Since the population is finite and our sample size is more than 30, we can construct a normal distribution for wood lengths up to 30 inches having $\mu = 13.95$ inches and $\sigma = 5.028$ inches. Figure 2–6 is a graph of the distribution.

Now suppose we wanted to find the probability that any board selected at random would have a length X between 20 and 22 inches. Calculating the z values:

$$z_{22} = \frac{22 - 13.95}{5.028} = 1.6010$$

$$z_{20} = \frac{20 - 13.95}{5.028} = 1.2033$$

$$P(20 \leq X \leq 22) = N(1.6010) - N(1.2033)$$

$$P(20 \leq X \leq 22) = .9453 - .8856 = 5.97\%$$

We would expect to find a board of length 20 to 22 inches only about 6 percent of the time. To find the probability that a board selected at random would be *over* 20 inches, we subtract the probability that X will be at least 20 (.8856) from 1, which yields 11.4 percent.

THE LOG-NORMAL DISTRIBUTION

There are many measurements such as heights, weights, lengths, and asset prices (stocks, etc.) that by their nature cannot be negative. A normal distribution of such measurements may, however, provide for some negative values depending on the size of the standard deviation. To overcome this anomaly, the *log-normal distribution* is often substituted for the normal curve. The lower bound of the log-normal distribution is zero—consistent with the lower bound of the preceding measurements. The log-normal distribution covers cases in which the elements them-

TABLE 2-6

Scrap sample

x Length (inches)	f No. of pieces	xf	$f(x - \mu)^2$
5	1	5	80.103
7	3	21	144.908
8	3	24	106.208
9	1	9	24.503
10	2	20	31.205
11	3	33	26.108
12	2	24	7.605
13	3	39	2.708
14	2	28	0.005
15	6	90	6.615
16	5	80	21.013
17	5	85	46.513
25	4	100	488.410
	40	558	985.900

Mean $\bar{x} = 13.950$
Std dev $s = 5.028$

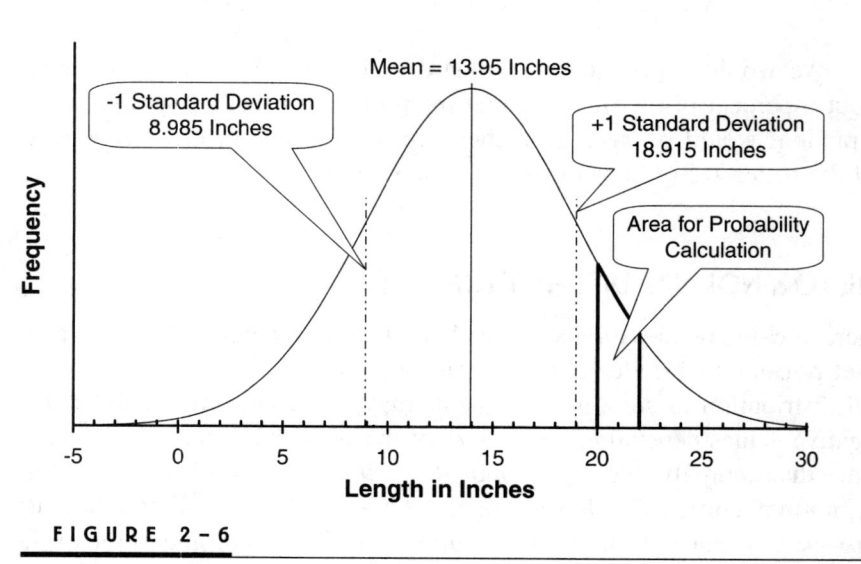

FIGURE 2-6

Normal distribution of scrap wood lengths

selves are not necessarily normally distributed, but their logarithms are. The probability density function $f(x)$ for the log-normal distribution is given by

$$f(x) = \frac{1}{x\sigma\sqrt{2\pi}} e^{-[\ln(x)-\mu]^2/2\sigma^2} \qquad (2.35)$$

Converting to the z scale, where

$$z = \frac{\ln(x) - \mu}{\sigma}$$

we have the probability density function:

$$f(z) = \frac{1}{x\sqrt{2\pi}} e^{-z^2/2} \qquad (2.36)$$

To convert the mean and standard deviation obtained for the z values (which are for the logarithms of the x values) back to the x scale, we have

$$\mu_x = e^{\mu_{\ln(x)} + (\sigma^2_{\ln(x)}/2)} \qquad (2.37)$$

$$\sigma_x^2 = e^{2\mu_{\ln(x)} + \sigma^2_{\ln(x)}}(e^{\sigma^2_{\ln(x)}} - 1) \qquad (2.38)$$

Taking the scrap wood example, we can find the log-normal distribution by expanding Table 2–6 and completing Table 2–7. Here we find the sample mean $\bar{x}_{\ln(x)}$ of the logs of the x values is 2.5694 and the sample standard deviation $s_{\ln(x)}$ of the logs is .3775.

Figure 2–7 shows the comparison between the normal and the log-normal distributions for the scrap wood example. This time the x scale has been extended to 40 inches to accommodate the longer tail of the log-normal distribution. The probability that X will fall between 20 and 22 inches is calculated by

$$z_{22} = \frac{\ln(22) - 2.5694}{.3775} = 1.3818$$

$$z_{20} = \frac{\ln(20) - 2.5694}{.3775} = 1.1294$$

$$P(20 \leq X \leq 22) = N(1.3818) - N(1.1294) = 4.6\%$$

TABLE 2-7

Sample of scrap wood

x Length (inches)	f No. of pieces	Normal distribution		Log-normal distribution		
		xf	$f(x - \mu)^2$	$\ln(x)$	$f \ln(x)$	$f[\ln(x) - \mu]^2$
5	1	5	80.103	1.61	1.609	0.9216
7	3	21	144.908	1.95	5.838	1.1663
8	3	24	106.208	2.08	6.238	0.7203
9	1	9	24.503	2.20	2.197	0.1385
10	2	20	31.205	2.30	4.605	0.1424
11	3	33	26.108	2.40	7.194	0.0883
12	2	24	7.605	2.48	4.970	0.0143
13	3	39	2.708	2.56	7.695	0.0001
14	2	28	0.005	2.64	5.278	0.0097
15	6	90	6.615	2.71	16.248	0.1153
16	5	80	21.013	2.77	13.863	0.2064
17	5	85	46.513	2.83	14.166	0.3479
25	4	100	488.410	3.22	12.876	1.6871
	40	558	985.900	31.75	102.777	5.5581

Mean $\bar{x} = 13.950$ (Normal); Std dev $s = 5.028$

Mean $\bar{x} = 2.5694$ (Log-normal); Std dev $s = 0.3775$

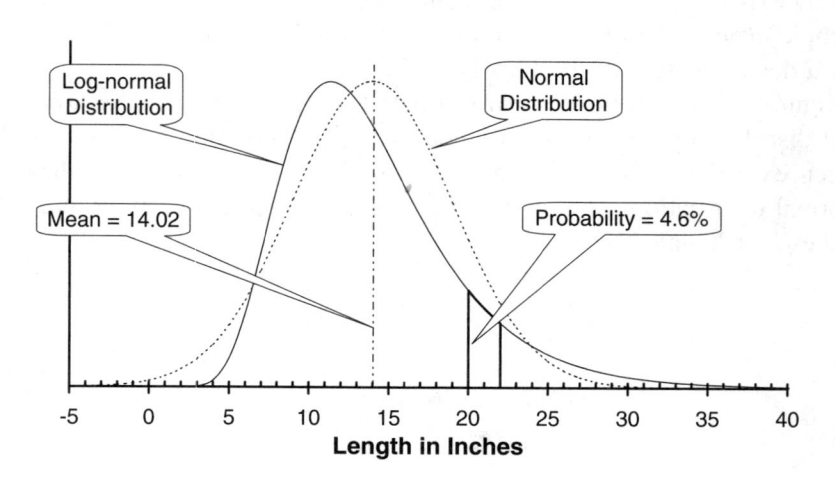

FIGURE 2-7

Comparison of normal and log-normal distributions

Contrast the 4.6 percent with the 6 percent obtained from the normal distribution. From Equations (2.45) and (2.46) we calculate the mean and standard deviation of the sample assumed to be log-normally distributed. Substituting $\bar{x}$ for μ and s for σ, we have

$$\bar{x}_x = e^{\bar{x}_{\ln(x)} + (s^2_{\ln(x)}/2)} = e^{2.6407} = 14.02$$

$$s_x = \sqrt{e^{2\bar{x}_{\ln(x)} + s^2_{\ln(x)}} (e^{s^2_{\ln(x)}} - 1)} = \sqrt{196.6273(0.1532)} = 5.49$$

The means of the two distributions are fairly close (14.02 versus 13.95), but there appears to be more variability in the log-normal distribution with its standard deviation of 5.49 versus 5.03 for the normal distribution. Table 2–8 reveals that the log-normal distribution is probably a more suitable descriptor, particularly in view of the negative lengths obtained for z greater than 3 standard deviations.

Because values of equities, indices, and futures never can be negative, the log-normal distribution will be assumed for options trading.

TABLE 2-8

Shortest and longest boards

z	Percent of cases	Normal distribution Shortest	Normal distribution Longest	Log-normal distribution Shortest	Log-normal distribution Longest
−1 to +1	68.3%	8.92	18.98	8.95	19.05
−1.96 to +1.96	95.0%	4.10	23.80	6.23	27.37
−2 to +2	95.4%	3.89	24.01	6.14	27.78
−2.58 to +2.58	99.0%	0.98	26.92	4.93	34.58
−3 to +3	99.7%	−1.13	29.03	4.21	40.52
−4 to +4	100.0%	−6.16	34.06	2.88	59.11

CHAPTER 3

Visualizing Option Structures and Strategies

There are two times in a man's life when he should not speculate: when he can't afford it, and when he can.

—Mark Twain (1835–1910)

Notwithstanding Mr. Twain's sage advice, presumably, you have decided to speculate—or at the very least to learn about speculating in options. The basic nature of options gives rise to geometric interpretations, making *visualization* of the basic strategies not only instructive but also an indispensable first step. Let's review the basics from Chapter 1.

Options are one of the most popular derivatives employed in the financial markets today. Options may be purchased or sold on a wide variety of instruments such as equities, commodity futures, indices, or even futures on indices. An *option* is the right but not the obligation to purchase or sell an underlying instrument, future, or index at a predetermined price (strike price) some time in the future. A Call option is the right to purchase the instrument, whereas a Put option is the right to sell the underlying instrument. The *option buyer* pays a premium for these rights, whereas the *option writer* collects the premium. An option buyer's losses are limited to the premium paid. The writer of an option is exposed to substantial downside risk. All options have an expiration date—usually the third Saturday of each expiration month. A European-style option is one that cannot be exercised prior to expiration. An American-style option is one that may be exercised at any time on or before expiration.

69

As a speculator, one simply may purchase or sell Puts and Calls (the *naked options*), one may use options to *hedge* other positions in the same or related underlying instruments, or one may construct combinations of options to make limited-risk trades. The results of a selected trade are, of course, a function of the price behavior of the underlying instrument or index over time. A Call is said to be *in the money* if the current price of the underlying instrument is greater than the strike price and *out of the money* otherwise. For a Put, just the reverse is true. The price of an option consists of an *intrinsic value* equal to the amount such option is in the money and a *time value* representing the difference between the total price and the intrinsic value. An out-of-the-money option has no intrinsic value, and its price consists solely of time value. Options are often referred to as *wasting assets* because their time value decreases as the expiration date approaches. If, on the expiration date, the price of the underlying instrument is unchanged from the transaction date, the entire time value of the price paid for the option will have been lost.

Why would one prefer to trade in options rather than the underlying instruments themselves? One reason is that option premiums are generally a fraction of the price of the underlying instrument, and another is that the margin requirements are considerably lower. As with most derivatives, leverage opportunities abound. Another, less obvious reason is that option contracts have a beginning (inception date) and an end (expiration date), representing a *closed system* for analysis. The analytical framework for options involves statistics and probability theory and is not limited to price behavior alone. An options trade always implies a forecast of the *magnitude* of a price change—whether or not the trader consciously thought about it. Depending on the strategy employed, a forecast of the price *direction* may or may not be implied. Contrast this feature with trading in the stock market, which is essentially open-ended from an analytical standpoint—success being entirely dependent on the ability to forecast the direction of prices in a never-ending time series.

SOURCES OF OPTIONS DATA

Each day the financial press and the online brokerages provide a plethora of easily accessible options price quotes. Table 3–1 summarizes the data for the IBM January 2003 Puts and Calls for strike prices between 30 and 120 for December 29, 2002. The price of IBM common stock on that day was $77.36.

TABLE 3-1

IBM Jan 03 options
(Prices on December 29, 2002)

Strike price	Call price	Put price
30	47.68	0.05
35	42.48	0.03
40	37.49	0.03
45	32.49	0.03
50	27.45	0.03
55	22.45	0.08
60	17.56	0.18
65	12.75	0.42
70	8.35	0.92
75	4.55	2.10
80	1.83	4.35
85	0.55	8.15
90	0.13	12.76
95	0.03	17.70
100	0.03	22.71
105	0.03	27.65
110	0.03	32.64
115	0.03	37.65
120	0.03	42.57

Source (data): E*Trade.

Figure 3-1 is a graph of the data contained in Table 3-1 with certain other information added. The solid straight lines forming the *V* represent the *limiting* prices of the Puts and Calls—always linear functions of the current market price. The two solid-line curves represent the prices quoted in Table 3-1. The dashed-line curves represent the *theoretical* option prices for the same stock prices, the derivation of which will be covered shortly.

These options expire in 19 days. The *volatility* of the IBM common stock is 25.4 percent. Volatility and remaining time are perhaps the most important concepts for options traders—so much so that an entire chapter (Chapter 5) is devoted to their meaning and derivation. For now, regard volatility as a measure of the annual *variability* of the returns for a given financial instrument. From Figure 3-1, the difference between the the-

FIGURE 3-1

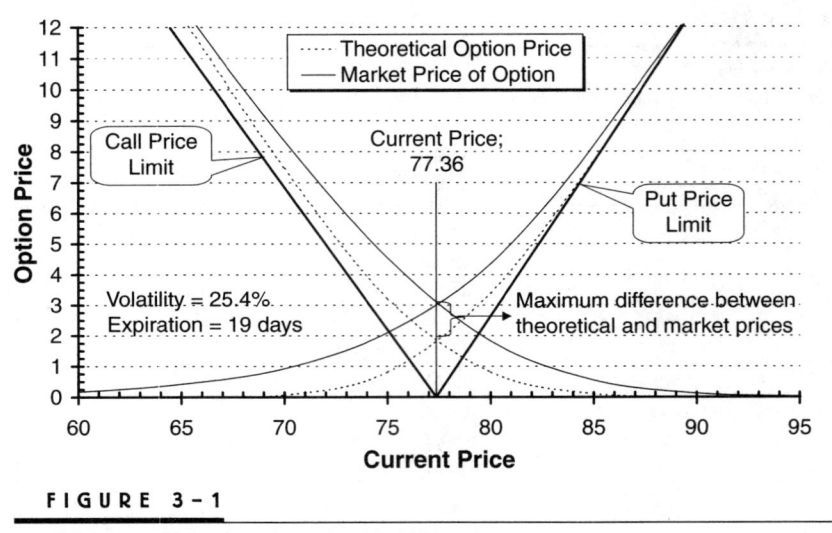

IBM Call and Put options, December 29, 2002

oretical and market prices at the money ($77.36) is approximately $1.24 ($3.04 − $1.80).

THEORETICAL OPTIONS PRICES

An important question for any options trader is, of course, How does the quoted option price compare with its "fair" value? A fair value for an option exists when the expected profit is zero for both buyer and seller. In general, the fair value of an option is a function of four variables:

- Price of the underlying instrument relative to the strike price
- Time until expiration of the option
- Volatility of the returns
- Level of interest rates

There are two basic forms of options pricing models—the *binomial options pricing model,* developed by Cox, Ross, and Rubenstein (1979), and the *Black-Scholes options pricing model* (1973). The binomial pricing model involves only two possible outcomes and refers to *discrete* price changes (either up or down from the current price). The binomial model typically is not used by traders to calculate stock option prices.

Before moving on to the Black-Scholes model, we list the notations for many of the variables used throughout this and future chapters:

S = current price of underlying instrument reduced by the present value of dividends, if any; see the following section on effects of dividends; also may be a target price chosen by the trader
x = price of the underlying instrument at expiration
K = strike price of any option
P = price of any option
P_C = fair value of a Call
P_P = fair value of a Put
K_{PC} = strike price of a purchased Call
K_{SC} = strike price of a sold Call
K_{PP} = strike price of a purchased Put
K_{SP} = strike price of a sold Put
P_{PC} = price of a purchased Call
P_{SC} = price of a sold Call
P_{PP} = price of a purchased Put
P_{SP} = price of a sold Put
BEP = break-even x value
t = time to expiration expressed as a proportion of one year
r = risk-free interest rate for period t
σ_s = standard deviation of returns (volatility)
G_{max} = maximum gain from an options strategy
L_{max} = maximum loss from an options strategy
$N(a)$ = cumulative normal probability to the left of a (see Chapter 2)
$N'(a)$ = normal probability distribution = $\dfrac{1}{\sqrt{2\pi}} e^{-a^2/2}$

The Black-Scholes options pricing model was developed in 1973 and it, along with its many variations, has become an important part of the financial landscape. It is based on a *continuous* distribution of the logs of investment returns. While its derivation is based on differential equations, the model itself is solved easily on a programmable calculator. Options traders on the floor of the exchanges frequently carry calculators with a variation of the model programmed in. With the background of mathematics presented in Chapter 2, solving the model should be relatively straightforward. The fair value of a European-style Call option on a non-dividend paying asset is given by

$$P_C = SN(d) - Ke^{-rt}N(d - \sigma_s\sqrt{t}) \qquad (3.1)$$

where

$$d = \frac{\ln\left(\frac{S}{K}\right) + t\left(r + \frac{\sigma_s^2}{2}\right)}{\sigma_s \sqrt{t}}$$

The Black-Scholes fair value of a European-style Put is given by

$$P_P = -SN(-d) + Ke^{-rt}N(\sigma_s\sqrt{t} - d) \qquad (3.2)$$

where all the other variables remain the same.

What causes options prices to fluctuate continually around their fair values? *Arbitrage* is the fundamental causal relationship. It simply refers to the simultaneous buying and selling of the same thing in different forms. The arbitrageur seeks out positive price differentials between what she buys and sells, thus ensuring a risk-free profit. One example is to buy a Call and sell a Put (equivalent to being long the underlying stock) and then sell the stock (see "Conversions" at end of this chapter). The risk-free profit is generally very small, and the opportunity to garner it is fleeting. Only floor traders and others not subject to commissions engage in this type of trading. If an instrument becomes mispriced relative to its fair value, arbitrage profits become available but soon disappear as the arbitrageurs jump in. Consequently, this practice tends to drive prices to their fair values and provides liquidity to the marketplace. *Put-Call parity* exists because of the potential for arbitrage. It equates the buying of a Call together with placing the present value of the strike price into a risk-free instrument with buying the stock and a Put. Equation (3.3) shows the equivalency.

$$P_C + Ke^{-rt} = P_P + S \qquad (3.3)$$

Therefore, by rearranging the terms in Equation (3.3), we may express the theoretical Put price in terms of the theoretical Call price.

$$P_P = P_c - S + Ke^{-rt} \qquad (3.4)$$

Equation (3.4) yields the same results as Equation (3.2).

THE EFFECT OF DIVIDENDS

Dividends were not listed as an input to the Black-Scholes model because they only affect equity options and then only for those based on stocks that actually pay dividends. Because the price of a stock will fall (jump down) by the amount of the dividend on the *ex-dividend date* (the last day the holder of the stock is entitled to the dividend), the current value of the stock must be reduced by the present value of such dividends. Dividends increase Put values and decrease Call values.

There are two methods for handling dividends—the *discrete method* and the *continuous method*.

Discrete Method

The discrete method looks at *actual* ex-dividend dates that occur during the life of the option. Letting

D = amount of periodic dividend
T = time to ex-dividend date (proportion of one year)
i = subscript denoting an individual dividend entitlement
n = number of dividends during life of the option

if only one dividend is expected during the life of the option,

$$S = S - De^{-rT} \tag{3.5}$$

If multiple dividends are expected, then

$$S = S - \sum_{i=1}^{n} D_i e^{-rT_i} \tag{3.6}$$

This method deals only with actual dividends that are discounted from the ex-dividend date to the present by the risk-free interest rate. Many times, especially for options held for 30 days or less, there will be no dividend, and the effect of dividends may be ignored.

Continuous Method

The continuous method assumes a constant accrual of dividends throughout the year. Letting

D = annual dividend amount
q = dividend yield = $\dfrac{D}{S}$

$$S = Se^{-qt} \tag{3.7}$$

Note that for the continuous method, q is treated like a discount rate over the time to expiration (t, not T). This method is more suited to index options, where it would be impractical to deal with many dividends on numerous stocks. The dividend yield for indices can be found using the *Valueline* service and on certain other brokerage Web sites.

When the S from Equation (3.7) is used to evaluate a Call in Equation (3.1), the expression for d changes slightly.

$$d = \frac{\ln\left(\frac{S}{K}\right) + t\left(r - q + \frac{\sigma_s^2}{2}\right)}{\sigma_s \sqrt{t}} \quad (3.8)$$

And the expression for P_C becomes

$$P_C = Se^{-qt}N(d) - Ke^{-rt}N(d - \sigma s\sqrt{t}) \quad (3.9)$$

The Put/Call parity relationship is then

$$P_P = P_C - Se^{-qt} + Ke^{-rt} \quad (3.10)$$

EARLY EXERCISE (THE AMERICAN-STYLE OPTION)

All equity options traded in the United States are American-style options. Some index options are American-style (OEX), whereas others are European-style (DJX, $INX, XEO, MNX, etc.). Two questions arise with respect to early exercise of an option: when to do it and what are the effects on option prices. The optimal time to exercise is left for Chapter 8.

Because early exercise is a privilege not afforded to holders of European-style options, there exists an *early exercise premium* on American-style options. For non-dividend-paying assets, it is never optimal to exercise an American-style Call early, and such premium is zero. In-the-money American-style Puts, however, usually will command a premium over their European-style counterparts. Letting

P_{CA} = fair value of an American-style Call
P_{CE} = fair value of a European-style Call
P_{PA} = fair value of an American-style Put
P_{PE} = fair value of a European-style Put

for non-dividend-paying assets,

$$P_{CA} = P_{CE} \tag{3.11}$$

$$P_{PA} \geq P_{PE} \quad \text{when } r > 0 \tag{3.12}$$

Figure 3-2 shows the relationship between hypothetical American-style and European-style Puts on a non-dividend-paying asset.

American-style Calls on dividend-paying assets may be exercised early—especially just prior to an ex-dividend date. Both American-style Calls and Puts generally will command a premium over their European-style counterparts when dividends are involved.

$$P_{CA} > P_{CE} \tag{3.13}$$

$$P_{PA} > P_{PE} \tag{3.14}$$

Although many studies have been conducted, there is no general agreement about the size of these premiums. One such study published in 2002 found early exercise premiums ranging from 5.04 to 5.9 percent for Calls and from 7.97 to 10.86 percent for Puts.

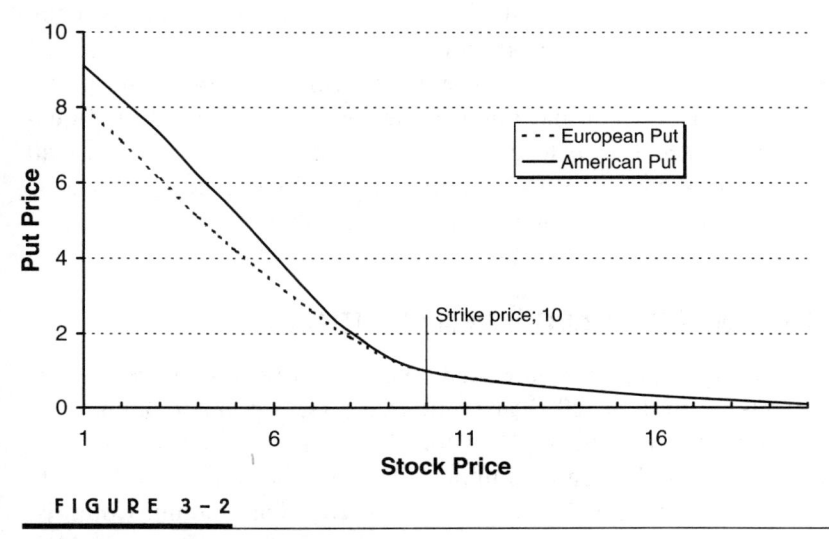

FIGURE 3-2

American-style versus European-style Puts

FIGURE 3–3

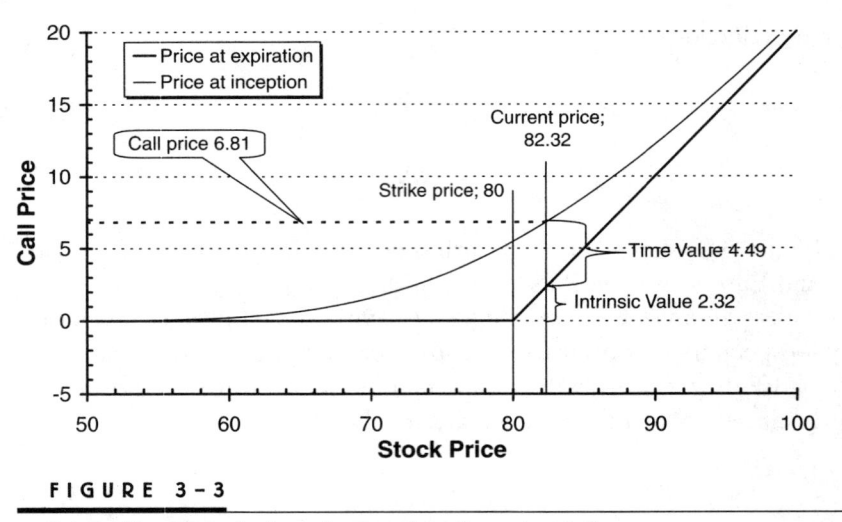

Relationship of Call price to stock price at inception and expiration

FUNDAMENTAL RELATIONSHIP BETWEEN CALL PRICE AND STOCK PRICE

At expiration, the Call price is zero up to the strike price and rises one for one with the stock price thereafter. At inception, the Call price is the market price. For example, assume a $6.81 Call option with a strike price of 80 on an underlying asset whose current price is $82.32. The volatility of the underlying asset is .335, the risk-free interest rate is 1.135 percent, and there are 90 days until expiration.

Figure 3–3 shows the relationship between Call prices and prices for the underlying stock at inception (trade date) and at expiration. Equation (3.1) was used to create the inception price curve. Since the Call option is in the money, its price of $6.81 can be divided into an intrinsic value of $2.32 ($82.32 − $80.00) and a time value of $4.49.

COMMISSIONS AND MARGIN REQUIREMENTS

Commissions and margin requirements vary from broker to broker. The requirements as of June 2003 at OptionsXpress, a popular online brokerage, are assumed to be in effect for all options transactions contemplated in this book. Basically, commissions for stocks are $14.95 up to 1,001 shares and $0.15 per share for trades over that amount. Commissions on options are $1.50 per contract, with a minimum of $14.95. Although multiple option strategies may be established with a single order, commissions are charged on each option in the combination. Margin requirements will be covered in the sections describing specific strategies.

CONTINGENT ORDERS

Since option prices are a function of the price of the underlying stock, they may change as rapidly as the stock price changes. Once a trader has identified an appropriate option to trade and the strategy to be applied, he would not want the stock price to move against him while he waits for his option order to be filled. The use of a *contingent order* prevents the option prices from becoming *uncoupled* from the underlying stock price. The contingent order specifies that the option be purchased or sold if and only if the stock price is at, above, or below a certain value—usually the value of the stock from which the option prices were quoted or derived. OptionsXpress provides a contingent order form.

NAKED OPTIONS

Options that are purchased or sold without any other position in the underlying securities, futures, or indices are called *naked options*. When these options are purchased, risk is limited to the purchase price (margin requirement). Writing naked options provides a maximum gain limited to the selling price while subjecting the seller to substantial downside risk—theoretically unlimited in the case of a sold Call. The four basic naked options transactions are

- Purchasing a Call
- Purchasing a Put
- Writing a Call
- Writing a Put

Except where specific actual options are investigated, for the remainder of this chapter it will be assumed that options transactions at inception (the trade date) will be 90 days prior to expiration on a non-dividend-paying stock having a volatility of 30 percent and when the risk-free interest rate is 1.2 percent. Such options will be based on a hypothetical stock selling at between $75 and $85. Options prices thereon at inception are calculated by Equation (3.1). The gain/loss profile for the inception options price curve will, of course, always be zero at the current stock price. We also introduce a function R (results function) that equals the gain or loss on any option trade *at expiration* for any value of the stock price x.

PURCHASING A CALL

Figure 3–4 shows the gain/loss profile for a purchase of an 80 Call for $2.55 at inception and at expiration when the current stock price is $77.00. The break-even stock price *BEP* for purchased Calls is given by

$$BEP = K_{PC} + P_{PC} \tag{3.15}$$

For the Call in Figure 3–4, we have

$$BEP = 80 + 2.55 = 82.55$$

The formula for the Call price for all possible values of the stock price x on the expiration date (results function R) for all purchased Calls is

$$R = f(x) = \begin{cases} -P_{PC} & \text{for } x \leq K_{PC} \\ x - BEP & \text{for } x > K_{PC} \end{cases} \tag{3.16}$$

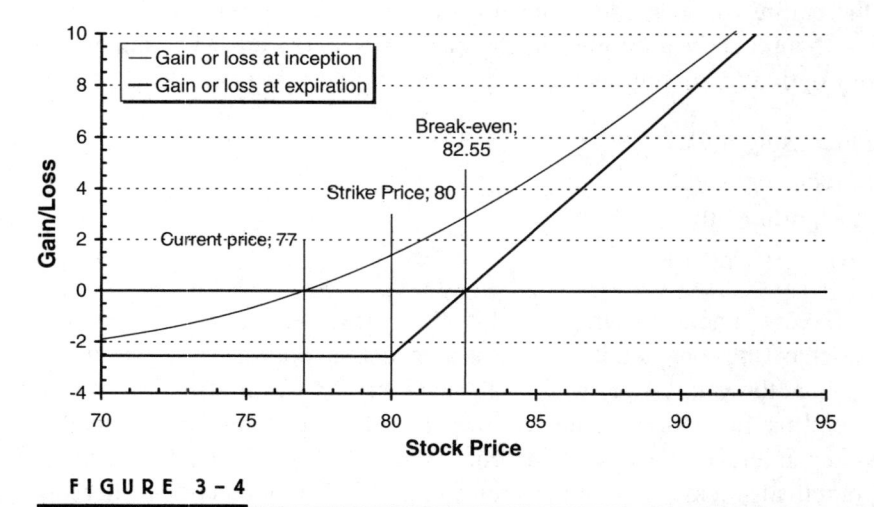

FIGURE 3-4

Purchasing a $2.55 naked Call with a strike price of 80

And for this Call,

$$R = f(x) = \begin{cases} -2.55 & \text{for } x \leq 80 \\ x - 82.55 & \text{for } x > 80 \end{cases}$$

The maximum gain or loss for purchasing this Call is

$$G_{max} = \text{unlimited}$$

$$L_{max} = -P_{PC} = -2.55$$

One contract of this purchased Call would be ordered by specifying the company, expiration month, and year and "buy one 80 Call at $2.55 contingent on stock price being *at or above* $77.00." The margin required for purchasing naked Calls is 100 times the Call price and, for the preceding example, is $255 per contract.

Purchasing a Call is a bullish strategy. The long Call position is best entered and held in periods of high or increasing volatility. Since the leverage is so high, it is also a somewhat aggressive strategy. A trader may lose all her investment in a fairly short time if the option expires worthless. Leverage, of course, works both ways. Consider the January 2003 IBM 75 and 80 Calls listed in Table 3–1. The 75 Call at $4.55 is in the money, having an intrinsic value of $2.36 and a time value of $2.19. The 80 Call is out of the money, with its price of $1.83 representing time value only. Figure 3–5 shows the dollar profit/loss profiles (at the expiration date) of a stock player who purchases 100 shares of IBM at $77.36 per share and purchasers of one contract (100 shares) each of the 75 and 80 Calls for $455 and $183, respectively. If the stock price moves up by 2.8 percent, the stock player makes $217, whereas the holder of the 75 Call breaks even. The holder of the 80 Call loses his entire investment of $183. For the holder of the 80 Call to break even, the stock price must move up 5.6 percent, which would produce a $214 profit for the holder of the 75 Call and $433 in profits for the stock player.

The absolute dollar profiles only tell part of the story. Figure 3–6 shows the same information for the *percentage* profit/loss profiles. For a 5.6 percent gain by the stock player, the holder of the 75 Call makes 47 percent on his investment, whereas the holder of the 80 Call breaks even. For an 8 percent gain by the stock player, the holder of the 75 Call makes 88 percent, whereas the holder of the 80 Call makes an astonishing 94 percent.

FIGURE 3-5

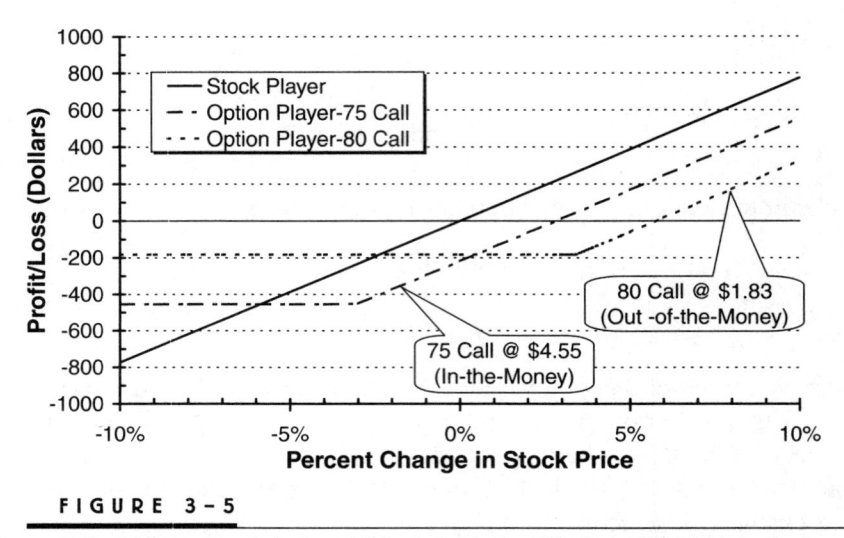

Option player versus stock player (dollars) (purchasing 100 shares at $77.36 per share)

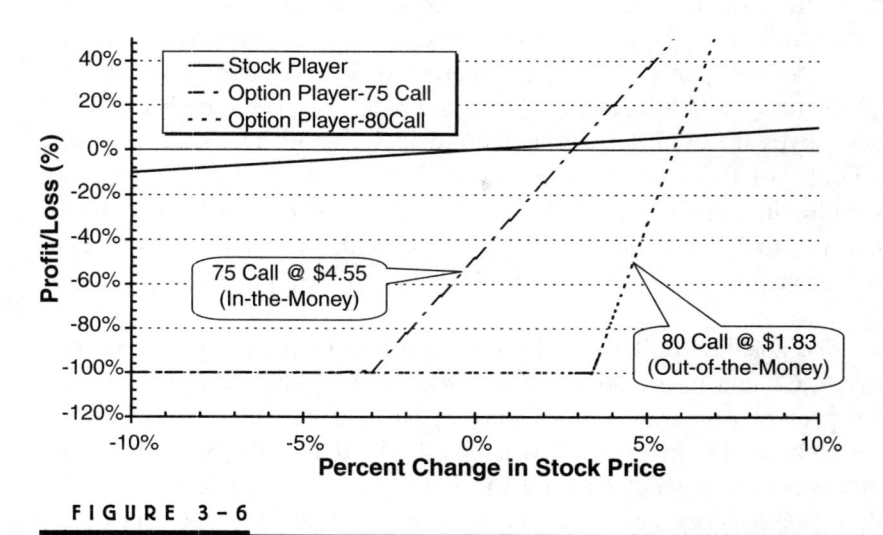

FIGURE 3-6

Option player versus stock player (percentage) (purchasing 100 shares at $77.36 per share)

Visualizing Option Structures and Strategies

What conclusions can be drawn from the preceding profiles? Remember, these options have only 19 days until expiration. Clearly, for small expected advances in the stock price (3 to 6 percent), purchasing an in-the-money Call is preferable. When large advances in the stock price are anticipated, purchasing an out-of-the-money Call is the preferred strategy. With only 19 days left, time value will decrease rapidly. It should be noted that a trader must forecast the *direction* of a price move in the underlying stock correctly if she is to be successful buying naked options. If the stock price drops, *a trader cannot profit from a Call option purchase—no matter which Call is selected.*

PURCHASING A PUT

Much of what has been said about purchasing Calls also applies to purchasing Puts—except in reverse. Purchasing naked Puts is a bearish strategy in which the trader profits from declines in the price of the underlying instrument. The long Put position is best entered and held in periods of high or rising volatility. Figure 3–7 shows the gain/loss profile at inception and expiration for purchasing a $2.57 naked Put with an 80 strike price when the current stock price is $83.00.

The break-even stock price *BEP* for purchased Puts is

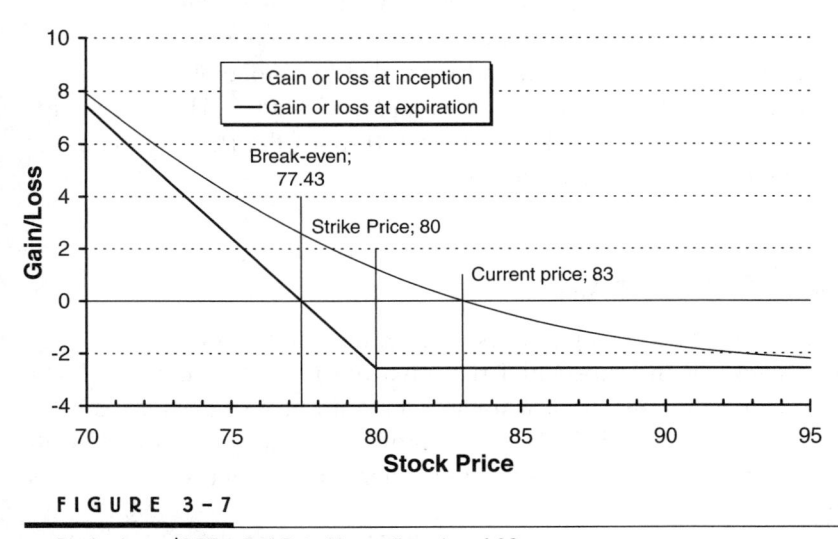

FIGURE 3-7

Purchasing a $2.57 naked Put with a strike price of 80

$$BEP = K_{PP} - P_{PP} \qquad (3.17)$$

For the Put in Figure 3–7, we have

$$BEP = 80 - 2.57 = 77.43$$

The results function at expiration for purchasing Puts is given by

$$R = f(x) = \begin{cases} -P_{PP} & \text{for } x \geq K_{PP} \\ BEP - x & \text{for } x < K_{PP} \end{cases} \qquad (3.18)$$

And for the Put in Figure 3–7,

$$R = f(x) = \begin{cases} -2.57 & \text{for } x \geq 80 \\ 77.43 - x & \text{for } x < 80 \end{cases}$$

The maximum gain or loss from purchasing this Put is

$$G_{max} = K_{PP} - P_{PP} = 77.43$$

$$L_{max} = -P_{PP} = -2.57$$

The Put shown in Figure 3–7 is out of the money, and the stock price would have to drop 5.57 points just to break even. As with Calls, it is much more conservative to purchase in-the-money Puts.

One contract of this purchased Put would be ordered by specifying the company, expiration month and year, and "buy one 80 Put at $2.57 contingent on stock price being *at or below* $83.00." The margin requirement for purchasing naked Puts is 100 times the Put price and, for the preceding example, $257 per contract.

WRITING (SELLING) A CALL

In many ways, writing options is simply the mirror image of buying them. Because of the substantial risk involved in writing options, however, margin requirements at a trader's favorite brokerage are likely to be much larger. Figure 3–8 shows the profile of writing a naked 80 Call for $2.55 at inception and expiration when the current stock price is $77.00.

Writing a Call is a bearish strategy. The short Call position is best entered and held in periods of low or declining volatility. Because the upside price moves on the underlying stock are theoretically unlimited,

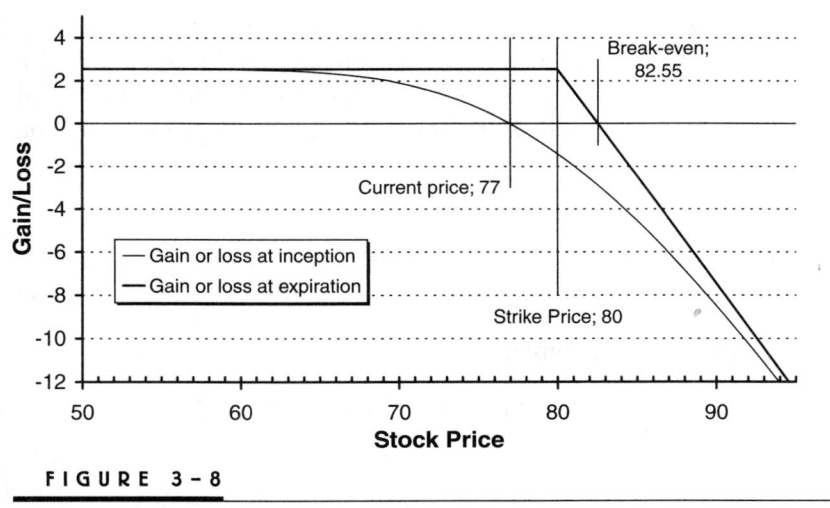

Visualizing Option Structures and Strategies

FIGURE 3-8

Selling a $2.55 naked Call with a strike price of 80

the downside risk in writing Calls is also unlimited. The break-even stock price *BEP* for sold Calls is

$$BEP = K_{SC} + P_{SC} \quad (3.19)$$

And for the sold Call in Figure 3–8,

$$BEP = 80 + 2.55 = 82.55$$

The results function at expiration for writing Calls is

$$R = f(x) = \begin{cases} P_{SC} & \text{for } x \leq K_{SC} \\ BEP - x & \text{for } x > K_{SC} \end{cases} \quad (3.20)$$

And for this Call,

$$R = f(x) = \begin{cases} 2.55 & \text{for } x \leq 80 \\ 82.55 - x & \text{for } x > 80 \end{cases}$$

The maximum gain or loss from writing this Call is given by

$$G_{max} = P_{SC} = 2.55$$

$$L_{max} = \text{unlimited}$$

One contract of this sold Call would be ordered by specifying the company, expiration month and year, and "sell one 80 Call at $2.55

contingent on stock price being *at or above* $77.00." The margin requirement for selling one contract of naked Calls is 25 percent of the price of the underlying stock plus the premium less the amount the Call is out of the money multiplied by 100 *or* 10 percent of the price of the underlying stock plus the premium multiplied by 100, whichever is greater. In equation form,

$$\text{Margin} = 100\{\max[.25S + P_{SC} - \max(K_{SC} - S, 0), .1S + P_{SC}]\} \quad (3.21)$$

In the preceding example, since

$$\max(K_{SC} - S, 0) = \max(80 - 77, 0) = 3$$

and

$$\max(.25S + P_{SC} - 3, .1S + P_{SC}) = .25(77) + 2.55 - 3 = 18.80$$

the margin requirement would be 100 times $18.80, or $1,880 per contract.

WRITING (SELLING) A PUT

Figure 3–9 shows the gain/loss profile for writing a naked 80 Put for $2.57 at inception and expiration when the current stock price is $83.

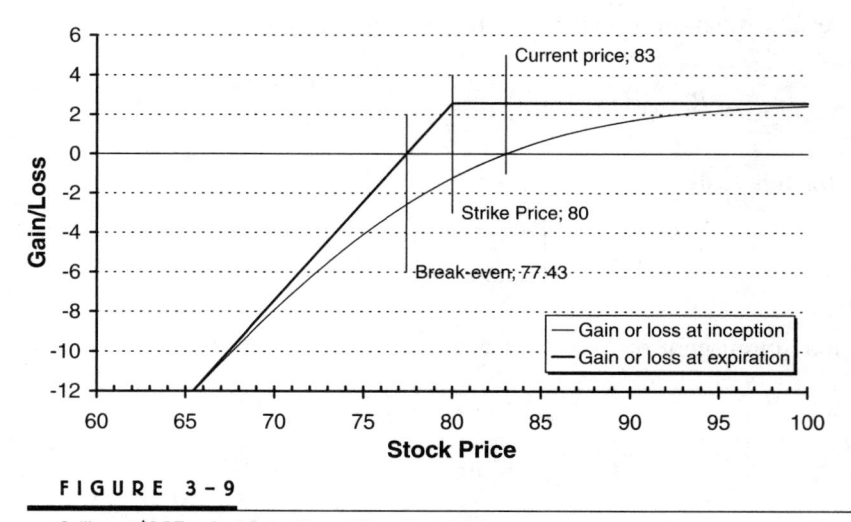

FIGURE 3-9

Selling a $2.57 naked Put with a strike price of 80

Visualizing Option Structures and Strategies

Writing Puts also has substantial risk, but the downside is not unlimited, as with writing Calls. The maximum loss from writing Puts occurs when the stock price falls to zero, at which point the writer of a Put loses an amount equal to the break-even stock price.

The break-even stock price *BEP* for writing Puts is

$$BEP = K_{SP} - P_{SP} \qquad (3.22)$$

And for the sold Put in Figure 3–9,

$$BEP = 80 - 2.57 = 77.43$$

The results function at expiration for writing Puts is

$$R = f(x) = \begin{cases} P_{SP} & \text{for } x \geq K_{SP} \\ x - BEP & \text{for } x < K_{SP} \end{cases} \qquad (3.23)$$

And for this Put,

$$R = f(x) = \begin{cases} 2.57 & \text{for } x \geq 80 \\ x - 77.43 & \text{for } x < 80 \end{cases}$$

The maximum gain or loss from selling this Put is given by

$$G_{max} = P_{SP} = 2.57$$

$$L_{max} = -BEP = -77.43$$

One contract of this sold Put would be ordered by specifying the company, expiration month and year, and "sell one 80 Put at $2.57 contingent on stock price being *at or below* $83.00." The margin requirement for writing naked Puts is similar to selling naked Calls earlier.

$$\text{Margin} = 100 \{\max[.25S + P_{SP} - \max(S - K_{SP}, 0), .1S + P_{SP}]\} \qquad (3.24)$$

In the preceding example, since

$$\max(S - K_{SP}, 0) = \max(83 - 80, 0) = 3$$

and

$$\max(.25S + P_{SP} - 3, .1S + P_{SP}) = .25(83) + 2.57 - 3 = 20.32$$

the margin requirement would be $2,032 per contract.

Writing a Put is a bullish strategy. The short Put position is best entered and held during periods of low or declining volatility. The maximum loss from writing a Put occurs when the price of the underlying stock falls to zero (Equation 3.23). The downside risk is not unlimited (as with writing a Call) and can be no more than an amount equal to the break-even stock price.

Writing American-style options exposes the seller to *early exercise* and *assignment*. The holder of an American-style option has the right to exercise his option at any time prior to the expiration date. This is done most often when little or no time value is left and the option is in the money. The holder's notice of exercise is sent to the Options Clearing Corporation, which randomly "assigns" a day's worth of such exercises to its member brokerage firms. The next day the brokerage firms, in turn, assign the exercises to their customers who are short the options. A Call writer of stock options on assignment is required to deliver the shares of the underlying stock for the strike price of the Call. Such delivery may be made from his own portfolio or from buying the shares at the then-existing market price. Conversely, the Put option writer on assignment is required to accept delivery of the shares of the underlying stock and pay the strike price. Such acceptance may be made by delivering a short instrument from his portfolio or by going short in the market and then delivering the instrument.

To be successful buying or writing naked options, the trader must have some idea of the magnitude and direction of expected price moves between the trade date and the expiration date. He also must be able to "beat the clock"—that is, to correctly anticipate the effects of time value. The appropriate naked option strategies are set forth in Table 3–2.

TABLE 3-2

Strategies for naked options

Anticipated move	Buy an option	Sell an option
Large upside	Out-of-the-money Call	
Large downside	Out-of-the-money Put	
Small upside	In-the-money Call	Out-of-the-money Put
Small downside	In-the-money Put	Out-of-the-money Call
No change		Out-of-the-money Call or Put

THE BASIC COMBINATIONS

Combining options with other options or instruments gives rise to some interesting and profitable strategies. The basic combination strategies are

- The covered Call
- The covered Put
- The protective Put
- The bull Call spread
- The bear Call spread
- The bull Put spread
- The bear Put spread
- The straddle
- The strangle

Combinations are put on to effect a particular strategy during specific market conditions. The basic combinations may be entered as a single order with most brokerages but will require additional margin depending on the number and type of instruments employed. Commissions will be charged on each leg of the combination. In the following strategies, *selling* is synonymous with *writing*.

COVERED CALL

The structure and profit profile of a covered Call from the list in Table 3–1 are shown in Figure 3–10. The covered Call was constructed by simultaneously buying 100 shares of IBM stock at $77.36 per share on December 29, 2002, and selling one January 2003 80 IBM Call for $4.55.

The break-even stock price *BEP* for covered Calls is

$$BEP = S - P_{SC} \qquad (3.25)$$

And for the covered Call in Figure 3–10,

$$BEP = 77.36 - 4.55 = 72.81$$

The results function at expiration for covered Calls is

$$R = f(x) = \begin{cases} K_{SC} + P_{SC} - S & \text{for } x \geq K_{SC} \\ x - BEP & \text{for } x < K_{SC} \end{cases} \qquad (3.26)$$

FIGURE 3-10

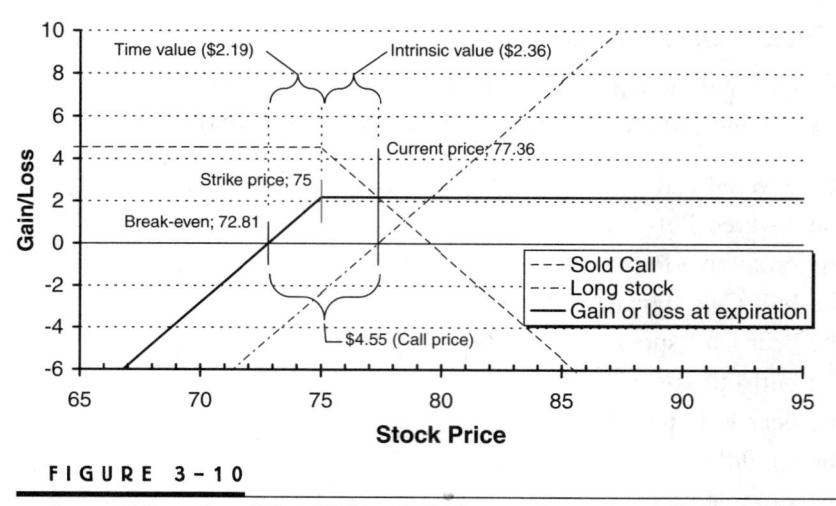

Covered Call: purchase IBM at $77.36; sell IBM January 2003 75 Call at $4.55

And for this covered Call,

$$R = f(x) = \begin{cases} 2.19 & \text{for } x \geq 75 \\ x - 72.81 & \text{for } x < 75 \end{cases}$$

The maximum gain or loss for this covered Call is given by

$$G_{max} = K_{SC} + P_{SC} - S = 2.19$$

$$L_{max} = -BEP = -72.81$$

One contract of this covered Call would be ordered by specifying the company, expiration month and year, and "buy 100 shares of IBM at $77.36; sell one 80 Call at $2.55 contingent on IBM's price being *at or below* $77.36." The margin requirement for writing covered Calls is a long position in the stock equal to the number of exercisable Calls that can be initiated with 50 percent margin. In the preceding example, the margin requirement would be $3,868 per contract.

In this case, the sold Call was in the money by $2.36—leaving a time value of $2.19. The maximum profit for any covered Call is also equal to the time value of the sold Call.

The intent of a covered Call writer is to exploit the "wasting asset" attributes of options and collect the premium when the option expires worthless while, at the same time, reducing downside risk. Covered Call writers come in two flavors. The first type operates the covered Call as a complete strategy—buying the stock and selling the Call. The second type merely writes Calls against a long position already held in hopes of garnering some additional income while also partially protecting her stock position on the downside. There is less risk in a covered Call than simply owning the stock outright because the break-even point is lowered by the price of the sold Call. Of course, the upside potential is limited, which means this strategy should be used only when anticipating a small upside move or no change at all. Writing covered Calls is thought to be a conservative, mildly bullish strategy—especially if in-the-money Calls are sold. It is best established during periods of declining or stable volatility.

Covered Call writing produces a gain/loss profile identical to selling a naked Put (see Figure 3-9). The two strategies are said to be *equivalent,* and the covered Call is sometimes referred to as a *synthetic Put*. Generally, there is a small positive difference between writing a covered Call and selling the naked Put at the same strike price. For example, the January 2003 IBM 75 Put in Table 3-1 was priced at $2.10, whereas the covered Call in Figure 3-10 showed a maximum gain of $2.19. If a trader is not already long the stock, it is generally preferable to sell naked Puts. There is only one bid-ask spread to contend with, the margin requirement will be considerably less, and commissions are paid on only one transaction.

COVERED PUT

Covered Put writing also may be established by writing naked Puts against a short stock position, initiating a mildly bearish strategy. The price of the sold Put partially protects the trader from upside stock price movements in the same way that a covered Call protects against declining prices. Covered Put writing is the equivalent of selling a naked Call (see Figure 3-8). Much of the discussion of covered Call writing applies to covered Put writing—except in reverse. Because it is harder to short stock (uptick rule, borrowing the stock, etc.), there are few covered Put writing programs today.

PROTECTIVE PUT

Another combination of options and stock is the protective Put. It is established by purchasing a naked Put against a long stock position currently held. A protective Put is a hedging (insurance) strategy implemented to protect the trader from price declines in individual stocks in her portfolio (stock option Put) or the entire portfolio itself (market index Put). The gain/loss profile is identical to buying a Call (see Figure 3–4), but the motivations are entirely different. A long Call is purchased by a speculator investing a limited amount of capital with the expectation of large gains in a short period of time. The hedger purchasing a Put might wish to be protected against a possible adverse court ruling, a potential poor earnings report, or a failed merger and is willing to pay for such protection.

THE SPREADS

Spreads are initiated by simultaneously buying and selling options on the same underlying instrument where both options are either Calls or Puts. Spreads are designed to limit risk while limiting profit potential as well. A *vertical* spread is one in which both options have the same expiration date with different strike prices. Although there are two transactions, spreads can be initiated with a single order specifying the net price difference between the purchased and sold options—a *debit* if the purchased Call or Put price is greater than the sold Call or Put price and a *credit* otherwise.

BULL CALL SPREAD

A bull Call spread is constructed by purchasing a Call at one strike price and selling another Call at a higher strike price. It is a hedged, mildly bullish strategy best entered during periods of declining or stable volatility. The bull Call spread is a *debit* spread; that is, the trader must deposit the difference between the premium paid for the lower strike Call and the premium received for the higher strike Call as margin with a broker.

Figure 3–11 shows the gain/loss profile at inception and expiration for a bull Call spread established by purchasing a 75 Call for $9.20 and selling an 80 Call for $5.72 when the current stock price is $83.

The break-even stock price *BEP* for a bull Call spread is

$$BEP = K_{PC} - P_{SC} + P_{PC} \qquad (3.27)$$

Visualizing Option Structures and Strategies

FIGURE 3-11

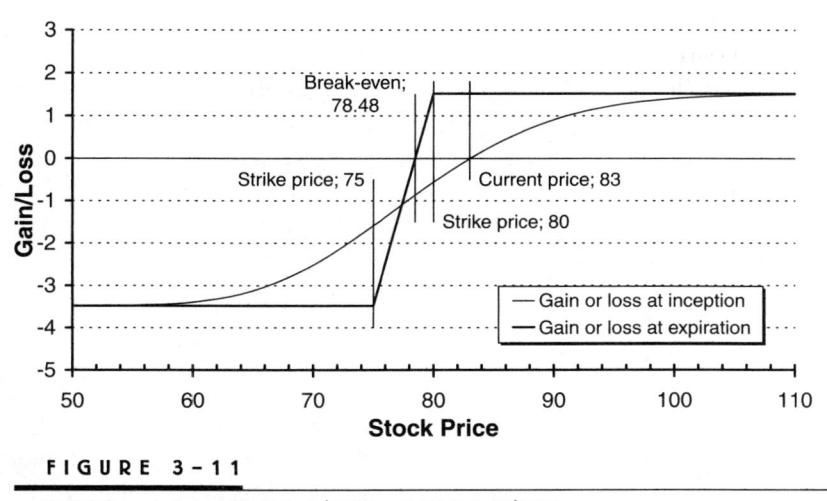

Bull Call spread: buy 75 Call at $9.20; sell 80 Call at $5.72

And for the bull Call spread in Figure 3–11,

$$BEP = 75 - 5.72 + 9.20 = 78.48$$

In Figure 3–11, the ratio of potential gain to potential loss is less than 1. To obtain a higher gain/loss ratio, the spread would be established with the underlying stock at a price close to the lower strike price. However, having a high gain/loss ratio means the distance the underlying stock price must move to the upside to produce a profit is far greater. Imagine the current stock price as the mean of a normal distribution with a 50 percent chance of an upside move and a 50 percent chance of going lower. This is the classic case of the undecided trader. There is a greater chance for profit when the current price is $83 than for an initial price of $75. There are tradeoffs between the gain/loss ratio, the probability of profit, and the amount of profit. The highest probability for profit occurs when both Calls are in the money, as in Figure 3–11.

The results function at expiration for the bull Call spread is

$$R = f(x) = \begin{cases} P_{SC} - P_{PC} & \text{for } x \leq K_{PC} \\ x - BEP & \text{for } K_{PC} < x < K_{SC} \\ K_{SC} - BEP & \text{for } x \geq K_{SC} \end{cases} \quad (3.28)$$

And for this bull Call spread,

$$R = f(x) = \begin{cases} -3.48 & \text{for } x \leq 75 \\ x - 78.48 & \text{for } 75 < x < 80 \\ 1.52 & \text{for } x \geq 80 \end{cases}$$

The maximum gain or loss for this bull Call spread is

$$G_{max} = K_{SC} - BEP = 1.52$$

$$L_{max} = P_{SC} - P_{PC} = -3.48$$

One contract of this spread would be ordered by specifying the company, expiration month and year, and "buy one 75 Call and sell one 80 Call for a net debit of $3.48 contingent on stock price being *at or above* $83.00." The margin requirements for debit spreads is equal to 100 times the absolute difference between the two option prices and for the preceding example would be $348 per contract.

BEAR CALL SPREAD

The bear Call spread is just the reverse of the bull Call spread. It is a hedged, mildly bearish strategy best entered during periods of declining or stable volatility. For the bear Call spread, the trader sells a Call at one strike price and buys another Call at a higher strike price. Figure 3–12 shows the gain/loss profile at inception and expiration for a bear Call spread established by selling a 75 Call for $9.20 and buying an 80 Call for $5.72 when the current stock price is $83.00. Both Calls are in the money.

The bear Call spread in Figure 3–12 shows a favorable gain/loss ratio because the Calls are in the money. Switching to out-of-the-money Calls would increase the *probability* of profit while decreasing the gain/loss ratio and the *amount* of potential profit.

The break-even stock price *BEP* for a bear Call spread is

$$BEP = K_{SC} + P_{SC} - P_{PC} \qquad (3.29)$$

And for the bear Call spread in Figure 3–12,

$$BEP = 75 + 9.20 - 5.72 = 78.48$$

Visualizing Option Structures and Strategies

FIGURE 3-12

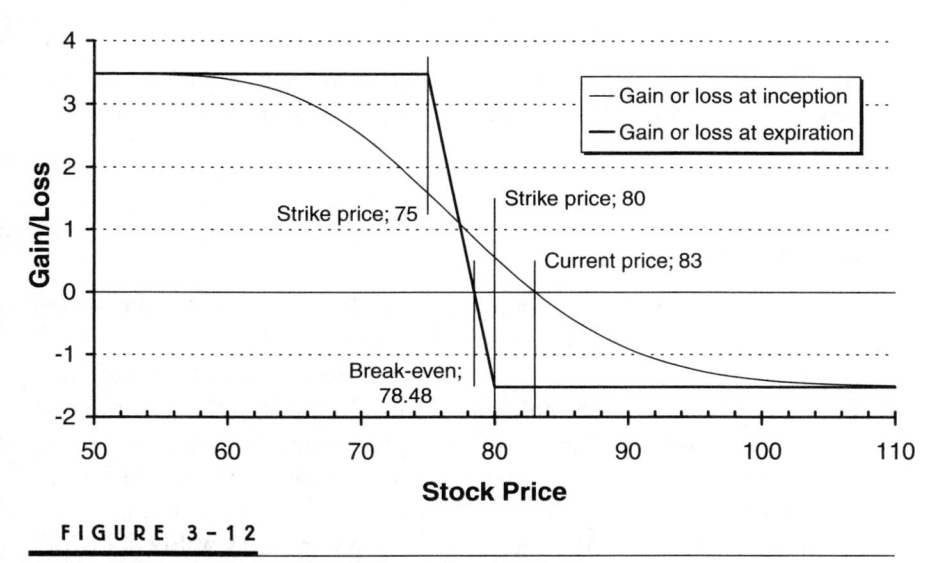

Bear Call spread: buy 80 Call at $5.72; sell 75 Call at $9.20.

The results function at expiration for the bear Call spread is

$$R = f(x) = \begin{cases} P_{SC} - P_{PC} & \text{for } x \leq K_{SC} \\ BEP - x & \text{for } K_{SC} < x < K_{PC} \\ BEP - K_{PC} & \text{for } x \geq K_{PC} \end{cases} \quad (3.30)$$

And for this bear Call spread,

$$R = f(x) = \begin{cases} 3.48 & \text{for } x \leq 75 \\ 78.48 - x & \text{for } 75 < x < 80 \\ -1.52 & \text{for } x \geq 80 \end{cases}$$

The maximum gain or loss for this bear Call spread is

$$G_{max} = P_{SC} - P_{PC} = 3.48$$

$$L_{max} = BEP - K_{PC} = -1.52$$

The bear Call spread is a *credit* spread; that is, the trader will receive more from selling the Call than he paid for the purchased Call. One contract of this spread would be initiated by specifying the company, expiration month and year, and "buy one 80 Call and sell one 75 Call for a net credit of $3.48 contingent on stock price being *at or below*

BULL PUT SPREAD

The gain/loss profile for the bull Put spread is identical to that of the bull Call spread when the Puts are calculated from Equation (3.4). It is a hedged, mildly bullish strategy best entered during periods of declining or stable volatility. For the bull Put spread, the trader sells a Put at one strike price and buys another at a lower strike price. Figure 3–13 shows the gain/loss profile at inception and expiration for selling an 80 Put for $2.57 and buying a 75 Put for $1.05. Both Puts are out of the money.

The bull Put spread in Figure 3–13 shows an unfavorable gain/loss ratio. Switching to in-the-money Puts would increase the gain/loss ratio and the *amount* of potential gain but would *decrease* the *probability* of a gain at expiration.

The break-even stock price *BEP* for a bull Put spread is

$$BEP = K_{SP} - P_{SP} + P_{PP} \qquad (3.31)$$

And for the bull Put spread in Figure 3–13,

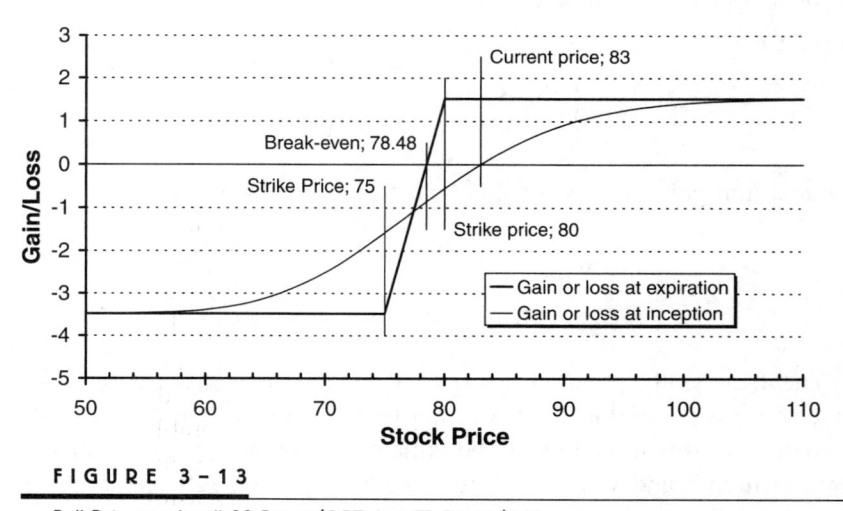

FIGURE 3–13

Bull Put spread: sell 80 Put at $2.57; buy 75 Put at $1.05

$$BEP = 80 - 2.57 + 1.05 = 78.48$$

The results function at expiration for the bull Put spread is

$$R = f(x) = \begin{cases} K_{PP} - BEP & \text{for } x \leq K_{PP} \\ x - BEP & \text{for } K_{PP} < x < K_{SP} \\ P_{SP} - P_{PP} & \text{for } x \geq K_{SP} \end{cases} \quad (3.32)$$

And for this bull Put spread,

$$R = f(x) = \begin{cases} -3.48 & \text{for } x \leq 75 \\ x - 78.48 & \text{for } 75 < x < 80 \\ 1.52 & \text{for } x \geq 80 \end{cases}$$

The maximum gain or loss from this bull Put spread is

$$G_{max} = P_{SP} - P_{PP} = 1.52$$

$$L_{max} = K_{PP} - BEP = -3.48$$

The bull Put spread is a *credit* spread. One contract of this spread would be initiated by specifying the company, expiration month and year, and "sell one 80 Put and buy one 75 Put for a net credit of $1.52 contingent on stock price being *at or above* $83.00." The margin requirement for credit spreads is the absolute difference in strike prices less the credit received multiplied by 100. For the preceding example, the margin would be $348.

BEAR PUT SPREAD

The gain/loss profile for the bear Put spread is identical to that of a bear Call spread when the Puts are calculated from Equation (3.4). It is a mildly bearish strategy best entered during periods of declining or stable volatility. For the bear Put spread, the trader sells a Put at one strike price and buys another at a higher strike price. Figure 3–14 shows the gain/loss profile at inception and expiration for buying an 80 Put for $2.57 and selling a 75 Put for $1.05. Both Puts are out of the money.

The bear Put spread in Figure 3–14 shows a favorable gain/loss ratio because the Puts are out of the money. Switching to in-the-money Puts would increase the *probability* of profit while decreasing the gain/loss ratio and the *amount* of potential profit.

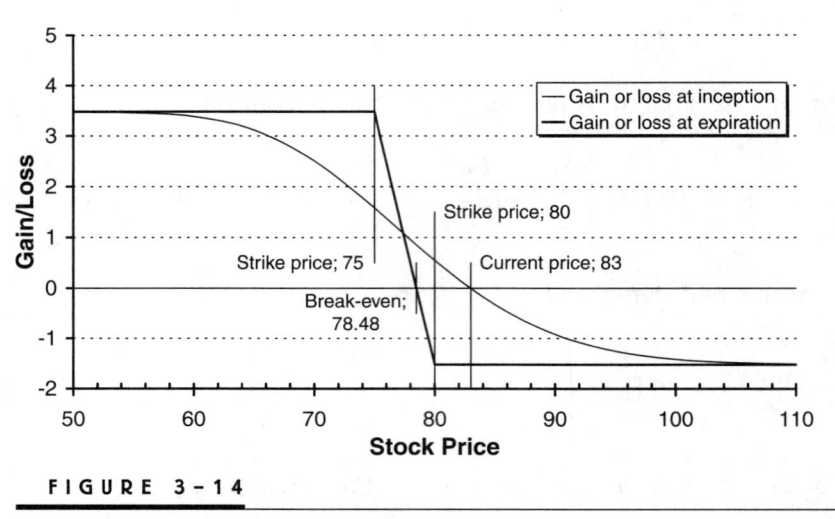

[Figure 3-14: Gain/Loss vs Stock Price chart showing Strike price 75, Strike price 80, Current price 83, Break-even 78.48, with curves for Gain or loss at inception and Gain or loss at expiration.]

FIGURE 3-14

Bear Put spread: sell 75 Put at $1.05; buy 80 Put at $2.57

The break-even stock price *BEP* for a bear Put spread is

$$BEP = K_{PP} - P_{PP} + P_{SP} \qquad (3.33)$$

The break-even stock price for the bear Put spread in Figure 3-14 is

$$BEP = 80 - 2.57 + 1.05 = 78.48$$

The results function at expiration for the bear Put spread is

$$R = f(x) = \begin{cases} BEP - K_{SP} & \text{for } x \leq K_{SP} \\ BEP - x & \text{for } K_{SP} < x < K_{PP} \\ P_{SP} - P_{PP} & \text{for } x \geq K_{PP} \end{cases} \qquad (3.34)$$

And for this bear Put spread,

$$R = f(x) = \begin{cases} 3.48 & \text{for } x \leq 75 \\ 78.48 - x & \text{for } 75 < x < 80 \\ -1.52 & \text{for } x \geq 80 \end{cases}$$

The maximum gain or loss from this bear Put spread is

$$G_{\max} = BEP - K_{SP} = 3.48$$

$$L_{\max} = P_{SP} - P_{PP} = -1.52$$

Visualizing Option Structures and Strategies

The bear Put spread is a *debit* spread. One contract of this spread would be initiated by specifying the company, expiration month and year, and "sell one 75 Put and buy one 80 Put for a net debit of $1.52 contingent on the stock price being *at or below* $83.00." The margin requirement for debit spreads is 100 times the absolute difference between the option prices, and for the preceding example, the margin requirement would be $152.

STRADDLES

A long straddle is established by purchasing a Call and a Put at the same strike price—generally the strike price closest to the current stock price. It is a hedged neutral strategy best entered during periods of increasing or high volatility when the stock price exhibits no particular trend. A trader will initiate this strategy when she anticipates a large move to either the upside or downside but is not confident of the direction. Figure 3–15 shows the gain/loss profile at inception and expiration for a long straddle established by purchasing an 80 Call for $5.10 and purchasing an 80 Put for $2.94 when the current stock price is $82.00. One of the options will be out of the money, whereas the other will be in the money.

The are two break-even points for this strategy—one for an upside move (BEP_{up}) and one for a downside move (BEP_{dn}). The break-even points are calculated by

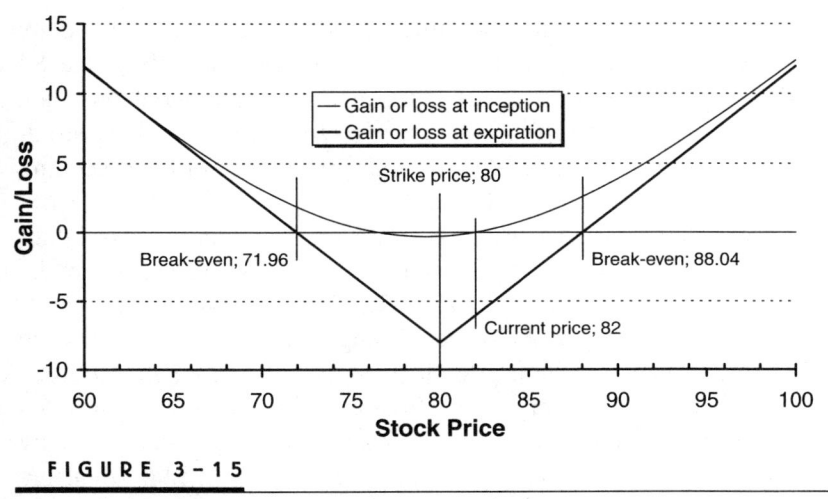

FIGURE 3–15

Long straddle: buy 80 Call at $5.10; buy 80 Put at $2.94

$$BEP_{up} = K_{PC} + P_{PC} + P_{PP} \qquad (3.35)$$

$$BEP_{dn} = K_{PP} - P_{PC} - P_{PP} \qquad (3.36)$$

And for the long straddle in Figure 3–15,

$$BEP_{up} = 80 + 5.10 + 2.94 = 88.04$$

$$BEP_{dn} = 80 - 5.10 - 2.94 = 71.96$$

The results function at expiration for the long straddle is

$$R = f(x) = \begin{cases} BEP_{dn} - x & \text{for } x < K_{PC} \\ x - BEP_{up} & \text{for } x \geq K_{PC} \end{cases} \qquad (3.37)$$

And for this long straddle,

$$R = f(x) = \begin{cases} 71.96 - x & \text{for } x < 80 \\ x - 88.04 & \text{for } x \geq 80 \end{cases}$$

The maximum gain or loss from this long straddle is

$$G_{max} = \begin{cases} BEP_{dn} & \text{for } x < K_{PC} = 71.96 \\ \text{unlimited} & \text{for } x \geq K_{PC} \end{cases}$$

$$L_{max} = -(P_{PC} + P_{PP}) = -8.04$$

An order for one contract of this straddle would be initiated by specifying the company, expiration month and year, and "buy one 80 Call and buy one 80 Put for a net debit of $8.04 contingent on stock price being *at or above* $82.00." The margin requirement for long straddles is 100 times the sum of the Put and Call prices, and for the preceding example, the margin requirement would be $804.

A short straddle is just the inverse of a long straddle. It is established by selling a Call and a Put at the same strike price, again the strike price closest to the current stock price. It is a hedged neutral strategy best entered during periods of decreasing or low volatility when the stock price exhibits no particular trend. A trader will initiate this strategy when he anticipates stagnant prices. Figure 3–15 shows the gain/loss profile at inception and expiration for a short straddle established by selling an 80 Call for $5.10 and selling an 80 Put for $2.94 when the

Visualizing Option Structures and Strategies 101

current stock price is $82.00. One of the options will be out of the money, and the other will be in the money.

The break-even points for a short straddle are

$$BEP_{up} = K_{SC} + P_{SC} + P_{SP} \qquad (3.38)$$

$$BEP_{dn} = K_{SP} - P_{SC} - P_{SP} \qquad (3.39)$$

And for the short straddle in Figure 3–16,

$$BEP_{up} = 80 + 5.10 + 2.94 = 88.04$$

$$BEP_{dn} = 80 - 5.10 - 2.94 = 71.96$$

The results function at expiration for the short straddle is

$$R = f(x) = \begin{cases} x - BEP_{dn} & \text{for } x < K_{SC} \\ BEP_{up} - x & \text{for } x \geq K_{SC} \end{cases} \qquad (3.40)$$

And for this short straddle,

$$R = f(x) = \begin{cases} x - 71.96 & \text{for } x < 80 \\ 88.04 - x & \text{for } x \geq 80 \end{cases}$$

The maximum gain or loss from this short straddle is

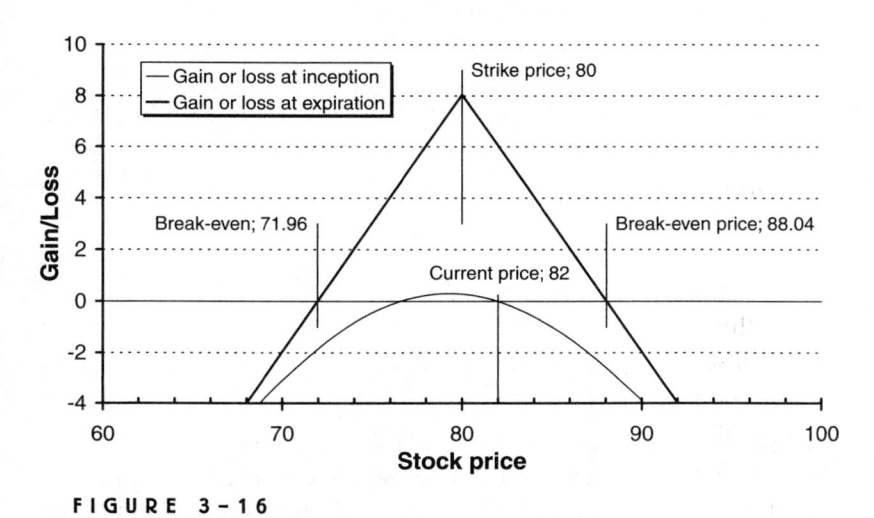

FIGURE 3–16

Short straddle: sell 80 Call at $5.10; sell 80 Put at $2.94

$$G_{max} = P_{SC} + P_{SP} = 8.04$$

$$L_{max} = \begin{cases} -BEP_{dn} & \text{for } x < K_{SC} = 71.96 \\ \text{unlimited} & \text{for } x \geq K_{SC} \end{cases}$$

An order for one contract of this short straddle would be initiated by specifying the company, expiration month and year, and "sell one 80 Call and sell one 80 Put for a net *credit* of $8.04 contingent on stock price being *at or below* $82.00." The margin requirement for selling one contract of a short straddle is 100 times the greater of the short Call or short Put requirement plus the current premium of the leg with the lower requirement. In the preceding example, the requirement for the short Call (from Equation 3.21) is

$$\text{Margin} = 100\{\max[.25S + P_{SC} - \max(K_{SC} - S, 0), .1S + P_{SC}]\}$$

Since

$$\max(K_{SC} - S, 0) = \max(80 - 82, 0) = 0$$

and

$$\max(.25S + P_{SC} - 0, .1S + P_{SC}) = .25(82) + 5.1 - 0 = 25.60$$

the short Call requirement is 100 times $25.60, or $2,560.

Requirement for the short Put (from Equation 3.24) is

$$\text{Margin} = 100\{\max[.25S + P_{SP} - \max(S - K_{SP}, 0), .1S + P_{SP}]\}$$

Since

$$\max(S - K_{SP}, 0) = \max(82 - 80, 0) = 2$$

and

$$\max(.25S + P_{SP} - 2, .1S + P_{SP}) = .25(82) + 2.94 - 2 = 21.44$$

the short Put requirement is 100 times $21.44, or $2,144.

The margin requirement for the short straddle in Figure 3–16 is the requirement for the short Call of $2,560 plus 100 times the premium for the short Put of $294 for a total of $2,854.

STRANGLES

The long strangle is similar to the long straddle except that the Calls and Puts are purchased at *different* strike prices. It is also a hedged neutral strategy best entered during periods of increasing or high volatility when the stock price exhibits no particular trend. To put on a long strangle, a trader must believe there will be an explosive move to either the upside or the downside. Typically, both options will be out of the money, with the Put having the lower strike price. The cost of initiating a long strangle will be less than for an equivalent long straddle, but the *probability* of profit will be less because the underlying stock price will have to move further in either direction to break even. Figure 3–17 shows the gain/loss profile at inception and expiration for a long strangle established by purchasing an 85 Call for $2.79 and a 75 Put for $1.25 when the current stock price is $82.00.

The two break-even points for a long strangle are calculated from Equations (3.35) and (3.36).

$$BEP_{up} = K_{PC} + P_{PC} + P_{PP}$$

$$BEP_{dn} = K_{PP} - P_{PC} - P_{PP}$$

And for the long strangle in Figure 3–17,

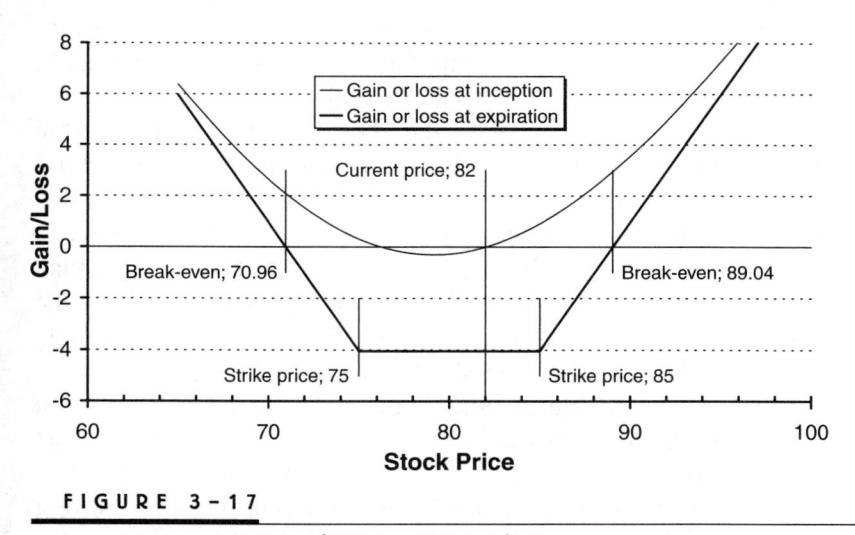

FIGURE 3-17

Long strangle: buy 85 Call at $2.79; buy 75 Put at $1.25

$$BEP_{up} = 85 + 2.79 + 1.25 = 89.04$$

$$BEP_{dn} = 75 - 2.79 - 1.25 = 70.96$$

The results function at expiration for the long strangle is

$$R = f(x) = \begin{cases} BEP_{dn} - x & \text{for } x \leq K_{PP} \\ -(P_{PC} + P_{PP}) & \text{for } K_{PP} < x < K_{PC} \\ x - BEP_{up} & x \geq K_{PC} \end{cases} \quad (3.41)$$

And for this long strangle,

$$R = f(x) = \begin{cases} 70.96 - x & \text{for } x \leq 75 \\ -4.04 & \text{for } K_{PP} < x < K_{PC} \\ x - 89.04 & \text{for } x \geq K_{PC} \end{cases}$$

The maximum gain or loss from this long strangle is

$$G_{max} = \begin{cases} BEP_{dn} & \text{for } x \leq K_{PP} = 70.96 \\ \text{unlimited} & \text{for } x \geq K_{PC} \end{cases}$$

$$L_{max} = -(P_{PC} + P_{PP}) = -4.04$$

An order for one contract of this long strangle would be initiated by specifying the company, expiration month and year, and "buy one 85 Call and buy one 75 Put for a net debit of $4.04 contingent on stock price being *at or above* $82.00." The margin requirement for long strangle is 100 times the sum of the Call and Put prices, and for the preceding example, the margin requirement would be $404.

The short strangle is similar to the short straddle except that the Calls and Puts are sold at *different* strike prices. It is also a hedged neutral strategy best entered during periods of decreasing or low volatility when the stock price exhibits no particular trend. To put on a short strangle, a trader must believe there will be stagnant prices—but less stagnant than for a short straddle strategy. Typically, both options will be out of the money. The *amount* of potential profit from initiating a short strangle will be less than for an equivalent short straddle, but the *probability* of profit will be greater because the underlying stock price has more room to move in either direction before a loss. Figure 3–18 shows the gain/loss profile at inception and expiration for a short strangle established by selling an 85 Call for $2.79 and a 75 Put for $1.25 when the current stock price is $82.00.

Visualizing Option Structures and Strategies

FIGURE 3-18

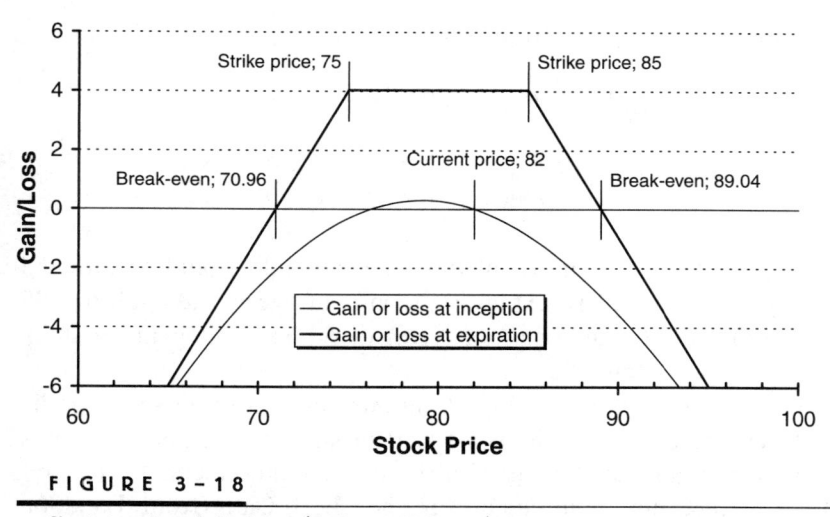

Short strangle: sell 85 Call at $2.79; sell 75 Put at $1.25

The two break-even points are calculated from Equations (3.38) and (3.39).

$$BEP_{up} = K_{SC} + P_{SC} + P_{SP}$$

$$BEP_{dn} = K_{SP} - P_{SC} - P_{SP}$$

And for the short strangle in Figure 3–18,

$$BEP_{up} = 85 + 2.79 + 1.25 = 89.04$$

$$BEP_{dn} = 75 - 2.79 - 1.25 = 70.96$$

$$R = f(x) = \begin{cases} x - BEP_{dn} & \text{for } x \leq K_{SP} \\ P_{SC} + P_{PP} & \text{for } K_{SP} < x < K_{SC} \\ BEP_{up} - x & \text{for } x \geq K_{SC} \end{cases} \quad (3.42)$$

And for this short strangle,

$$R = f(x) = \begin{cases} x - 70.96 & \text{for } x \leq 75 \\ 4.04 & \text{for } 75 < x < 85 \\ 89.04 - x & \text{for } x \geq 85 \end{cases}$$

The maximum gain or loss from this short strangle is:

$$G_{max} = P_{SC} + P_{SP} = 4.04$$

$$L_{max} = \begin{cases} -BEP_{dn} & \text{for } x < K_{SP} = 70.96 \\ \text{unlimited} & \text{for } x \geq K_{SC} \end{cases}$$

An order for one contract of this short strangle would be initiated by specifying the company, expiration month and year, and "sell one 85 Call and sell one 75 Put for a net *credit* of $4.04 contingent on stock price being *at or below* $82.00."

The margin requirement for selling one contract of a short straddle is 100 times the greater of the short Call or short Put requirement plus the current premium of the leg with the lower requirement. In the preceding example, the requirement for the short Call (from Equation 3.21) is

$$\text{Margin} = 100\{\max[.25S + P_{SC} - \max(K_{SC} - S, 0), .1S + P_{SC}]\}$$

Since

$$\max(K_{SC} - S, 0) = \max(85 - 82, 0) = 3$$

and

$$\max(.25S + P_{SC} - 3, .1S + P_{SC}) = .25(82) + 2.79 - 3 = 20.29$$

the short Call requirement is 100 times $20.29, or $2,029.

The requirement for the short Put (from Equation 3.24) is

$$\text{Margin} = 100\{\max[.25S + P_{SP} - \max(S - K_{SP}, 0), .1S + P_{SP}]\}$$

Since

$$\max(S - K_{SP}, 0) = \max(82 - 75, 0) = 5$$

and

$$\max(.25S + P_{SP} - 5, .1S + P_{SP}) = .25(82) + 1.25 - 5 = 16.75$$

the short Put requirement is 100 times $16.75, or $1,675.

The margin requirement for the short strangle in Figure 3–18 is the requirement for the short Call of $2,029 plus 100 times the premium for the short Put of $125 for a total of $2,154.

OTHER COMBINATIONS

Most other combination strategies except for the *calendar spread* (discussed later) are simply variations of the basic strategies set forth earlier. The most common of these are the ratio spreads, backspreads, synthetics, butterfly spreads, and condors. Since some of these spreads involve selling more options than purchased (or buying more options than sold), the *number* of options purchased or sold becomes important. Accordingly, we set up the following additional variables:

n_{PC} = number of purchased Calls
n_{SC} = number of sold Calls
n_{PP} = number of purchased Puts
n_{SP} = number of sold Puts

CALL RATIO SPREAD

A *Call ratio spread* involves buying Calls at one strike price and selling a greater number of Calls at a *higher* strike price. Thus, in essence, it is a bull Call spread with added sold Calls. The credit obtained from selling the extra Calls usually more than covers the cost of the Calls being purchased (a net credit). However, this is not always so, thus a Call ratio spread may be entered at a net credit or a net debit. This strategy has little or no downside risk—risk being limited to the net debit if the spread was entered at a debit. If the spread was established at a credit, there is *no* downside risk.

A Call ratio spread is a neutral to mildly bearish strategy best entered during periods of stable volatility with the stock price showing no particular trend. A trader may initiate this strategy if she is unsure about a directional move but believes there will *not* be an explosive move to the upside. Figure 3–19 shows a Call ratio spread entered for a credit where one 75 Call is purchased for $8.40 and two 80 Calls are sold for $5.10, each when the current stock price is $82.00.

The maximum gain for a Call ratio spread is

$$G_{max} = n_{PC}(K_{SC} - K_{PC} - P_{PC}) + n_{SC}P_{SC} \qquad (3.43)$$

And for the Call ratio spread in Figure 3–19,

$$G_{max} = 1(80 - 75 - 8.40) + 2(5.10) = 6.80$$

Note: The maximum gain for a Call ratio spread occurs when the stock price at expiration is equal to the higher strike price (K_{SC}).

FIGURE 3-19

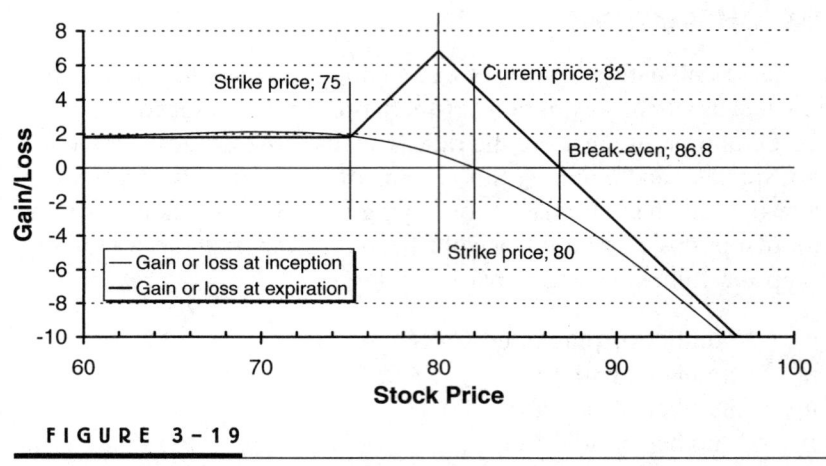

Call ratio spread: buy 75 Call at $8.40; sell two 80 Calls at $5.10

The break-even stock prices *BEP* for a Call ratio spread are

$$BEP_{up} = K_{SC} + \frac{G_{max}}{n_{SC} - n_{PC}} \quad (3.44)$$

$$BEP_{dn} = K_{PC} - n_{SC}P_{SC} + n_{PC}P_{PC} \quad (3.45)$$

Note: BEP_{dn} is a break-even point *only* if the spread was entered at a debit. Since this spread was entered at a credit, BEP_{dn} is only a quantity used in the results function to determine the value of the spread at expiration between the two strike prices. There is no downside risk for this spread.

The break-even stock prices *BEP* for this Call ratio spread are

$$BEP_{up} = 80 + \frac{6.80}{2 - 1} = 86.80$$

$$BEP_{dn} = 75 - 2(5.10) + 1(8.40) = 73.20$$

The results function at expiration for a Call ratio spread is

$$R = f(x) = \begin{cases} n_{SC}P_{SC} - n_{PC}P_{PC} & \text{for } x \leq K_{PC} \\ x - BEP_{dn} & \text{for } K_{PC} < x < K_{SC} \\ BEP_{up} - x & \text{for } x \geq K_{SC} \end{cases} \quad (3.46)$$

And for this Call ratio spread,

$$R = f(x) = \begin{cases} 1.80 & \text{for } x \leq K_{PC} \\ x - 73.20 & \text{for } K_{PC} < x < K_{SC} \\ 86.80 - x & \text{for } x \geq K_{SC} \end{cases}$$

The maximum loss for a Call ratio spread is

$$L_{max} = \begin{cases} n_{SC}P_{SC} - n_{PC}P_{PC} & \text{for } x \leq BEP_{dn} \text{ (only if negative)} \\ \text{unlimited} & \text{for } x \geq BEP_{up} \end{cases}$$

(3.47)

And for this spread,

$$L_{max} = \begin{cases} \text{no loss} & \text{for } x \leq 75 \\ \text{unlimited} & \text{for } x \geq 86.80 \end{cases}$$

A little scrutiny of this spread reveals that it is simply a bull Call spread with additional naked Calls sold. Its advantage is that it makes money all the way up to the upside break-even point with no downside risk. Its disadvantage is, of course, the extra margin required for the additional naked Calls sold. An order to enter this spread would be initiated by specifying the company, expiration month and year, and "buy one 75 Call and sell two 80 Calls for a net *credit* of $1.80 contingent on stock price being *at or below* $82.00."

The margin requirement for a Call ratio spread is the margin requirement for a bull Call spread plus the margin requirement for selling the extra naked Calls.

PUT RATIO SPREAD

A Put ratio spread is similar to a Call ratio spread but involves buying Puts at one strike price and selling a greater number of Puts at a *lower* strike price. In essence, it is a bear Put spread with added sold Puts. The credit obtained from selling the extra Puts usually more than covers the cost of the Puts being purchased (a net credit). However, this is not always so, thus a Put ratio spread may be entered at a net credit or a net debit. This strategy has little or no upside risk—risk being limited to the net debit if the spread was entered at a debit. If the spread was established at a credit, there is *no* upside risk.

A Put ratio spread is a neutral to mildly bullish strategy best entered during periods of stable volatility with the stock price showing no particular trend. A trader may initiate this strategy if he is unsure about a directional move but believes there will *not* be an explosive move to the downside. Figure 3–20 shows a Call ratio spread entered for a credit where one 80 Put is purchased for $8.09 and two 75 Puts are sold for $4.59, each when the current stock price is $73.00.

The maximum gain for a Put ratio spread is

$$G_{max} = n_{pp}(K_{PP} - K_{SP} - P_{PP}) + n_{SP}P_{SP} \qquad (3.48)$$

And for the Put ratio spread in Figure 3–20,

$$G_{max} = 1(80 - 75 - 8.09) + 2(4.59) = 6.09$$

Note: The maximum gain for a Put ratio spread occurs when the stock price at expiration is equal to the lower strike price (K_{SP}).

The break-even stock prices *BEP* for a Put ratio spread are

$$BEP_{dn} = K_{SP} - \frac{G_{max}}{n_{SP} - n_{PP}} \qquad (3.49)$$

$$BEP_{up} = K_{PP} + n_{SP}P_{SP} - n_{PP}P_{PP} \qquad (3.50)$$

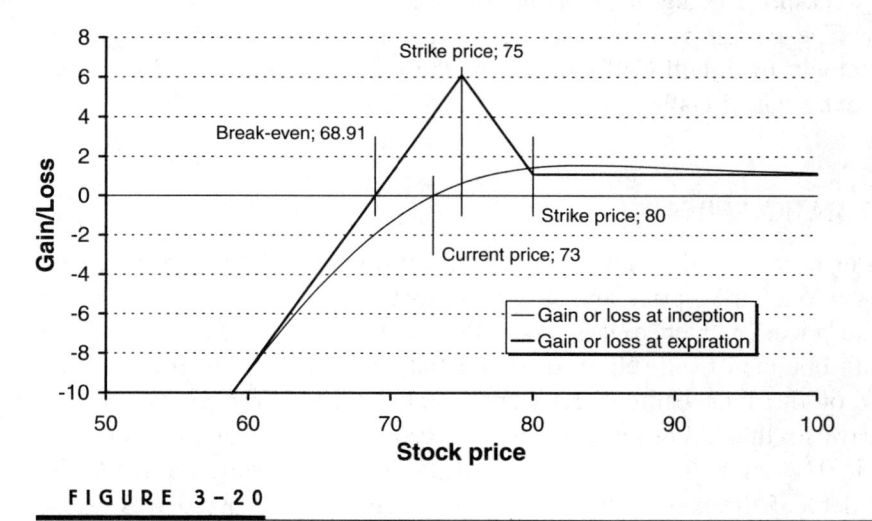

FIGURE 3–20

Put ratio spread: buy 80 Put at $8.09; sell two 75 Puts at $4.59

Note: BEP_{up} is a break-even point *only* if the spread was entered at a debit. Since this spread was entered at a credit, BEP_{up} is only a quantity used in the results function to determine the value of the spread at expiration between the two strike prices. There is no upside risk for this spread.

The break-even stock prices *BEP* for this Put ratio spread are

$$BEP_{dn} = 75 - \frac{6.09}{1} = 68.91$$

$$BEP_{up} = 80 + 2(4.59) - 1(8.40) = 81.09$$

The results function at expiration for a Put ratio spread is

$$R = f(x) = \begin{cases} x - BEP_{dn} & \text{for } x \leq K_{SP} \\ BEP_{up} - x & \text{for } K_{SP} < x < K_{PP} \\ n_{SP}P_{SP} - n_{PP}P_{PP} & \text{for } x \geq K_{PP} \end{cases} \quad (3.51)$$

And for this Put ratio spread,

$$R = f(x) = \begin{cases} x - 68.91 & \text{for } x \leq K_{SP} \\ 81.09 - x & \text{for } K_{SP} < x < K_{PP} \\ 1.09 & \text{for } x \geq K_{PP} \end{cases}$$

The maximum loss for a Put ratio spread is

$$L_{max} = \begin{cases} \text{unlimited} & \text{for } x \leq BEP_{dn} \\ n_{SP}P_{SP} - n_{PP}P_{PP} & x \geq BEP_{up} \text{ (only if negative)} \end{cases} \quad (3.52)$$

And for this Put ratio spread,

$$L_{max} = \begin{cases} \text{unlimited} & \text{for } x \leq 68.91 \\ \text{no loss} & \text{for } x \geq 81.90 \end{cases}$$

This spread is simply a bull Put spread with additional naked Puts sold. Its advantage is that it makes money all the way down to the downside break-even point with no upside risk. Its disadvantage is, of course, the extra margin required for the additional naked Puts sold. An order to enter this spread would be initiated by specifying the company, expiration month and year, and "buy one 80 Put and sell two 75 Puts for a net *credit* of $1.09 contingent on stock price being *at or above* $73.00."

The margin requirement for a Put ratio spread is the margin requirement for a bull Put spread plus the margin requirement for selling the extra naked Puts.

CALL BACKSPREADS

Call backspreads are simply the *inverse* of Call ratio spreads. They are also a combination of a bear Call spread and purchasing additional Calls. A Call backspread is established by selling Calls at one strike price and purchasing a greater number of Calls at a *higher* strike price and may be put on for debit or a credit. Figure 3–21 shows a Call backspread entered for a credit where two 85 Calls are purchased for $0.63 each and one 75 Call is sold for $3.20 when the current stock price is $74.

A Call backspread is bullish strategy that also provides protection on the downside best entered during periods of rising or high volatility. A trader may initiate this strategy if she anticipates a large move to the upside but wants protection against a sharp move to the downside.

The maximum loss for a Call backspread occurs when the stock price at expiration equals the higher strike price (K_{PC}) and is given by

$$L_{max} = n_{SC}(K_{SC} - K_{PC} + P_{SC}) - n_{PC}P_{PC} \qquad (3.53)$$

And for this Call backspread,

$$L_{max} = 1(75 - 85 + 3.20) - 2(.63) = -8.06$$

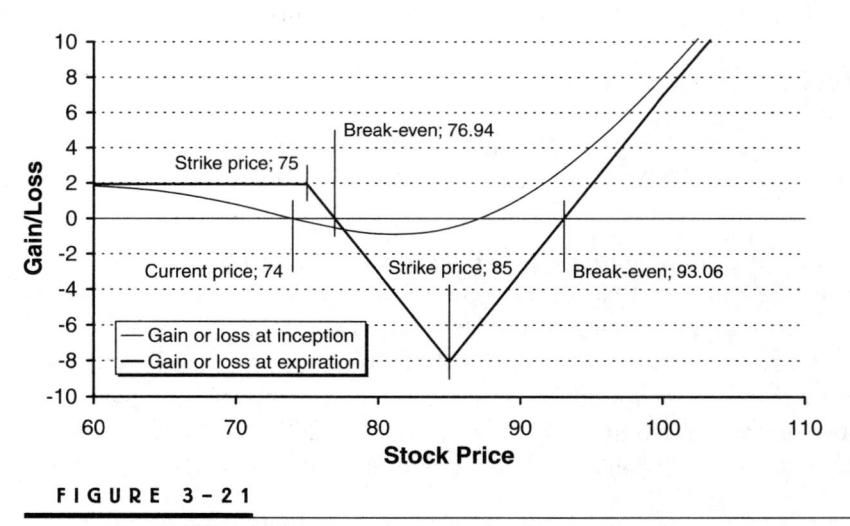

FIGURE 3-21

Call backspread: buy two 85 Calls at $0.63; sell 75 Call at $3.20

Visualizing Option Structures and Strategies

The break-even stock prices *BEP* for a Call backspread are

$$BEP_{up} = K_{PC} + \frac{L_{max}}{n_{SC} - n_{PC}} \quad (3.54)$$

$$BEP_{dn} = K_{SC} + n_{SC}P_{SC} - n_{PC}P_{PC} \quad (3.55)$$

The break-even stock prices *BEP* for the Call backspread in Figure 3–21 are

$$BEP_{up} = 85 + \frac{-8.06}{-1} = 93.06$$

$$BEP_{dn} = 75 + 1(3.20) - 2(.63) = 76.94$$

The results function at expiration for a Call backspread is

$$R = f(x) = \begin{cases} n_{SC}P_{SC} - n_{PC}P_{PC} & \text{for } x \leq K_{SC} \\ BEP_{dn} - x & \text{for } K_{SC} < x < K_{PC} \\ x - BEP_{up} & \text{for } x \geq K_{PC} \end{cases} \quad (3.56)$$

And for this Call backspread,

$$R = f(x) = \begin{cases} 1.94 & \text{for } x \leq 75 \\ 76.94 - x & \text{for } 75 < x < 85 \\ x - 93.06 & \text{for } x \geq 85 \end{cases}$$

The maximum gain for a Call backspread is

$$G_{max} = \begin{cases} n_{SC}P_{SC} - n_{PC}P_{PC} & \text{for } x \leq K_{SC} \text{ (only if positive)} \\ \text{unlimited} & \text{for } x \geq BEP_{up} \end{cases} \quad (3.57)$$

And for this Call backspread,

$$G_{max} = \begin{cases} 1.94 & \text{for } x \leq 75 \\ \text{unlimited} & \text{for } x \geq 93.06 \end{cases}$$

An order to enter this spread would be initiated by specifying the company, expiration month and year, and "buy two 85 Calls and sell one 75 Call for a net *credit* of $1.94 contingent on stock price being *at or below* $74.00."

The margin requirement for a Call backspread is the margin requirement for a bear Call spread plus the margin requirement for purchasing the extra naked Calls. The margin requirement for the bear Call spread would be $7.43 and, together with the margin requirement for purchasing the extra Call of $0.63, yields a total margin of $8.06—the maximum loss.

PUT BACKSPREADS

Put backspreads are the *inverse* of Put ratio spreads and are a combination of a bull Put spread and additional purchased Puts. A Put backspread is established by selling Puts at one strike price and purchasing a greater number of Puts at a *lower* strike price and may be established for a debit or a credit. It is a bearish strategy affording protection to the upside in case the market moves against the trader. Figure 3–22 shows a Put backspread entered for a *debit* where two 75 Puts are purchased for $4.59 each and one 80 Call is sold for $8.09 when the current stock price is $73.

The maximum loss for a Put backspread occurs when the stock price at expiration equals the lower strike price (K_{PP}) and is given by

$$L_{max} = n_{SP}(K_{PP} - K_{SP} + P_{SP}) - n_{PP}P_{PP} \qquad (3.58)$$

And for this Put backspread,

$$L_{max} = 1(75 - 80 + 8.09) - 2(4.59) = -6.09$$

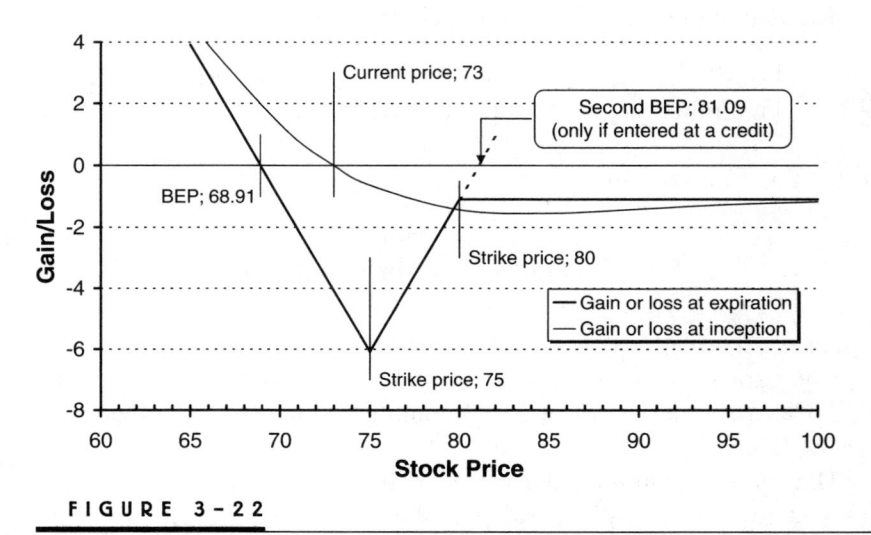

FIGURE 3-22

Put backspread: buy two 75 Puts at $4.59; sell 80 Put at $8.09

The break-even stock prices *BEP* for a Put backspread are

$$BEP_{dn} = K_{PP} - \left(\frac{L_{max}}{n_{SP} - n_{PP}}\right) \quad (3.59)$$

$$BEP_{up} = K_{SP} + n_{PP}P_{PP} - n_{SP}P_{SP} \quad (3.60)$$

The break-even stock prices *BEP* for the Put backspread in Figure 3–22 are

$$BEP_{dn} = 75 - \left(\frac{-6.09}{-1}\right) = 68.91$$

$$BEP_{up} = 80 + 2(4.59) - 1(8.09) = 81.09$$

Note: BEP_{up} is not a real break-even point when a Put backspread is entered for a debit, as is the case for this Put backspread. It is used only in further calculations of the results function. In Figure 3–22, a dashed line is plotted representing an extension of the function to show where the break-even point would be if this strategy had been entered for a credit.

The results function at expiration for a Put backspread is

$$R = f(x) = \begin{cases} BEP_{dn} - x & \text{for } x \leq K_{PP} \\ x - BEP_{up} & \text{for } K_{PP} < x < K_{SP} \\ n_{SP}P_{SP} - n_{PP}P_{PP} & \text{for } x \geq K_{SP} \end{cases} \quad (3.61)$$

And for this Put backspread,

$$R = f(x) = \begin{cases} 68.91 - x & \text{for } x \leq 75 \\ x - 81.09 & \text{for } 75 < x < 80 \\ -6.09 & \text{for } x \geq 80 \end{cases}$$

The maximum gain for a Put backspread is

$$G_{max} = \begin{cases} n_{SP}P_{SP} - n_{PP}P_{PP} & \text{for } x \geq K_{SP} \text{ (only if positive)} \\ \text{unlimited} & \text{for } x \leq BEP_{dn} \end{cases} \quad (3.62)$$

And for this Put backspread,

$$G_{max} = \text{unlimited} \quad \text{for } x \leq 68.91$$

An order to enter this spread would be initiated by specifying the company, expiration month and year, and "buy two 75 Puts and sell one

80 Put for a net *debit* of $1.09 contingent on stock price being *at or below* $73.00."

The margin requirement for a Put backspread is the margin requirement for a bull Put spread plus the margin requirement for purchasing the extra naked Puts. The margin requirement for the bull Put spread would be $1.50 and, together with the margin requirement for purchasing the extra Put of $4.59, yields a total margin of $6.09—the maximum loss.

BUTTERFLY SPREAD

The butterfly spread is a strategy that is the combination of both a bull spread and a bear spread. It is also the same as selling a straddle and limiting risk by purchasing both an out-of-the-money Call and an out-of-the-money Put. It may be established with all Calls or all Puts using three different strike prices in either case. Both long and short butterfly spreads may be initiated. We will concentrate on the long butterfly spread using all Calls, which is a neutral strategy best entered during periods of declining or stable volatility when the stock price is exhibiting no particular trend. It is established by

- Purchasing one low-strike-price Call
- Selling two medium-strike-price Calls
- Purchasing one high-strike-price Call

Figure 3–23 shows a long Call butterfly spread entered for a net debit where two 80 Calls are sold for $5.73 each, one 75 Call is purchased for $9.20, and one 85 Call is purchased for $3.22 when the current stock price is $83.00.

Since there are two purchased Calls, each at a different strike price, we need to differentiate between the two. We shall use H to designate the higher strike price and L for the lower strike price. Thus

LK_{PC} = the lower strike price for a purchased Call
HK_{PC} = the higher strike price for a purchased Call
LP_{PC} = the price of a purchased Call at the lower strike price
HP_{PC} = the price of a purchased Call at the higher strike price
Ln_{PC} = the number of purchased Calls at the lower strike price
Hn_{PC} = the number of purchased Calls at the higher strike price

The break-even stock prices *BEP* for a long Call butterfly spread are

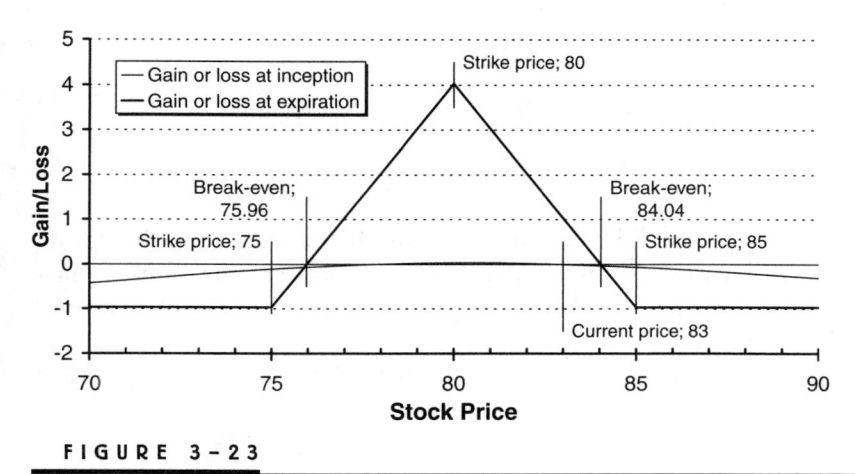

Visualizing Option Structures and Strategies

FIGURE 3-23

Long Call butterfly spread: buy 75 Call at $9.20; buy 85 Call at $3.22; sell two 80 Calls at $5.73 each

$$BEP_{up} = n_{SC}(K_{SC} + P_{SC}) - Ln_{PC}(LK_{PC} + LP_{PC}) - Hn_{PC}HP_{PC} \quad (3.63)$$

$$BEP_{dn} = LK_{PC} + n_{PC}LP_{PC} + n_{PC}HP_{PC} - n_{SC}P_{SC} \quad (3.64)$$

And for the long Call butterfly spread in Figure 3–23,

$$BEP_{up} = 2(80 + 5.73) - (75 + 9.2) - 3.22 = 84.04$$

$$BEP_{dn} = 75 + 9.20 + 3.22 - 2(5.73) = 75.96$$

The maximum gain for a long Call butterfly spread is

$$G_{max} = K_{SC} - LK_{PC} - n_{PC}LP_{PC} - n_{PC}HP_{PC} + n_{SC}P_{SC} \quad (3.65)$$

And for this long Call butterfly spread,

$$G_{max} = 80 - 75 - 9.2 - 3.22 + 2(5.73) = 4.04$$

There are two possible loss amounts for a long Call butterfly spread if the strategy is entered at a debit. For the upside loss,

$$L_{max} = BEP_{up} - Hn_{PC}HK_{PC} \quad (3.66)$$

For the downside loss,

$$L_{max} = n_{SC}P_{SC} - Ln_{PC}LP_{PC} - Hn_{PC}HP_{PC} \quad (3.67)$$

And for this long Call butterfly spread,

$$L_{max} = 84.04 - 85 = -.96 \quad \text{for the upside loss}$$

$$L_{max} = 2(5.73) - 9.2 - 3.22 = -.96 \quad \text{for the downside loss}$$

The actual maximum loss, of course, would be the greater of the upside or downside losses. In this example, both losses are the same, which occurs when the high and low strike prices are equidistant from the middle strike price.

The results function at expiration for the long Call butterfly spread is

$$R = f(x) = \begin{cases} n_{SC}P_{SC} - Ln_{PC}LP_{PC} + Hn_{PC}HP_{PC} & \text{for } x \leq LK_{PC} \\ x - BEP_{dn} & \text{for } LK_{PC} < x < K_{SC} \\ BEP_{up} - x & \text{for } K_{SC} < x < HK_{PC} \\ BEP_{up} - Hn_{PC}HK_{PC} & \text{for } x \geq HK_{PC} \end{cases}$$

(3.68)

And for this long Call butterfly spread,

$$R = f(x) = \begin{cases} -.96 & \text{for } x \leq 75 \\ x - 75.96 & \text{for } 75 < x < 80 \\ 84.04 - x & \text{for } 80 < x < 85 \\ -.96 & \text{for } x \geq 85 \end{cases}$$

This spread would be ordered by specifying the company, expiration month and year and "buy one 75 Call, buy one 85 Call, and sell two 80 Calls for a net *debit* of $96.00 contingent on stock price being *at or above* $83.00." The margin requirement for this long Call butterfly spread would be 100 times the sum of the margin requirements for the associated bull Call spread ($1.53 debit) and the bear Call spread ($2.51 credit), or $98.00.

Whereas the long Call butterfly spread studied earlier calls for selling two Calls at the same strike price, they could have been sold at different strike prices—resulting in a special case of the butterfly spread called a *condor*. Condor spreads have four strike prices instead of three. A long Call condor spread would look like a purchased strangle with limited losses on both the upside and the downside.

SYNTHETICS

Two positions are said to be *equivalent* if their profit profiles are identical or nearly so. One position would be a *synthetic* of the other. Earlier we showed that a covered Call is a synthetic Put, and a covered Put is a synthetic Call. We shall limit further investigation of synthetics to a long or short position in an underlying stock. To establish a synthetic long position in an underlying stock, a trader simply would buy a Call and sell a Put at the same strike price. Using the Call and Put prices employed to construct Figure 3–16, the 80 Call was priced at $5.10, whereas the 80 Put was priced at $2.94. The assumed stock price was $82.00. Table 3–3 shows the equivalency. Note that the synthetic is not an exact replica of the long stock position (being plus or minus $16 different) but is certainly close.

Why would the synthetic be preferable to the long stock position? The difference is in the margin requirements and commissions.

Purchasing 100 shares of the stock outright on 50 percent margin requires an outlay of $4,100 plus a $15 commission. Table 3–4 shows the comparison of margin and commission requirements for the synthetic.

TABLE 3-3

Synthetic long stock
Gain/loss comparison

Price at expiration	Gain/loss on long stock	Gain/loss on long Call	Gain/loss on short Put	Total option profit
55	(2,700)	(510)	(2,206)	(2,716)
60	(2,200)	(510)	(1,706)	(2,216)
65	(1,700)	(510)	(1,206)	(1,716)
70	(1,200)	(510)	(706)	(1,216)
75	(700)	(510)	(206)	(716)
80	(200)	(510)	294	(216)
85	300	(10)	294	284
90	800	490	294	784
95	1,300	990	294	1,284
100	1,800	1,490	294	1,784
105	2,300	1,990	294	2,284
110	2,800	2,490	294	2,784

TABLE 3-4

Synthetic long stock
Margin and commission comparison

Strategy	Margin	Commission	Total investment
Long stock	4,100	15	4,115
Synthetic:			
Long Call	510	15	525
Short Put:		15	15
25% of stock price	2,050		2,050
Premium	294		294
Out-of-the-money	(200)		(200)
Total	2,654	30	2,684
Savings using synthetic	1,446	(15)	1,431

Suppose that on the expiration date the stock is trading at $90 per share. Selling the stock outright would produce a gain of $800, or a 19 percent profit. Closing out the synthetic would produce a gain of $784, or a *29 percent profit*! Because of the reduced margin requirement, trading the synthetic produces an additional 10 percentage points of profit. Of course, this leverage works both ways.

As with the example set forth earlier, the profit profile generally will not be *exactly* the same as purchasing the underlying stock. Since there are two bid-ask spreads involved in the synthetic, the net debit could be different from the theoretical values. To get as close as is possible to the profit profile of the long stock, a trader should use the options pricing model (Equations 3.1 and 3.4) to determine the Call and Put values and enter the position with a single spread order; for example "buy one 80 Call and sell one 80 Put for a net debit of $2.16."

Another difference between the synthetic and the long stock position is that the trader of the options is not entitled to any dividends that might be paid to the holder of the stock. Also, the options trader must pay two commissions, whereas the purchaser of the stock is subject to only one.

Similarly, a short position in the underlying stock may be established by purchasing a Put and selling a Call with the same terms. The leverage in terms of reduced margin requirements is the same as for the long stock position. Two additional advantages accrue to the holder of

TABLE 3-5

Synthetic positions

Option positons	Synthetic
Long Call	Long Put, long stock
Long Put	Long Call, short stock
Short Call	Short Put, short stock
Short Put	Short Call, long stock
Long stock	Long Call, short Put
Short stock	Long Put, short Call
Long straddle	Long 2 Calls, short stock
Short straddle	Short 2 Calls, long stock

the short synthetic: A trader need not wait for an uptick before entering the position, and she does not have to actually borrow the stock.

All basic options strategies have an equivalent synthetic position. The expiration months, strike prices, and number of shares all must be equal to establish a synthetic. Table 3–5 shows the basic synthetic positions.

CONVERSIONS

Earlier in this chapter we indicated that *Put/Call parity* (the relationship between Put and Call prices) exists because of the potential for arbitrage. If the Puts and Calls on a given asset are not in parity, an arbitrageur could establish a conversion and thereby have a risk-free trade. A *conversion* is a position that has a long Put and a short Call at the same strike price while being long the underlying. Likewise, a *reverse conversion* could be established by shorting the underlying while simultaneously buying a Call and selling a Put at the same strike price. These opportunities are rare and generally suitable only for market makers and floor traders whose trading costs are negligible.

THE COLLAR

The collar strategy is established by combining a synthetic short position in a stock with a long position in the same stock. The trader sells out-of-the-money Calls against the long stock (covered Calls) while simultaneously purchasing at-the-money Puts. Another way to look at this strategy is to assume a trader purchases protective Puts against the long stock and lowers the cost of the "insurance" by selling out-of-the-money Calls. The collar behaves just like a bull spread—limited risk at or below the Put strike price and limited profit potential at or above the Call strike price. The collar differs from a conversion because the strike prices of the options typically are different.

CALENDAR SPREADS

Calendar spreads are established by purchasing a Call or Put with a particular expiration date and selling a Call or Put having a closer expiration date at the same strike price. Also called *time spreads* or *horizontal spreads*, these strategies are employed to take advantage of the faster time decay of the nearby option as compared with the option with the later expiration.

Unfortunately, the profit profile at expiration of the combined options is nonlinear, and no simple formula for break-even stock prices exists. Moreover, the nonlinearity of the profit profile precludes the use of calendar spreads in the "expectation analysis" derived in later chapters.

OPTION PRICES

Throughout this chapter we have used theoretical option prices derived from the options pricing formulas (Equations 3.1 and 3.4). In reality, option prices are quoted with a *bid* price at which a trader could sell the option and an *ask* price at which a trader could buy the option. The difference is called the *bid-ask spread*. A *last price* is generally also quoted, referring to the last price at which an option traded. For thinly traded options, the last price may be quite old.

When evaluating actual options that are trading currently, a trader could use the ask price when contemplating a purchase and the bid price if contemplating a sale. However, the true market price is typically somewhere in between. For the remainder of this book we will take *market* to mean

$$\text{Market} = \frac{\text{last} + 10(\text{bid}) + 10(\text{ask})}{21}$$

And the same market price will be used for purchases and sales.

CHAPTER 4

Mathematical Expectation and Optimal Position Size

The race is not always to the swift, nor the battle to the strong—but that's the way to bet.

—Damon Runyon (1884–1946)

Runyon's oft-repeated tongue-in-cheek parody of Ecclesiastes 9:11 refers to expectations of outcomes based on records of past performance that are likely to provide an advantage to one wagering on future events. It allows that outcomes will not *always* follow expectations but, in the long run, will adhere to established patterns of probability.

Mathematical expectation is the basis for developing profitable options trading strategies and the cornerstone of the approach presented in later chapters. In general, *mathematical expectation* is defined as the product of the *value* of an event and the *probability* of the event's occurrence. When a "game" consists of a set of events whose probabilities can be estimated, the mathematical expectation of the entire game may be determined. This requires a *results function* and a *probability density function*—both of which have been introduced in previous chapters.

Any function of the form

$$R = f(x)$$

may be a results function, where

x = outcome of a device of decision (e.g., a roll of the dice, the value of an equity on the option expiration date, etc.)
R = results (payoff) for a given value of x

As shown in Chapter 2, a probability density function $g(x)$ must sum up to 1. If x is a discrete variable,

$$\sum_{i=1}^{n} g(x_i) = 1 \qquad \text{for } n \text{ discrete values of } x$$

If x is a continuous variable,

$$\int_a^b g(x)\,dx = 1 \qquad \text{for all values of } x \text{ in the interval } a \text{ to } b$$

If a results function $R = f(x)$ is known and x has the probability density function $g(x)$, the expected value of R, denoted by $E(R)$, may be determined for any interval a to b by

$$E(R) = \sum_{i=a}^{b} f(x_i) g(x_i) \qquad \text{for the discrete case} \qquad (4.1)$$

$$E(R) = \int_a^b f(x) g(x)\,dx \qquad \text{for the continuous case} \qquad (4.2)$$

A SIMPLE DISCRETE MODEL

If a linear results function is coupled with the tossing of a pair of dice, we can construct an almost perfect discrete analog of the Call option discussed in Chapter 3 by designing a hypothetical game in which the player pays the house $2 if a 2, 3, 4, or 5 is rolled and receives from the house an amount equal to the sum of the dice less $7 if any other number is rolled. The results function is

$$R = f(x) = \begin{cases} -2 & \text{for } x = 2, 3, 4, 5 \\ x - 7 & \text{for } = 6, 7, 8, 9, 10, 11, 12 \end{cases}$$

The probability density function for tossing a pair of dice is

$$g(x) = \begin{cases} \dfrac{x-1}{36} & \text{for } x = 2, 3, 4, 5, 6, 7 \\ \dfrac{13-x}{36} & \text{for } x = 8, 9, 10, 11, 12 \end{cases}$$

Proof that $g(x)$ is a probability density function is as follows:

$$\sum_{i=2}^{12} g(x_i) = \frac{1}{36}\left[\sum_{i=2}^{7}(x_i - 1) + \sum_{i=8}^{12}(13 - x_i)\right] = 1$$

The expected value of the game now may be determined:

$$E(R) = \sum_{2}^{12} f(x)g(x)$$

$$E(R) = \frac{1}{36}\left[-2\sum_{2}^{5}(x-1) + \sum_{6}^{7}(x-7)(x-1)\right.$$

$$\left. + \sum_{8}^{12}(x-7)(13-x)\right]$$

$$E(R) = \frac{1}{36}(-20 - 5 + 35) = .2778$$

The expected value of R means that if this game were played a large number of times, the player could expect to win $0.28 on average for each toss—not the type of game we would expect to find in a casino. Graphically, the results function is shown in Figure 4–1, whereas the density function is shown in Figure 4–2.

In the discrete case, only the dots represent legitimate outcomes. The connecting line in Figure 4–1 was drawn to show the graphic similarity to a purchased Call option at expiration (see Figure 3–4).

In a discrete model, the mathematical expectation of each event can be set forth in a table. Table 4–1 shows the details for the hypothetical two-dice game. See Table 2–4 for the source of $g(x)$.

The column for $g(x)$ sums to 1, as expected, and the column $f(x)g(x)$ sums to .2778—precisely the result obtained earlier. Table 4–1 has introduced new information, namely, that $E(R)$ has two components—a gain portion and a loss portion. The $0.28 expected result is made up of an expected gain $E(G)$ of $0.97 (should a gain occur) and an expected loss $E(L)$ of $0.69 (should a loss occur). Since no money

FIGURE 4-1

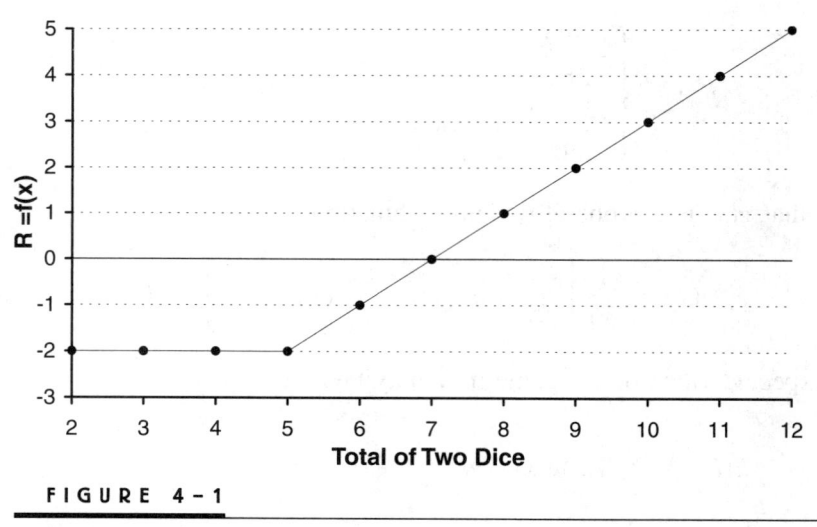

Results of two-dice game

changes hands when a 7 is rolled, its probability (.1667) is divided equally between a gain and a loss. The table indicates a gain will occur for tosses of 7 through 12 (with a probability of 50 percent), whereas a loss will occur for tosses of 2 through 7 (also with a probability of 50 percent).

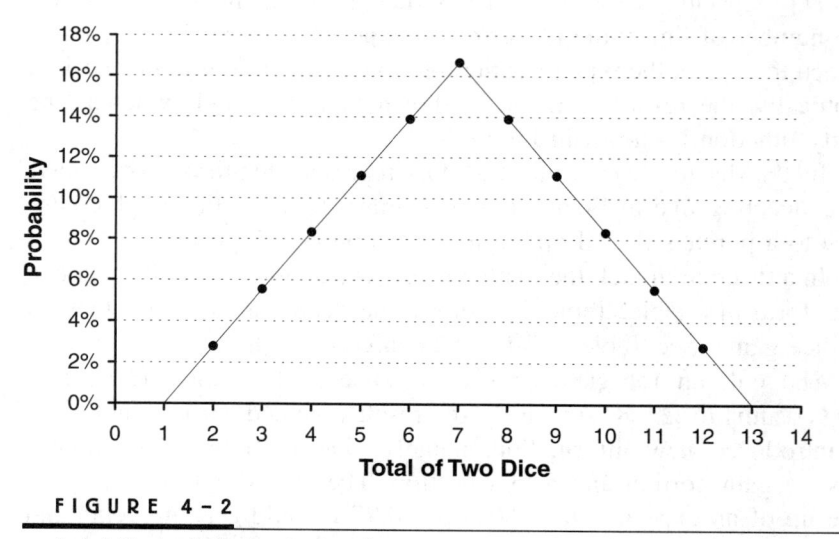

FIGURE 4-2

Probability density function for two dice

TABLE 4-1

Results of two-dice game

x	f(x)	g(x)	f(x)g(x)	Probability Loss	Probability Gain	Amount Loss	Amount Gain
2	−2	0.0278	−0.0556	0.0278		−0.0556	
3	−2	0.0556	−0.1111	0.0556		−0.1111	
4	−2	0.0833	−0.1667	0.0833		−0.1667	
5	−2	0.1111	−0.2222	0.1111		−0.2222	
6	−1	0.1389	−0.1389	0.1389		−0.1389	
7	0	0.1667	0	0.0833	0.0833		
8	1	0.1389	0.1389		0.1389		0.1389
9	2	0.1111	0.2222		0.1111		0.2222
10	3	0.0833	0.25		0.0833		0.25
11	4	0.0556	0.2222		0.0556		0.2222
12	5	0.0278	0.139		0.0278		0.139
		1.0000	0.2778	0.5000	0.5000	−0.6944	0.9722

To find the *actual probability weighted average gain G* in the gain interval, let p_G be the probability of a gain. Then

$$G = \frac{E(G)}{p_G} = \frac{.9722}{.5} = 1.9444$$

Likewise, the *actual probability weighted average loss L* in the loss interval is

$$L = \frac{|E(L)|}{1 - p_G} = \frac{.6944}{.5} = 1.3888$$

Thus

$$E(R) = E(G) - E(L)$$

$$E(R) = p_G(G + L) - L \qquad (4.3)$$

Which for our hypothetical game is

$$E(R) = .5(1.9444 + 1.3888) - 1.3888 = .2778$$

Precisely the same answer as obtained in Table 4–1.

This makes intuitive sense because, in the long run, we can expect to win $1.94 with a probability of 50 percent and lose $1.38 with a probability of 50 percent.

MATHEMATICAL ADVANTAGE

While we have developed a technique for measuring expected values in absolute dollar terms, we still do not know how this game would compare with other similar games. A yardstick is needed. *Mathematical advantage MA* provides such a yardstick for measuring individual events. If we think of L as the amount we are willing to risk on an event and $E(R)$ as the return on that event, then

$$MA = \frac{E(R)}{L}$$

or the expected rate of return for the event.

To obtain a general expression for *MA* where $E(R)$ is not required, we divide Equation (4.3) by L and get

$$\frac{E(R)}{L} = p_G\left(\frac{G+L}{L}\right) - 1$$

Therefore,

$$MA = p_G\left(\frac{G}{L} + 1\right) - 1 \qquad (4.4)$$

The term G/L sometimes is replaced by Q, which is defined as "the payoff odds to 1."

For the hypothetical two-dice game,

$$MA = .5\left(\frac{1.9444}{1.3888} + 1\right) - 1 = 20.0\%$$

As we shall see, this is a tremendous advantage.

MA may be used to evaluate the relative merits of any gambling, speculative, or investment opportunity. Some examples are listed below:

- We know from Chapter 2 the probability of a win on the pass line at craps is .493. What is the *MA*? Since a player wins or loses 1 unit,

$$\frac{G}{L} = 1$$

$$MA = .493(1 + 1) - 1 = -1.4\%$$

A negative *MA* is a *disadvantage* to the player.
- On an American-style double-zero roulette wheel, what is the *MA* for a wager on a single number? Since there are 38 slots into which the spinning ball may fall, the probability on any single number is 1/38, or .02632. The house pays 35 to 1 when a single number hits.

$$MA = .02632\left(\frac{35}{1} + 1\right) - 1 = -5.26\%$$

This is one of the worst games in a casino.
- Over the years, a player has developed a system for handicapping horse races that consistently selects winners 35 percent of the time at average odds of 2 to 1. What is the *MA* of the system?

$$MA = .35\left(1 + \frac{2}{1}\right) - 1 = 5\%$$

This player likely will do well.

Mathematical advantage *MA* also may be described as the *arithmetic mean rate of return per event* (not to be confused with *RTN*, which is the *geometric mean return per event*).

Remember that *L* is the probability weighted average loss—not the expected loss. Therefore, in the special case where $L = 1$, *MA* and $E(R)$ are identical except that *MA* is expressed as a percentage, whereas $E(R)$ is a dollar amount. In the third example above, the *MA* is 5 percent, and the $E(R)$ is $0.05.

INVESTMENT RETURNS

While *MA* is useful in comparing *similar* activities (which casino game has the least disadvantage, which options should be bought or sold today, which strategy should be employed with a given device of decision, etc.), it is not *time-dependent*. In other words, it specifies the mathematical advantage for a *single* event. A given speculative activity, however, typically consists of a series of events over time. An options trader may make an average of 25 trades per month. A horse player may wager on 1,000 races in a year's time. A casino may accept hundreds of thousands of bets on the pass line at its craps tables during the course of a year.

One way to compare such diverse activities is to determine their *annual compound returns*. From basic financial mathematics,

$$FV = PV(1 + r)^n \qquad (4.5)$$

where n = number of periods
PV = beginning capital (present value)
FV = ending capital after n periods (future value)
r = rate of return on capital (growth rate)

Equation (4.5) is the familiar compound interest formula where the rate is compounded once in n periods. If the rate of return is compounded more often, say, m times in n periods, the formula becomes

$$FV = PV\left(1 + \frac{r}{m}\right)^{mn} \qquad (4.6)$$

If the return is compounded *continuously*,

$$FV = PVe^{rn} \qquad (4.7)$$

The result of continuous compounding is approximately the same as daily compounding.

Since investment returns generally are compared on an annual basis, we will concentrate on annual returns; that is, the n in the preceding formulas will always be 1. The series of events comprising a specific activity will be measured by the number of times they occur in one year (m in Equation 4.6). An event may be interpreted as the risking of an amount w *one time* on the chosen device of decision.

OPTIMAL POSITION SIZE (TWO OUTCOMES)

A question plaguing traders and gamblers alike for decades is how much to risk (what percentage of capital) on a given event (toss of the dice, horse race, option trade, etc.). A gambler wants to know the best *bet-to-bank ratio,* whereas the options trader needs the appropriate *position size* (number of contracts) to put on.

Suppose the horse player mentioned earlier plays an average of 1,000 races per year. Recall that he had a 35 percent win probability at

2 to 1 odds, giving him an MA of 5 percent and an E(R) of $.05. The gaming literature suggests that professional gamblers usually risk between 1 and 2 percent of their capital on a single event when *flat betting* (wagering the same *amount* on each event). With an initial stake of $20,000 and wanting to adhere to professional standards, our player decides to wager $300 on each race (1.5 percent of initial capital). What is his expected annual return?

Letting

Q = odds to 1
RTN = geometric mean return (per event)
$E(R)$ = expected result of event
m = number of events per year
RTN_A = annual return = RTN^m
r = annual *rate* of return = $RTN^m - 1$
w = fixed *amount* of wager
$f = w/PV$ = ratio of wager to starting capital

for flat betting, the annual return may be expressed as

$$RTN_A = \frac{FV}{PV} = 1 + fmE(R)$$

$$RTN_A = 1 + .015(1000).05 = 1.75 \qquad (4.8)$$

Thus, if our horse player bets $300 on each of 1,000 races during one year, he would expect to increase his starting capital by a factor of 1.75. To prove this, consider that he would expect to win 350 races at 2 to 1 odds while losing 650 races. He would expect to win $15,000 as follows:

$$2(300)(350) - 300(650) = 210,000 - 195,000 = 15,000$$

$$FV = 20,000 + 15,000 = 35,000$$

$$RTN_A = \frac{FV}{PV} = \frac{35,000}{20,000} = 1.75$$

And this agrees with the answer obtained with Equation (4.8).

By inspection, it is obvious that increasing f (which increases w) will result in ever-increasing annual returns. While this practice tends to maximize returns, it also maximizes risk. Depending how the 650 losing races are distributed among the 1,000 races, it is possible to drive the capital to zero (wipe out) before completing the sequence. As the fixed amount of the wager is increased, the probability of a wipeout losing streak also increases. For example, suppose our horse player decided to wager $5,000 per race. From Equations (2.19) and (2.20), we may determine the probability of *no* wins in four trials (which would wipe out the capital):

$$_4C_0 = \frac{4!}{0!(4-0)!} = 1$$

$$P(0:4) = {}_4C_0(p)^0(1-p)^4 = (.65)^4 = 17.9\%$$

And this makes betting $5,000 per race a risky proposition.

Is there a way to select a bet size that would both *maximize* return and *minimize* risk? One method is to fix the *percentage f* instead of the wager *w*. In this approach, each wager is a fixed fraction of the then-existing capital. After a gain, the dollar wager is increased; after a loss, it is decreased. Theoretically, assuming fractional betting is possible, there is no way the capital may be driven to zero.

In 1956, J. L. Kelly, an engineer at Bell Laboratories, produced some interesting formulas to solve a problem with random noise in long-distance telephone transmissions. Surprisingly, Kelly's work provided insight into geometric growth rates that could be applied to money management techniques for investing, trading, and gambling. Known as the *Kelly criterion,* these concepts began to appear in the gaming literature in the 1960s to address the age-old dilemma of picking the appropriate bet-to-bank ratio. The theory was later embraced by the investment community as a viable money management technique.

Kelly's theory was developed for *Bernoulli trials,* which must be independent events with only *two* possible outcomes—win or lose. Wagering on the toss of a coin and betting on horse races are examples of events having only two possible outcomes. We first will discuss the properties of the Kelly formula, and then we will apply it to the horse race example. Finding the correct fraction to wager on events with *multiple* outcomes is covered later under the section on money management.

Recall that

p_G = probability of a gain

RTN = geometric mean return per event

Letting f now be the fixed fraction of capital to risk, the Kelly formula for the return *RTN* is

Mathematical Expectation and Optimal Position Size

$$RTN = (1 + f)^{P_G}(1 - f)^{1-P_G}$$

Since the ratio of gains to losses is rarely, if ever, equal to 1 (i.e., an even payoff), the formula must be modified slightly for uneven payoffs:

$$RTN = (1 + Qf)^{P_G}(1 - f)^{1-P_G} \quad (4.9)$$

where Q = odds to 1.

With this formula, the geometric mean return on capital *RTN* may be calculated for any fixed-fraction f risked. The question now becomes, How is f chosen to maximize *RTN*? Mathematically, the derivative of the expression for *RTN* is set equal to zero and then solved for f. The result of that exercise is

$$f^* = \frac{P_G(1 + Q) - 1}{Q} \quad (4.10)$$

where f^* = the optimal f.

However, the expression in the numerator is simply the *MA* derived earlier. Thus, the optimal fixed fraction f^* of trading capital may be calculated easily from

$$f^* \Leftarrow \frac{MA}{Q} \quad (4.11)$$

The $\Leftarrow$ symbol in Equation (4.11) means "is derived from," so the formula only works in one direction. Since *MA* is independent of f^*, the expression $MA = f^*Q$ is meaningless. Also, Equation (4.11) only works for a *positive MA* when there are *only two possible outcomes* (Bernoulli trials).

Returning to our horse player's concern about how much to bet, his *MA* was .05, his Q was 2, his initial stake was $20,000, and there are only two possible outcomes for any race—win or lose. From Equation (4.11),

$$f^* = \frac{.05}{2} = .025$$

Thus the first bet would be $500 (.025 × $20,000). If the first race were won, the next bet would be $525 (.025 × $21,000). If the first race were lost, the next bet would be $488 ($487.50 rounded to the nearest

$2). Figure 4–3 is a graph of Equation (4.9). The maximum per-event return *RTN* calculated at f^* is

$$RTN = [1 + 2(.025)]^{.35}(1 - .025)^{.65} = 1.00062$$

Note that any betting fraction *above or below* .025 reduces the per-event return *RTN*. Risking more than 5 percent actually produces a loss.

Having the maximum *RTN* per event, we can now calculate the annual return RTN^m.

$$RTN^m = 1.00062^{1000} = 1.86$$

$$FV = 20,000(1.86) = 37,200$$

With annual return RTN^m, we have a yardstick that measures the relative merits of *dissimilar* games and opportunities that have two possible outcomes. In the horse-racing example, the annual return from optimal f betting is slightly better than for the flat betting example (1.86 versus 1.75) and produces $2,200 more gain. This benefit is in addition to using an approach that *minimizes* risk while maximizing capital growth. The player expects to lose 650 races. If a string of, say, 20 losses occurs early on, flat betting could call for as much as a 5 percent wager compared with the desired 1.5 percent.

Actually, the superiority (or inferiority) of optimal f betting over flat betting depends on the number of trials. Early on in the sequence of the preceding horse bets, flat betting holds a slight edge. As Table 4–2

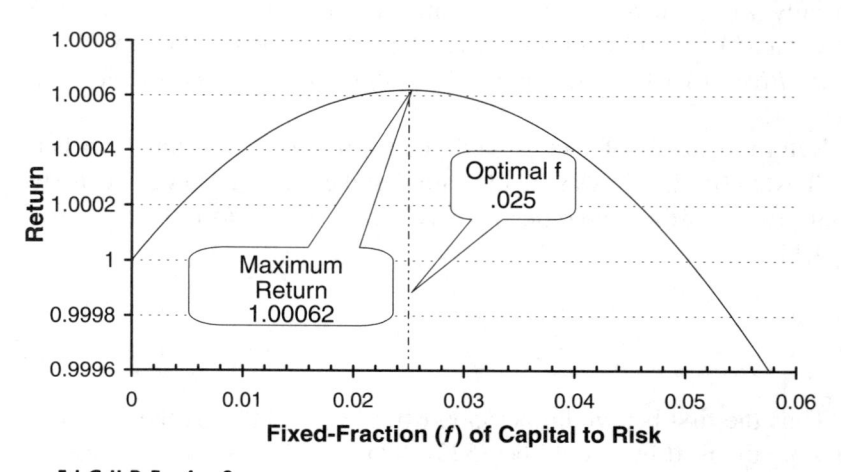

FIGURE 4-3

Compound growth rate for gain probability of .35 and odds of 2 to 1

TABLE 4-2
Comparison of flat bets with optimal f bets

	Annual returns	
Races	Optimal f bets	Flat bets
10	1.006	1.008
100	1.064	1.075
500	1.363	1.375
1,000	1.859	1.750
2,000	3.450	2.500
5,000	22.177	4.750

illustrates, optimal f betting produces significantly faster growth after 1,000 races.

By inspection, Figure 4–3 reveals that the return is driven to zero at about 5 percent. To determine the precise fraction f_c above which there is a loss (negative return), the following formula is solved by computer numerically:

$$p \ln(1 + Qf) + (1 - p) \ln(1 - f) = 0$$

For our case,

$$f_c = 5.037\%$$

It is also interesting to note that the *order* of gains and losses in a sequence of events has no impact on the result. To demonstrate this phenomenon in a simple sequence of 10 events, assume a gain probability of .4 (four gains and six losses). Assume 2 to 1 payoff odds (a Q of 2). In this hypothetical case, *MA* will be 20 percent, the optimal percentage to risk will be 10 percent, and the maximum per event return will be 1.00976. Therefore, $10,000 of risk capital should grow to $11,020 after 10 trades under the preceding assumptions.

$$FV = 10,000(1.00976)^{10} = 11,020$$

Table 4–3 shows two sequences of 10 trials. No matter how the wins and losses are distributed among the 10 trials, *FV* will always be approximately $11,020.

TABLE 4-3

Sequence inconsequential

Trial	Sequence 1				Sequence 2			
	Wager	W/L	Result	Stake	Wager	W/L	Result	Stake
1	1,000	W	2,000	12,000	1,000	L	(1,000)	9,000
2	1,200	L	(1,200)	10,800	900	W	1,800	10,800
3	1,080	L	(1,080)	9,720	1,080	L	(1,080)	9,720
4	972	L	(972)	8,748	972	L	(972)	8,748
5	875	L	(875)	7,873	875	L	(875)	7,873
6	787	W	1,574	9,447	787	L	(787)	7,086
7	945	W	1,890	11,337	709	L	(709)	6,377
8	1,134	L	(1,134)	10,203	638	W	1,276	7,653
9	1,020	W	2,040	12,243	765	W	1,530	9,183
10	1,224	L	(1,224)	11,019	918	W	1,836	11,019

There is a long-standing controversy concerning *progressive betting* versus flat betting. Optimal f betting is just one of a myriad of progressive betting schemes. The best known progressive sequence is called the *martingale,* in which the player doubles her bet after each loss until a win occurs. She is thus guaranteed of winning one betting unit per sequence. The obvious fallacy lies in the very strong probability that the player will exhaust her bankroll or hit the house limits before completing a long sequence of losing wagers. Consider that with a $1 betting unit and losing 10 times, the next bet will be $1,024 and, after 20 losses, over $1 million.

Another progressive scheme called simply the *1, 3, 2, 6 sequence* is rumored to have broken the bank at Monte Carlo. As the sequence name suggests, the player attempts to win four bets in a row betting one unit and then three, two, and six units, assuming each previous bet was won. After the fourth bet, win or lose, the sequence is repeated beginning with one betting unit. An interesting feature of this system is that the fourth bet is always "free," so after three wins, the outcome of the four bet sequence is either break even or a profit of 12 units.

Many other progressive betting schemes have been touted, with some claiming almost mystical properties. Intuitively, betting more during winning streaks and less during losing streaks has a certain appeal. Indeed, most progressive betting schemes in vogue today are of the antimartingale type. Optimal f betting is one such system and does not depend on numerology or the occult for its success. It was designed to maximize the *return* on capital—rather than the capital itself.

The *RTN* in Equation (4.9) represents the per-event return produced by wagering a fixed fraction f on Bernoulli events. We maximized the return by choosing f appropriately. What about optimal f betting on events having more than two outcomes? When we consider events with multiple outcomes, we also want to maximize the return—but Equation (4.9) will not work!

OPTIMAL POSITION SIZE (MULTIPLE OUTCOMES)

Ralph Vince, in his excellent book on money management,[1] correctly pointed out that a sequence of gains and losses cannot simply be averaged into two quantities and used as inputs to the Kelly formula. He went on to develop a formula for determining the correct optimal f for multiple outcomes.

When working with growth-rate expressions such as the one contained in Equation (4.5),

$$(1 + r)^n$$

it is good practice to ensure that the quantity in the parentheses is always nonnegative, that is, $r > -1$. Otherwise, equations containing the growth-rate expression occasionally may "blow up" when attempting to take the log of a negative number or to raise a negative number to a fractional power. Accordingly, Vince defined his return (using our notation R_i for results) as

$$R'_i = \frac{-R_i}{L_{max}} \qquad (4.12)$$

where L_{max} is always negative.

This means that when we include a fixed fraction between 0 and 1 (we'll call it g), the expression

$$1 + gR'_i$$

---

[1] Ralph Vince, *The Mathematics of Money Management*, (New York: Wiley, 1992), pp. 29–34; this material is used by permission of John Wiley & Sons, Inc.

will never be negative. Note that Vince uses the term *optimal f* for the *g* in the preceding expression. Since we want optimal *f* to stand for the fixed fraction of capital to risk (the same as in the Kelly formula), we introduced *g* as an interim step.

The *per-event return RTN* (or geometric mean return) on any given sequence of results having the same probability of occurrence is then

$$RTN = \prod_{i=1}^{n} (1 + g*R'_i) \quad (4.13)$$

Once a $g*$ is found that maximizes *RTN* in Equation (4.13), an interim step is needed to find optimal *f*—the fixed fraction of capital to risk. $g*$ is actually the divisor of the largest loss, meaning a trader should risk $1.00 for every $L_{max}/g*$ in his capital account. Therefore, the fixed fraction $f*$ of capital to risk is

$$f* = \frac{-g*}{L_{max}} \quad (4.14)$$

Vince considered a particular sequence of trading results to demonstrate the development of his formula and to prove that using the Kelly formula produces incorrect results. This sequence is

$$+9, +18, +7, +1, +10, -5, -3, -17, -7$$

Vince's sequence represents a hypothetical series of results from trading a particular system. All the results are equally probable. He is interested in finding the optimal fixed fraction that will maximize the growth of profits for that system. The problem we want to investigate later on is slightly different. We want to be able to analyze a sequence of events, each of which has a *different* probability. To convert Vince's formula (Equation 4.13) into one that will account for probabilities, we have

$$RTN = \prod_{i=1}^{n} (1 + gR'_i)^{p_i}$$

where

$$\sum_{i=1}^{n} p_i = 1$$

and its logarithmic equivalent:

$$RTN = e^{\sum_{i=1}^{n} p_i \ln(1+g*R'_i)} \qquad (4.15)$$

Unfortunately, there is no closed-form solution for finding $g*$ in Equations (4.13) or (4.15). The solution may be found by iteration, that is, by looping through all values of g between .001 and 1, finding the g that produces the highest *RTN*. Alternatively, the binary, golden ratio or the parabolic search algorithms covered in Chapter 8 also may be employed.

Returning to Vince's sequence to prove the simple Kelly formula will not produce the correct optimal f, we find that if the gains and losses were simply averaged, there would be an average gain of 9 and an average loss of 8 for a Q of 1.125. Since each outcome is equally likely and there are nine possible outcomes, the probability of any particular outcome is .111, and the probability of a gain is .555. Using the Kelly formula (Equation 4.10) produces an $f*$ of .159.

$$f* = \frac{p_G(1+Q) - 1}{Q} = \frac{.555(2.125) - 1}{1.125} = .159$$

To show that .159 *cannot* be the optimal f, we now solve Equation (4.15). For Vince's nine-element sequence,

$$L_{max} = -17$$

By iteration, we find from Equation (4.15) that $g*$ lies between .23 and .24 at .23664, which produces the maximum geometric mean return of 1.010208.

Table 4–4 shows the calculations using Equation (4.15) for g = .159, .23, .23664, and .24. Obviously, g = .159 (the result obtained from Equation 4.10) does *not* maximize *RTN*. Note that g = .23 and g = .24 also produce a smaller *RTN* than when $g*$ = .23664.

Since we transformed R_i to R'_i in order to find $g*$, we must transform $g*$ back to find optimal f or $f*$. This is done by solving Equation (4.14):

$$f* = \frac{-g*}{L_{max}} = \frac{-.23664}{-17} = .01392$$

And the fixed-fraction to risk for the *incorrect* Kelly solution would be

$$f* = \frac{-g*}{L_{max}} = \frac{-.159}{-17} = .00935$$

Converting Equation (4.15) for use with $f*$, we have

TABLE 4-4

Return per sequence: Vince's sequence
Using different fixed fractions

R_i	R_i^*	P_i	$g = .159$	$g = .23$	$g^* = .23664$	$g = .24$
9	0.5294118	0.11111	0.008980	0.012767	0.013115	0.013290
18	1.0588235	0.11111	0.017288	0.024217	0.024843	0.025159
7	0.4117647	0.11111	0.007046	0.010054	0.010331	0.010471
1	0.0588235	0.11111	0.001034	0.001493	0.001536	0.001558
10	0.5882353	0.11111	0.009934	0.014099	0.014481	0.014673
−5	−0.294118	0.11111	(0.005321)	(0.007783)	(0.008016)	(0.008134)
−3	−0.176471	0.11111	(0.003162)	(0.004604)	(0.004740)	(0.004808)
−17	−1	0.11111	(0.019240)	(0.029040)	(0.030003)	(0.030493)
−7	−0.411765	0.11111	(0.007524)	(0.011055)	(0.011391)	(0.011561)
ln(RTN)			0.009036	0.010148	0.010157	0.010155
RTN			1.009077	1.010200	1.010208	1.010206

$$RTN = e^{\sum_{i=1}^{n} p_i \ln(1+f^*R_i')} \quad (4.16)$$

Table 4–5 provides solutions to Equation (4.16) for various values of f^*.

Note that the *RTN* obtained at optimal f in Table 4–5 (1.010208) is the same *RTN* obtained at g^* in Table 4–4.

The purpose of this last exercise was to demonstrate that the Kelly formula (Equation 4.10) produces *incorrect* results for optimal f in events consisting of multiple outcomes and to derive an approach that *would* work in such cases. From Table 4–5, the Kelly optimal f produced a maximum return of 1.009077, whereas using Equation (4.16) to determine optimal f produced a maximum return of 1.010208. These are per-event returns, and while the differences may not appear material in the short run, they can be extremely significant as the number of events played increases. Table 4–6 shows a comparison of the returns for the number of events played between 1 and 1,000.

THEORETICAL OPTIMAL f FOR THE TWO-DICE GAME

The two-dice game examined earlier is a perfect example of an event with multiple outcomes. Although there are only 8 possible monetary results (from a $2 loss to a $5 gain), there are 11 possible outcomes

Mathematical Expectation and Optimal Position Size

TABLE 4-5

Return per sequence: equation (4.16)
Using different fixed fractions

R_i	P_i	$f = .00935$	$f = .013$	$f^* = .01392$	$f = .0145$
9	0.11111	0.008980	0.012294	0.013115	0.013629
18	0.11111	0.017288	0.023362	0.024843	0.025767
7	0.11111	0.007046	0.009677	0.010331	0.010741
1	0.11111	0.001034	0.001435	0.001536	0.001600
10	0.11111	0.009934	0.013580	0.014481	0.015045
−5	0.11111	(0.005321)	(0.007468)	(0.008016)	(0.008362)
−3	0.11111	(0.003162)	(0.004420)	(0.004740)	(0.004942)
−17	0.11111	(0.019240)	(0.027749)	(0.030003)	(0.031447)
−7	0.11111	(0.007524)	(0.010601)	(0.011391)	(0.011892)
ln(RTN)		0.009036	0.010110	0.010157	0.010138
RTN		1.009077	1.010161	1.010208	1.010190

from tossing two dice—each with different probabilities of occurrence that sum to 1.

For the two-dice game, the maximum per toss loss is 2. Table 4–7 shows the solutions to Equation (4.15) for the two-dice game by iteration on a computer by which g^* is found to be .147.

From Equation (4.14), f^* is found to be .0735—the optimal f for the two-dice game with a geometric mean return RTN of 1.01 (rounded) over the full probability spectrum. Table 4–8 shows the solutions to Equation (4.16).

TABLE 4-6

Comparison of Kelly returns
With returns from equation (4.16)

Events	1.009007 Return	1.010208 Return	Percent difference
1	1.009	1.010	0.11%
10	1.095	1.107	1.13%
50	1.571	1.662	5.76%
100	2.468	2.761	11.85%
1,000	8,400.543	25,751.554	206.55%

TABLE 4-7

Return per sequence: two-dice game
Equation (4.15) using different fixed fractions

Outcome	R_i	R_j	P_i	$g = .14$	$g^* = .147$	$g = .16$
2	−2	−1	0.0278	(0.004193)	(0.004420)	(0.004847)
3	−2	−1	0.0556	(0.008386)	(0.008840)	(0.009694)
4	−2	−1	0.0833	(0.012564)	(0.013244)	(0.014524)
5	−2	−1	0.1111	(0.016756)	(0.017664)	(0.019371)
6	−1	−0.5	0.1389	(0.010080)	(0.010604)	(0.011582)
7	0	0	0.1667	0.000000	0.000000	0.000000
8	1	0.5	0.1389	0.009398	0.009851	0.010690
9	2	1	0.1111	0.014557	0.015237	0.016489
10	3	1.5	0.0833	0.015879	0.016598	0.017919
11	4	2	0.0556	0.013725	0.014330	0.015436
12	5	2.5	0.0278	0.008343	0.008701	0.009354
			1.00000			
ln(*RTN*)				0.009923	0.009946	0.009871
RTN				1.009973	1.009995	1.009920

TABLE 4-8

Return per sequence: two-dice game
Equation (4.16) using different fixed fractions

Outcome	R_i	P_i	$f = .07$	$f^* = .0735$	$f = .08$
2	−2	0.0278	(0.004193)	(0.004420)	(0.004847)
3	−2	0.0556	(0.008386)	(0.008840)	(0.009694)
4	−2	0.0833	(0.012564)	(0.013244)	(0.014524)
5	−2	0.1111	(0.016756)	(0.017664)	(0.019371)
6	−1	0.1389	(0.010080)	(0.010604)	(0.011582)
7	0	0.1667	0.000000	0.000000	0.000000
8	1	0.1389	0.009398	0.009851	0.010690
9	2	0.1111	0.014557	0.015237	0.016489
10	3	0.0833	0.015879	0.016598	0.017919
11	4	0.0556	0.013725	0.014330	0.015436
12	5	0.0278	0.008343	0.008701	0.009354
		1.00000			
ln(*RTN*)			0.009923	0.009946	0.009871
RTN			1.009973	1.009995	1.009920

SIMULATING RESULTS

Thus far we have dealt with *theoretical* probabilities that yield theoretical results. What happens when we cross over into the real world? If we were *actually* to toss two dice and record the results, how would such results compare with the theoretical outcomes? We have now moved from the theoretical world to the empirical world—where data are collected by observation and experiment. Conceptually, this is the most difficult area for a nonstatistician to understand. When we flip a coin 100 times, we expect to get something close to 50 percent heads, but the *actual* number of heads and tails will differ by some amount. If we flipped the same coin 100,000 times, the percentage of heads would be much closer to 50 percent, but the absolute difference in heads and tails would be much greater. So it is with the tossing of two dice. We know the outcomes (2 through 12) are theoretically normally distributed, but how many tosses are necessary for the outcomes to exhibit this behavior? To find out, we must be able to *simulate* the tossing of two dice a great many times.

EMPIRICAL OPTIMAL f FOR THE TWO-DICE GAME

We know from the *theoretical* calculations that

Optimal f = 7.35% (Equation 4.16)
Maximum return RTN = 1.01 (Table 4–9)
Expected results $E(R)$ = .278 (Equation 4.3)

Tables 4–9 and 4–10 contain the results of over 11 million independent simulations of the two dice game to obtain optimal f, maximal RTN, and $E(R)$.

From Table 4–10 (1 million tosses), the mean optimal f is 7.4 percent, and we may assert with a probability of 99.7 percent that the actual long-run optimal f will lie in the interval 7.23 to 7.57 percent (compared with the theoretical value of 7.35 percent). Next, there is a 99.7 percent chance that the interval from 1.0094 to 1.0106 will contain the maximal growth RTN, whose mean value is 1.01 (compared with the theoretical value of 1.01). We also can be 99.7 percent sure that the expected result $E(R)$, whose mean is .279, will be between $0.273 and $0.284 (compared with the theoretical value of $0.2778).

The simulations (particularly the 1-million-toss case) track the theory remarkably well. However, the two tables demonstrate dramatically

TABLE 4-9

Simulations of two-dice game

Trial	1,000 Tosses $f^*\%$	RTN	Win	10,000 Tosses $f^*\%$	RTN	Win
1	6.0	1.0063	0.214	7.2	1.0094	0.271
2	8.6	1.0138	0.330	6.4	1.0076	0.245
3	6.2	1.0069	0.229	7.9	1.0116	0.299
4	6.7	1.0086	0.263	7.5	1.0103	0.280
5	9.9	1.0186	0.387	7.4	1.0099	0.278
6	6.6	1.0077	0.240	7.0	1.0088	0.261
7	7.5	1.0106	0.288	6.8	1.0084	0.255
8	4.1	1.0031	0.154	7.5	1.0103	0.283
9	7.0	1.0088	0.259	7.7	1.0109	0.288
10	7.2	1.0097	0.277	7.3	1.0097	0.273
	69.8	10.0941	2.641	72.7	10.0969	2.733
μ	7.0	1.0094	0.264	7.3	1.0097	0.273
σ	1.548	0.00428	0.064	0.442	0.0012	0.016

TABLE 4-10

Simulations of two-dice game

Trial	100,000 Tosses $f^*\%$	RTN	Win	1 Million tosses $f^*\%$	RTN	Win
1	7.5	1.0102	0.280	7.4	1.0099	0.277
2	7.3	1.0098	0.277	7.4	1.0102	0.280
3	7.7	1.0110	0.291	7.4	1.0102	0.281
4	7.5	1.0102	0.281	7.5	1.0103	0.281
5	7.5	1.0104	0.283	7.3	1.0098	0.276
6	7.5	1.0102	0.281	7.3	1.0098	0.276
7	7.6	1.0105	0.285	7.4	1.0102	0.280
8	7.4	1.0102	0.279	7.4	1.0102	0.280
9	7.5	1.0105	0.284	7.4	1.0099	0.278
10	7.6	1.0107	0.284	7.4	1.0099	0.277
	75.1	10.1037	2.825	73.9	10.1004	2.786
μ	7.5	1.0104	0.283	7.4	1.0100	0.279
σ	0.110	0.00033	0.004	0.057	0.0002	0.002

the difference between the law of *large numbers* (1 million tosses) and the law of *small numbers* (1,000 tosses). Note the large variability in optimal f for sequences under 100,000 events. While it is clear that 7.4 percent is the true empirical optimal f in the long run, consider that even if you traded five options per day for 252 trading days in a year, the sequence would be only 1,260 events. The options trader operates in the short run (the law of *small numbers*), where the *variability* in optimal f and the *RTN* values is substantially greater.

The enormous power of compounding can now be demonstrated. With a compound return *RTN* of 1.01, after 1,000 tosses, a $100 stake is expected to grow to $2,095,916. The calculation is

$$100(1.01)^{1000} = 2,095,916$$

Of course, not all random sequences of 1,000 tosses will produce an *RTN* of 1.01. Indeed, because of the extreme variability associated with only 1,000 tosses (see Table 4–10), it should come as no surprise that at a confidence level of 99.7 percent, *RTN* can vary between .9966 (a loss) and 1.0222. Likewise, with only 1,000 tosses, optimal f will lie somewhere between 2.36 and 11.64 percent. Table 4–11 demonstrates the effect of using 11 different fixed fractions from 2 to 12 percent on the *same sequence* of 1,000 tosses. A small beginning capital of only $100 was used for the analysis.

For this particular sequence of 1,000 tosses, optimal f turns out to be somewhere around 6 percent—well within the expected range but

TABLE 4-11

Effect of different fixed fractions on same sequence of 1,000 tosses

Trial	f %	Ending capital	Maximum gain	Maximum loss	Maximum drawdown	RTN
1	2	36,378	3,353	1,579	8,878	1.0036
2	3	120,076	16,394	8,154	44,137	1.0048
3	4	270,209	53,277	26,126	136,145	1.0056
4	5	418,245	119,589	59,795	306,772	1.0061
5	6	443,939	187,431	105,668	563,886	1.0061
6	7	327,043	210,130	158,255	792,158	1.0058
7	8	167,940	212,774	183,025	860,360	1.0051
8	9	59,498	182,620	162,577	718,575	1.0041
9	10	14,903	124,670	114,063	474,631	1.0027
10	11	2,523	66,025	60,723	238,197	1.0009
11	12	302	28,184	25,871	95,796	0.9988

different from the empirical 7.4 percent and the theoretical 7.35 percent. All fixed fractions between 2 and 11 percent produced gains. Over 11 percent betting produced losses. This is additional support for limiting betting fractions to the long-run optimal f (7.4 percent) or less. Also, the largest *RTN* (at 6 percent optimal f) was only 1.0061, which produced an ending capital of $443,939—a far cry from $2 million.

Table 4–11 includes the maximum single gain and the maximum single loss experienced in the sequence. It also introduces a new concept—*drawdowns*. There will be significant drawdowns in any system no matter what betting strategy is employed. A *drawdown* is defined as a series of capital reductions occurring before the next win within a sequence of events. Drawdowns are a fact of trading life. They cannot be avoided—only managed. Strategies such as optimal f betting tend to maximize drawdowns because of their aggressive posture.

The use of the long-run optimal f (7.4 percent) in *different* independent trials consisting of only 1,000 tosses also produces widely different results. Table 4–12 shows the variation.

Here also, the beginning capital was limited to $100. In these 10 *independent* trials, the returns ranged from 72 to 134,472 times the initial stake—proving once again that extreme variation can occur in a mere 1,000-event sequence. Notably, however, there were *no* losses—not surprising with an *MA* of over 20 percent. Rarely, if ever, will a trader be offered such an attractive deal. Note the large drawdowns associated with the largest returns—some even larger than the ending capital itself.

TABLE 4–12

Effect of betting 7.4% in 10 independent sequences of 1,000 tosses each

Trial	Ending capital	Maximum gain	Maximum loss	Maximum drawdown	RTN
1	7,701,657	1,513,939	974,518	1,804,807	1.0113
2	36,116	73,805	51,919	132,448	1.0059
3	7,225	6,047	3,296	7,883	1.0043
4	13,447,191	8,993,898	7,121,872	34,673,568	1.0119
5	7,940,584	4,741,345	3,072,392	12,818,820	1.0113
6	987,854	217,898	141,198	195,456	1.0092
7	7,673,293	2,432,335	1,332,920	1,414,726	1.0113
8	17,203	289,315	235,695	1,070,199	1.0052
9	330,700	266,830	172,906	435,972	1.0081
10	20,252	8,790	5,290	11,983	1.0053

From the study of the two-dice game (whose geometry looks a lot like a Call option), we can deduce that optimal f betting is probably the best money management technique for betting on events with a limited number of *discrete* outcomes such as the two-dice game and horse-racing example, assuming the bettor is able to stomach the occasional crushing drawdown. What remains to be shown is that the same is true for events with continuous outcomes such as option trades.

OPTIMAL f FOR THE TWO-DICE GAME: NORMAL PROBABILITY APPROXIMATION

Moving from the discrete case to the continuous one, we can show the two-dice game analyzed earlier can be closely approximated by a normal curve. From the information in Table 2–4 and the methods described in Chapter 2, the mean and standard deviation of the discrete distribution of the results of tossing two dice are 7 and 2.4152, respectively. Since

$$R = f(x) = \begin{cases} -2 & \text{for } x = 2, 3, 4, 5 \\ x - 7 & \text{for } 6, 7, 8, 9, 10, 11, 12 \end{cases}$$

and since, for a normal distribution,

$$z = \frac{x - \mu}{\sigma} \quad \text{(therefore, } x = \sigma z + 7)$$

for $x = 5$ (upper boundary of $2 loss interval),

$$z = \frac{5 - 7}{2.4152} = -.82809$$

Then, by substitution,

$$R = f(z) = \begin{cases} -2 & \text{for } -4 \leq z \leq -.82809 \\ 2.4152z & \text{for } -.82809 \leq z \leq 4 \end{cases}$$

The −4 and +4 refer to the number of standard deviations to be included.

Figure 4–4 shows a normal curve superimposed over the results function. The original triangular discrete density function is also shown by the dotted lines. We are interested in results for three different inter-

FIGURE 4-4

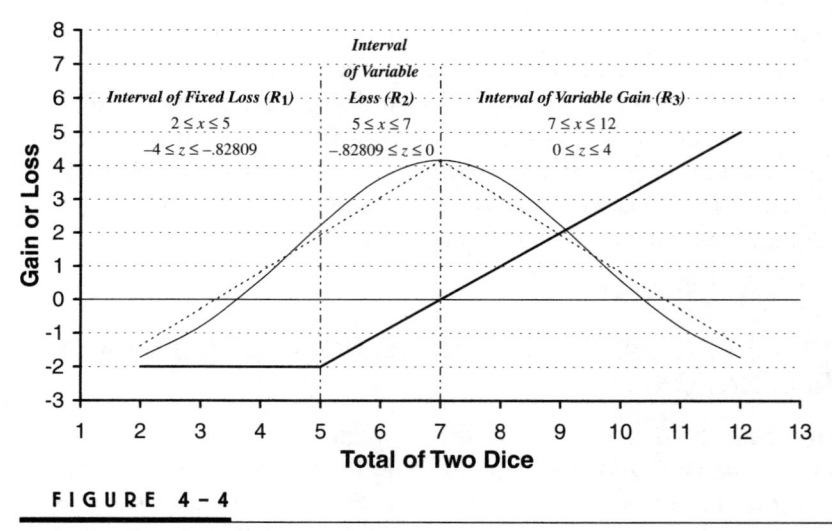

Results of two-dice game

vals R_1 (the fixed-loss interval), R_2 (the variable-loss interval), and R_3 (the variable-gain interval).

We now have a results function and a density function—both in terms of z. Because mathematical expectation is the product of the results function and the density function, we have for the fixed $2 loss outcomes R_1,

$$E(R_1) = -2[N(-.82809) - N(-4)] = -.40763$$

Since the intervals R_2 and R_3 contain the variable z in their results function, we cannot simply multiply the normal density function by a constant as we did for R_1. The normal density function (from Equation 2.29) can be stated as

$$g(z) = \frac{1}{\sqrt{2\pi}} e^{-z^2/2}$$

The product $f(z)g(z)$ is

$$2.4152z \left(\frac{1}{\sqrt{2\pi}}\right) e^{-z^2/2}$$

Integrating over the interval a to b, we have

Mathematical Expectation and Optimal Position Size

$$E(R) = \frac{2.4152}{\sqrt{2\pi}} \int_a^b ze^{-z^2/2} \, dz \tag{4.17}$$

Letting $u = -z^2/2$, from the rules of differentiation (Equation 2.23), we have

$$\frac{du}{dz} = -z \quad \text{or} \quad du = -zdz$$

From the rules for integration (Equation 2.28),

$$\int e^u \, du = e^u$$

Therefore,

$$\int_a^b e^{-z^2/2}(-zdz) = -e^{-z^2/2}\Big|_a^b = e^{-z^2/2}\Big|_b^a = (e^{-a^2/2} - e^{-b^2/2})$$

The vertical line containing a and b means that the preceding expression is to be evaluated between a and b (or b and a, as the case may be). Thus the full expression for $E(R_2)$ and $E(R_3)$ is now given by

$$E(R_2, R_3) = \frac{2.4152}{\sqrt{2\pi}} (e^{-a^2/2} - e^{-b^2/2}) \tag{4.18}$$

Since for R_2, $5 \leq x \leq 7$,

$$a = z_5 = \frac{5-7}{2.4152} = -.82809$$

$$b = z_7 = \frac{7-7}{2.4152} = 0$$

The solution is

$$E(R_2) = \frac{2.4152}{2.5066} [e^{-(-.82809)^2/2} - e^{-0^2/2}] = -.27968$$

Since for R_3, $7 \leq x \leq \infty$,

$$a = z_7 = \frac{7 - 7}{2.4152} = 0$$

Since we are using plus and minus 4 standard deviations from the mean, infinity (∞) will be represented by $+4$:

$$b = z_\infty = 4$$

And the solution is

$$E(R_3) = .96354(e^{-0^2/2} - e^{-4^2/2}) = .96322$$

As might be expected,

$$E(R) = E(R_1) + E(R_2) + E(R_3)$$

And

$$E(R) = -.40763 - .27968 + .96322 = .27591, \text{ or } \$0.28$$

Not surprisingly, the normal approximation yields roughly the same expected results for the game as the discrete model. This has been an extremely long-winded presentation of the proof that when a simple linear results function is present (as is the case for most option trades), expected results may be calculated using a probability density function suitable to the distribution of the game's elements. Each step along the way is important to the understanding of the process. Although a *normal distribution* was used here to analyze the two-dice game, a *log-normal distribution* will be employed for asset prices. While use of the log-normal distribution presents some additional math challenges, all the *basic elements* necessary for the development of a profitable options trading strategy are covered in this chapter.

For calculation of *MA*, when the loss or gain intervals contain subintervals with different probabilities and results, we must average the subinterval results. In the normal approximation to the two-dice game, there were three intervals. The loss interval contained subintervals R_1 and R_2, whereas the gain interval was represented by interval R_3. Table 4–13 contains all the information we know about the three intervals.

Thus, for the normal approximation to the game, the rounded losses average $1.37, whereas the rounded gain is 1.93—slightly different from the discrete case, where the losses averaged $1.39 and the gain was $1.94. *MA* for the normal approximation is

TABLE 4-13
Interval information: two-dice game

Interval	R	Probability	E(R)
R_1	−2.00015	0.2038	−0.40763
R_2	−0.94423	0.2962	−0.27968
Losses	−1.37462	0.5000	−0.68731
R_3	1.92644	0.5000	0.96322
		1.0000	0.27591

$$MA = p_G\left(\frac{G}{L} + 1\right) - 1 = .5\left(1 + \frac{1.92644}{1.37462}\right) - 1 = 20.07\%$$

which is very close to the 20.0 percent obtained for the discrete case.

How do we find optimal f and RTN from the continuous probability distribution? First, it should be noted the continuous outcomes are really discrete outcomes because all values are measured to the nearest cent. The trick is to divide the range of outcomes into a large number of *intervals* whose probability can be calculated and the midpoint of each interval used to calculate the R_i.

For the two-dice game, a normal probability density function was constructed with its mean μ at 7 and its standard deviation σ at 2.4152 (the mean and standard deviation, respectively, of the outcomes of the discrete version). For the approximation exercise, we divided the range of outcomes into 1,000 intervals, calculated the midpoint of each interval, determined the result R_i at each midpoint, calculated the probability p_i associated with each interval, and used Equation (4.16) to find the optimal f. The optimal f was determined to be 7.6 percent, with a geometric mean return RTN of 1.0102 and an $E(R)$ of $0.27591. Employing more than 1,000 intervals does *not* appear to enhance the accuracy.

COMPARISON OF METHODS USED WITH THE RESULTS OF THE TWO-DICE GAME

Table 4–14 shows the comparison of the three methods used to determine optimal f, $E(R)$, MA, and geometric mean return RTN. As may be seen from Table 4–14, the discrete two-dice game may be approximated by a continuous version with fairly accurate results.

TABLE 4-14

Comparison of methods used to determine results associated with the two-dice game

Item	SYM	Calculated theoretical results	Empirical (experimental) results	Continuous probability distribution results
Optimal f	f^*	7.35%	7.40%	7.6%
Expected result	$E(R)$	$0.2778	$0.279	$0.2759
Geometric mean return	RTN	1.0100	1.0100	1.0102
Matematical advantage	MA	0.2000	[a]	0.2007

[a]MA was not estimated for the experiment.

Optimal f betting is not without its critics. Some people claim it calls for uncomfortably large wagers during a winning streak (large drawdowns, which were discussed earlier). An argument for optimal f actually being suboptimal in financial markets is the price variability (volatility) of the underlying instrument. If the *actual* standard deviation of stock returns turns out to be materially different from the estimate used to calculate the expected returns of options trades (see Chapter 6), there is a good chance the calculated optimal f will differ from the actual optimal f. We have seen that overbetting is far worse than underbetting, and if the fraction exceeds f_c, a loss actually may occur despite a positive MA. In view of the foregoing, it appears that the rational approach would be to risk something less than the calculated optimal f. Some researchers have opined that using half optimal f makes good sense. More about this in Chapter 6.

Whether to trade option A or option B is a simple choice of the highest MA. However, the annual return always should be calculated because RTN will vary within similar MA's. Whether to speculate in the options market or bet on horses is, of course, a personal preference. There may be overwhelming *qualitative* reasons to prefer one device or decision over the other. If, however, one is intellectually indifferent as to the activity in which to participate, the choice may be made based on the highest RTN. Methods for determining expected results, MA and RTN, for options trades are covered in Chapter 6.

CHAPTER 5

Volatility and Sensitivity to Change

The more things change, the more they remain the same.
—Alphonse Karr (1808–1890)

In Chapter 4 we evaluated the two-dice game—a game extremely favorable to the player. Any financial advisor worth her salt would recommend that her client play this game as often as possible not only because of the high *MA* (20 percent) and *RTN* (1.01) but also because the *variability* of the results is known and, more important, *fixed*. The game's standard deviation is always 2.4152—we never have to estimate it. The standard deviation of the two-dice game is a constant and never changes. In statistical terms, it is said to be *stationary*. In contrast, the variability in the results of options trades (called *volatility*) is always changing, is said to be nonstationary, and must be estimated. In short, volatility itself will vary over time, which amplifies risk.

The term *volatility* seems to mean different things to different people. While most traders recognize that volatility may be the single most important component for evaluating risk in futures and options trading, there appears to be a cloud of mystery surrounding its definition and use. Generally speaking, there are two types of volatility—*historical* (statistical) and *implied*.

HISTORICAL VOLATILITY

First, let's attempt a general working definition of historical volatility and then proceed to a more formal description. In general, most people would agree that *volatility is a measure of the rate and magnitude of price fluctuations* (*in percentage terms*) *over a specified time period*. Volatility describes how far and how fast prices are likely to change per unit of time. Time units may be days, weeks, months, or even years.

The rate of return r on an investment is a function of volatility. To understand just what this relationship is, recall Equation (4.7):

$$FV = PVe^{rn}$$

Substituting x (the price of the underlying stock at expiration) for the future value FV and S (current stock price) for the present value PV, we have

$$x = Se^{rn} \qquad (5.1)$$

where x = the future price of an asset
S = the current price of an asset
r = rate of return on the asset
n = number of periods

Solving for r in Equation (5.1) for one year ($n = 1$) gives

$$r = \ln\left(\frac{x}{S}\right) \qquad (5.2)$$

The quantity inside the parentheses (investment return) is also known as a *price relative*. It is the relative price change in one time period—in this case, one year. Equation (5.2) says that the annual *rate of return* is a function of the natural logarithm of the price relatives. The price relatives for any asset are changing constantly over time. To predict a future rate of return (which enables one to predict a future price), it is necessary to know just how the rate of return r is distributed over time.

Fortunately, there is general agreement about the distribution of r. It has the familiar bell-shaped curve known as the *normal distribution*, which is the basis for the Black-Scholes options pricing model discussed in Chapter 3. Since the natural logarithms of the price relatives are normally distributed, the actual prices themselves are said to be *log-normally distributed*. This distinction is important. A normal distribution is not used for the actual prices because it provides for negative values as well as positive ones. Obviously, an asset cannot have a negative price. The lower bound of the log-normal distribution is zero—consistent with the lower bound of asset prices.

As we learned previously, a normal distribution is completely defined by two parameters—its *mean,* denoted by μ, and its *standard deviation,* denoted by σ. For work with futures and options, the *annual* standard deviation is used because it may be converted easily to any other time frame of interest. One way to obtain an estimate of the annual standard deviation of the *r* values is to take a sample of equally time-spaced price relatives from a stock's price history. Most texts suggest using weekly observations because they are, by definition, equally time spaced. Daily observations, by contrast, are not equally time spaced owing to weekends and holidays. This problem can be overcome by using the number of trading days in a year (252) instead of 365 calendar days.

Having said there is general agreement about the distribution of returns, it is necessary to point out that many traders and academicians believe the log-normal distribution does not describe the real-world distribution adequately, which, according to them, has fatter tails (is more *leptokurtic;* see Chapter 8 under "Kurtosis"). More about this later in the section on implied volatility.

CALCULATING HISTORICAL VOLATILITY

Table 5–1 shows calculation of the mean and standard deviation of a sample of IBM week-ending stock prices over the 11-week period October 4, 2002, through December 13, 2002 (77 days). Table 5–1 employs the formulas from Chapter 2 for the sample mean $\bar{x}$ and the sample standard deviation *s,* where *i* denotes a single weekly observation:

$$\bar{x}_{77} = \frac{1}{n} \sum_{i=1}^{n} \ln\left(\frac{S_i}{S_{i-1}}\right) \tag{5.3}$$

$$s_{77} = \sqrt{\frac{n \sum \left[\ln\left(\frac{S_i}{S_{i-1}}\right)\right]^2 - \left[\sum \ln\left(\frac{S_i}{S_{i-1}}\right)\right]^2}{n(n-1)}} \tag{5.4}$$

Note the *mean* of the sample $\bar{x}$ is not used. The trader is usually interested in a distribution centered around the current price *S*. In trending markets, *S* can represent a target price chosen by the trader that may be above or below the current price. Thus the mean of the distribution

TABLE 5-1

Sample of IBM weekly stock prices

No.	Friday date	Weekly Stock price S_i	Return (price relative) S_i/S_{i-1}	Rate of return (log of price relative) $\ln(S_i/S_{i-1})$	Square $[\ln(S_i/S_{i-1})]^2$
1	4-Oct-02	56.60			
2	11-Oct-02	63.92	1.1293	0.121623316	0.014792231
3	18-Oct-02	74.25	1.1616	0.149805476	0.022441681
4	25-Oct-02	74.56	1.0042	0.004166393	0.000017359
5	1-Nov-02	80.40	1.0783	0.075410006	0.005686669
6	8-Nov-02	77.59	0.9650	−0.035575623	0.001265625
7	15-Nov-02	80.10	1.0323	0.031837301	0.001013614
8	22-Nov-02	84.43	1.0541	0.052646935	0.002771700
9	29-Nov-02	86.92	1.0295	0.029065367	0.000844796
10	6-Dec-02	82.32	0.9471	−0.054374064	0.002956539
11	13-Dec-02	80.00	0.9718	−0.028587457	0.000817243
				0.346017649	0.052607455
	Mean			0.034601765	
	Std Dev			0.067193447	

is always assumed to be S. The *annual* standard deviation is proportional to the square root of the quotient of 365 divided by the number of days between observations. The time factor in Table 5-1 is $\sqrt{365/7}$, or 7.221. To obtain the *annual* standard deviation σ, the sample standard deviation s (.0672) is multiplied by 7.221, which results in .4852. This procedure is known as the *close-to-close method* of calculating historical volatility.

The precise formal definition of annual historical volatility is simply *the annual standard deviation of the natural logarithms of the price relatives expressed as a percentage.* For IBM, the annual volatility is 48.5 percent.

VOLATILITY AND TIME

Options are said to be *wasting assets;* that is, their value declines over time. More specifically, the *time-value portion* of an option's price declines as expiration approaches. To visualize the impact volatility has on this time decay, Figure 5-1 was prepared for an at-the-money Call option with an 80 strike price with 60 days prior to expiration. As may be seen

Volatility and Sensitivity to Change 157

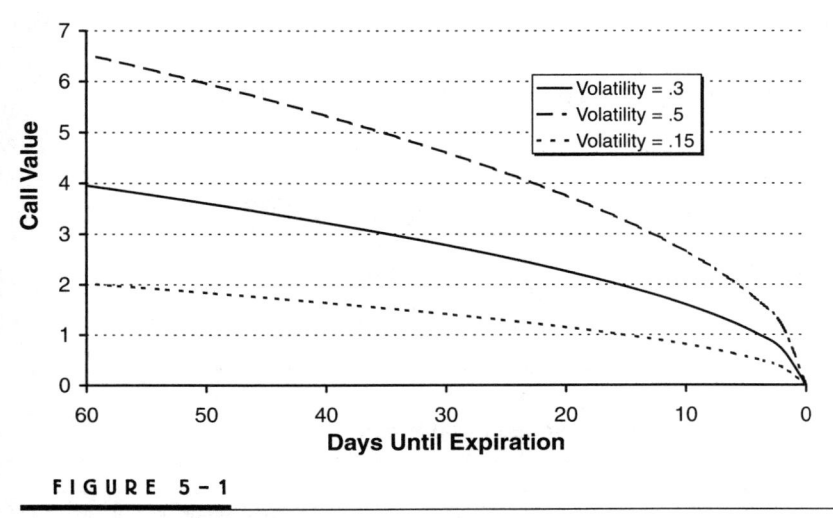

FIGURE 5-1

Time decay: buy at-the-money 80 Call

from Figure 5–1, the steepest price declines occur for the highest volatility.

To be useful, annual historical volatility generally is converted to the time period of interest. Thus, if an option is expiring in 10 days, the 10-day volatility (standard deviation) is needed. To convert annual volatility to any other time period,

$$\sigma_D = \sigma\sqrt{t} \qquad (5.5)$$

where D = number of days in the time period
σ_D = period volatility for specified number of days
σ = annual standard deviation
$t = \dfrac{D}{365}$

For the IBM example, σ_{10} = .485(.16552) = .0803. Figure 5–2 shows a graph of the log-normal distribution of the IBM returns over a 10-day period.

To calculate a future price x from the current price S when the standard deviation is known,

$$x = Se^{z\sigma_D} \qquad (5.6)$$

where z is the number of standard deviations of interest.

```
                                                                    Chapter 5
```

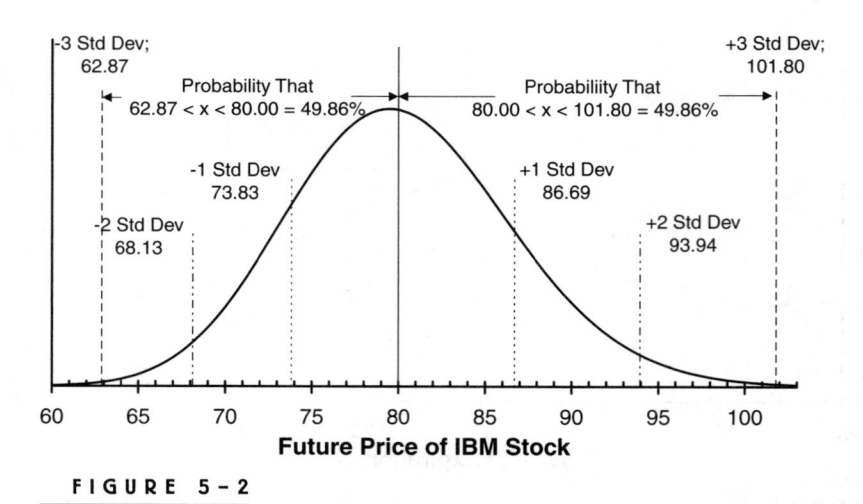

```
-3 Std Dev;                                                +3 Std Dev;
62.87                                                      101.80
         Probability That              Probabiliity That
         62.87 < x < 80.00 = 49.86%    80.00 < x < 101.80 = 49.86%

              -1 Std Dev          +1 Std Dev
              73.83               86.69
     -2 Std Dev                              +2 Std Dev
     68.13                                   93.94

60      65      70      75      80      85      90      95     100
                       Future Price of IBM Stock
```

FIGURE 5-2

IBM stock: log-normal distribution of prices from 10-week sample (for a 10-day period)

For example, the future prices of IBM contained within plus and minus 1 standard deviation (68.3 percent of the cases) may be determined from Equation (5.6). For plus 1 standard deviation,

$$x = 80e^{(1)(.0803)} = 86.69$$

For minus 1 standard deviation,

$$x = 80e^{(-1)(.0803)} = 73.83$$

These calculations may be verified by reference to Figure 5-2. Note that after 10 days, the price of IBM stock is expected to wind up between $62.87 and $101.80 with a probability of 99.7 percent.

What about the rate of return r? What is the growth or discount rate for any given number of standard deviations? Replacing n from Equation (5.1) with z gives

$$x = S(1 + r)^z$$

And from Equation (5.6),

$$x = Se^{z\sigma_D}$$

It follows that

Volatility and Sensitivity to Change

$$(1 + r)^z = e^{z\sigma_D}$$

Therefore,

$$r = e^{\sigma_D} - 1$$

For the IBM case, $r = e^{.0803} - 1 = .0836$. For the plus and minus 1 standard deviation situation,

$$80(1.0836)^1 = 86.69$$

$$80(1.0836)^{-1} = 73.83$$

which agrees with the previous results.

HISTORICAL VOLATILITY AND PROBABILITY

The most common use of historical volatility is as an input to one of the popular options pricing models such as the Black-Scholes model to determine if a quoted option is priced fairly. Another important use of volatility is in calculating probabilities. For example, consider the IBM January 2003 70 Put option priced at $1.32 on December 6, 2002. On that date, IBM stock closed at $82.32, and the option had 42 days to run. The break-even point for writing this Put was $68.68, meaning that if IBM stock price closed anywhere *above* $68.68, the trader won. What is the probability of IBM finishing above the break-even point?

First, the 42-day standard deviation is calculated from Equation (5.5):

$$\sigma_{42} = \sigma\sqrt{t} = .485\sqrt{\frac{42}{365}} = .1645$$

Rearranging terms from Equation (5.6) to solve for z gives

$$z = \frac{\ln\left(\frac{x}{S}\right)}{\sigma_D} = \frac{\ln\left(\frac{68.68}{82.32}\right)}{.1645} = -1.10125$$

From Chapter 2, the probability that z will lie between a and b is given by

$$N(b) - N(a)$$

For plus and minus 3 standard deviations, we have

$$a = -1.110125$$

$$b = 3$$

Therefore,

$$N(b) - N(a) = N(3) - N(-1.110125) = .99865 - .1354 = .8633$$

The probability that x will lie above $68.68 is equal to 86.3 percent. Once the standard deviation (volatility) is known, the probability of x finishing between any two values may be determined.

Many traders prefer to use a sample period equal to the number of days prior to expiration, believing that data from too far in the past are not relevant. If, instead of 10 weeks of data, the 6 weeks of price relatives prior to December 6, 2002, were used as the sample (a period equal to the 42 days prior to expiration), the estimate of the annual standard deviation would be 36.7 percent instead of 48.5 percent. The calculated probability of a winning trade in the preceding example would increase from 86.3 to 92.7 percent.

SOURCES FOR HISTORICAL VOLATILITY

Several sites on the Internet provide volatility information. E*Trade makes the average 30-day volatility available to customers on its detailed stock quotes. Dr. Robert Lum furnishes volatility quotes for one to nine months and one to five years at www.intrepid.com/~robertl/stock-vols1.html. At the time of this writing, a historical volatility calculator may be found at www.rutterassociates.com/htmls/calculator/classes/histVol.htm. Care must be taken to ensure that any downloaded volatilities are calculated properly. On December 20, 2002, Robert Lum posted an annual volatility of 29.3 percent for IBM, whereas E*Trade posted 33.7 percent. Compare these quotes with the 48.5 percent just computed for IBM.

SHORTCUT METHODS FOR CALCULATING HISTORICAL VOLATILITY

There is no reliable and accurate shortcut method of calculating volatility; however, at least two texts and one investment course suggest that annual volatility can be obtained from the 52-week high price H and the 52-week low price L for a stock. They rely on the following formula:

$$\sigma = \frac{2(H - L)}{H + L}$$

This oversimplified formula completely ignores the log-normal nature of stock prices and yields unreliable results. This formula should *not* be used! For example, the 52-week high and low prices for IBM on December 13, 2002, were $126.39 and $54.01, respectively. If the preceding relationship were true:

$$\sigma = \frac{2(126.39 - 54.01)}{126.39 + 54.01} = .802$$

which is a far cry from the 48.5 percent from the 10-week sample or the 36.7 percent from the 6-week sample.

Using the *range* of a distribution to calculate standard deviation is not generally recommended because it deals only with extreme values and includes nothing of the dispersion of the remaining data. There is, however, a way to express the high and low prices as a price relative and use Equation (5.6) to solve for σ. From Equation (5.6), assuming *one* year and *one* standard deviation,

$$H = Se^{z\sigma\sqrt{t}}$$

$$L = Se^{-z\sigma\sqrt{t}}$$

Since z and $\sqrt{t}$ both $= 1$,

$$S = He^{-\sigma}$$

$$S = Le^{\sigma}$$

Therefore,

$$He^{-\sigma} = Le^{\sigma}$$

$$(e^{\sigma})^2 = \frac{H}{L}$$

$$\sigma = \ln\left(\sqrt{\frac{H}{L}}\right) \qquad (5.7)$$

For the IBM case, $\sigma = .425$, which is reasonably close to the 48.5 percent obtained from the 10-week sample. For the Cisco case (see below), $\sigma = .439$, which is quite close to the implied volatility of .433 and reasonably close to the .398 historical volatility. However, Equation (5.7) should be used only as a last resort.

Another procedure for determining volatility from the high and low asset prices is known as the *extreme-value method*. It is useful when no reliable settlement prices are available for the time periods t under scrutiny. Each data point S_i is calculated by Equation (5.8), and Equation (5.4) is used to calculate the standard deviation. The standard deviation is then multiplied by the square root of the number of periods t in one year to obtain the desired volatility.

$$S_i = .601 \ln\left(\frac{H_t}{L_t}\right) \tag{5.8}$$

As with the range method, Equation (5.8) should be used only when no other data are available.

IMPLIED VOLATILITY

Implied volatility is the market's best guess at what future volatility will be. It is determined by inputting actual options quotes into an options pricing model and solving it backwards for volatility (the *brute-force method*). Another method for calculating implied volatility uses the Newton-Raphson search technique and is covered in Chapter 8. These methods produce the volatility that must have been used to arrive at the quoted options prices. Although theoretically inconsistent, in reality, implied volatilities typically will be slightly different for Calls and Puts at the same strike price and also will vary according to the strike price used in the pricing model. Such variation is known as the *volatility skew* and suggests that some sort of averaging may be necessary to obtain a single value for implied volatility for any given time period.

For example, E*Trade reported the historical annual volatility of Cisco Systems, Inc., on July 11, 2003, at 39.8 percent based on the most recent 30 days. The price of Cisco stock closed at $18.57 on that day, with the closest strike price being 17.5. The market price of the 17.5 Call was $1.60, and the 17.5 Put was priced at $0.50. Solving Equations (3.1) and (3.3) backwards by iteration using $1.60 and $0.50 as the Call and Put inputs, we find the implied Call volatility to be 43.3 percent and the implied Put volatility to be 43.4 percent—fairly close to each other and the historical volatility. However, if we move to the 12.5 strike price, we find the Call implied volatility to be 54.2 percent, whereas the Put implied volatility is 34.4 percent—an *average* of 44.3 percent. These individual implied volatilities are contrasted with the 39.8 percent historical volatility. More about these "skewed" volatilities will be provided later.

Whether to use historical or implied volatility is a personal choice. It depends on whether you believe recent historical volatility is a better forecasting tool than the market's own guess about variability. In either case, volatility is said to be *mean-reverting;* that is, the further volatility strays from its mean, the more likely it will reverse direction. Generally, shifts in implied volatility result from shifts in historical volatility as traders become aware of the new historical data and adjust their thinking; however, the magnitude of the implied volatility changes is usually less.

Implied volatility is published for certain market indices. A popular index is the OEX (S&P 100), which contains the 100 largest companies tracked by Standard & Poor's. The OEX index options are the most actively traded of all index options. Introduced by the Chicago Board of Options Exchange (CBOE) in 1993, the VIX was a weighted measure of the implied volatility for 8 OEX Calls and Puts. A hypothetical at-the-money OEX option was created based on time remaining and the degree to which the actual 8 options were either in or out of the money. VIX represented the implied volatility for this hypothetical OEX option and could be tracked intraday, daily, weekly, or monthly. In September 2003, the CBOE upgraded the VIX, which is now based on the broader S&P 500 index ($INX).

DELTA

In options trading, there exists a set of measurements called *the Greeks*—Greek letters that stand for calculations representing relationships among the variables used to describe an option (price of underlying asset, volatility, time, etc.). The best known of the Greeks is *delta* (Δ), which stands for the instantaneous rate of change in an option price given a 1-point change in the price of the underlying asset.

A rule of thumb is that an at-the-money Call option has a delta of approximately .5; that is, when the strike price and the current price are equal, the Call price will move ½ point for a 1-point price move in the underlying asset or index. Call deltas are expressed as positive numbers ranging from 0 to 1. Put deltas are expressed as negative numbers ranging from -1 to 0. The deltas of a Put and Call at the same strike price and expiration date are related by the formula

$$\Delta_{Put} = \Delta_{Call} - 1 \tag{5.9}$$

Geometrically, delta is the slope of the straight line that is tangent to the option price curve at any given underlying price. It is the first partial derivative of the option price with respect to the price of the underlying asset or index.

$$\Delta = \frac{\partial P}{\partial S} \tag{5.10}$$

Call delta is equal to the expression $N(d)$ in Equation (3.1) [or Equation (3.9) if a dividend using the continuous method is involved]. An option's delta is also known as the *hedge ratio*, which may be used in a trading strategy known as *delta-neutral trading*, which is discussed below. For the entirety of the discussion of the remaining Greeks, we will consider a European-style Call option (we'll call it the *example Call*) on a non-dividend-paying stock selling for \$82.32 with strike price 80, volatility of .335, risk-free interest rate of 1.135 percent, and 90 days until expiration. From Equations (3.1) and (3.4), we have

$$d = \frac{\ln\left(\frac{82.32}{80}\right) + .2466\left[.01135 + \frac{.335(.335)}{2}\right]}{.335(.4966)} = .27185$$

The theoretical option prices are

$$P_C = 82.32 N(.27185) - 80(.99721) N(.10549) = 6.74$$

$$P_p = 6.74 - 82.32 + 80(.99721) = 4.20$$

The at-the-money Call delta is calculated by

$$\Delta_{Call} = N(d) \tag{5.11}$$

Therefore,

$$d = \frac{\ln\left(\frac{82.32}{82.32}\right) + .2466\left[.01135 + \frac{.335(.335)}{2}\right]}{.335(.4966)} = .1$$

$$\Delta_{Call} = N(.1) = .54$$

And the at-the-money Put delta is

$$\Delta_{Put} = \Delta_{Call} - 1 = .54 - 1 = -.46$$

Figure 5–3 shows the relationship between the Call price and the price of the underlying asset.

The relationship between Call delta and stock price is shown in Figure 5–4. It is common practice to write delta without the decimal point. A purchaser of the Call in Figure 5–3 is said to be long 54 deltas.

The relationship between Put delta and stock price is shown in Figure 5–5. Figure 5–6 shows how delta varies with time to expiration.

GAMMA

Delta itself changes when the price of the underlying asset changes. The *rate* at which delta changes with respect to a change in the underlying's

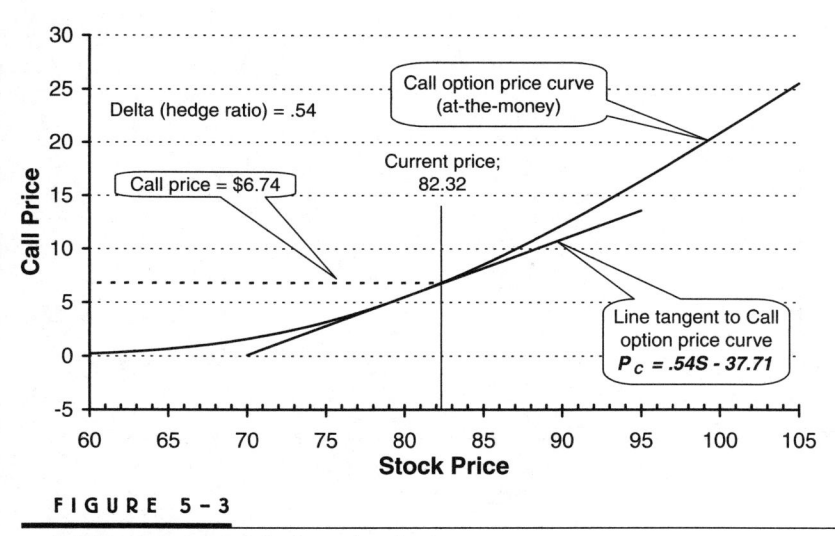

FIGURE 5-3

Relationship between Call price and stock price

FIGURE 5-4

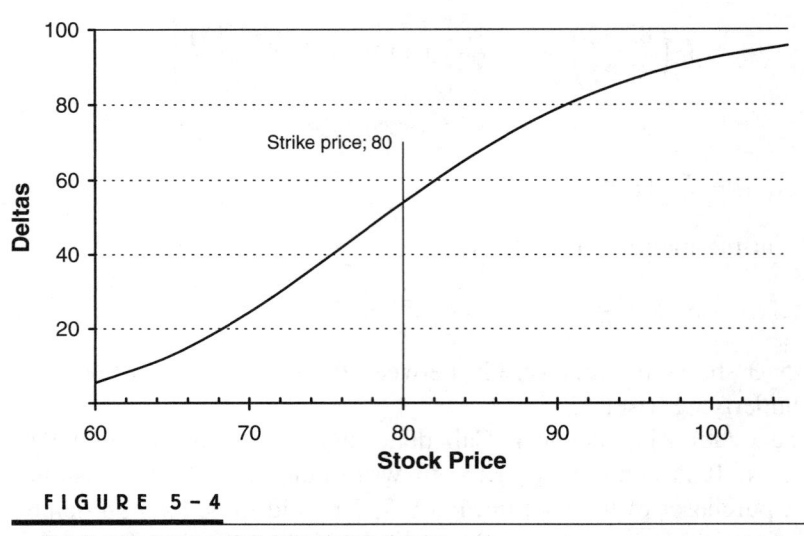

Relationship between Call delta and stock price

price is denoted by gamma. *Gamma* generally is expressed as the number of deltas lost or gained for a 1-point change in the price of the underlying and is the same for a Put and a Call having identical strike prices and expiration dates. If an option has a gamma of 7, a 1-point change in the price of the underlying will cause the option to gain or lose 7 deltas.

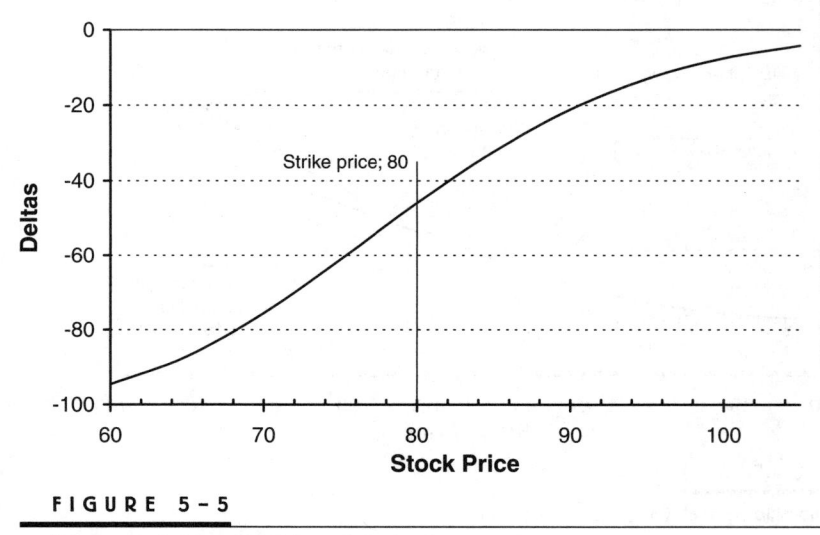

FIGURE 5-5

Relationship between Put delta and stock price

Volatility and Sensitivity to Change

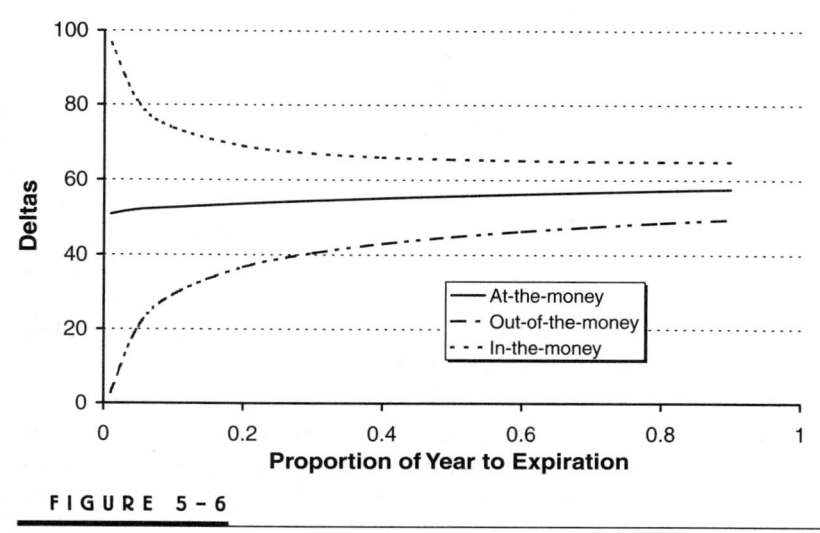

FIGURE 5-6

Delta versus time to expiration

Irrespective of whether a Put or Call is being evaluated, gamma is *added* when the underlying price rises and *subtracted* when the price falls. The gamma of an underlying contract is zero because its delta never changes.[1]

Because gamma is a rate of change of a change, it is the second partial derivative of an option's price with respect to the underlying price, holding all other variables constant. The gamma of a Call option on a non-dividend-paying stock is expressed as

$$\Gamma = \frac{\partial^2 P}{\partial S^2} = \frac{\partial \Delta}{\partial S} = \frac{N'(d)}{S\sigma\sqrt{t}} \quad (5.12)$$

or

$$\Gamma = \frac{e^{-d^2/2}}{S\sigma\sqrt{2\pi t}} \quad (5.13)$$

Gamma for a dividend-paying stock is

$$\Gamma = \frac{e^{-[qt+(d^2/2)]}}{S\sigma\sqrt{2\pi t}} \quad (5.14)$$

For the example Call option,

---

[1] Shelton Natenberg, *Option Volatility and Pricing* (New York: McGraw-Hill, 1994), pp. 103–111.

$$N'(d) = \frac{e^{-(.27185)^2/2}}{\sqrt{2\pi}} = .38447$$

From Equation (5.12),

$$\Gamma = \frac{.38447}{82.32(.335)\sqrt{.2466}} = \frac{.38447}{13.69452} = .02807$$

This means that this Call will gain or lose approximately 3 deltas for each 1-point change in the price of the underlying asset. Figure 5–7 shows the gamma plot for the example Call option.

Gamma is always positive for long positions and negative for short positions. It is the same for Puts and Calls having the same strike price and time to expiration and is at a maximum for an at-the-money strike price.

Figure 5–8 shows the relationship between gamma and time to expiration for the example Call.

Gamma increases as time to expiration decreases for at-the-money options (value of option highly sensitive to underlying asset price). Gammas for in-the-money and out-of-the-money options decrease to zero (the option will or will not be exercised).

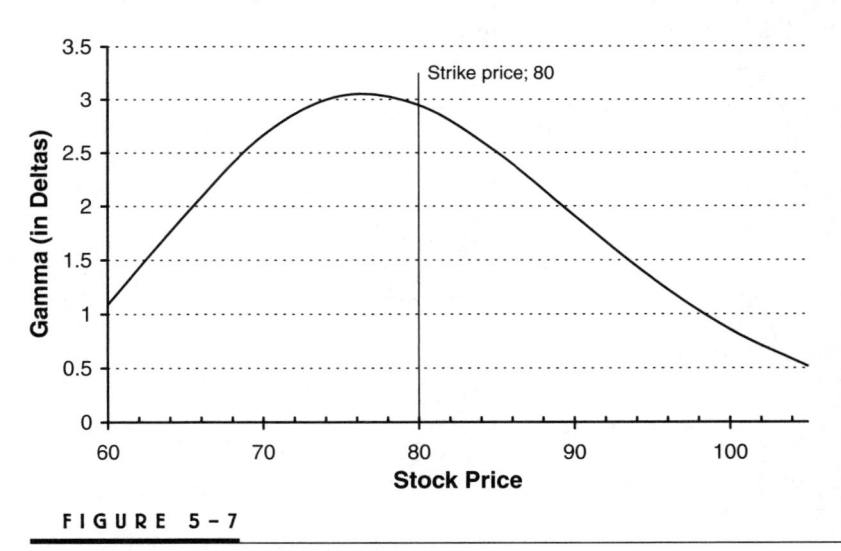

FIGURE 5-7

Relationship between gamma and stock price

Volatility and Sensitivity to Change

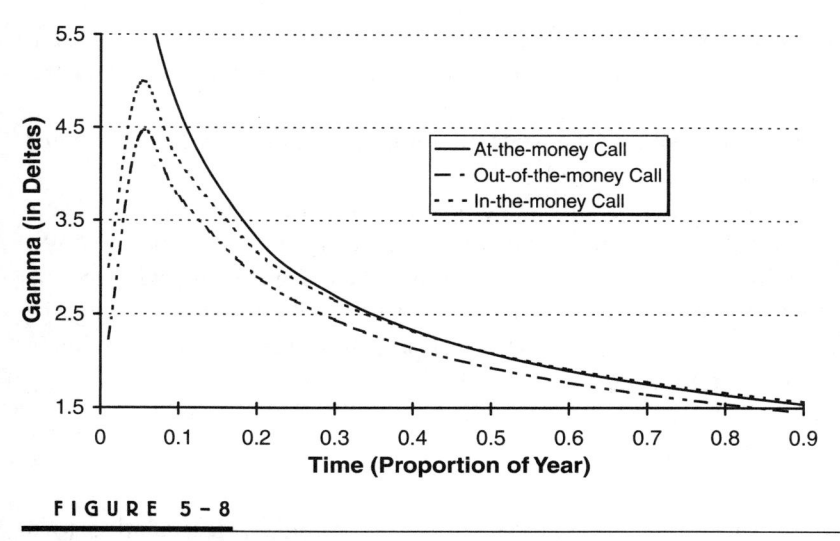

FIGURE 5-8

Gamma versus time to expiration

VEGA

Another important sensitivity measure is *vega* (not a Greek letter), sometimes denoted as *kappa,* which *is* a Greek letter. Vega measures the likely change in an option's price for a one percentage point (.01) change in an option's implied volatility. In effect, vega tells us the likely option price consequences of being wrong in our volatility estimate. Vega is the partial derivative of an option's price with respect to its implied volatility:

$$\text{Vega} = \frac{\partial P}{\partial \sigma} = S\sqrt{t}N'(d) \qquad (5.15)$$

or

$$\text{Vega} = \frac{S\sqrt{t}}{\sqrt{2\pi}} e^{-d^2/2} \qquad (5.16)$$

where d is calculated from Equation (3.8) if dividends are involved and from Equation (3.1) otherwise.

Vega for the example Call option shown in Figure 5–3 is

$$\text{Vega} = \frac{82.32(.4966)}{2.50663} e^{-.03695} = 15.72$$

which means the option's price will move approximately $0.16 for each 1-point change (.01) in implied volatility when the strike price is at the money.

Figure 5–9 shows the vega plot for the example Call option for strike prices between 60 and 105.

Vega is always positive and is the same for both Put and Calls having the same strike price and time to maturity. Vega will be the highest (in point change) for the at-the-money strike price and will decline thereafter for both increasing and decreasing strike prices. The vega of all options declines as expiration approaches. Chapter 8 contains a method for determining implied volatility from vega.

THETA

Theta measures the rate of change of an option's price relative to a decrease in the time to maturity (expiration). Theta is the time decay factor or the rate at which an option loses value as time passes. It is usually expressed in points per day lost when all the other variables remain constant. Thus a long option with a theta of −.07 priced at $1.75 today is expected to be worth $1.68 tomorrow and $1.61 the next day, and so on. By convention, long options have negative thetas, whereas short options have positive ones.[2]

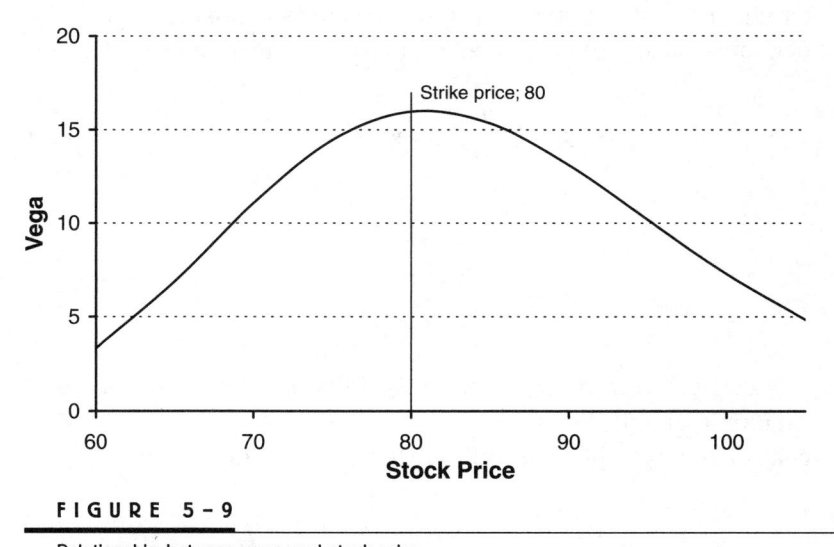

FIGURE 5-9

Relationship between vega and stock price

---

[2] *Ibid.*, p. 111.

Volatility and Sensitivity to Change

For a non-dividend-paying asset, the European-style Call theta is

$$\Theta_{Call} = -\frac{SN'(d)\sigma}{2\sqrt{t}} - rKe^{-rt}N(d - \sigma\sqrt{t}) \quad (5.17)$$

And for a non-dividend-paying asset, the European-style Put theta is

$$\Theta_{Put} = -\frac{SN'(d)\sigma}{2\sqrt{t}} + rKe^{-rt}N(\sigma\sqrt{t} - d) \quad (5.18)$$

where d is calculated from Equation (3.1).

For a dividend-paying asset (continuous method), the European-style Call theta is

$$\Theta_{Call} = -\frac{SN'(d)\sigma}{2\sqrt{t}} + qSN(d)e^{-qt} - rKe^{-rt}N(d - \sigma\sqrt{t}) \quad (5.19)$$

And for a dividend-paying asset (continuous method), the European-style Put theta is

$$\Theta_{Put} = -\frac{SN'(d)\sigma}{2\sqrt{t}} - qSN(-d)e^{-qt} + rKe^{-rt}N(\sigma\sqrt{t} - d) \quad (5.20)$$

where d is calculated from Equation (3.8).

Since t is measured in years, theta is also expressed in years. To obtain theta in days, divide the calculated theta by 365.

Theta for the example Call option is calculated from Equation (5.17):

$$\Theta_{Call} = -\frac{82.32(.38447))(.335)}{2(.4966)} - \ldots$$
$$- .01135(80)(.99721)N(.27185 - .16636) = -11.16422$$

$$\Theta_{Call} \text{ (in days)} = \frac{-11.16422}{365} = -.03$$

meaning that at 90 days prior to expiration, this Call is expected to *lose* $0.03 per day; that is, the value of the Call will be worth $6.71 tomorrow, $6.68 the next day, and so on. Figure 5–10 shows the variation in Call theta for changes in the stock price.

Theta for the Put counterpart of the example Call is calculated from Equation (5-18):

FIGURE 5-10

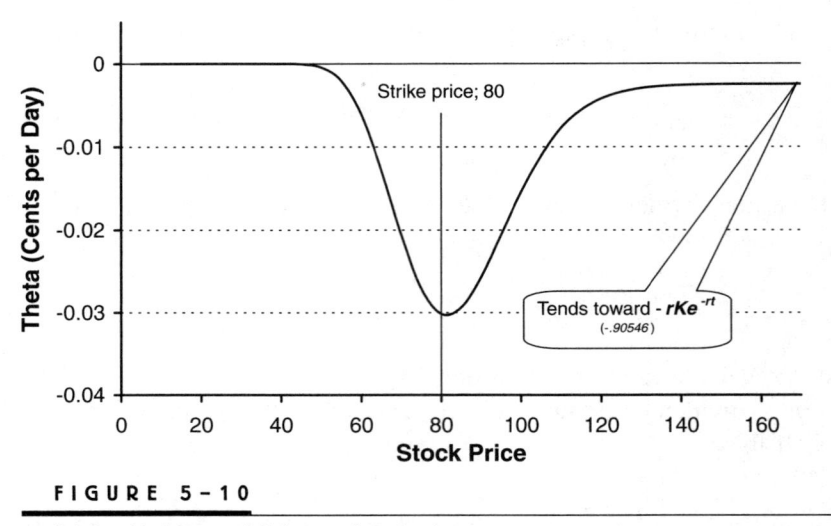

Relationship between Call theta and stock price

$$\Theta_{Put} = -\frac{80(.38447)(.335)}{2(.4966)} + \cdots$$
$$+ .01135(80)(.99721)N(.16636 - .27185) = -10.26051$$

$$\Theta_{Put} \text{ (in days)} = \frac{-10.26051}{365} = -.02811$$

meaning that at 90 days prior to expiration, the Put (corresponding to the example Call) is expected to *lose* $0.028 per day. Figure 5–11 shows how the Put theta varies with changes in the underlying stock price. Figure 5–12 shows how theta varies with time to expiration.

RHO

The sensitivity of an option's theoretical value to changes in interest rates is given by *rho*.[3] Although interest rates are the least significant input to the options pricing model and rho frequently is ignored by options traders, we will discuss it briefly.

---

[3] *Ibid.*, p. 116.

Volatility and Sensitivity to Change 173

FIGURE 5-11

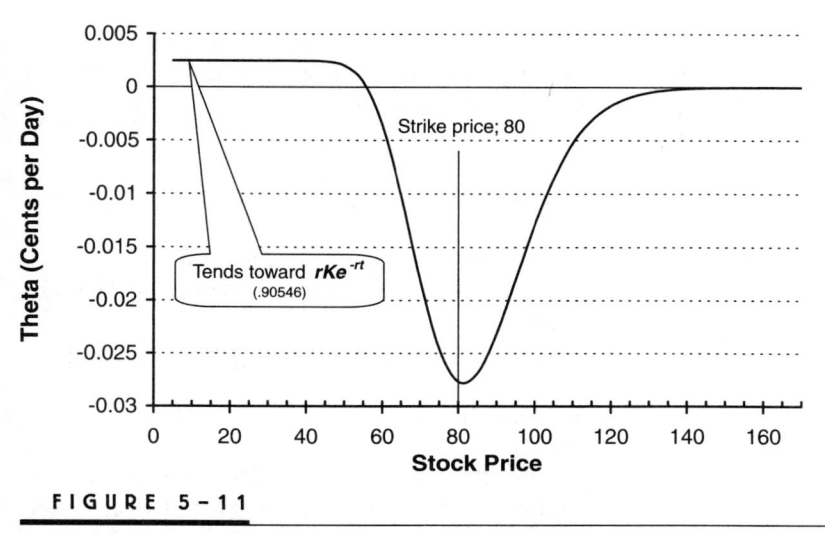

Relationship between Put theta and stock price

For a Call on a non-dividend-paying asset,

$$\rho = tKe^{-rt}N(d - \sigma\sqrt{t}) \qquad (5.21)$$

For a Put on a non-dividend-paying asset,

$$\rho = -tKe^{-rt}N(\sigma\sqrt{t} - d) \qquad (5.22)$$

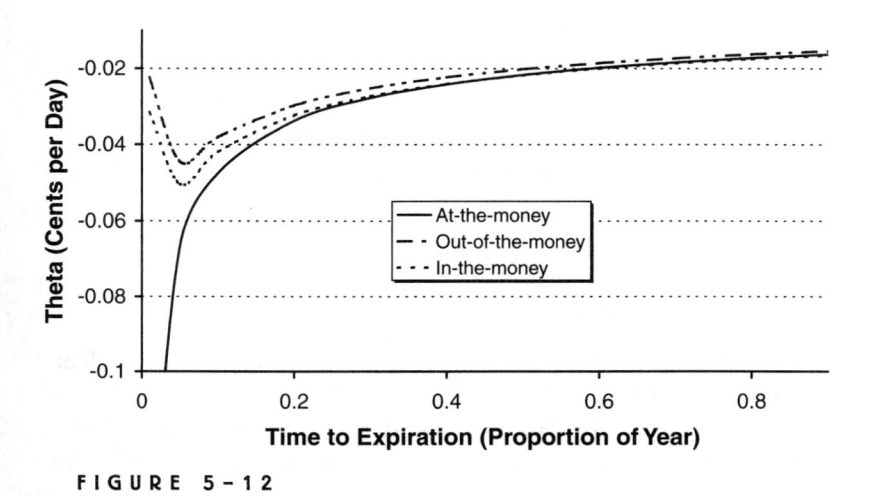

FIGURE 5-12

Relationship between Call theta and time to expiration

For non-dividend-paying assets, d is defined by Equation (3.1). For dividend-paying stocks (continuous method), both Equations (5.21) and (5.22) may be used, except that d is defined by Equation (3.8).

For the example Call, rho is calculated by

$$\rho = .2466(80)(.99721)N(.271847 - .16636) = 10.66282$$

which means that for each one percentage point (.01) increase or decrease in the interest rate, the Call's theoretical value will increase or decrease by .10663.

For the Put associated with the example Call, rho is calculated by

$$\rho = -.2466(80)(.99721)N(.16636 - .271847) = -9.01004$$

which means that for each one percentage point (.01) *increase* in the interest rate, the Put's theoretical value will *decrease* by .0901, and vice versa.

Figure 5–13 shows how the rhos for the example Call and associated Put vary with the stock price.

ELASTICITY

Elasticity[4] refers to the *leverage* of the option position and is denoted by the Greek letter lambda (λ). It measures the percentage change in the option price for a 1 percent change in the underlying asset price.

$$\lambda = \Delta_C\left(\frac{S}{P_C}\right) \quad \text{or} \quad \lambda = \Delta_P\left(\frac{S}{P_P}\right)$$

A lambda of 8 means that a 1 percent increase in the price of the stock causes an 8 percent increase in the price of the option. Typically, elasticity values range from 8 to 10.

DELTA-NEUTRAL HEDGING

Hedging is technique employed by traders and investors to protect an open position or investment. Simple hedges such as protective Puts and covered Calls are relatively straightforward and are easily understood. Delta-neutral hedging is a hedging strategy designed to minimize (or

---
[4] Robert T. Daigler, *Advanced Options Trading* (New York: McGraw-Hill, 1994), p. 125.

Volatility and Sensitivity to Change   175

FIGURE 5-13

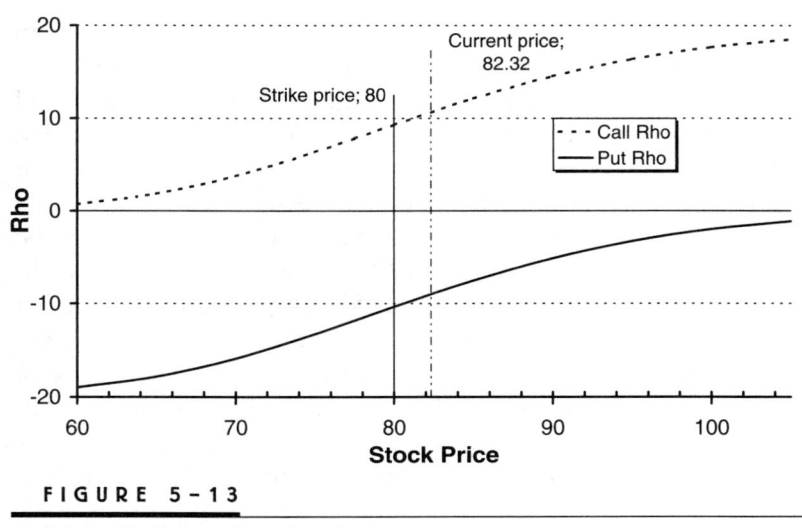

Relationship between rho and stock price

neutralize) a position's exposure to market price changes. In short, it allows a potential profit without having to forecast the direction of prices.

Earlier we introduced delta, which measures the change in an option's price for a 1-point change in the underlying asset price. Typically, an at-the-money Call has a delta of approximately +.5 or slightly higher, whereas an at-the-money Put has a delta of approximately −.5. The deltas of the Puts and Calls are changing constantly throughout the life of an option. The underlying asset is said to have a delta of 1 and is *fixed*. In the customary parlance of the marketplace, a position having a +.5 delta is said to be "long 50 deltas." An underlying asset consisting of 100 shares is said to have a "fixed 100 deltas" (one delta per share). Thus a position consisting of 100 owned shares of an underlying stock and one at-the-money Put on that stock would be long 50 deltas.

Out-of-the-money options have very low deltas, whereas in-the-money options have deltas in excess of 50. As the price of an underlying stock rises, a deep in-the-money option's delta tends toward 100, and the option begins to behave like the stock itself. At the same time, the out-of-the-money option's delta will tend toward zero as it appears the option will expire worthless.

To illustrate how delta-neutral hedging works, suppose you buy 500 shares of XYZ stock selling for $25 per share and simultaneously buy 10 XYZ 25 Puts each having a delta of 50. You would be short 500 deltas with the Puts and long 500 deltas with the stock—delta-neutral.

For small movements in the price of XYZ, the position would remain delta-neutral; however, if the price rises or falls by any significant amount, the deltas themselves would change, and the position would become unbalanced. For example, if the price of XYZ rose to $28 and the Put delta fell to 45, the position then would be long 500 deltas and short 450 deltas for a net long position of 50 deltas. To rebalance (get back to delta-neutral), 50 deltas would have to be sold. This could be accomplished by selling 50 shares of XYZ. Subsequently, if the price of XYZ fell to $23 and the Put delta rose to 55, the position would be net short 50 deltas and could be rebalanced by buying 50 shares of XYZ.

Notice how this hedge forces you to sell deltas when the stock price increases and buy deltas when it falls (buy low, sell high). In the latter case, we also could have sold one Put and sold five shares of XYZ, as shown in Table 5-2. Generally speaking, the information in Table 5-3 holds true.

Delta-neutral hedging does not have to involve an underlying asset. A position of options only also can be made delta-neutral. Straddles and strangles established with at-the-money options will be, by definition, delta-neutral. Ratio spreads and backspreads are easily made delta-neutral with a disproportionate number of contracts of Puts or Calls.

Delta-neutral hedging can be profitable if a trader buys underpriced options and sells overpriced options. The downside is that continuously

TABLE 5-2

Example of delta-neutral hedging

	Deltas	
	10 XYZ Puts	500 shares XYZ
Original delta position	−500	500
Change due to price increase	50	0
Sell 50 shares of XYZ @ 28		−50
New position	−450	450
Change due to price decrease	−50	0
Rebalance:		
Sell l Put	55	0
Sell 5 shares of XYZ @ 23	0	−5
Position delta neutral	−445	445

TABLE 5-3
Delta-neutral hedging

Delta-neutral	Market goes up	Market goes down
Long underlying, long Put	Profit on underlying Smaller loss on Put	Loss on underlying Larger profit on Put
Short underlying, long Call	Loss on underlying Larger profit on Call	Profit on underlying Smaller loss on Call

rebalancing a portfolio can be very expensive and is really suitable only for market makers or other professionals subject to small transaction costs. The amount of rebalancing can be controlled by trading only in those options having a low gamma.

THE VOLATILITY SKEW

Theoretically, Put and Call options ought to have the same implied volatility for a given strike price and time to expiration. In addition, because there can be only one actual or historical volatility (calculated after the fact for a specified time period), an option's implied volatility should be fairly constant over the range of strike prices as well.

Prior to the market crash in October 1987, this was most often the case. Subsequently, with the realization that extreme short-term movements in the underlying asset prices occur more often than originally anticipated, we see implied volatilities skewing in one direction from lower strikes to higher ones, and vice versa. They also may rise on both side of the at-the-money strike price (the *volatility smile*). A good example of this kind of skew (smile) is shown in Figure 5–14 for the S&P 100 Index (OEX) options on October 14, 2003, which stood at 519.56 with three days to expiration. Historical volatility was .169, and the interest rate employed was .02.

Fitted parabolas (see Chapter 8 under "Second-Order Equations: The Parabola") for both Calls and Puts exhibit R^2 of .99 and .98, respectively, which suggests an extremely good fit.

Note that in addition to the skewed effect, implied volatilities for Calls and Puts having the same strike price are *not* the same. This might be due to errors in the quotes at the end of the day or simply a reflection of arbitrage opportunities about to be corrected. Remember, *there can be*

FIGURE 5-14

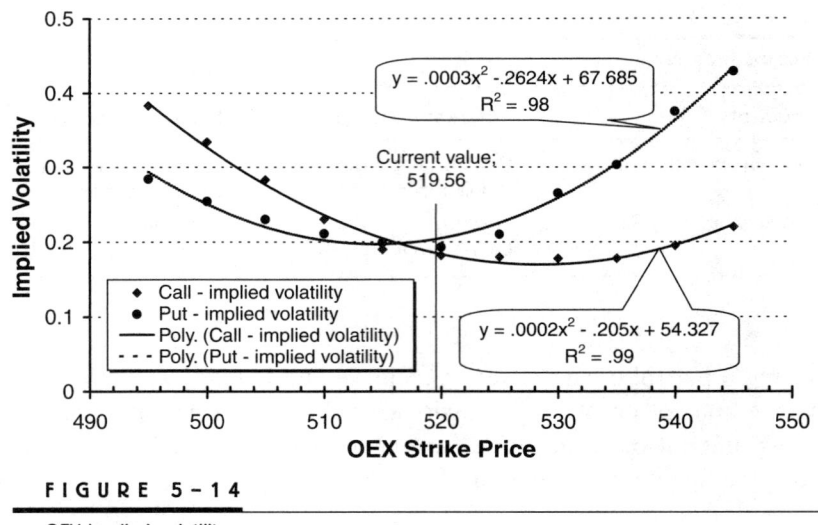

OEX implied volatility

only one actual volatility that reflects the price behavior of the underlying asset between the trade and expiration dates. The actual volatility for the three remaining days was .104.

The typical explanation for the skew phenomenon is that the Black-Scholes model assumes returns are distributed log-normally and are subject to a *diffusion* process; that is, prices progress smoothly from one level to another without significant intervening jumps along the way. However, such jumps *do* occur frequently enough that the Black-Scholes model tends to underprice options that are either deeply in the money or deeply out of the money. This is equivalent to saying that the actual distribution of returns has "fatter tails" than are provided by a simple log-normal distribution. The actual distribution of returns is said to be more *leptokurtic* (see Chapter 8 under "Kurtosis"). Others attribute the skew to increased demand from professional money managers for out-of-the-money options to protect large stock portfolios.

There have been many academic attempts to account for the volatility smile and/or skews, but as yet, none has completely described the real-world process. The trader is much better off employing the Black-Scholes model with the knowledge that certain options away from the at-the-money strike price may be mispriced and acting accordingly. The trader actually may *choose* to trade the volatility skew by using ratio spreads and backspreads.

TRADING THE VOLATILITY SKEW

Volatility skews will be either *forward* (positive), *reverse* (negative), or both, as in the "smile" depicted in Figure 5-14. A forward skew has implied volatilities increasing with the strike prices, whereas a reverse skew is just the opposite. A forward or positively skewed distribution differs from the log-normal distribution in that the rightmost tail indicates a greater probability that the price of the underlying asset will increase by a large amount. The distribution's leftmost tail indicates a lower probability of a large price decrease. A negatively skewed distribution exhibits the opposite characteristics when compared with a log-normal distribution—higher probability of a large price decrease coupled with a lower probability of a large price increase.

If, as some suggest, the higher and lower implied volatilities are the result of professional money managers acting to protect large portfolios, such actions would not necessarily affect the actual *asset price distribution,* which is what volatility is all about. In such a case, the at-the-money implied volatility would be more representative of true volatility, and options away from the money would be mispriced.

To take advantage of the mispricing in a forward skew, a trader could establish a bull spread, whereby he buys the option with the lower strike price (lower implied volatility) and sells the option with the higher strike (higher implied volatility). In effect, the trader is buying cheap options while selling expensive ones. In a reverse-skew situation, the trader could establish a bear spread to accomplish the same goals.

Since bull and bear spreads imply a forecast of price direction, they may not be the best strategies for a trader who is neutral on the direction of potential price movements. In such case, the trader could establish a Call ratio spread or a Put backspread for the forward skew (see Figures 3-19 and 3-22). Likewise, for a reverse or negative skew, the trader could establish a Put ratio spread or a Call backspread (see Figures 3-20 and 3-21).

Both historical volatility and implied volatility are best understood when viewed in relation to past values rather than as a single unadorned measure. Typically, volatility measures adhere to a much narrower range of values than do asset prices. It is necessary to determine where volatility has been relative to where it is now. The mean reverting characteristic of volatility (discussed previously) is important in determining whether the instant volatility is high or low relative to mean volatility. Table 5-4 shows which strategy to use based on the relative volatility.

TABLE 5-4

Volatility skew

	Volatility	
Skew	High	Low
Forward	Put ratio spread Bear spread	Call backspread Bear spread
Reverse	Put backspread Bull spread	Call ratio spread Bull spread

FORECAST VOLATILITY

We have spent a considerable amount of time describing the two types of volatility—historical and implied. These measures are not so important in and of themselves. They are important mainly as an aid in forecasting future volatility. *Forecast volatility* is not a new type of volatility—it is the trader's best estimate of what the *actual* volatility will be between the trade date and the expiration date (only known after the fact). Most traders will want an accurate forecast of volatility to use in their pricing models. We want a reasonably good forecast of volatility to make the kind of probability calculations demonstrated earlier in this chapter. Moreover, we need reasonable volatility estimates to determine expected results of options trades, as shown in Chapters 6 and 7.

There is no one correct way to estimate future volatility. The common place to start is to look at historical volatility. Some traders will argue that the appropriate period to look at for valuing a three-month option is the immediate past three months of asset prices. Others will calculate historic volatilities for a range of periods and then take some kind of weighted average. Still others will select a period of between 90 and 180 days and use the associated volatility for all expiration periods.

Certain other traders will argue that using some form of implied volatility as an estimate of future volatility is appropriate. After all, isn't it implied volatility that gets you to the current market price? It has been our experience, however, that actual volatility calculated after the expiration date differs widely from the collection of implied volatilities existing on the trade date.

Figure 5–15 shows a one-year price history of the OEX between November 19, 2002, and the same day in 2003. During that one-year period, the OEX price varied between 406.74 and 524.19. A quick and dirty estimate of the annual volatility may be obtained from Equation (5.7):

Volatility and Sensitivity to Change

[Figure: OEX one-year price history chart from 11/19/2002 to 11/4/2003, Price ranging from 400 to 520]

FIGURE 5-15

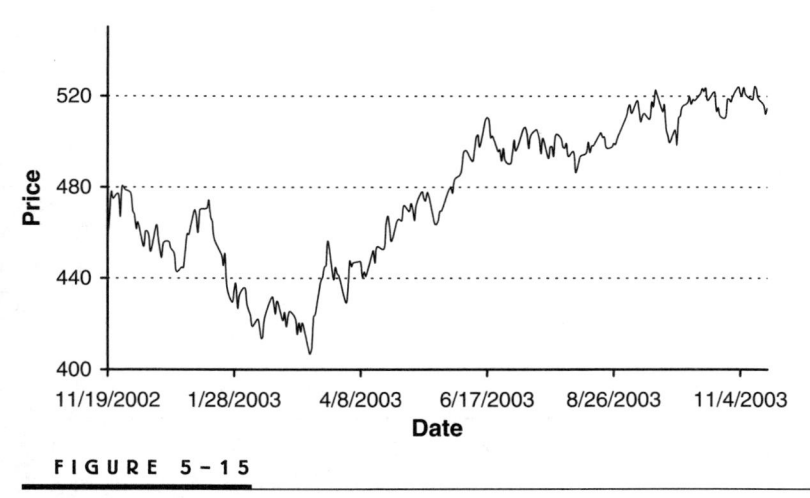

OEX one-year price history (11/19/02–11/19/03)

$$\sigma = \ln\left(\sqrt{\frac{H}{L}}\right) = \ln\left(\sqrt{\frac{524.19}{406.74}}\right) = .126$$

The actual annual volatility was calculated from Equation (5.4), which yields .186. From a list of the OEX prices for the 252 trading days in the one-year period, volatility was calculated for each successive 30-day period. For example, the volatility of .233 for January 3, 2003, was calculated based on the 30 preceding trading days (November 20, 2002–January 3, 2003); the January 6, 2003, figure of .236 was calculated on the 30 trading days between November 21, 2002 and January 6, 2003; and so on. Figure 5-16 shows a time plot of the sample 30-day periods and their associated volatilities.

The mean of the samples was .182 (close to the actual volatility of .186). Figure 5-16 demonstrates the phenomenon known as *reversion to the mean,* which implies that the further a given volatility strays from the mean, the more likely it will reverse direction. We would expect the volatility (which was .106 on the last day of the period) to begin trending upward toward .186 in the near future.

What does all this have to do with projecting volatility into future periods? We saw from Figure 5-14 that an actual three-day volatility of .104 was matched with implied volatilities that varied from under .2 to over .4. Clearly, the historical volatility of .169 is a better forecast of .104 than the implied volatilities. Just how good is historical volatility as an estimate of future volatility? From the 30-day sample periods shown in Figure 5-16, each historical volatility was used to forecast the

FIGURE 5-16

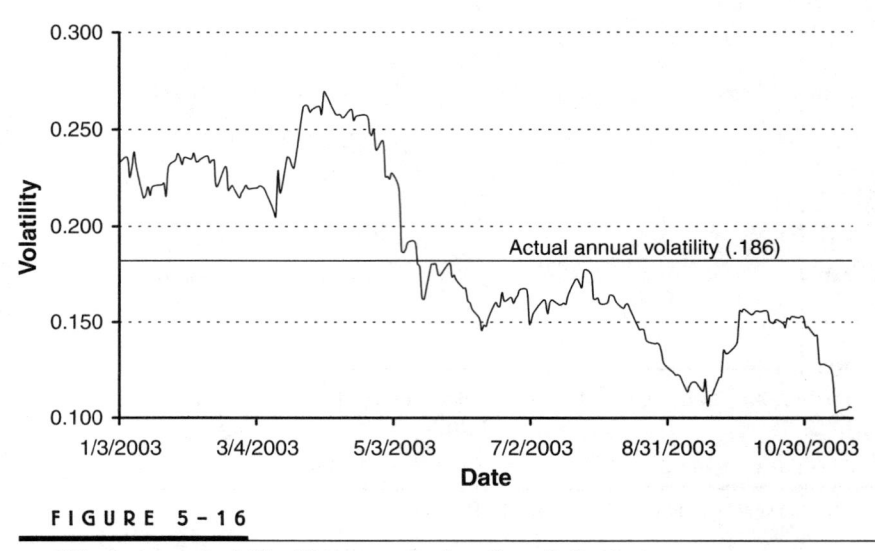

OEX actual annual volatility (30-day samples from Figure 5-15 prices)

volatility 30 days ahead. Figure 5–17 shows how projected volatility compared with historical volatility.

Only a little better than 50 percent of the variation in the forecast volatility is accounted for by the historical volatility ($R^2 = .53$). The regression line is fairly close to the "perfect forecast" line for lower values of historical volatility but begins to stray as the values increase.

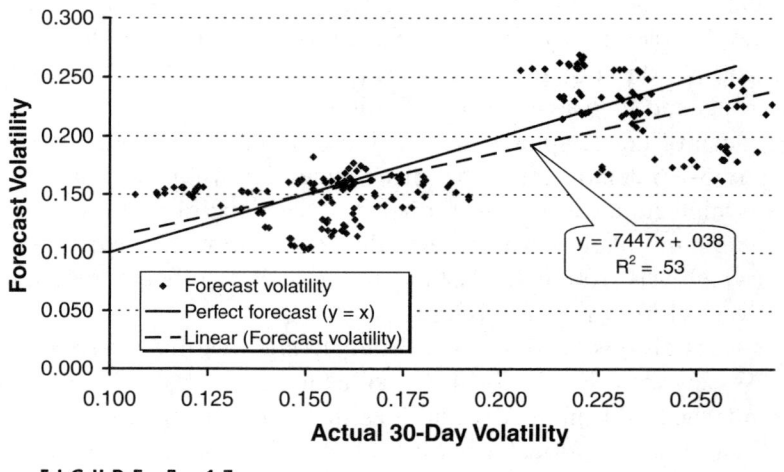

FIGURE 5-17

Forecast of annual OEX volatility (from 30-day samples in Figure 5-16)

In this example, we were only marginally successful in forecasting future volatility using past history.

The problem (mentioned earlier) is that the variance (volatility squared) of the time series is not constant over the option's life, as the Black-Scholes model assumes. As can be seen from Figure 5–16, volatility is changing constantly over time. This property of the variance is called *heteroscedasticity*. If the variance was constant, as many traders assume, it would be *homoscedastic*. Any model of a time series using past data in a forecast of future values is said to be *autoregressive*. Statistical models making use of both properties have been developed over the past decade and are widely known as *autoregressive conditional heteroscedasticity* (ARCH) *models*. Finally, to cure certain problems of memory and lag structure associated with ARCH models, generalized ARCH (GARCH) models have been developed more recently. GARCH models tend to produce distributions that have fatter tails and that are more leptokurtic than a log-normal distribution, thus overcoming some of the criticisms of the Black-Scholes model.

CHAPTER 6

Determining Expected Results of Options Trades: Naked Options and Basic Spreads

> *As far as the laws of mathematics refer to reality, they are not certain, and as far as they are certain, they do not refer to reality.*
> —Albert Einstein (1879–1955)

If you have made it this far, Einstein's paradox must seem hopelessly accurate. However, what we have covered so far does, indeed, refer to the reality of the options markets, and its uncertainty is mitigated somewhat through the use of probability theory.

The accompanying CD contains two programs for determining expected results of options trades and the optimal position size. *Expectation.exe* produces the results for a *single* trade for any strategy covered in this book—both on screen and in a printed report. *DailyCheck.exe* produces a printed report covering all available trades within all strategies for a given underlying instrument, including the ability to choose to print out all trades or just those trades having a positive $E(R)$. Instructions for the use of these two programs are set forth in Chapter 9.

All examples in Chapters 6 and 7 are based on the Cisco Systems, Inc., options quoted on July 11, 2003, for the August 15 expiration when the current price of Cisco stock was $18.57 and the historical volatility was 39.8 percent. Using an initial trade date of July 13, 2003, there were 34 days until expiration. Although solving the equations by hand is somewhat tedious, at least one solved example for each strategy is presented so that you may make use of the mathematics in your own programs or spreadsheets.

The power of these programs is evident from the first report from *DailyCheck.exe,* whereby trades with negative expectation can be abandoned immediately. Table 6–1 shows *all* available trades for Cisco Systems, Inc., on July 11, 2003, together with trades having a positive expectation. Note that over 160 trades can be dropped from consideration immediately. Details of the 144 positive-expectation trades are set forth in Appendix B.

In the first solved example below—that of a purchased Call—every detailed step of the solution process is shown. Thereafter, some of the detail arithmetic is omitted, assuming that you will have grasped the fundamentals.

In Chapter 3 we learned how to express the results of an options trade at expiration in terms of simple linear results functions. In Chapter 4 we learned how to combine *normal* probability distributions with linear functions to produce expected results. It remains only to discover how

TABLE 6–1

Cisco Systems, Inc., option strategies, July, 11 2003

Strategy	All	Positive $E(R)$
Purchase naked Calls	8	6
Sell naked Calls	8	2
Purchase naked Puts	7	0
Sell naked Puts	7	7
Bull Call spreads	28	24
Bear Call spreads	27	0
Bull Put spreads	21	16
Bear Put spreads	21	2
Covered Calls	8	5
Long straddles	4	0
Short straddles	4	4
Long strangles	6	0
Short strangles	6	6
Call ratio spreads	27	22
Put ratio spreads	20	19
Call backspreads	27	6
Put backspreads	21	2
Butterfly spreads	56	23
Totals	306	144

to combine the results functions with *log-normal* probability distributions to produce expected results of options trades.

A log-normal distribution function is plotted on each chart for each strategy with its height arbitrarily scaled to fit the region of interest. Remember, probability relates to the area under the curve of the distribution function—not the height or the linear distance from the mean.

If you are not interested in the *derivation* of the closed-form solution for expected results, you should skip over the next few pages to the section entitled, "Maximum Gains and Losses."

DERIVATION OF THE CLOSED-FORM SOLUTION FOR EXPECTED RESULTS

We start the derivation process by examining the purchase of a naked Call. We want to construct a log-normal probability distribution having a mean equal to the current price S of the underlying stock. This is the case for which the probability of the stock's price at expiration being either above or below the current price is 50 percent. Recall the results function for purchasing a naked Call (Equation 3.16):

$$R = f(x) = \begin{cases} -P_{PC} & \text{for } x \le K_{PC} \\ x - BEP & \text{for } x > K_{PC} \end{cases}$$

We construct a log-normal distribution function from the standard normal probability distribution function by defining the z scale in terms of the *logs* of the returns. From Equation (2.29) we have the standard normal probability distribution as a function of z. We call this function $g(z)$.

$$g(z) = \frac{1}{\sqrt{2\pi}} e^{-z^2/2} \qquad (6.1)$$

We now define z as

$$z = \frac{\ln\left(\dfrac{x}{S}\right)}{\sigma \sqrt{t}} \qquad (6.2)$$

Since R is a function of x, we must transform $f(x)$ into a function of z so that the two functions may multiplied together. The transformation is made by solving Equation (6.2) for x. Rearranging the terms in Equation (6.2), we have

$$\ln\left(\frac{x}{S}\right) = z\sigma\sqrt{t}$$

Taking the exponential of both sides and solving for x, we have

$$x = Se^{\sigma z\sqrt{t}} \qquad (6.3)$$

Rewriting the results function in terms of z, we have

$$R = f(z) = \begin{cases} -P_{PC} & \text{for } z \leq z_{K_{PC}} \\ Se^{\sigma z\sqrt{t}} - BEP & \text{for } z > z_{K_{PC}} \end{cases} \qquad (6.4)$$

where $z_{K_{PC}}$ is the z value of K_{PC} obtained from Equation (6.2) by substituting for K_{PC} for x.

To obtain the expected results $E(R)$, we must find the integral of the product of the two functions:

$$E(R) = \int f(z)g(z)\,dz \qquad (6.5)$$

Multiplying the two functions together, we get

$$(Se^{\sigma z\sqrt{t}} - BEP)\left(\frac{1}{\sqrt{2\pi}}e^{-z^2/2}\right)$$

Simplifying, we have (remember the laws of exponents)

$$\frac{S}{\sqrt{2\pi}}e^{\sigma\sqrt{t}z - z^2/2} - BEP\left(\frac{1}{\sqrt{2\pi}}e^{-z^2/2}\right)$$

Integrating the product, we get

$$\frac{S}{\sqrt{2\pi}}\int e^{\sigma\sqrt{t}z - z^2/2}\,dz - \frac{BEP}{\sqrt{2\pi}}\int e^{-z^2/2}\,dz$$

Recall from Chapter 2 that whenever $1/\sqrt{2\pi}\int e^{-z^2/2}\,dz$ appears in the solution, it will be denoted as $N(b) - N(a)$, meaning "the probability that z will lie between a and b." The final form of the expression to be evaluated is

$$\frac{S}{\sqrt{2\pi}} \int e^{\sigma\sqrt{t}z - z^2/2} \, dz - BEP[N(b) - N(a)] \qquad (6.6)$$

It is now necessary to find a generalized solution to the integral contained in Equation (6.6). This is done by searching through tables of integrals found in most complete mathematical handbooks. We look for a solved integral that has the same form as the integral in Equation (6.6). From a table of integrals, the general solution that "fits" Equation (6.6) is

$$\int e^{-(ax^2 + 2bx + c)} \, dx = \frac{1}{2}\sqrt{\frac{\pi}{a}} \, e^{(b^2 - 4ac)/a} \, \text{erf}\left(\sqrt{ax} + \frac{b}{\sqrt{a}}\right) \qquad (6.7)$$

where erf represents the widely tabulated error function. In the general solution, a and b are coefficients of the unknown terms and c is a constant (they are *not* interval boundaries). In Equation (6.6), there is no constant term in the exponent for e; therefore, $c = 0$. In order to evaluate the integral in Equation (6.6), we substitute z for x and determine the values of the coefficients a and b for use in Equation (6.7).

For the coefficient of the z^2 term

$$-a = -\frac{1}{2}$$

and

$$a = \frac{1}{2}$$

For the coefficient of the z term

$$-2b = \sigma\sqrt{t}$$

and

$$b = -\frac{\sigma\sqrt{t}}{2}$$

Substituting the coefficients a and b and the constant c into Equation (6.7), we get the solution

$$\int e^{\frac{1}{2}z^2 - \frac{\sigma\sqrt{t}}{2}z} \, dz = \frac{1}{2}\sqrt{2\pi} \, e^{\sigma^2 t/2} \, \text{erf}\left(.70711z - \frac{\sigma\sqrt{t}}{1.4142}\right) \quad (6.8)$$

The error function erf has emerged in the solution. It is closely related to the area under the standard normal curve and may be calculated using Equation (6.9).

$$\text{erf}(x) = 2[N(x\sqrt{2}) - .5] \quad (6.9)$$

where N is the operator for the standard normal density function, as described previously (NORMSDIST in Excel). For example, letting

$$x = .5$$

we have

$$\text{erf}(x) = 2[N(.5\sqrt{2}) - .5]$$

$$= 2(.76025 - .5) = .5205$$

which may be verified by reference to any table of error functions.

Evaluating the error function from Equation (6.8), we have

$$\text{erf}\left(.70711z - \frac{\sigma\sqrt{t}}{1.4142}\right)$$

$$= 2\left\{N\left[1.4142(.70711)z - \frac{1.4142\sigma\sqrt{t}}{1.4142}\right] - .5\right\}$$

which reduces to

$$2[N(z - \sigma\sqrt{t}) - .5]$$

Simplifying, the solution to the integral in Equation (6.6) is

$$\int e^{\frac{1}{2}z^2 - \frac{\sigma\sqrt{t}}{2}z} \, dz = \sqrt{2\pi} \, e^{\sigma^2 t/2}[N(z - \sigma\sqrt{t}) - .5] \quad (6.10)$$

Multiplying the integral by the constant $S/\sqrt{2\pi}$ from Equation (6.6), the general form of Equation (6.6) to be evaluated becomes

$$E(R) = Se^{\sigma^2 t/2}[N(z - \sigma\sqrt{t}) - .5] - BEP[N(b) - N(a)]$$

Letting there be an interval from $z = a$ to $z = b$ and letting $c = \sigma\sqrt{t}$, the $-.5$ constants cancel out, and the solution becomes

$$E(R) = Se^{c^2/2}[N(b-c) - N(a-c)] - BEP[N(b) - N(a)] \quad (6.11)$$

And the full equation for expected results of purchasing Calls is

$$E(R) \begin{cases} -P_{PC}[N(b) - N(a)] & \text{for } z \leq z_{K_{PC}} \\ Se^{c^2/2}(N^*) - BEP[N(b) - N(a)] & \text{for } z > z_{K_{PC}} \end{cases}$$

where

$$N^* = N(b-c) - N(a-c) \quad (6.12)$$

Since Equation (6.11) was developed for purchased Calls, the variable portion of the results function has a *positive slope* (upward and to the right). For results functions with *negative slopes* (purchased Puts, sold Calls, etc.), the expression for the variable portion is simply the reverse of Equation (6.11).

$$E(R) = BEP[N(b) - N(a)] - Se^{c^2/2}[N(b-c) - N(a-c)] \quad (6.13)$$

MAXIMUM GAINS AND LOSSES

Before moving on to the solved examples, it should be noted that maximum gains and losses set forth in Chapter 3 are the *theoretical* limits. While the maximum gain for purchasing Calls and the maximum loss for selling Calls are theoretically unlimited, a practical or *statistical* limit exists at a stock price that is plus 4 standard deviations from the current price. Likewise, the maximum gain for purchasing Puts and the maximum loss for selling Puts, while theoretically limited to an amount equal to the break-even stock price (stock worthless at expiration), has a statistical limit at a stock price that is 4 standard deviations below the current stock price. For the Cisco options quoted on July 11, 2003, the limits are calculated by

At +4 standard deviations,

$$\ln\left(\frac{x}{S}\right) = 4\sigma\sqrt{t} = 4(.398)\sqrt{\frac{34}{365}} = .4859$$

And since $x/S = e^{.4859}$, therefore,

$$x = 1.62564S = 30.19$$

At −4 standard deviations,

$$\frac{x}{S} = e^{-.4859} \quad \text{and} \quad x = 11.42$$

Based on the foregoing, the statistical maximum gain for purchasing Calls and the statistical maximum loss for selling Calls would occur when the Cisco stock price was $30.19 at expiration. Additionally, the statistical maximum gain for purchasing Puts and the statistical maximum loss for selling Puts would occur when the Cisco stock price was $11.42 at expiration. The same range holds true for any combination of Cisco options purchased or sold on July 12, 2003 (see information accompanying Figure 6–1 below). The probabilities set forth in the following examples are based on the $11.42 to $30.19 range of prices at expiration. When applicable, G_{max} and L_{max} will refer to the *statistical* maximums and minimums.

EXPECTED RESULTS FOR PURCHASED CALLS

Table 6–2 contains quotes for the most active Call options for Cisco Systems, Inc., on July 11, 2003. Recall from Chapter 3 that *market* means

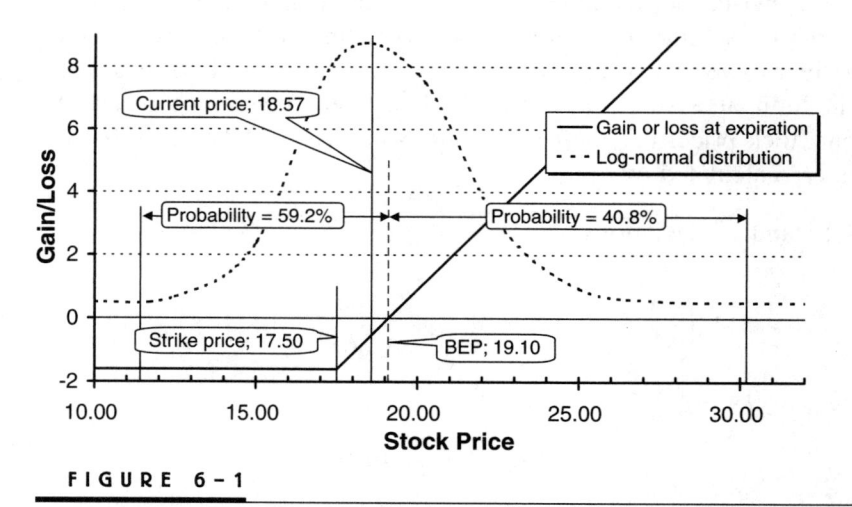

$$\text{Market} = \frac{\text{last} + 10(\text{bid}) + 10(\text{ask})}{21}$$

FIGURE 6-1

Purchasing a $1.60 Cisco Call with a strike price of 17.5

TABLE 6-2

Cisco Systems, Inc., August 2003 Calls
Call option prices on July 11, 2003

Strike	Bid	Ask	Last	Market
5.00	13.50	13.70	12.80	13.56
7.50	11.00	11.20	10.40	11.07
10.00	8.50	8.70	8.70	8.60
12.50	6.00	6.20	6.10	6.10
15.00	3.60	3.80	3.60	3.70
17.50	1.55	1.65	1.60	1.60
20.00	0.40	0.45	0.45	0.43
22.50	0.10	0.15	0.10	0.12

Source (data): E*Trade.

Figure 6–1 shows the particulars of purchasing the August 2003 17.5 Call for $1.60. The equivalent values of other variables relating to x on the x scale in Figure 6–1 are shown in Table 6–3.

In all examples, plus and minus 4 standard deviations is used to encompass the entire probability spectrum. As may be seen, plus and minus 4 standard deviations from the current price of $18.57 encompasses all potential stock prices at expiration from $11.42 to $30.19. This table is applicable to all solutions for the Cisco options.

First, we calculate the time variables, which will be the same for all examples having the same trade and expiration dates.

$$t = \frac{34}{365} = .093151$$

$$c = \sigma\sqrt{t} = .398(.30521) = .12147$$

Next, we begin the calculations specific to purchasing Calls.

TABLE 6-3

Equivalent values for Figure 6–1

x	11.42	12.90	14.56	16.45	**18.57**	20.97	23.68	26.73	30.19
x/S	0.615	0.695	0.784	0.886	**1**	1.129	1.275	1.440	1.626
$\ln(x/S)$	−0.486	−0.364	−0.243	−0.121	**0**	0.121	0.243	0.364	0.486
z	−4	−3	−2	−1	**0**	1	2	3	4

$$BEP = K_{PC} + P_{PC} = 17.50 + 1.60 = 19.10$$

$$L_{max} = -P_{PC} = -1.60$$

$$G_{max} = 30.19 - BEP = 11.09$$

The results function for purchasing Calls is Equation (3.16):

$$R = f(x) = \begin{cases} -P_{PC} & \text{for } x \le K_{PC} \\ x - BEP & \text{for } x > K_{PC} \end{cases}$$

And the expected results are given by Equation (6.12).

$$E(R) = \begin{cases} -P_{PC}[N(b) - N(a)] & \text{for } -4 < z \le z_{K_{PC}} \\ Se^{c^2/2}(N^*) - BEP[N(b) - N(a)] & \text{for } z_{K_{PC}} < z < 4 \end{cases}$$

where $N^* = N(b - c) - N(a - c)$.

For purchasing Calls, the interval R_1 is the fixed-loss interval for which $a = -4$ and $b = z_{K_{PC}}$ ($x < 17.50$).

$$z_{K_{PC}} = \frac{\ln\left(\frac{K_{PC}}{S}\right)}{c} = \frac{\ln\left(\frac{17.50}{18.57}\right)}{.12147} = -.48857$$

The probability that x will wind up in the R_1 interval is given by

$$N(b) - N(a)$$

where

$$N(b) = N(-.48857) = .31257$$

$$N(a) = N(-4) = .00003$$

Therefore, the probability that x will be less than 17.50 is 31.3 percent, and the expected result for the R_1 interval is

$$E(R_1) = -P_{PC}[N(b) - N(a)] = -1.6(.31254) = -.50$$

For purchasing Calls, the interval R_2 is the variable loss interval for which $a = $ and $z_{K_{PC}}$ and $b = z_{BEP}$ ($17.50 \le x \le 19.10$).

$$z_{BEP} = \frac{\ln\left(\frac{BEP}{S}\right)}{c} = \frac{\ln\left(\frac{19.10}{18.57}\right)}{.12147} = .23167$$

The probability that x will wind up in the R_2 interval is given by

$$N(b) - N(a)$$

where

$$N(b) = N(.23167) = .59160$$

$$N(a) = N(-.48857) = .31257$$

Therefore, the probability that x will lie between 17.50 and 19.10 is 27.9 percent. The R_2 calculations necessary for Equation (6.11) are

$$N(b - c) = N(.23167 - .12147) = N(.11020) = .54388$$

$$N(a - c) = N(-.48857 - .12147) = N(-.61004) = .27092$$

$$N(b - c) - N(a - c) = .54388 - .27092 = .27296$$

$$Se^{c^2/2} = 18.57e^{.00738} = 18.57(1.00741) = 18.70760$$

Substituting the preceding quantities into Equation (6.11), we have

$$E(R_2) = 18.7076(.27296) - 19.1(.59160 - .31257) = -.223$$

For purchasing Calls, the interval R_3 is the variable gain interval for which $a = z_{BEP}$ and $b = 4$ ($x \geq 19.10$). The probability that x will wind up in the R_3 interval is given by

$$N(b) - N(a)$$

where

$$N(b) = N(4) = .99997$$

$$N(a) = N(.23167) = .59160$$

Therefore, the probability that x will be greater than 19.10 is 40.8 percent. Since R_3 is the variable gain interval, the probability of a gain

p_G is also 40.8 percent. The R_3 calculations necessary for Equation (6.11) are

$$N(b - c) = N(4 - .12147) = N(3.87853) = .99995$$

$$N(a - c) = N(.23167 - .12147) = N(.11020) = .54388$$

$$N(b - c) - N(a - c) = .99995 - .54388 = .45607$$

Substituting the preceding quantities into Equation (6.11), we have

$$E(R_3) = 18.7076(.45607) - 19.1(.99997 - .59160) = .732$$

The overall expected results are

$$E(R) = E(R_1) + E(R_2) + E(R_3)$$

$$E(R) = -.50 - .223 + 732 = .009$$

Thus, purchasing this Call over the long run will result in a $0.01 gain per trade. Not particularly exciting. Let's check the *MA* for this trade. From Chapter 4, we have

$$MA = p_G\left(\frac{G}{L} + 1\right) - 1 = .40837\left(1 + \frac{1.79249}{1.22217}\right) - 1 = .73\%$$

Optimal f and *RTN* are produced by *Expectation.exe* using the methods covered in Chapter 4.

$$\text{Optimal } f = .25\%$$

$$RTN = 1.00001$$

What about the other Calls in Table 6–2? Table 6–4 compares the purchased Call just investigated with other Calls from Table 6–2.

Sometimes the calculations shown in the text may differ from the solutions in the tables for the same variable (produced by the computer program) owing to rounding and truncating.

As may be seen from Table 6–4, the Call with the largest *MA* is the 5 Call at $13.56. But at only 8.85 percent *MA* and an *RTN* of 1.00212, this option is not really a candidate for trading. Note how close the theoretical prices (Black-Scholes) are to the market prices.

TABLE 6-4

Cisco Systems, Inc., August 2003 Calls

Comparison of expected results of purchasing on July 11, 2003

Strike	Market price	Black-Scholes	$E(R)$	p_G	MA	f^*	RTN
5.00	13.56	13.58	0.15	0.502	8.84%	2.89%	1.00212
7.50	11.07	11.08	0.14	0.500	8.22%	2.69%	1.00184
10.00	8.60	8.59	0.11	0.495	6.37%	2.09%	1.00112
12.50	6.10	6.09	0.11	0.495	6.38%	2.10%	1.00113
15.00	3.70	3.63	0.04	0.477	2.08%	0.70%	1.00012
17.50	1.60	1.53	0.01	0.408	0.73%	0.25%	1.00001
20.00	0.43	0.40	0.00	0.216	N/A	N/A	N/A
22.50	0.12	0.06	(0.05)	0.052	N/A	N/A	N/A

THE E(R)-VOLATILITY CURVE

In Chapter 5 we introduced the Greeks, which measured the sensitivity of an option's price to other variables such as volatility. Since we are now concentrating on expected results, it helpful to understand the relationship between $E(R)$ and volatility. We will call this relationship *omega*—another Greek. Just as vega measures the degree to which an option's price will vary given a change in volatility, omega measures the likely change in $E(R)$ given a change in volatility. In short, omega tells us how $E(R)$ will likely react if we are wrong in our estimate of volatility.

The $E(R)$-volatility curve is based on fitting a parabola to three data points consisting of our original volatility estimate and two additional volatility values 80 percent above and below the original estimate together with the associated values of $E(R)$. Curve-fitting tests of numerous data points ranging from 20 to 180 percent of the original volatility estimates indicated a parabola is the best fit with an R^2 very close to 1 (see Chapter 8 for fitting a parabola and determining goodness of fit). Omega is the slope of the line that is tangent to the $E(R)$-volatility curve at the original volatility estimate and indicates the relative change (in both direction and magnitude) for a given change in volatility.

For the purchased Call just analyzed, the equation of the $E(R)$-volatility curve is

$$E(R) = 1.5789\sigma^2 + .9185\sigma - .6067$$

And its derivative is

$$\frac{dE(R)}{d\sigma} = 3.1578\sigma + .9185$$

At .398 (the original volatility estimate), omega (the slope) is

$$\frac{dE(R)}{d\sigma} = 3.1578(.398) + .9185 = 2.18$$

Using the point-slope form of a linear first-order equation from Chapter 8, the *intercept* for the tangent line is $-.94$, and the equation of the tangent is

$$E(R) = 2.18\sigma - .86$$

An omega of 2.18 means that for an *increase* in volatility, $E(R)$ will increase at a rate 2.18 times as fast as the increase in volatility. For a *decrease* in volatility, $E(R)$ will decrease 2.18 times as fast. Therefore, when purchasing Calls, it is far better to *underestimate* volatility. The omegas for the solved strategies were produced by *Expectation.exe*.

THE BERNOULLI EQUIVALENT

Recalling that Bernoulli outcomes mean only two outcomes of an event are possible, that is, win-lose, success-failure, and so on, it is possible to construct a *Bernoulli equivalent* of an options strategy even though there are multiple outcomes. The value of a gain G is calculated by summing the gains in the gain intervals and dividing by the sum of the gain probabilities. Likewise, the value of a loss L is calculated by summing the losses in the loss intervals and dividing by the sum of the loss probabilities. For the purchased Call analyzed earlier, we have

$$G = \frac{E(R_3)}{p(R_3)} = \frac{.732}{.40837} = 1.79249$$

$$L = \frac{E(R_1) + E(R_2)}{p(R_1) + p(R_2)}$$

$$= \frac{.5 + .223}{.31254 + .27903} = 1.22217$$

Note that the preceding values for G and L were used in the prior calculation of MA. Table 6–5 shows the Bernoulli equivalent for Figure 6–1.

Although the Bernoulli equivalent is suitable for calculating MA, it *cannot* be used for determining optimal f, as explained in Chapter 4. In

TABLE 6-5

Bernoulli equivalent for Figure 6-1

	Prob.	Average result	Expected value
Gain (underlying is greater than or equal to $19.10)	0.408	1.792	0.732
Loss (underlying is less than $19.10)	0.592	−1.222	−0.723
The expected result of this trade is			0.009

the following solved examples of potential option trades, optimal f, RTN, and omega were determined by running *Expectation.exe*.

EXPECTED RESULTS OF PURCHASING PUTS

Table 6–6 contains the Cisco Puts expiring in August 2003 trading on July 11, 2003, which had a transaction that day. Choosing the 17.50 Put priced at $0.50, we get the following:

$$BEP = K_{PP} - P_{PP} = 17.50 - .50 = 17.00$$

$$G_{max} = BEP - 11.42 = 5.58$$

$$L_{max} = -P_{PP} = -.50$$

The results function at expiration for purchasing Puts is Equation (3.18):

$$R = f(x) = \begin{cases} -P_{PP} & \text{for } x \geq K_{PP} \\ BEP - x & \text{for } x < K_{PP} \end{cases}$$

And the expected results are

$$E(R) = \begin{cases} -P_{PP}[N(b) - N(a)] & \text{for } -4 < z \leq z_{K_{PP}} \\ BEP[N(b) - N(a)] - Se^{c^2/2}(N*) & \text{for } z_{K_{PP}} < z < 4 \end{cases}$$

where

TABLE 6-6

Cisco Systems, Inc., August 2003 Puts
Put option prices on July 11, 2003

Strike	Bid	Ask	Last	Market
15.00	0.05	0.15	0.10	0.10
17.50	0.45	0.55	0.55	0.50
20.00	1.80	1.90	1.85	1.85
22.50	3.90	4.10	4.00	4.00
25.00	6.30	6.50	6.50	6.40
27.50	8.80	9.00	10.00	8.95
30.00	11.30	11.50	12.50	11.45

Source (data): E*Trade.

$$N^* = N(b - c) - N(a - c) \qquad (6.14)$$

Figure 6–2 shows the particulars for purchasing this Cisco Put.

Note that the formula for the variable portion of $E(R)$ for purchasing Puts (negative slope) is Equation (6.13)—just the reverse of Equation (6.11) for the variable portion of $E(R)$ for purchasing Calls (positive slope). For purchasing Puts, R_1 is the variable gain interval where $x \leq 17$. R_2 is the variable loss interval where $17 \leq x \leq 17.5$. R_3 is the fixed loss interval where $x \geq 17.5$.

The z value of the break-even stock price BEP is

$$z_{BEP} = \frac{\ln\left(\dfrac{BEP}{S}\right)}{c} = \frac{\ln\left(\dfrac{17}{18.57}\right)}{.12147} = -.72721$$

The probability of a gain (R_1 interval) is given by

$$P_G = N(z_{BEP}) - N(-4) = N(-.72721) - .00003 = .23352$$

And the probability of a loss ($R_2 + R_3$ intervals) is

$$p_L = 1 - p_G = .76648$$

Solving Equation (6.14), we have

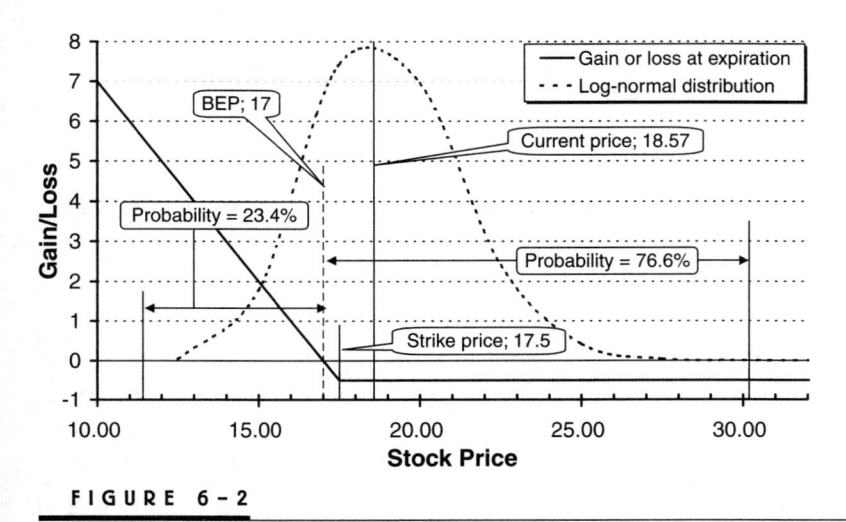

FIGURE 6-2

Purchasing a $0.50 Cisco Put with a strike price of 17.5

$$E(R_1) = 17(.23355) - 18.7076(.19801) = .266$$

$$E(R_2) = 17(.07902) - 18.7076(.07289) = -.020$$

$$E(R_3) = -.5(.6874) = -.344$$

$$E(R) = .266 - .02 - .344 = -.098$$

Table 6–7 shows the Bernoulli equivalent for Figure 6–2. The expected result of this trade is a *loss* of $0.10. Since the expectation is negative, no further calculations need be made. Table 6–8 was prepared showing a comparison of the purchased Put just analyzed (highlighted) with other purchased August 2003 Puts from Table 6–6.

This time there are *no* Puts with a positive *MA*—thus no candidates for a trade. Note that the Puts are somewhat *overpriced* relative to the Calls (comparison of market prices with theoretical prices). Clearly, no trader would want to be a buyer of these naked options—particularly the Puts.

EXPECTED RESULTS OF SELLING CALLS

Choosing the same Call just analyzed for a purchase and selling it, we have

$$BEP = K_{SC} + P_{SC} = 17.50 + 1.60 = 19.10$$

$$G_{max} = P_{SC} = 1.60$$

$$L_{max} = BEP - 30.19 = -11.09$$

Figure 6–3 shows the results of selling the 17.5 Cisco August 2003 Call for $1.60.

TABLE 6-7

Bernoulli equivalent for Figure 6-2

	Prob.	Average result	Expected value
Gain (underlying is less than or equal to $17)	0.234	1.137	$0.26
Loss (underlying is greater than $17)	0.766	−0.475	−$0.36
The expected result of this trade is			−$0.10

TABLE 6-8

Cisco Systems, Inc., August 2003 Puts

Comparison of expected results of purchasing on July 11, 2003

Strike	Market price	Black-Scholes	E(R)	p_G	MA	f*	RTN
15.00	0.10	0.03	(0.07)	0.035	N/A	N/A	N/A
17.50	0.50	0.43	(0.10)	0.234	N/A	N/A	N/A
20.00	1.85	1.79	(0.13)	0.425	N/A	N/A	N/A
22.50	4.00	3.95	(0.14)	0.488	N/A	N/A	N/A
25.00	6.40	6.39	(0.10)	0.505	N/A	N/A	N/A
27.50	8.95	8.88	(0.16)	0.496	N/A	N/A	N/A
30.00	11.45	11.37	(0.16)	0.496	N/A	N/A	N/A

FIGURE 6-3

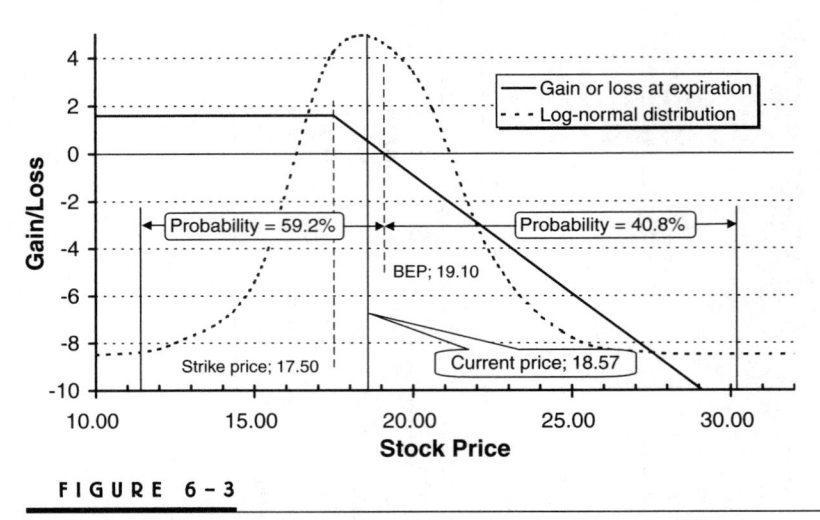

Selling a $1.60 Cisco Call with a strike price of 17.5

The results function at expiration for selling Calls is Equation (3.20).

$$R = f(x) = \begin{cases} P_{SC} & \text{for } x \leq K_{SC} \\ BEP - x & \text{for } x > K_{SC} \end{cases}$$

And the expected results are

$$E(R) = \begin{cases} P_{SC}[N(b) - N(a)] & \text{for } -4 < z \geq z_{K_{SC}} \\ BEP[N(b) - N(a)] - Se^{c^2/2}(N^*) & \text{for } z_{K_{SC}} < z < 4 \end{cases}$$

where

$$N^* = N(b - c) - N(a - c) \qquad (6.15)$$

For selling Calls, R_1 is the fixed gain interval where $x \leq 17.5$. R_2 is the variable gain interval where $17.5 < x \leq 19.10$. R_3 is the variable loss interval where $x > 19.10$.

The probability of a gain ($R_1 + R_2$ intervals) is given by

$$p_G = N(z_{BEP}) - N(-4) = .59160 - .00003 = .59157$$

And the probability of a loss (R_3 interval) is

$$p_L = 1 - p_G = .40834$$

Solving Equation (6.15), we have

$$E(R_1) = 1.6(.31254) = .500$$

$$E(R_2) = 19.1(.27903) - 18.7076(.27296) = .223$$

$$E(R_3) = 19.1(.40837) - 18.7076(.45607) = -.732$$

$$E(R) = .5 + .223 - .732 = -.009$$

$$\text{Omega} = -2.18$$

Table 6–9 shows the Bernoulli equivalent for Figure 6–3. The expected result of this trade is a *loss* of $0.01. Since the expectation is negative, no further calculations need be made. Table 6–10 was prepared showing a comparison of the sold Call just analyzed with other sold Calls from Table 6–2.

The only sold Call with a positive expectation is the 22.5 Call at $0.12, with an expected return of 1.00471. Let's look at selling Puts.

EXPECTED RESULTS OF SELLING PUTS

Figure 6–4 shows the results of selling a 17.5 Put for $0.50. Selling this Put, we have

$$BEP = K_{SP} - P_{SP} = 17.50 - .50 = 17.00$$

$$G_{max} = P_{SP} = .50$$

$$L_{max} = 11.42 - BEP = -5.58$$

The results function for selling Puts is Equation (3.23).

TABLE 6-9

Bernoulli equivalent for Figure 6-3

	Prob.	Average result	Expected value
Gain (underlying is less than or equal to $19.10)	0.592	1.222	0.720
Loss (underlying is greater than $19.10)	0.408	−1.793	−0.730
The expected result of this trade is			−0.010

TABLE 6-10

Cisco Systems, Inc., August 2003 Calls

Comparison of expected results of selling on July 11, 2003

Strike	Market price	Black-Scholes	E(R)	p_G	MA	f*	RTN
5.00	13.56	13.58	0.15	0.498	N/A	N/A	N/A
7.50	11.07	11.08	(0.14)	0.500	N/A	N/A	N/A
10.00	8.60	8.59	(0.11)	0.505	N/A	N/A	N/A
12.50	6.10	6.09	(0.11)	0.505	N/A	N/A	N/A
15.00	3.70	3.63	(0.04)	0.523	N/A	N/A	N/A
17.50	1.60	1.53	(0.01)	0.592	N/A	N/A	N/A
20.00	0.43	0.40	0.00	0.784	0.0001	12.00%	1.00000
22.50	0.12	0.06	0.05	0.948	0.0404	13.20%	1.00471

Determining Expected Results of Options Trades: Naked Options and Basic Spreads   207

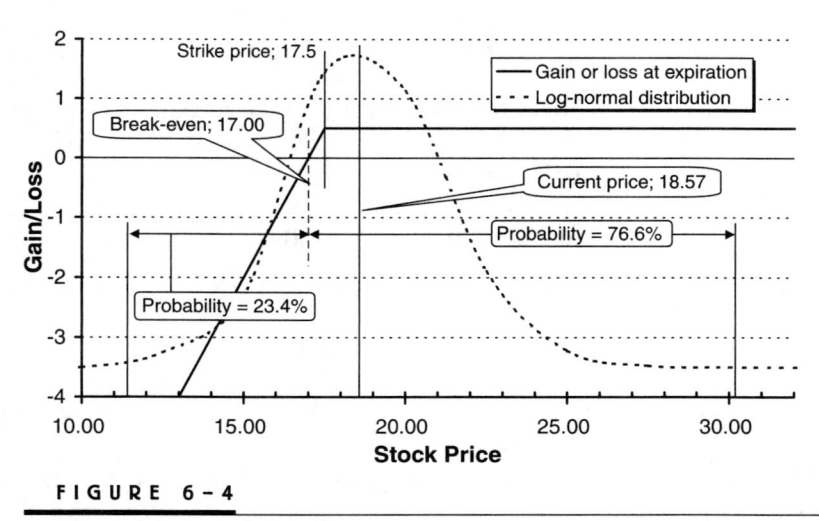

FIGURE 6-4
Selling a $0.50 Cisco Put with a strike price of 17.5

$$R = f(x) = \begin{cases} P_{SP} & \text{for } x \geq K_{SP} \\ x - BEP & \text{for } x < K_{SP} \end{cases}$$

And the expected results are

$$E(R) = \begin{cases} P_{SP}[N(b) - N(a)] & \text{for } z_{K_{SP}} < z < 4 \\ Se^{c^2/2}(N^*) - BEP[N(b) - N(a)] & \text{for } -4 < x < z_{K_{SP}} \end{cases}$$

where

$$N^* = N(b - c) - N(a - c) \qquad (6.16)$$

For selling Puts, R_1 is the variable loss interval where $x \leq 17$. R_2 is the variable gain interval where $17 < x \leq 17.5$. R_3 is the fixed gain interval where $x > 17.5$.

The probability of a gain (R_2 and R_3 intervals) is given by

$$p_G = N(4) - N(z_{BEP}) = .99997 - .23355 = .76642$$

And the probability of a loss (R_1 interval) is

$$p_L = 1 - p_G = .23358$$

Solving Equation (6.16), we have

$$E(R_1) = 18.7076(.19801) - 17(.23352) = -.266$$

$$E(R_2) = 18.7076(.07289) - 17(.07902) = .020$$

$$E(R_3) = .5(.6874) = .343$$

$$E(R) = -.266 + .020 + .343 = .097$$

$$\text{Optimal } f = 11.42\%$$

$$RTN = 1.00615$$

$$\text{Omega} = -1.48$$

Table 6–11 shows the Bernoulli equivalent for Figure 6–4. The *MA* of the trade is given by

$$MA = p_G\left(1 + \frac{G}{L}\right) - 1 = .76642\left(1 + \frac{.47389}{1.13675}\right) - 1 = 8.59\%$$

Table 6–12 was prepared showing a comparison of the sold Put just analyzed with other sold August 2003 Puts from Table 6–6. All the sold Puts have positive expected results.

EXPECTED RESULTS OF COVERED CALLS

Simultaneously selling the 17.5 Call for $1.60 and purchasing 100 shares of Cisco stock for $18.57 per share sets up a covered Call strategy. The basic values are

TABLE 6-11

Bernoulli equivalent for Figure 6-4

	Prob.	Average result	Expected value
Gain (underlying is greater than $17)	0.766	0.475	0.360
Loss (underlying is less than or equal to $17)	0.234	−1.137	−0.260
The expected result of this trade is			0.100

TABLE 6-12

Cisco Systems, Inc., August 2003 Puts

Comparison of expected results of selling on July 11, 2003

Strike	Market price	Black-Scholes	$E(R)$	p_G	MA	f^*	RTN
15.00	0.10	0.03	0.07	0.965	10.57%	6.70%	1.00478
17.50	0.50	0.43	0.10	0.766	8.64%	5.88%	1.00455
20.00	1.85	1.79	0.13	0.575	8.52%	4.46%	1.00293
22.50	4.00	3.95	0.14	0.512	8.39%	3.05%	1.00211
25.00	6.40	6.39	0.10	0.495	5.94%	1.99%	1.00099
27.50	8.95	8.88	0.16	0.505	9.43%	3.08%	1.00241
30.00	11.45	11.37	0.16	0.504	9.46%	3.09%	1.00242

$$BEP = S - P_{SC} = 18.57 - 1.60 = 16.97$$

$$G_{max} = K_{SC} + P_{SC} - S = 17.5 + 1.60 - 18.57 = .53$$

$$L_{max} = 11.42 - BEP = -5.55$$

The results function for a covered Call is Equation (3.26).

$$R = f(x) = \begin{cases} K_{SC} + P_{SC} - S & \text{for } x \geq K_{SC} \\ x - BEP & \text{for } x < K_{SC} \end{cases}$$

Figure 6–5 shows the results of this covered Call assuming the Cisco stock is sold on the expiration date. The expected results are

$$E(R) = \begin{cases} (K_{SC} + P_{SC} - S)[N(b) - N(a)] & \text{for } x \geq K_{SC} \\ Se^{c^2/2}(N^*) - BEP[N(b) - N(a)] & \text{for } x < K_{SC} \end{cases}$$

where

$$N^* = N(b - c) - N(a - c) \tag{6.17}$$

For covered Calls, R_1 is the variable loss interval where $x \leq 16.97$. R_2 is the variable gain interval where $16.97 < x \leq 17.5$. R_3 is the fixed gain interval where $x > 17.5$.

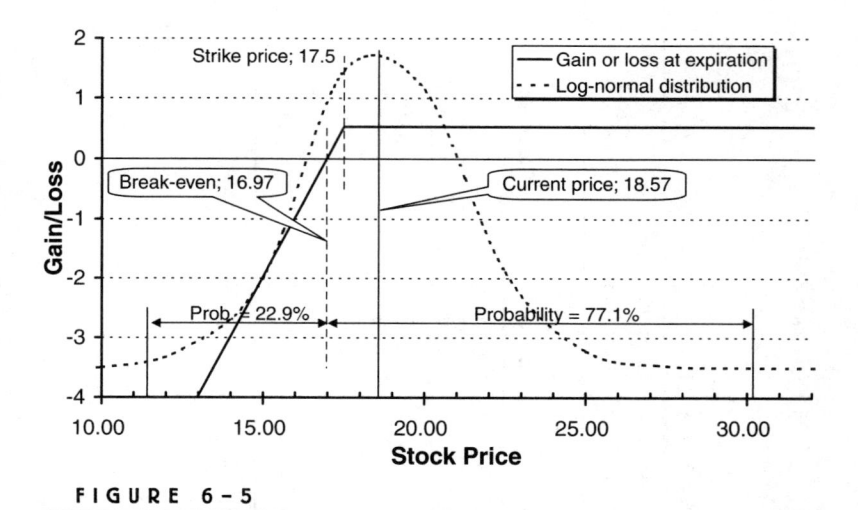

FIGURE 6-5

Covered Call: buy stock at $18.57; sell 17.5 Call at $1.60

The probability of a gain (R_2 and R_3 intervals) is given by

$$p_G = N(4) - N(z_{BEP}) = .99997 - .22912 = .77085$$

And the probability of a loss (R_1 interval) is

$$p_L = 1 - p_G = .22915$$

Solving Equation (6.17), we have

$$E(R_1) = 18.7076(.19399) - 16.97(.22909) = -.259$$

$$E(R_2) = 18.7076(.07691) - 16.97(.08345) = .023$$

$$E(R_3) = .53(.6874) = .364$$

$$E(R) = -.259 + .023 + .364 = .128$$

Optimal $f = 13.81\%$

$RTN = 1.00998$

Omega $= -1.48$

Table 6–13 shows the Bernoulli equivalent for Figure 6–5. The *MA* of the trade is given by

$$MA = p_G\left(1 + \frac{G}{L}\right) - 1 = .771\left(1 + \frac{.50195}{1.13100}\right) - 1 = 11.3\%$$

Table 6–14 shows a comparison of the covered Call just analyzed (highlighted) with other covered Call combinations from Table 6–2.

TABLE 6-13

Bernoulli equivalent for Figure 6-5

	Prob.	Average result	Expected value
Gain (underlying is greater than $16.97)	0.771	0.502	0.390
Loss (underlying is less than or equal to $16.97)	0.229	-1.127	-0.260
The expected result of this trade is			0.130

TABLE 6-14

Cisco Systems, Inc., August 2003 Calls
Comparison of covered Calls as of July 11, 2003

Strike	Market	E(R)	P_G	MA	f*	RTN
7.50	11.07	0.00	1.000	N/A	N/A	N/A
10.00	8.60	0.03	1.000	N/A	N/A	N/A
12.50	6.10	0.03	0.999	8.09%	8.01%	1.00239
15.00	3.70	0.10	0.966	15.07%	6.72%	1.00680
17.50	1.60	0.13	0.771	11.36%	5.89%	1.00632
20.00	0.43	0.14	0.576	9.21%	4.79%	1.00339
22.50	0.12	0.19	0.521	11.57%	4.15%	1.00392

EXPECTED RESULTS OF BULL CALL SPREAD

Choosing the bull Call spread consisting of purchasing the 5 Call for $13.56 and selling the 17.5 Call for $1.60 (from Table 6–1), we have

$$BEP = K_{PC} - P_{SC} + P_{PC} = 5 - 1.60 + 13.56 = 16.96$$

$$G_{max} = K_{SC} - BEP = 17.5 - 16.96 = .54$$

$$L_{max} = P_{SC} - P_{PC} = 1.60 - 13.56 = -11.96$$

The results are shown in Figure 6–6.

Although a trader theoretically can lose $11.96 on this trade, such a loss is extremely unlikely. At minus 4 standard deviations from the current price, the stock price at expiration would be $11.42, at which price the loss would be only $5.54. This is why knowing the probabilities is so important to trading success.

The results function for a bull Call spread is Equation (3.28).

$$R = f(x) = \begin{cases} P_{SC} - P_{PC} & \text{for } x \leq K_{PC} \\ x - BEP & \text{for } K_{PC} < x < K_{SC} \\ K_{SC} - BEP & \text{for } x \geq K_{SC} \end{cases}$$

And the expected results are

$$E(R) = \begin{cases} (P_{SC} - P_{PC})[N(b) - N(a)] & \text{for } -4 < z \leq z_{K_{PC}} \\ Se^{c^2/2}(N^*) - BEP[N(b) - N(a)] & \text{for } z_{K_{PC}} < z < z_{K_{SC}} \\ (K_{SC} - BEP)[N(b) - N(a)] & \text{for } z_{K_{SC}} \leq z < 4 \end{cases}$$

Determining Expected Results of Options Trades: Naked Options and Basic Spreads

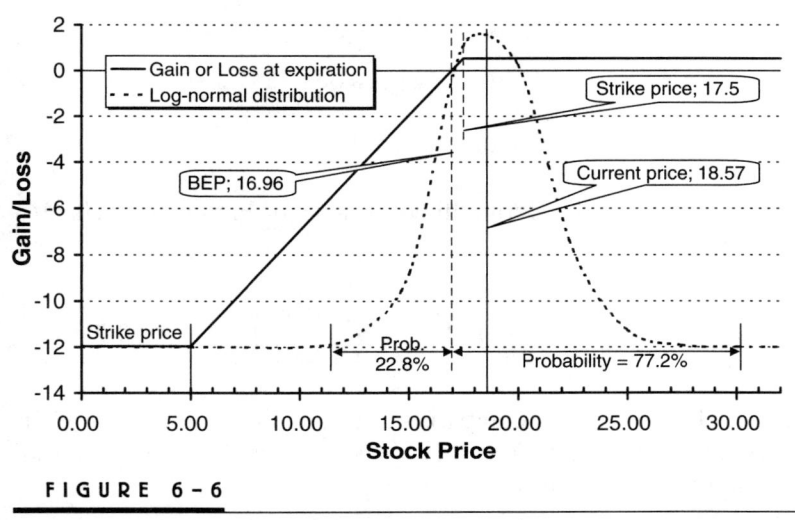

FIGURE 6-6

Bull Call spread: buy 5 Call at $13.56; sell 17.5 Call at $1.60

where

$$N^* = N(b - c) - N(a - c) \qquad (6.18)$$

When analyzing the basic spreads, there are four intervals of interest. For the bull Call spread, R_1 is the fixed loss interval where $x \leq 5$. R_2 is the variable loss interval where $5 < x \leq 16.96$. R_3 is the variable gain interval where $16.96 < x < 17.5$. R_4 is the fixed gain interval where $x \geq 17.5$.

The probability of a gain (R_3 and R_4 intervals) is given by

$$p_G = N(4) - N(z_{BEP}) = .99997 - .22765 = .77232$$

And the probability of a loss (R_1 and R_2 intervals) is

$$p_L = 1 - p_G = .22768$$

Solving Equation (6.18), we have

$$E(R_1) = -11.96(.00003) = 0$$

$$E(R_2) = 18.7076(.19268) - 16.96(.22765) = -.256$$

$$E(R_3) = 18.7076(.07824) - 16.96(.08492) = .023$$

$$E(R_4) = .54(.6874) = .371$$

$$E(R) = 0 - .256 + .023 + .371 = .138$$

$$\text{Optimal } f = 8.35\%$$

$$RTN = 1.00899$$

$$\text{Omega} = -1.48$$

Table 6–15 shows the Bernoulli equivalent for Figure 6–6. The *MA* of the trade is given by

$$MA = p_G\left(1 + \frac{G}{L}\right) - 1 = .772\left(1 + \frac{.51036}{1.12281}\right) - 1 = 12.29\%$$

Table 6–16 sets forth a comparison of other combinations of Calls making up bull Call spreads from the Calls listed in Table 6–2. Not all possible combinations are listed in Table 6–16.

EXPECTED RESULTS OF BEAR CALL SPREAD

Looking at the bear Call spread consisting of purchasing the 20 Call for $0.43 and selling the 17.5 Call for $1.60 (from Table 6–1), we have

$$BEP = K_{SC} + P_{SC} - P_{PC} = 17.5 + 1.6 - .43 = 18.67$$

$$G_{max} = P_{SC} - P_{PC} = 1.6 - .43 = 1.17$$

$$L_{max} = BEP - K_{PC} = 18.67 - 20 = -1.33$$

The results are shown in Figure 6–7.

The results function for a bear Call spread is Equation (3.30)

TABLE 6–15

Bernoulli equivalent for Figure 6–6

	Prob.	Average result	Expected value
Gain (underlying is greater than $16.96)	0.772	0.511	0.390
Loss (underlying is less than or equal to $16.96)	0.228	−1.125	−0.250
The expected result of this trade is			0.140

TABLE 6-16

Cisco Systems, Inc., August 2003 Calls

Comparison of bull Call spreads as of July 11, 2003

Purchased Call		Sold Call		$E(R)$	P_G	MA	f^*	RTN
Strike	Market	Strike	Market					
5.00	13.56	17.50	1.60	0.14	0.772	12.30%	8.35%	1.00899
5.00	13.56	20.00	0.43	0.15	0.578	9.91%	5.12%	1.00389
7.50	11.07	17.50	1.60	0.13	0.771	11.38%	10.55%	1.00929
7.50	11.07	20.00	0.43	0.14	0.576	9.22%	4.79%	1.00339
10.00	8.60	17.50	1.60	0.10	0.766	8.64%	11.43%	1.00615
10.00	8.60	20.00	0.43	0.11	0.571	7.16%	3.81%	1.00210
12.50	6.10	17.50	1.60	0.10	0.766	8.66%	11.49%	1.00619
12.50	6.10	20.00	0.43	0.11	0.571	7.17%	3.81%	1.00211
15.00	3.70	17.50	1.60	0.03	0.751	2.45%	4.76%	1.00063
17.50	1.60	20.00	0.43	0.01	0.482	1.09%	0.94%	1.00005

FIGURE 6-7

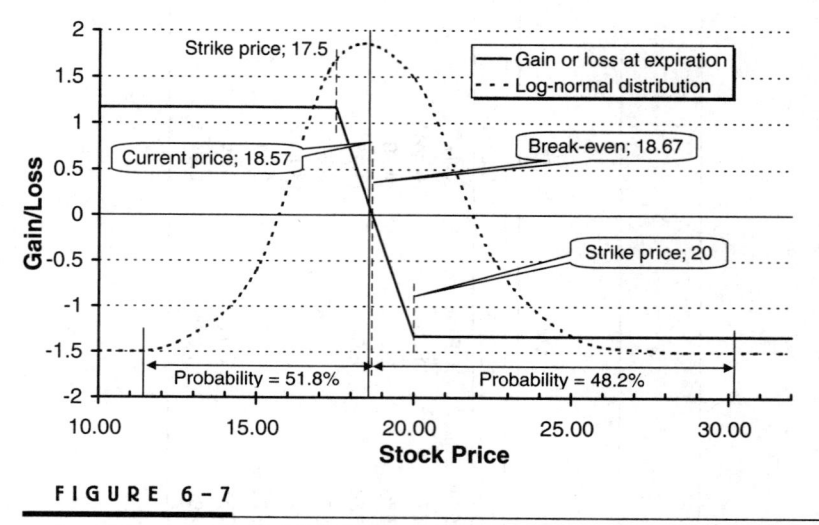

Bear Call spread: buy 20 Call at $0.43; sell 17.5 Call at $1.60

$$R = f(x) = \begin{cases} P_{SC} - P_{PC} & \text{for } x \leq K_{SC} \\ BEP - x & \text{for } K_{SC} < x < K_{PC} \\ BEP - K_{PC} & \text{for } x \geq K_{PC} \end{cases}$$

And the expected results are

$$E(R) = \begin{cases} (P_{SC} - P_{PC})[N(b) - N(a)] & \text{for } -4 < z \leq z_{K_{SC}} \\ BEP[N(b) - N(a)] - Se^{c^2/2}(N^*) & \text{for } z_{K_{SC}} < z < z_{K_{PC}} \\ (BEP - K_{PC})[N(b) - N(a)] & \text{for } z_{K_{PC}} \leq z < 4 \end{cases}$$

where

$$N^* = N(b - c) - N(a - c) \tag{6.19}$$

For the bear Call spread, R_1 is the fixed gain interval where $x \leq 17.5$. R_2 is the variable gain interval where $17.5 < x \leq 18.67$. R_3 is the variable loss interval where $18.67 < x < 20$. R_4 is the fixed loss interval where $x \geq 20$. The probability of a gain (R_1 and R_2 intervals) is given by

$$p_G = N(z_{BEP}) - N(-4) = .51763 - .00003 = .5176$$

And the probability of a loss (R_3 and R_4 intervals) is

Determining Expected Results of Options Trades: Naked Options and Basic Spreads 217

$$p_L = 1 - p_G = .4824$$

Solving Equation (6.19) gives

$$E(R_1) = 1.17(.31254) = .366$$

$$E(R_2) = 18.67(.20506) - 18.7076(.19829) = .119$$

$$E(R_3) = 18.67(.21168) - 18.7076(.21846) = -.135$$

$$E(R_4) = -1.33(.27066) = -.356$$

$$E(R) = .366 + .119 - .135 - .356 = -.006$$

Table 6–17 shows the Bernoulli equivalent for Figure 6–7.

Since the expectation is negative, no further calculations are necessary. The *MA* of the trade is given by

$$MA = p_G\left(1 + \frac{G}{L}\right) - 1 = .518\left(1 + \frac{.93702}{1.01783}\right) - 1 = -.5\%$$

Not only is the *MA* for this bear Call spread negative, there also are *no* combinations of Calls (from Table 6–1) that produce a positive *MA*. The trader should ignore bear Call spreads for Cisco on July 11, 2003.

EXPECTED RESULTS OF BULL PUT SPREAD

Considering the bull Put spread consisting of purchasing the 15 Put at $0.10 and selling the 30 Put for $11.45 (from Table 6–3), we have

TABLE 6-17

Bernoulli equivalent for Figure 6-7

	Prob.	Average result	Expected value
Gain (underlying is less than or equal to $18.67)	0.518	0.936	0.480
Loss (underlying is greater than $18.67)	0.482	−1.026	−0.490
The expected result of this trade is			−0.010

$$BEP = K_{SP} - P_{SP} + P_{PP} = 30 - 11.45 + .10 = 18.65$$

$$G_{\max} = P_{SP} - P_{PP} = 11.45 - .10 = 11.35$$

$$L_{\max} = K_{PP} - BEP = 15 - 18.65 = -3.65$$

Figure 6–8 shows the results of establishing this bull Put spread. Although a trader theoretically can make $11.35 on this trade, such a gain is extremely unlikely. It requires a stock price of more than $30.00 to be in the fixed gain interval of $11.35, which is almost plus 4 standard deviations from the current stock price. Most of the action will take place much closer to the break-even stock price of $18.65 Again, this is why knowing the probabilities is so important to trading success.

The results function for a bull Put spread is Equation (3.32).

$$R = f(x) = \begin{cases} K_{PP} - BEP & \text{for } x \leq K_{PP} \\ x - BEP & \text{for } K_{PP} < x < K_{SP} \\ P_{SP} - P_{PP} & \text{for } x \geq K_{SP} \end{cases}$$

And the expected results are

$$E(R) = \begin{cases} (K_{PP} - BEP)[N(b) - N(a)] & \text{for } -4 < z \leq z_{K_{PP}} \\ Se^{c^2/2}(N^*) - BEP[N(b) - N(a)] & \text{for } z_{K_{PP}} < z < z_{K_{SP}} \\ (P_{SP} - P_{PP})[N(b) - N(a)] & \text{for } z_{K_{SP}} \leq z < 4 \end{cases}$$

where

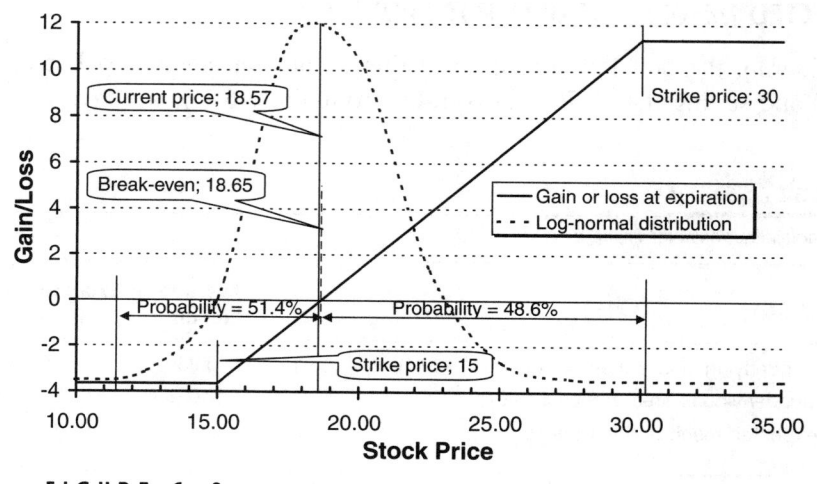

FIGURE 6-8

Bull Put spread: buy 15 Put at $0.10; sell 30 Put at $11.45

Determining Expected Results of Options Trades: Naked Options and Basic Spreads

$$N^* = N(b - c) - N(a - c) \quad (6.20)$$

Again, there are four intervals of interest. R_1 is the fixed loss interval where $x \leq 15$. R_2 is the variable loss interval where $15 < x \leq 18.65$. R_3 is the variable gain interval where $18.65 < x < 30$. R_4 is the fixed gain interval where $x \geq 30$.

The probability of a gain (R_3 and R_4 intervals) is given by

$$p_G = N(4) - N(z_{BEP}) = .99997 - .51412 = .48585$$

And the probability of a loss (R_1 and R_2 intervals) is

$$p_L = 1 - p_G = .51415$$

Solving Equation (6.20) gives

$$E(R_1) = -3.65(.03938) = -.143$$

$$E(R_2) = 18.7076(.43558) - 18.65(.47471) = -.705$$

$$E(R_3) = 18.7076(.53424) - 18.65(.48584) = .933$$

$$E(R_4) = 11.35(.00001) = 0$$

$$E(R) = -.143 - .705 + .933 + 0 = .085$$

Optimal $f = 1.75\%$

$RTN = 1.00074$

Omega $= 1.05$

Table 6–18 shows the Bernoulli equivalent for Figure 6–8. The *MA* of the trade is given by

TABLE 6-18

Bernoulli equivalent for Figure 6-8

	Prob.	Average result	Expected value
Gain (underlying is greater than $18.65)	0.486	1.921	0.930
Loss (underlying is less than or equal to $18.657)	0.514	−1.650	−0.850
The expected result of this trade is			−0.080

$$MA = p_G\left(1 + \frac{G}{L}\right) - 1 = .48585\left(1 + \frac{1.92035}{1.64942}\right) - 1 = 5.15\%$$

Table 6–19 sets forth a comparison of certain other combinations of Puts making up bull Put spreads from the Puts listed in Table 6–6. The spread just analyzed is highlighted.

EXPECTED RESULTS OF BEAR PUT SPREAD

Constructing a bear Put spread by purchasing the 25 Put for $6.40 and selling the 22.5 Put for $4.00, we have

$$BEP = K_{PP} - P_{PP} + P_{SP} = 25.00 - 6.40 + 4.00 = 22.60$$

$$G_{max} = BEP - K_{SP} = 22.60 - 22.50 = .10$$

$$L_{max} = P_{SP} - P_{PP} = 4.00 - 6.40 = -2.40$$

Figure 6–9 shows the results of establishing this bear Put spread. Again, a trader theoretically can lose $2.40 on this trade, but such a loss is extremely unlikely. It requires a stock price of more than $25.00 to be in the fixed loss interval of $2.40, which is almost plus 2.5 standard deviations from the current price. Most of the action will take place much closer to the current stock price of $18.57. The probabilities tell the real story.

For the bear Put spread, R_1 is the fixed gain interval where $x \leq 22.5$. R_2 is the variable gain interval where $22.5 < x \leq 22.6$. R_3 is the variable loss interval where $22.6 < x < 25$. R_4 is the fixed loss interval where $x \geq 25$.

The results function for a bear Put spread is Equation (3.34).

$$R = f(x) = \begin{cases} BEP - K_{SP} & \text{for } x \leq K_{SP} \\ BEP - x & \text{for } K_{SP} < x < K_{PP} \\ P_{SP} - P_{PP} & \text{for } x \geq K_{PP} \end{cases}$$

And the expected results are

$$E(R) = \begin{cases} (BEP) - K_{SP})[N(b) - N(a)] & \text{for } -4 < z \leq z_{K_{SP}} \\ BEP[N(b) - N(a)] - Se^{c^2/2}(N^*) & \text{for } z_{K_{SP}} < z < z_{K_{PP}} \\ (P_{SP} - P_{PP})[N(b) - N(a)] & \text{for } z_{K_{PP}} \leq z < 4 \end{cases}$$

where

TABLE 6-19

Cisco Systems, Inc., August 2003 Puts

Comparison of bull Put spreads as of July 11, 2003

Purchased Put		Sold Put		E(R)	P_G	MA	f*	RTN
Strike	Market	Strike	Market					
15.00	0.10	17.50	0.50	0.03	0.751	2.45%	4.76%	1.00063
15.00	0.10	20.00	1.85	0.06	0.557	3.78%	2.18%	1.00062
15.00	0.10	30.00	11.45	0.09	0.486	5.14%	1.75%	1.00074
17.50	0.50	20.00	1.85	0.03	0.486	3.27%	2.70%	1.00041
17.50	0.50	27.50	8.95	0.06	0.417	4.92%	1.87%	1.00054
17.50	0.50	30.00	11.45	0.06	0.417	4.96%	1.87%	1.00055

FIGURE 6-9

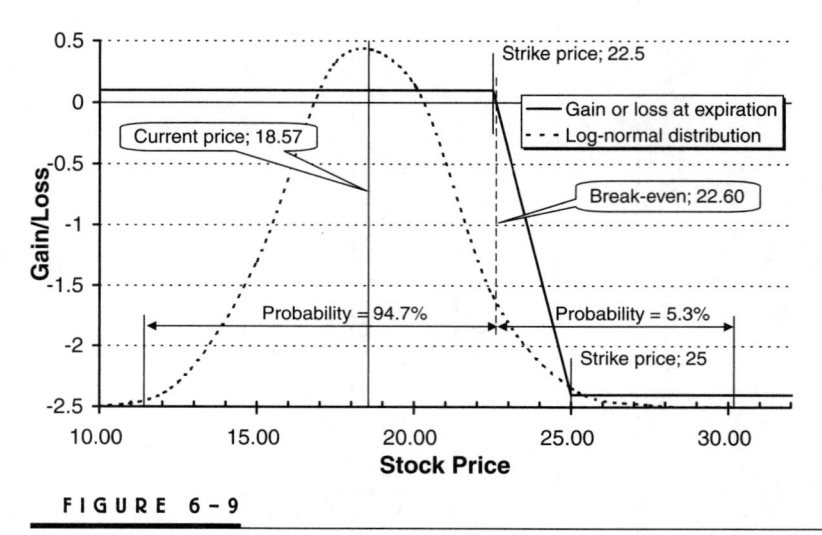

Bear Put spread: buy 25 Put at $6.40; sell 22.5 Put at $4.00

$$N^* = N(b - c) - N(a - c) \qquad (6.21)$$

The probability of a gain (R_1 and R_2 intervals) is given by

$$p_G = N(z_{BEP}) - N(-4) = .94705 - .00003 = .94702$$

And the probability of a loss (R_3 and R_4) intervals is

$$p_L = 1 - p_G = .05298$$

Solving Equation (6.21) gives

$$E(R_1) = .1(.94296) = .094$$

$$E(R_2) = 22.6(.00406) - 18.7076(.0049) = 0$$

$$E(R_3) = 22.6(.04576) - 18.7076(.0574) = -.04$$

$$E(R_4) = -2.4(.00716) = -.017$$

$$E(R) = .094 + 0 - .04 - .017 = .037$$

Optimal $f = 21.38\%$

$$RTN = 1.00479$$

$$\text{Omega} = -.52$$

Table 6–20 shows the Bernoulli equivalent for Figure 6–9. The *MA* of the trade is given by

TABLE 6-20

Bernoulli equivalent for Figure 6-9

	Prob.	Average result	Expected value
Gain (underlying is less than or equal to $22.60)	0.947	0.1	0.090
Loss (underlying is greater than $22.60)	0.053	−1.072	−0.050
The expected result of this trade is			0.040

$$MA\ p_G\left(1 + \frac{G}{L}\right) - 1 = .947\left(1 + \frac{.09926}{1.07587}\right) - 1 = 3.4\%$$

Not only is the *MA* for this bear Put spread only 3.4 percent, but there is also only one other combination of Puts (from Table 6–6) that produces a positive *MA* (2 percent). The trader also should ignore bear Put spreads for Cisco on July 11, 2003.

CHAPTER 7

Determining Expected Results of Options Trades: Straddles and Other Strategies

> *I never guess. It is a shocking habit—destructive to the logical facility.*
> —Sir Arthur Conan Doyle (1859–1930)

By now you should be aware that guessing is, indeed, destructive to one's capital account—especially when probabilities are available to reduce much of the risk. In this chapter we continue on with solved examples of more advanced strategies.

EXPECTED RESULTS OF A LONG STRADDLE

The results of establishing a long straddle by purchasing the 20 Call for $0.43 and purchasing the 20 Put for $1.85 are shown in Figure 7–1. Recall from Chapter 3 that straddles have two break-even stock prices:

$$BEP_{up} = K_{PC} + P_{PC} + P_{PP} = 20 + .43 + 1.85 = 22.28$$

$$BEP_{dn} = K_{PP} - P_{PC} - P_{PP} = 20 - .43 - 1.85 = 17.72$$

The maximum gain or loss from this long straddle is as follows:

Theoretical maximum gain:

$$G_{max} = \begin{cases} BEP_{dn} & \text{for } x < K_{PC} = 17.72 \\ \text{unlimited} & \text{for } x \geq K_{PC} \end{cases}$$

225

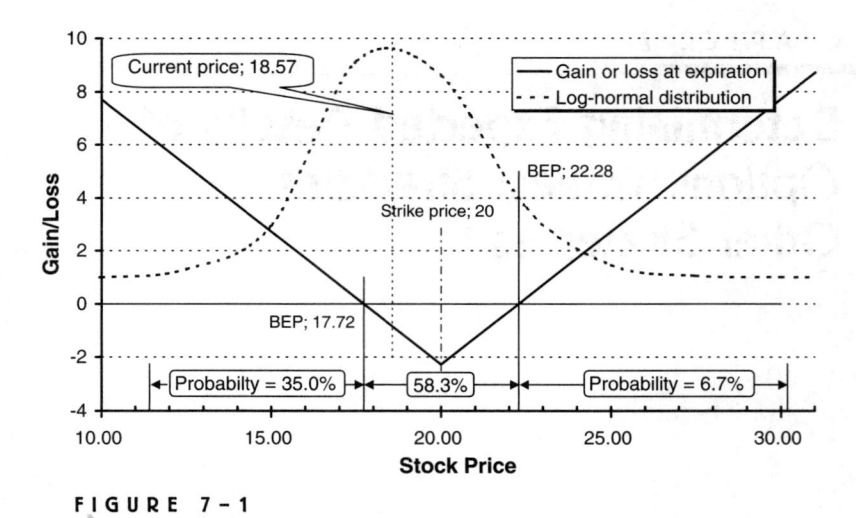

![Figure 7-1: Long straddle gain/loss diagram with current price 18.57, strike price 20, BEP 17.72 and BEP 22.28, probabilities 35.0%, 58.3%, 6.7%]

FIGURE 7-1

Long straddle: buy 20 Call at $0.43; buy 20 Put at $1.85

Statistical maximum gain:

$$G_{max} = \begin{cases} BEP_{dn} - 11.42 & \text{for } x < K_{PC} = 6.3 \\ 30.19 - BEP_{up} & \text{for } x \geq K_{PC} = 7.91 \end{cases}$$

Maximum loss:

$$L_{max} = -(P_{PC} + P_{PP}) = -2.28$$

For the long straddle, R_1 is a variable gain interval where $x \leq 17.72$. R_2 is a variable loss interval where $17.72 < x \leq 20$. R_3 is a variable loss interval where $20 < x < 22.28$. R_4 is a variable gain interval where $x \geq 22.28$.

The results function for a long straddle is Equation (3.37).

$$R = f(x) = \begin{cases} BEP_{dn} - x & \text{for } x < K_{PC} \\ x - BEP_{up} & \text{for } x \geq K_{PC} \end{cases}$$

And the expected results are

$$E(R) = \begin{cases} BEP_{dn}[N(b) - N(a)] - Se^{c^2/2}(N^*) & \text{for } -4 \leq z < z_{K_{PC}} \\ Se^{c^2/2}(N^*) - BEP_{up}[N(b) - N(a)] & \text{for } z_{K_{PC}} < z \leq 4 \end{cases}$$

where

$$N^* = N(b - c) - N(a - c) \qquad (7.1)$$

The probability of a gain (R_1 and R_4 intervals) is given by

$$p_G = N(z_{BEP_{dn}}) - N(-4) + N(4) - N(z_{BEP_{up}})$$

$$= .34985 - .00003 + .99997 - .93312 = .41667$$

And the probability of a loss (R_2 and R_3 intervals) is

$$p_L = 1 - p_G = .58333$$

Solving Equation (7.1) gives

$$E(R_1) = 17.72(.34982) - 18.7076(.306) = .474$$

$$E(R_2) = 17.72(.37945) - 18.7076(.38165) = -.416$$

$$E(R_3) = 18.7076(.22823) - 22.28(.20381) = -.271$$

$$E(R_4) = 18.7076(.08405) - 22.28(.06685) = .083$$

$$E(R) = .474 - .416 - .271 + .083 = -.13$$

$$\text{Omega} = 3.23$$

Table 7–1 shows the Bernoulli equivalent for Figure 7–1.

The *MA* of the trade is given by

$$MA = p_G\left(1 + \frac{G}{L}\right) - 1 = .41667\left(1 + \frac{1.33680}{1.17772}\right) - 1 = -11\%$$

TABLE 7-1

Bernoulli equivalent for Figure 7–1

	Prob.	Average result	Expected value
Gain (underlying < $17.72 or > $22.28)	0.417	1.338	0.560
Loss (underlying between $17.72 and $22.28)	0.583	−1.178	−0.690
The expected result of this trade is			−0.130

Clearly, this is a trade to avoid. With a negative *MA* and a negative *E(R)*, there is no need for any further calculations. There were *no* long straddles with positive expectation on July 11, 2003, for Cisco Systems, Inc.

EXPECTED RESULTS OF A SHORT STRADDLE

Establishing a short straddle by selling the 22.5 Call for $0.12 and selling the 22.5 Put for $4.00, we have

$$BEP_{up} = K_{SC} + P_{SC} + P_{SP} = 22.5 + .12 + 4 = 26.62$$

$$BEP_{dn} = K_{SP} - P_{SC} - P_{SP} = 22.5 - .12 - 4 = 18.38$$

Figure 7–2 shows the results of selling this straddle.

The maximum gain or loss from this short straddle is as follows:

Theoretical maximum loss:

$$L_{max} = \begin{cases} -BEP_{dn} & \text{for } x < K_{SC} = -18.38 \\ \text{unlimited} & \text{for } x \geq K_{SC} \end{cases}$$

Statistical maximum loss:

$$L_{max} = \begin{cases} 11.42 - BEP_{dn} & \text{for } x < K_{PC} = -6.96 \\ BEP_{up} - 30.19 & \text{for } x \geq K_{PC} = -3.57 \end{cases}$$

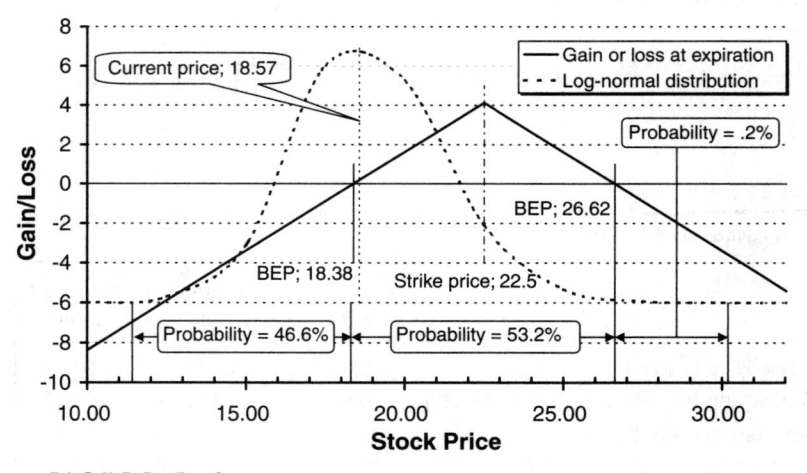

FIGURE 7-2

Short straddle: sell 22.5 Call at $0.12; sell 22.5 Put at $4.00

Maximum gain:

$$G_{max} = P_{SC} + P_{SP} = 4.12$$

For the short straddle, R_1 is a variable loss interval where $x \leq 18.38$. R_2 is a variable gain interval where $18.38 < x \leq 22.5$. R_3 is a variable gain interval where $22.5 < x < 26.62$. R_4 is a variable loss interval where $x \geq 26.62$.

The results function for a short straddle is Equation (3.40).

$$R = f(x) = \begin{cases} x - BEP_{dn} & \text{for } x < K_{SC} \\ BEP_{up} - x & \text{for } x \geq K_{SC} \end{cases}$$

And the expected results are

$$E(R) = \begin{cases} Se^{c^2/2}(N^*) - BEP_{dn}[N(b) - N(a)] & \text{for } -4 < z < z_{K_{SC}} \\ BEP_{up}[N(b) - N(a)] - Se^{c^2/2}(N^*) & \text{for } z_{K_{SC}} < z \leq 4 \end{cases}$$

where

$$N^* = N(b - c) - N(a - c) \quad (7.2)$$

The probability of a gain (R_2 and R_3 intervals) is given by

$$p_G = N(z_{BEP_{up}}) - N(z_{BEP_{dn}}) = .99848 - .46627 = .53221$$

And the probability of a loss (R_1 and R_4 intervals) is

$$p_L = 1 - p_G = .46779$$

Solving Equation (7.2) gives

$$E(R_1) = 18.7076(.41832) - 18.38(.46624) = -.744$$

$$E(R_2) = 18.7076(.50935) - 18.38(.47672) = .767$$

$$E(R_3) = 16.62(.05554) - 18.7076(.07007) = .168$$

$$E(R_4) = 26.62(.00149) - 18.7076(.00218) = -.001$$

$$E(R) = -.744 + .767 + .168 - .001 = .19$$

Optimal $f = 4.51\%$

$RTN = 1.00428$

Omega $= -1.1$

Table 7–2 shows the Bernoulli equivalent for Figure 7–2.

TABLE 7-2

Bernoulli equivalent for Figure 7-2

	Prob.	Average result	Expected value
Gain (underlying between $18.38 and $26.62)	0.532	1.754	0.930
Loss (underlying < $18.38 or > $26.62)	0.468	−1.593	−0.740
The expected result of this trade is			0.190

The *MA* of the trade is given by

$$MA = p_G \left(1 + \frac{G}{L}\right) - 1 = .53221\left(1 + \frac{1.75683}{1.59259}\right) - 1 = 11.9\%$$

This appears to be a trade we might consider. Table 7–3 shows the short straddles with positive $E(R)$.

EXPECTED RESULTS OF A LONG STRANGLE

Constructing a long strangle by purchasing the 20 Call for $0.43 and purchasing the 17.5 Put for $0.50, we have

$$BEP_{up} = K_{PC} + P_{PC} + P_{PP} = 20 + .43 + .5 = 20.93$$

$$BEP_{dn} = K_{PP} - P_{PC} - P_{PP} = 17.5 - .43 - .5 = 16.57$$

Figure 7–3 shows the results of purchasing this strangle.

The maximum gain or loss from this long strangle is as follows:

TABLE 7-3

Cisco Systems, Inc., August 2003 Puts and Calls
Comparison of short straddles as of July 11, 2003

Sold Call		Sold Put						
Strike	Market	Strike	Market	E(R)	P_G	MA	f*	RTN
15.00	3.70	15.00	0.10	0.0375	0.5403	1.99%	0.77%	1.00015
17.50	1.60	17.50	0.50	0.0893	0.6100	5.84%	3.18%	1.00146
20.00	0.43	20.00	1.85	0.1298	0.5833	9.69%	5.43%	1.00360
22.50	0.12	22.50	4.00	0.1884	0.5322	11.83%	4.51%	1.00428

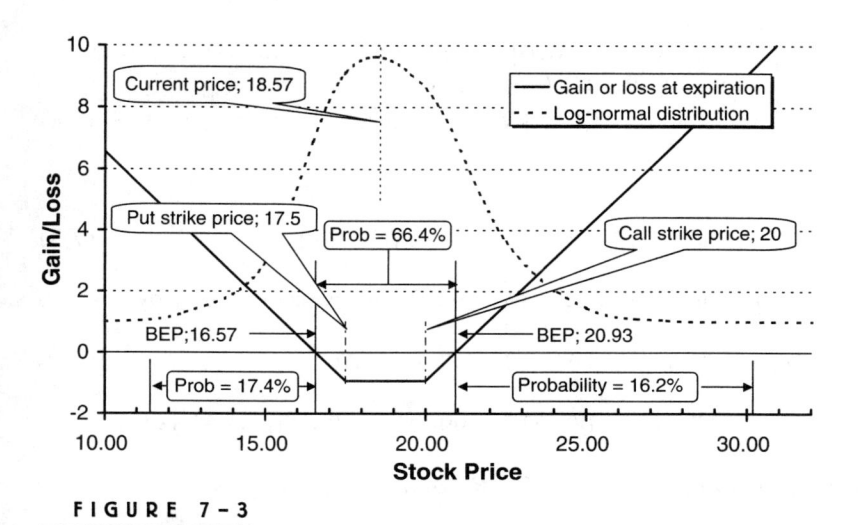

Determining Expected Results of Options Trades: Straddles and Other Strategies 231

FIGURE 7-3

Long strangle: buy 20 Call at $0.43; buy 17.5 Put at $0.50

Theoretical maximum gain:

$$G_{max} = \begin{cases} BEP_{dn} & \text{for } x \leq K_{PP} = 16.57 \\ \text{unlimited} & \text{for } x \geq K_{PC} \end{cases}$$

Statistical maximum gain:

$$G_{max} = \begin{cases} BEP_{dn} - 11.42 & \text{for } x < K_{PP} = 5.12 \\ 30.19 - BEP_{up} & \text{for } x \geq K_{PC} = 9.26 \end{cases}$$

Maximum loss:

$$L_{max} = -(P_{PC} + P_{PP}) = -.93$$

For the long strangle, we have five intervals of interest. R_1 is a variable gain interval where $x \leq 16.57$. R_2 is a variable loss interval where $16.57 < x \leq 17.5$. R_3 is a fixed loss interval where $17.5 < x \leq 20$. R_4 is a variable loss interval where $20 < x < 20.93$. R_5 is a variable gain interval where $x \geq 20.93$.

The results function for a long strangle is Equation (3.41).

$$R = f(x) = \begin{cases} BEP_{dn} - x & \text{for } x \leq K_{PP} \\ -(P_{PC} + P_{PP}) & \text{for } K_{PP} < x < K_{PC} \\ x - BEP_{up} & \text{for } x \geq K_{PC} \end{cases}$$

And the expected results are

$$E(R) = \begin{cases} BEP_{dn}\,[N(b) - N(a)] - Se^{c^2/2}(N^*) & \text{for } -4 \le z < z_{K_{PP}} \\ -(P_{PC} + P_{PP})[N(b) - N(a)] & \text{for } z_{K_{PP}} \le z < z_{K_{PC}} \\ Se^{c^2/2}(N^*) - BEP_{up}[N(b) - N(a)] & \text{for } z_{K_{PC}} < z \le 4 \end{cases}$$

where

$$N^* = N(b - c) - N(a - c) \tag{7.3}$$

The probability of a gain (R_1 and R_5 intervals) is given by

$$p_G = N(z_{BEP_{dn}}) - N(-4) + N(4) - N(z_{BEP_{up}})$$

$$= .17409 - .00003 + .99997 - .83766 = .33637$$

And the probability of a loss (R_2, R_3, and R_4 intervals) is

$$p_L = 1 - p_G = .66363$$

Solving Equation (7.3) gives

$$E(R_1) = 16.57(.17406) - 18.7076(.14465) = .178$$

$$E(R_2) = 16.57(.13849) - 18.7076(.12625) = -.067$$

$$E(R_3) = -.93(.41673) = -.388$$

$$E(R_4) = 18.7076(.11837) - 20.93(.10835) = -.053$$

$$E(R_5) = 18.7076(.19391) - 20.93(.16231) = .230$$

$$E(R) = .178 - .067 - .388 - .053 + .23 = -.10$$

$$\text{Omega} = 3.44$$

Table 7–4 shows the Bernoulli equivalent for Figure 7–3.

TABLE 7-4

Bernoulli equivalent for Figure 7-3

	Prob.	Average result	Expected value
Gain (underlying < $16.57 or > $20.93)	0.336	1.214	0.410
Loss (underlying between $16.57 and $20.93)	0.664	−0.766	−0.510
The expected result of this trade is			−0.100

Determining Expected Results of Options Trades: Straddles and Other Strategies   233

The *MA* of the trade is given by

$$MA = p_G\left(1 + \frac{G}{L}\right) - 1 = .33637\left(1 + \frac{1.21295}{.76506}\right) - 1 = -13\%$$

Clearly, this is another trade to avoid. There were no Cisco long strangles with positive expectation on July 11, 2003.

EXPECTED RESULTS OF A SHORT STRANGLE

Constructing a short strangle by selling the 22.5 Call for $0.12 and selling the 17.5 Put for $0.50, we have

$$BEP_{up} = K_{SC} + P_{SC} + P_{SP} = 22.5 + .12 + .5 = 23.12$$

$$BEP_{dn} = K_{SP} - P_{SC} - P_{SP} = 17.5 - .12 - .5 = 16.88$$

The maximum gain or loss from this short strangle is as follows:

Theoretical maximum loss:

$$L_{max} = \begin{cases} -BEP_{dn} & \text{for } x < K_{SP} = -16.88 \\ \text{unlimited} & \text{for } x \geq K_{SC} \end{cases}$$

Statistical maximum loss:

$$L_{max} = \begin{cases} 11.42 - BEP_{dn} & \text{for } x < 17.5 = -5.46 \\ BEP_{up} - 30.19 & \text{for } x \geq 23.12 = -7.07 \end{cases}$$

Maximum gain:

$$G_{max} = P_{SC} + P_{SP} = .62$$

Figure 7–4 shows the results of selling this strangle.

For the short strangle, R_1 is a variable loss interval where $x \leq 16.88$. R_2 is a variable gain interval where $16.88 < x \leq 17.5$. R_3 is a fixed gain interval where $17.5 < x \leq 22.5$. R_4 is a variable gain interval where $22.5 < x < 23.12$. R_5 is a variable loss interval where $x \geq 23.12$.

The results function for a short strangle is Equation (3.42).

$$R = f(x) = \begin{cases} x - BEP_{dn} & \text{for } x \leq K_{SP} \\ P_{SC} + P_{PP} & \text{for } K_{SP} < x < K_{SC} \\ BEP_{up} - x & \text{for } x \geq K_{SC} \end{cases}$$

And the expected results are

FIGURE 7-4

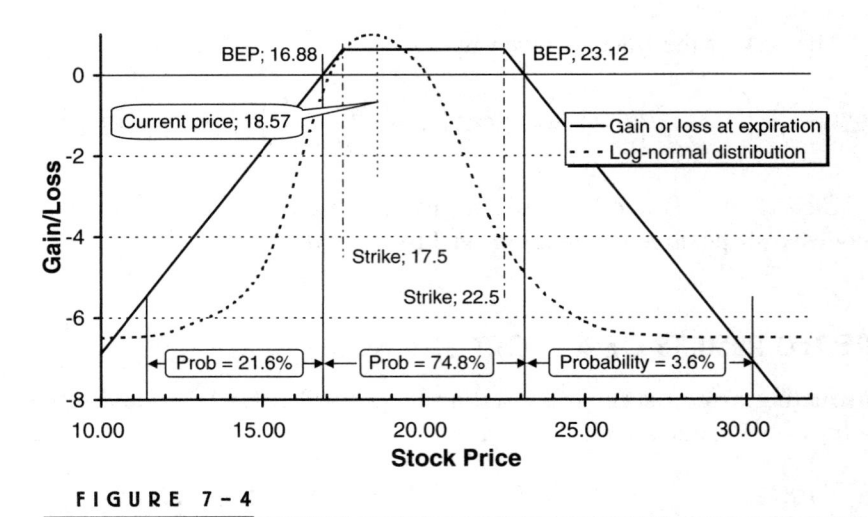

Short strangle: sell 22.5 Call at $0.12; sell 17.5 Put at $0.50

$$E(R) = \begin{cases} Se^{c^2/2}(N^*) - BEP_{dn}[N(b) - N(a)] & \text{for } -4 < z \leq z_{K_{SP}} \\ (P_{SC} + P_{PP})[N(b) - N(a)] & \text{for } z_{K_{SP}} < z \leq z_{K_{SC}} \\ BEP_{up}[N(b) - N(a)] - Se^{c^2/2}(N^*) & \text{for } z_{K_{SC}} < z \leq 4 \end{cases}$$

where

$$N^* = N(b - c) - N(a - c) \tag{7.4}$$

The probability of a loss (R_1 and R_5 intervals) is given by

$$p_L = N(z_{BEP_{dn}}) - N(-4) + N(4) - N(z_{BEP_{up}})$$

$$= .21608 - .00003 + .99997 - .96439 = .25163$$

And the probability of a gain (R_2, R_3, and R_4 intervals) is

$$p_G = 1 - p_L = .74837$$

Solving Equation (7.4) gives

Determining Expected Results of Options Trades: Straddles and Other Strategies

$$E(R_1) = 18.7076(.18219) - 16.88(.21598) = -.237$$

$$E(R_2) = 18.7076(.08869) - 16.88(.09657) = .029$$

$$E(R_3) = .62(.63041) = .39$$

$$E(R_4) = 23.12(.0214) - 18.7076(.02608) = .007$$

$$E(R_5) = 23.12(.03558) - 18.7076(.04617) = -.041$$

$$E(R) = -.237 + .029 + .39 + .007 - .041 = .148$$

Optimal $f = 13.68\%$

$RTN = 1.01164$

Omega $= -2.38$

Table 7–5 shows the Bernoulli equivalent for Figure 7–4.

The *MA* of the trade is given by

$$MA = p_G\left(1 + \frac{G}{L}\right) - 1 = .74837\left(1 + \frac{.56952}{1.10317}\right) - 1 = 13.5\%$$

We might consider this trade—especially with a return of 1.01164. Table 7–6 shows the short strangles with positive $E(R)$.

EXPECTED RESULTS OF A CALL RATIO SPREAD

We establish a Call ratio spread by purchasing one 15 Call for $3.70 and selling two 17.5 Calls for $1.60 each. Since the credit from selling the

TABLE 7-5

Bernoulli equivalent for Figure 7-4

	Prob.	Average result	Expected value
Gain (underlying < $16.88 or > $23.12)	0.748	0.573	0.430
Loss (underlying between $16.88 and $23.12)	0.252	-1.112	-0.280
The expected result of this trade is			0.150

TABLE 7-6

Cisco Systems, Inc., August 2003 Puts and Calls
Comparison of short strangles as of July 11, 2003

Purchased Put		Sold Put						
Strike	Market	Strike	Market	E(R)	P_G	MA	f^*	RTN
15.00	0.10	17.50	1.60	0.06	0.605	3.60%	1.90%	1.00061
15.00	0.10	20.00	0.43	0.07	0.776	5.23%	5.93%	1.00235
15.00	0.10	22.50	0.12	0.12	0.922	12.38%	13.38%	1.01417
17.50	0.50	20.00	0.43	0.10	0.664	8.19%	6.47%	1.00341
17.50	0.50	22.50	0.12	0.15	0.748	13.38%	13.68%	1.01164
20.00	1.85	22.50	0.12	0.18	0.584	12.33%	6.30%	1.00580

two Calls does not cover the cost of the purchased Call, this strategy will be entered at a debit, and there will be a *real* downside break-even stock price. First, we calculate the maximum gain from Equation (3.43).

$$G_{max} = n_{PC}(K_{SC} - K_{PC} - P_{PC}) + n_{SC}P_{SC}$$

$$= 1(17.5 - 15 - 3.7) + 2(1.6) = 2$$

$$BEP_{up} = K_{SC} + \frac{G_{max}}{n_{SC} - n_{PC}} = 17.5 + \frac{2}{1} = 19.5$$

$$BEP_{dn} = K_{PC} - n_{SC}P_{SC} + n_{PC}P_{PC} = 15 - 3.2 + 3.7 = 15.5$$

Figure 7–5 shows the results of establishing this Call ratio spread.

The maximum gain or loss from this Call ratio spread is as follows:

Theoretical maximum loss:

$$L_{max} = \begin{cases} n_{SC}P_{SC} - n_{PC}P_{PC} & \text{for } x \leq BEP_{dn} = -.5 \\ \text{unlimited} & \text{for } x \geq BEP_{up} \end{cases}$$

Statistical maximum loss:

$$L_{max} = \begin{cases} n_{SC}P_{SC} - n_{PC}P_{PC} & \text{for } x \leq BEP_{dn} = -.5 \\ BEP_{up} - 30.19 & \text{for } x \geq BEP_{up} = -10.69 \end{cases}$$

For the Call ratio spread, R_1 is a fixed loss (or fixed gain) interval where $x \leq 15$. R_2 is a variable gain (or variable loss) interval where $15 < x \leq 15.5$. R_3 is a variable gain interval where $15.5 < x \leq 17.5$.

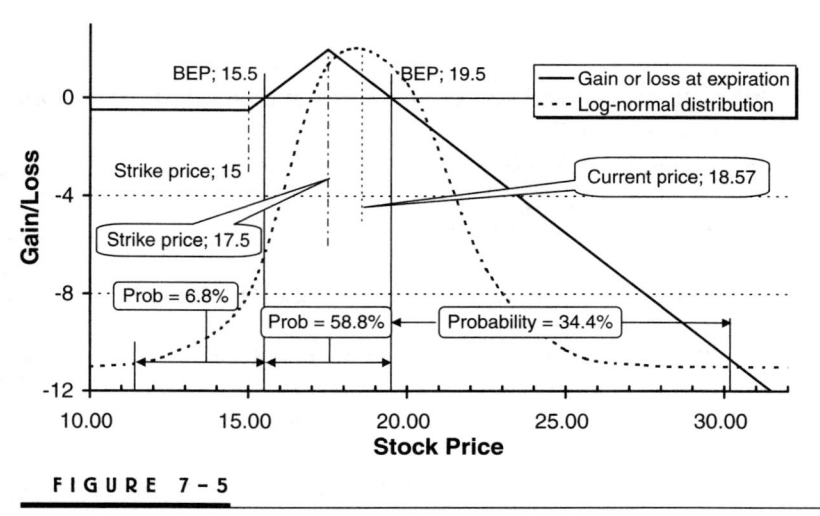

Determining Expected Results of Options Trades: Straddles and Other Strategies   237

FIGURE 7-5

Call ratio spread: buy 15 Call at $3.70; sell two 17.5 Calls at $1.60

R_4 is a variable gain interval where $17.5 < x < 19.5$. R_5 is a variable loss interval where $x \leq 19.5$.

The results function for a Call ratio spread is Equation (3.46):

$$R = f(x) = \begin{cases} n_{SC}P_{SC} - n_{PC}P_{PC} & \text{for } x \leq K_{PC} \\ x - BEP_{dn} & \text{for } K_{PC} < x < K_{SC} \\ BEP_{up} - x & \text{for } x \geq K_{SC} \end{cases}$$

And the expected results are

$$E(R) = \begin{cases} (n_{SC}P_{SC} - n_{PC}P_{PC})[N(b) - N(a)] & \text{for } -4 < z \leq z_{K_{PC}} \\ Se^{c^2/2}(N^*) - BEP_{dn}[N(b) - N(a)] & \text{for } z_{K_{PC}} \leq z < z_{K_{SC}} \\ BEP_{up}[N(b) - N(a)] - Se^{c^2/2}(N^*) & \text{for } z_{K_{SC}} < z \leq 4 \end{cases}$$

where

$$N^* = N(b - c) - N(a - c) \qquad (7.5)$$

Since this Call ratio spread was entered at a *debit,* the probability of a gain (R_3 and R_4 intervals) is given by

$$p_G = N(z_{K_{SC}}) - N(z_{BEP_{dn}}) + N(z_{BEP_{up}}) - N(z_{K_{SC}})$$

$$= .31258 - .06842 + .65627 - .31258 = .58785$$

And the probability of a loss (R_1, R_2, and R_5 intervals) is

$$p_L = 1 - p_G = .41215$$

Note: If this Call ratio spread had been entered at a credit, the only loss interval would have been R_5.

Solving Equation (7.5) gives

$$E(R_1) = .5(.03938) = -.02$$

$$E(R_2) = 18.7076(.02368) - 15.5(.02901) = -.007$$

$$E(R_3) = 18.7076(.21713) - 15.5(.24416) = .278$$

$$E(R_4) = 19.5(.34368) - 18.7076(.33966) = .348$$

$$E(R_5) = 19.5(.34371) - 18.7076(.38937) = -.582$$

$$E(R) = -.02 + .007 + .278 + .348 - .582 = .02$$

Optimal $f = .65\%$

$$RTN = 1.00006$$

Omega $= -3.25$

Table 7–7 shows the Bernoulli equivalent for Figure 7–5.

The *MA* of the trade is given by

$$MA = p_G\left(1 + \frac{G}{L}\right) - 1 = .58785\left(1 + \frac{1.064626}{1.47816}\right) - 1 = 1.1\%$$

Not an exciting prospect. Table 7–8 show selected other Call ratio spreads with positive expectation available on July 11, 2003.

TABLE 7-7

Bernoulli equivalent for Figure 7-5

	Prob.	Average result	Expected value
Gain (underlying between $15.50 and $19.503)	0.588	1.064	0.630
Loss (underlying < $15.50 or > $19.50)	0.412	−1.476	−0.610
The expected result of this trade is			0.020

Determining Expected Results of Options Trades: Straddles and Other Strategies   239

TABLE 7-8

Cisco Systems, Inc., August 2003 Calls
Comparison of Call ratio spreads as of July 11, 2003

Purchased Call		Sold Call						
Strike	Market	Strike	Market	E(R)	P_G	MA	f^*	RTN
5.00	13.56	15.00	3.70	0.0777	0.5473	4.16%	1.59%	1.00062
5.00	13.56	22.50	0.12	0.2486	0.5430	15.84%	5.91%	1.00742
7.50	11.07	20.00	0.43	0.1399	0.5855	10.47%	5.81%	1.00417
10.00	8.60	22.50	0.12	0.2085	0.5358	13.15%	4.98%	1.00523
12.50	6.10	20.00	0.43	0.1100	0.5789	8.18%	4.65%	1.00261
15.00	3.70	22.50	0.12	0.1360	0.5179	8.68%	3.51%	1.00238
15.00	3.70	17.50	1.60	0.0169	0.5878	1.14%	0.65%	1.00006
17.50	1.60	22.50	0.12	0.1101	0.4468	10.35%	5.09%	1.00275

EXPECTED RESULTS OF A PUT RATIO SPREAD

We construct a Put ratio spread by purchasing one 22.5 Put for $4.00 and selling two 20 Puts for $1.85 each. Since the credit from selling the two Puts does not cover the cost of the purchased Put, this strategy will be entered at a debit, and there will be a *real* upside break-even stock price.

First, we calculate the maximum gain from Equation (3.48).

$$G_{max} = n_{PP}(K_{PP} - K_{SP} - P_{PP}) + n_{SP}P_{SP}$$

$$= 1(22.5 - 20 - 4) + 2(1.85) = 2.2$$

The break-even stock prices *BEP* for this Put ratio spread are

$$BEP_{dn} = K_{SP} - \frac{G_{max}}{n_{SP} - n_{PP}} = 20 - \frac{2.2}{1} = 17.8$$

$$BEP_{up} = K_{PP} + n_{SP}P_{SP} - n_{PP}P_{PP} = 22.5 + 3.7 - 4 = 22.2$$

The maximum loss from this Put ratio spread is as follows:

Theoretical maximum loss:

$$L_{max} = \begin{cases} \text{unlimited} & \text{for } x \leq BEP_{dn} \\ n_{SP}P_{SP} - n_{PP}P_{PP} & \text{for } x \geq BEP_{up} \end{cases} = -.3$$

Statistical maximum loss:

$$L_{max} = \begin{cases} 11.42 - BEP_{dn} & \text{for } x \leq BEP_{dn} = -6.38 \\ n_{SP}P_{SP} - n_{PP}P_{PP} & \text{for } x \geq BEP_{up} = -.3 \end{cases}$$

Figure 7–6 shows the results of this Put ratio spread.

For the Put ratio spread, R_1 is a variable loss interval where $x \leq 17.8$. R_2 is a variable gain interval where $17.8 < x \leq 20$. R_3 is a variable loss interval where $20 < x \leq 22.2$. R_4 is a variable loss (or variable gain) interval where $22.2 < x \leq 22.5$. R_5 is a fixed loss (or fixed gain) interval where $x \geq 22.5$.

The results function for a Put ratio spread is Equation (3.51).

$$R = f(x) = \begin{cases} x - BEP_{dn} & \text{for } x \leq K_{SP} \\ BEP_{up} - x & \text{for } K_{SP} < x < K_{PP} \\ n_{SP}P_{SP} - n_{PP}P_{PP} & \text{for } x \geq K_{PP} \end{cases}$$

And the expected results are

$$E(R) = \begin{cases} Se^{c^2/2}(N^*) - BEP_{dn}[N(b) - N(a)] & \text{for } -4 < z \leq z_{K_{SP}} \\ BEP_{up}[N(b) - N(a)] - Se^{c^2/2}(N^*) & \text{for } z_{K_{SP}} < z < z_{K_{PP}} \\ (n_{SP}P_{SP} - n_{PP}P_{PP})[N(b) - N(a)] & \text{for } z_{K_{PP}} < z \geq 4 \end{cases}$$

where

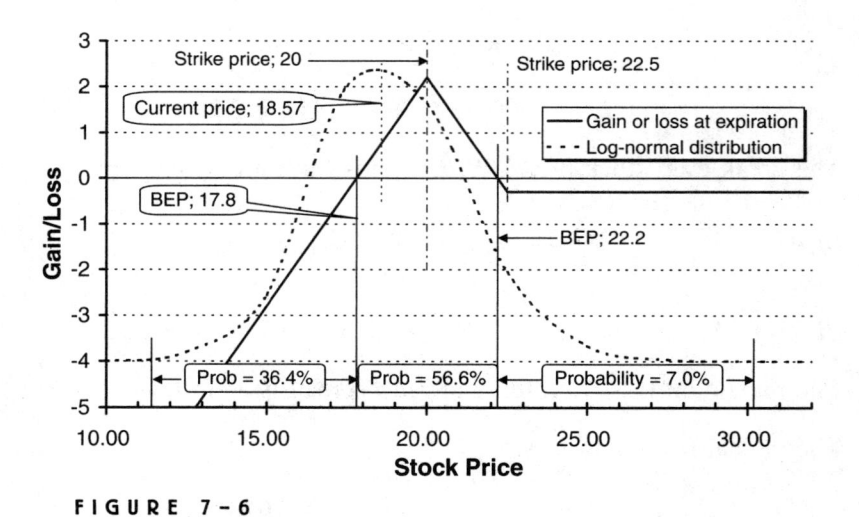

FIGURE 7-6

Put ratio spread: buy 22.5 Put at $4.00; sell two 20 Puts at $1.85

Determining Expected Results of Options Trades: Straddles and Other Strategies

$$N^* = N(b - c) - N(a - c) \qquad (7.6)$$

Since this Put ratio spread was entered at a *debit*, the probability of a gain (R_2 and R_3 intervals) is given by

$$p_G = N(z_{K_{SP}}) - N(z_{BEP_{dn}}) + N(z_{BEP_{up}}) - N(z_{K_{SP}})$$

$$= .61072 - .36369 + .9292 - .72931 = .56551$$

And the probability of a loss (R_1, R_4, and R_5 intervals) is

$$p_L = 1 - p_G = .43449$$

Note: If this Put ratio spread had been entered at a credit, the only loss interval would have been R_1.

Solving Equation (7.6) gives

$$E(R_1) = 18.7076(.31914) - 17.8(.36365) = -.503$$

$$E(R_2) = 18.7076(.36853) - 17.8(.36563) = .386$$

$$E(R_3) = 22.2(.19989) - 18.7076(.22356) = .255$$

$$E(R_4) = 17.8(.01379) - 18.7076(.01647) = -.002$$

$$E(R_5) = -.3(.05698) = -.017$$

$$E(R) = -.503 + .386 + .255 - .002 - .017 = .119$$

Optimal $f = 5.49\%$

$RTN = 1.00335$

Omega $= -2.34$

Table 7–9 shows the Bernoulli equivalent for Figure 7–6.
The *MA* of the trade is given by

$$MA = p_G\left(1 + \frac{G}{L}\right) - 1 = .56551\left(1 + \frac{1.13251}{1.20276}\right) - 1 = 9.8\%$$

Table 7–10 shows other selected Put ratio spreads with positive expectation on July 11, 2003.

TABLE 7-9

Bernoulli equivalent for Figure 7-6

	Prob.	Average result	Expected value
Gain (underlying between $17.80 and $22.20)	0.566	1.134	0.640
Loss (underlying < $17.80 or > $22.20)	0.434	−1.202	−0.520
The expected result of this trade is			0.120

EXPECTED RESULTS OF A CALL BACKSPREAD

A Call backspread may be established by purchasing two 15 Calls for $3.70 each and selling one 10 Call for $8.60. Since the proceeds from the sold Call exceed the total cost of the two purchased Calls, this trade will be entered at a credit. First, we calculate the maximum loss from Equation (3.53).

$$L_{max} = n_{SC}(K_{SC} - K_{PC} + P_{SC}) - n_{PC}P_{PC}$$

$$= 1(10 - 15 + 8.6) - 2(3.7) = -3.8$$

The break-even stock prices for this Call backspread are

TABLE 7-10

Cisco Systems, Inc., August 2003 Puts

Comparison of Put ratio spreads as of July 11, 2003

Purchased Put		Sold Put						
Strike	Market	Strike	Market	E(R)	P_G	MA	f^*	RTN
17.50	0.50	15.00	0.10	0.0465	0.2630	16.01%	12.64%	1.00280
25.00	6.40	15.00	0.10	0.0447	0.5403	2.40%	0.95%	1.00021
20.00	1.85	17.50	0.50	0.0681	0.5038	9.22%	8.25%	1.00281
25.00	6.40	17.50	0.50	0.0965	0.6100	6.39%	3.57%	1.00177
30.00	11.45	17.50	0.50	0.0393	0.5990	2.55%	1.46%	1.00029
22.50	4.00	20.00	1.85	0.1192	0.5655	9.91%	5.49%	1.00335
25.00	6.40	20.00	1.85	0.1569	0.5877	11.93%	6.68%	1.00538
27.50	8.95	22.50	4.00	0.1188	0.5197	7.33%	2.86%	1.00171

Determining Expected Results of Options Trades: Straddles and Other Strategies 243

$$BEP_{up} = K_{PC} + \frac{L_{max}}{n_{SC} - n_{PC}} = 15 + \frac{-3.8}{-1} = 18.8$$

$$BEP_{dn} = K_{SC} + n_{SC}P_{SC} - n_{PC}P_{PC} = 10 + 8.6 - 7.4 = 11.2$$

Figure 7–7 shows the results of this Call backspread.

The maximum gain from this Call backspread is as follows:

Theoretical maximum gain:

$$G_{max} = \begin{cases} n_{SC}P_{SC} - n_{PC}P_{PC} & \text{for } x \leq K_{SC} \text{ (only if positive)} \\ \text{unlimited} & \text{for } x \geq BEP_{up} \end{cases}$$

Statistical maximum gain:

$$G_{max} = \begin{cases} n_{SC}P_{SC} - n_{PC}P_{PC} & \text{for } x \leq 10 = 1.2 \\ 30.19 - BEP_{up} & \text{for } x \geq 18.8 = 11.39 \end{cases}$$

For the Call backspread, R_1 is a fixed loss (or fixed gain) interval where $x \leq 10$. R_2 is a variable gain (or variable loss) interval where $10 < x \leq 11.2$. R_3 is a variable loss interval where $11.2 < x \leq 15$. R_4 is a variable loss interval where $15 < x < 18.8$. R_5 is a variable gain interval where $x \geq 18.8$.

The results function for a Call backspread is Equation (3.56).

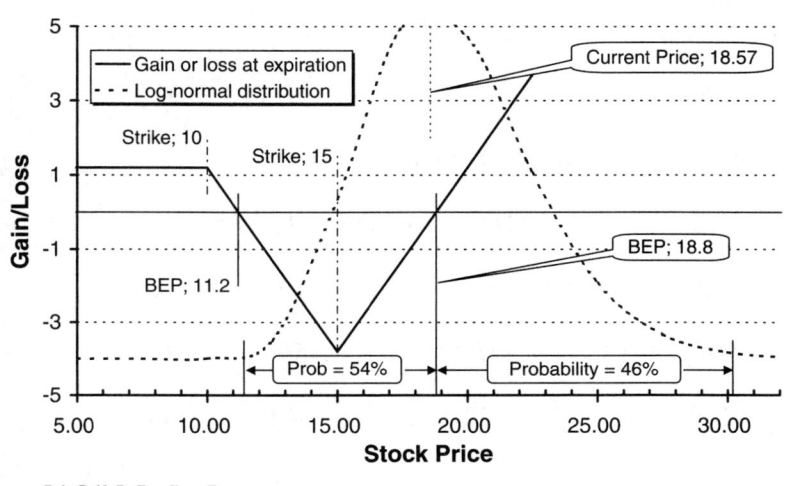

FIGURE 7–7

Call backspread: buy two 15 Calls at $3.70; sell 10 Call at $8.60

$$R = f(x) = \begin{cases} n_{SC}P_{SC} - n_{PC}P_{PC} & \text{for } x \leq K_{SC} \\ BEP_{dn} - x & \text{for } K_{SC} < x < K_{PC} \\ x - BEP_{up} & \text{for } x \geq K_{PC} \end{cases}$$

And the expected results are

$$E(R) = \begin{cases} (n_{SC}P_{SC} - n_{PC}P_{PC})[N(b) - N(a)] & \text{for } -4 < z \leq z_{K_{SC}} \\ BEP_{dn}[N(b) - N(a)] - Se^{c^2/2}(N^*) & \text{for } z_{K_{SC}} < z \leq z_{K_{PC}} \\ Se^{c^2/2}(N^*) - BEP_{up}[N(b) - N(a)] & \text{for } z_{K_{PC}} < z < 4 \end{cases}$$

where

$$N^* = N(b - c) - N(a - c) \tag{7.7}$$

Since this Call backspread was entered at a *credit,* the probability of a loss (R_3 and R_4 intervals) is given by

$$p_L = N(z_{K_{PC}}) - N(z_{BEP_{dn}}) + N(z_{BEP_{up}}) - N(z_{K_{PC}})$$

$$= .03941 - 0 + .54036 - .03491 = .54036$$

And the probability of a gain (R_1, R_2, and R_5 intervals) is

$$p_G = 1 - p_L = .45964$$

Note: If this Call backspread had been entered at a debit, the only gain interval would have been R_5.

Solving Equation (7.7) gives

$$E(R_1) = 1.2(0) = 0$$

$$E(R_2) = 11.2(0) - 18.7076(0) = 0$$

$$E(R_3) = 11.2(.03941) - 18.7076(.03012) = -.122$$

$$E(R_4) = 18.7076(.46185) - 18.8(.50095) = -.778$$

$$E(R_5) = 18.7076(.50798) - 18.8(.45961) = .862$$

$$E(R) = 0 + 0 - .122 - .778 + .862 = -.038$$

Omega = 1.51

Table 7–11 shows the Bernoulli equivalent for Figure 7–7.

TABLE 7-11
Bernoulli equivalent for Figure 7-7

	Prob.	Average result	Expected value
Gain (underlying < $11.20 or > $18.80)	0.46	1.876	0.860
Loss (underlying between $11.20 and $18.80)	0.54	−1.665	−0.900
The expected result of this trade is			−0.040

The *MA* of the trade is given by

$$MA = p_G\left(1 + \frac{G}{L}\right) - 1 = .45964\left(1 + \frac{1.87391}{1.66666}\right) - 1 = -2.3\%$$

Since the expected result is negative, no further calculations are necessary. Table 7–12 shows all other Call backspreads with positive expectation.

EXPECTED RESULTS OF A PUT BACKSPREAD

A Put backspread may be established by purchasing two 20 Puts for $1.85 each and selling one 22.5 Put for $8.60. Since the proceeds from the sold Put exceed the total cost of the two purchased Puts, this trade will be entered at a credit. First, we calculate the maximum loss from Equation (3.58).

TABLE 7-12
Cisco Systems, Inc., August 2003 Calls
Comparison of Call backspreads as of July 11, 2003

Purchased Call		Sold Call						
Strike	Market	Strike	Market	E(R)	P_G	MA	f*	RTN
10.00	8.60	5.00	13.56	0.0672	0.4876	3.95%	1.31%	1.00044
12.50	6.10	5.00	13.56	0.0675	0.4876	3.97%	1.32%	1.00044
10.00	8.60	7.50	11.07	0.0773	0.4894	4.55%	1.51%	1.00058
12.50	6.10	7.50	11.07	0.0776	0.4894	4.57%	1.52%	1.00059
12.50	6.10	10.00	8.60	0.1076	0.4947	6.39%	2.10%	1.00113

$$L_{\max} = n_{SP}(K_{PP} - K_{SP} + P_{SP}) - n_{PP}P_{PP}$$

$$= 1(20 - 22.5 + 4) - 2(1.85) = -2.2$$

The break-even stock prices BEP for this Put backspread are

$$BEP_{dn} = K_{PP} - \left(\frac{L_{\max}}{n_{SP} - n_{PP}}\right) = 20 - \frac{-2.2}{-1} = 17.8$$

$$BEP_{up} = K_{SP} + n_{PP}P_{PP} - n_{SP}P_{SP} = 22.5 + 3.7 - 4 = 22.2$$

The maximum gain from a Put backspread is as follows:

Theoretical maximum gain:

$$G_{\max} = \begin{cases} n_{SP}P_{SP} - n_{PP}P_{PP} & \text{for } x \geq K_{SP} \text{ (only if positive)} \\ \text{unlimited} & \text{for } x \leq BEP_{dn} \end{cases}$$

Statistical maximum gain:

$$G_{\max} = \begin{cases} n_{SP}P_{SP} - n_{PP}P_{PP} & \text{for } x \geq 22.5 = .3 \\ BEP_{dn} - 11.42 & \text{for } x \leq 17.8 = 6.38 \end{cases}$$

Figure 7–8 shows the results of this Put backspread.

For the Put backspread, R_1 is a variable gain interval where $x \leq 17.8$. R_2 is a variable loss interval where $17.8 < x \leq 20$. R_3 is a variable loss interval where $20 < x \leq 22.2$. R_4 is a variable gain (or variable

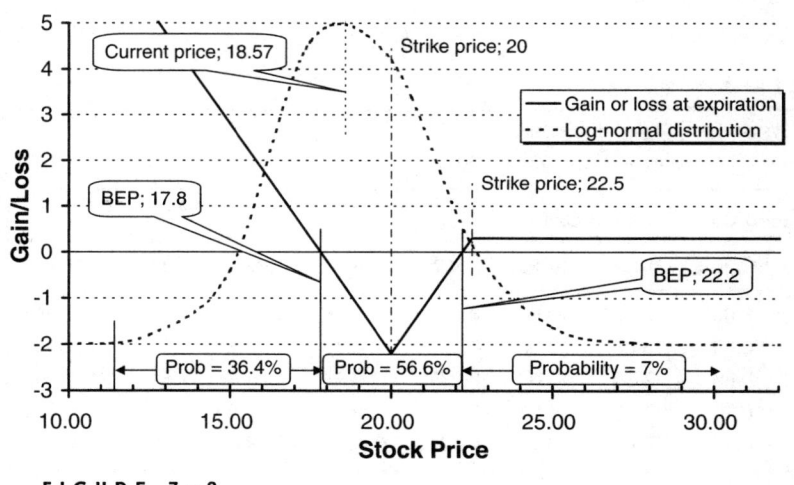

FIGURE 7-8

Put backspread: buy two 20 Puts at $1.85; sell 22.5 Put at $4.00

loss) interval where $22.2 < x < 22.5$. R_5 is a fixed gain (or fixed loss) interval where $x \geq 22.5$.

The results function for a Put backspread is Equation (3.61).

$$R = f(x) = \begin{cases} BEP_{dn} - x & \text{for } x \leq K_{PP} \\ x - BEP_{up} & \text{for } K_{PP} < x < K_{SP} \\ n_{SP}P_{SP} - n_{PP}P_{PP} & \text{for } x \geq K_{SP} \end{cases}$$

And the expected results are

$$E(R) = \begin{cases} BEP_{dn}[N(b) - N(a)] - Se^{c^2/2}(N^*) & \text{for } -4 < z \leq z_{K_{PP}} \\ Se^{c^2/2}(N^*) - BEP_{up}[N(b) - N(a)] & \text{for } z_{K_{PP}} < z < z_{K_{SP}} \\ (n_{SP}P_{SP} - n_{PP}P_{PP})[N(b) - N(a)] & \text{for } z_{K_{SP}} \leq z < 4 \end{cases}$$

where

$$N^* = N(b - c) - N(a - c) \qquad (7.8)$$

Since this Put backspread was entered at a *credit*, the probability of a loss (R_2 and R_3 intervals) is given by

$$p_L = N(z_{K_{PP}}) - N(z_{BEP_{dn}}) + N(z_{BEP_{up}}) - N(z_{K_{PP}})$$

$$= .72931 - .36368 + .92918 - .72931 = .5655$$

And the probability of a gain (R_1, R_4, and R_5 intervals) is

$$p_G = 1 - p_L = .4345$$

Note: If this Put backspread had been entered at a debit, the only gain interval would have been R_1.

Solving Equation (7.8) gives

$$E(R_1) = 17.8(.36365) - 18.7076(.31912) = .503$$

$$E(R_2) = 17.8(.36563) - 18.7076(.36853) = -.386$$

$$E(R_3) = 18.7076(.22356) - 22.2(.19987) = -.255$$

$$E(R_4) = 18.7076(.01647) - 22.2(.01381) = .002$$

$$E(R_5) = .3(.05698) = .017$$

$$E(R) = .5030 - .386 - .255 + .002 + .017 = -.119$$

Omega = 2.34

Table 7–13 shows the Bernoulli equivalent for Figure 7–8.

TABLE 7-13

Bernoulli equivalent for Figure 7-8

	Prob.	Average result	Expected value
Gain (underlying between $17.80 and $22.20)	0.434	1.202	0.520
Loss (underlying < $17.80 or > $22.20)	0.566	−1.134	−0.640
The expected result of this trade is			−0.120

The *MA* of the trade is given by

$$MA = p_G\left(1 + \frac{G}{L}\right) - 1 = .4345\left(1 + \frac{1.20276}{1.13251}\right) - 1 = -10.4\%$$

Since the *MA* is negative, no further calculations are necessary. Only 2 of the 21 available Put backspreads were marginally profitable.

EXPECTED RESULTS OF A LONG CALL BUTTERFLY SPREAD

A long Call butterfly spread may be established by purchasing one 12.5 Call for $6.10, purchasing one 22.5 Call for $0.12, and selling two 17.5 Calls for $1.60 each. Since the proceeds from the sold Calls do not exceed the total cost of the two purchased Calls, this trade will be entered at a *debit*. Figure 7–9 shows the results of this long Call butterfly spread.

The break-even stock prices *BEP* for a long Call butterfly spread are

$$BEP_{up} = n_{SC}(K_{SC} + P_{SC}) - Ln_{PC}(LK_{PC} + LP_{PC}) - Hn_{PC}HP_{PC}$$

$$BEP_{dn} = LK_{PC} + n_{PC}LP_{PC} + n_{PC}HP_{PC} - n_{SC}P_{SC}$$

And for this long Call butterfly spread

$$BEP_{up} = 2(17.5 + 1.6) - (12.5 + 6.1) - .12 = 19.48$$
$$BEP_{dn} = 12.5 + 6.1 + .12 - 2(1.6) = 15.52$$

The maximum gain for a long Call butterfly spread is

$$G_{max} = K_{SC} - LK_{PC} - n_{PC}LP_{PC} - n_{PC}HP_{PC} + n_{SC}P_{SC}$$

And for this long Call butterfly spread

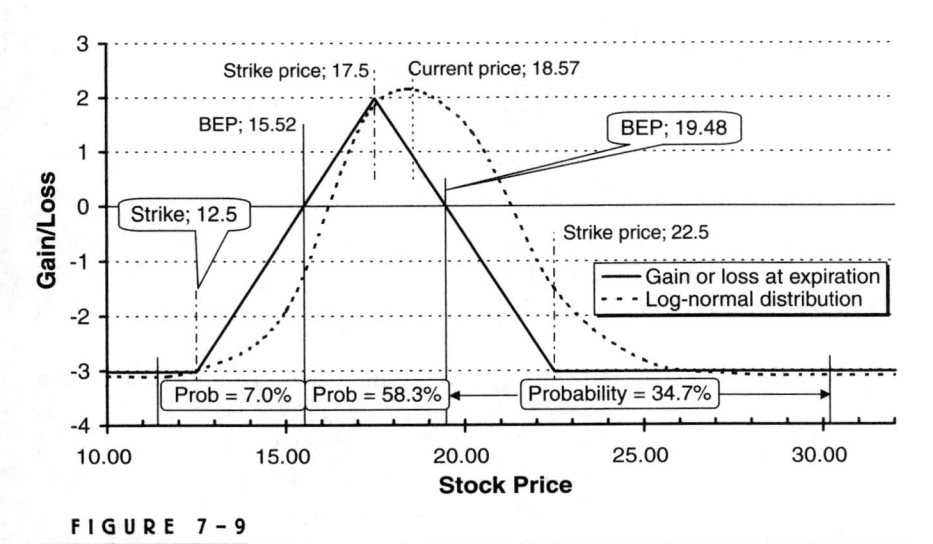

Determining Expected Results of Options Trades: Straddles and Other Strategies

FIGURE 7-9

Long Call butterfly spread: buy 12.5 Call at $6.10; buy 22.5 Call at $0.12; sell two 17.5 Calls at $1.60.

$$G_{max} = 17.5 - 12.5 - 6.1 - .12 + 2(1.6) = 1.98$$

There are two possible loss amounts if this strategy is entered at a debit:

Theoretical maximum loss:

$$L_{max} = BEP_{up} - Hn_{PC}HK_{PC}$$

for the upside loss and

$$L_{max} = n_{SC}P_{SC} - Ln_{PC}LP_{PC} - Hn_{PC}HP_{PC}$$

for the downside loss. And for this long Call butterfly spread,

$$L_{max} = 19.48 - 22.5 = -3.02$$

for the upside loss and

$$L_{max} = 2(1.6) - 6.1 - .12 = -3.02$$

for the downside loss.

Statistical maximum loss:

$$L_{max} = BEP_{up} - 30.19 = -10.17$$

$$L_{max} = 11.42 - BEP_{dn} = -4.1$$

For this strategy, the *theoretical* maximum loss controls because there can be no loss greater than $3.02 on either the downside or the upside. Other combinations will involve the use of the *statistical* maximum losses.

For the long Call butterfly spread, R_1 is a fixed loss interval where $x \leq 12.5$. R_2 is a variable gain interval where $12.5 < x \leq 15.52$. R_3 is a variable gain interval where $15.52 < x \leq 17.5$. R_4 is a variable gain interval where $17.5 < x < 19.48$. R_5 is a variable loss interval where $19.48 < x \leq 22.5$. R_6 is a fixed loss interval where $x > 22.5$.

The results function for the long Call butterfly spread is Equation (3.68).

$$R = \begin{cases} n_{SC}P_{SC} - Ln_{PC}LP_{PC} - Hn_{PC}HP_{PC} & \text{for } x \leq LK_{PC} \\ x - BEP_{dn} & \text{for } LK_{PC} < x < K_{SC} \\ BEP_{up} - x & \text{for } K_{SC} < x < HK_{PC} \\ BEP_{up} - Hn_{PC}HK_{PC} & \text{for } x \geq HK_{PC} \end{cases}$$

And the expected results for this long Call butterfly spread are

$$E(R) = \begin{cases} -3.02[N(b) - N(a)] & \text{for } -4 < z \leq z_{LK_{PC}} \\ Se^{c^2/2}(N^*) - BEP_{dn}[N(b) - N(a)] & \text{for } z_{LK_{PC}} < z < z_{K_{SC}} \\ BEP_{up}[N(b) - N(a)] - Se^{c^2/2}(N^*) & \text{for } z_{K_{SC}} \leq z < z_{HK_{PC}} \\ -3.02[N(b) - N(a)] & \text{for } z_{HK_{PC}} \leq z < 4 \end{cases}$$

where

$$N^* = N(b - c) - N(a - c) \qquad (7.9)$$

For a long Call butterfly spread, the probability of a gain (R_3 and R_4 intervals) is given by

$$p_G = N(z_{K_{SC}}) - N(z_{BEP_{dn}}) + N(z_{BEP_{up}}) - N(z_{K_{SC}})$$

$$= .31258 - .06983 + .65315 - .31258 = .58323$$

And the probability of a loss (R_1, R_2, R_5, and R_6 intervals) is

Determining Expected Results of Options Trades: Straddles and Other Strategies

$$p_L = 1 - p_G = .41677$$

Note: If this spread had been entered for a *credit*, the only loss intervals would have been R_5 and R_6.

Solving Equation (7.9) gives

$$E(R_1) = -3.02(.00053) = -.002$$

$$E(R_2) = 18.7076(.05461) - 15.52(.06927) = -.053$$

$$E(R_3) = 18.7076(.21592) - 15.52(.24275) = .272$$

$$E(R_4) = 19.48(.34057) - 18.7076(.33641) = .341$$

$$E(R_5) = 19.48(.28984) - 18.7076(.32037) = -.347$$

$$E(R_6) = -3.02(.05698) = -.172$$

$$E(R) = -.002 - .053 + .272 + .341 - .172 = .039$$

$$\text{Omega} = -2.7$$

$$RTN = 1.00037$$

Optimal $f = 1.89\%$

Table 7–14 shows the Bernoulli equivalent for Figure 7–9.

The *MA* of the trade is given by

$$MA = p_G\left(1 + \frac{G}{L}\right) - 1 = .58323\left(1 + \frac{1.05146}{1.3765}\right) - 1 = 2.9\%$$

Table 7–15 shows other selected long Call butterfly spreads with positive expectation available on July 11, 2003.

TABLE 7-14

Bernoulli equivalent for Figure 7-9

	Prob.	Average result	Expected value
Gain (underlying between $15.52 and $19.48)	0.583	1.052	0.610
Loss (underlying < $15.52 or > $19.48)	0.417	−1.379	−0.570
The expected result of this trade is			0.040

TABLE 7-15

Cisco Systems, Inc., August 2003 Calls

Comparison of long Call butterfly spreads as of July 11, 2003

Purchased Call		Sold Calls		Purchased Call		E(R)	P_G	MA	f*	RTN
Strike	Market	Strike	Market	Strike	Market					
5.00	13.56	15.00	3.70	17.50	1.60	0.0867	0.2693	34.33%	27.01%	1.01063
5.00	13.56	17.50	1.60	20.00	0.43	0.1283	0.5189	18.34%	15.41%	1.00996
7.50	11.07	17.50	1.60	20.00	0.43	0.1182	0.5164	16.74%	14.23%	1.00847
7.50	11.07	20.00	0.43	22.50	0.12	0.0893	0.5588	7.36%	4.18%	1.00190
10.00	8.60	20.00	0.43	22.50	0.12	0.0592	0.5520	4.83%	2.83%	1.00084
12.50	6.10	15.00	3.70	17.50	1.60	0.0467	0.2630	16.09%	12.67%	1.00282
15.00	3.70	17.50	1.60	20.00	0.43	0.0157	0.4832	2.13%	2.15%	1.00017

CHAPTER 8

Other Useful Techniques

Proverbial wisdom counsels against risk and change. But sitting ducks fare worst of all.
—Mason Cooley (1927–)

Although not essential to the understanding of options, the following mathematical concepts will be helpful to any serious student of financial markets. You are almost certain to encounter applications of most of these techniques in other texts on equities, futures, and options.

MOVING AVERAGES

Moving averages play a major role in technical analysis. Traders employ them to smooth historical price data and discern a *trend*. Moving averages are constructed by selecting a constant time period (usually in days), averaging the prices for that period beginning with the oldest data point, and then dropping the oldest data point while adding the newest data point and repeating the process until the most current price is reached. The resulting set of averages is called a *simple moving average* (SMA).

Letting:

F = forecast price
P = actual price
n = number of days in the period

t = forecast time period

w = weight assigned to data point

for the SMA, we have

$$F_t = \frac{1}{n} \sum_{i=t-n}^{t} P_i \qquad (8.1)$$

Since many traders believe that current data are more relevant than older data, they *weight* the data points, giving less weight to the older points. A set of weights equal in number to the number of data points in the period and whose sum equals 1 is selected. For the *weighted moving average* (WMA), we have

$$F_t = \sum_{i=t-n}^{t} w_i P_i \qquad (8.2)$$

where

$$\sum_{i=t-n}^{t} w_i = 1$$

For simple and weighted moving averages used in forecasting stock prices, 50- and 200-day periods are the most common. Many technical analysts believe that when the 50- and 200-day moving averages of stock prices cross, a strong buy or sell signal is given.

The SMA and WMA require that n data points be stored for calculating the next F_t. Another data-smoothing technique called *exponential moving average* (EMA) requires only the previous data point and previous forecasted price be stored. A constant smoothing factor α is chosen between 0 and 1 and is applied as follows:

$$F_t = F_{t-1} + \alpha(P_t - F_{t-1}) \qquad (8.3)$$

Since EMA is calculated by adding a percentage of yesterday's moving average to a percentage of today's closing value, EMA weights the more recent data more heavily than older data. Selecting α near 1 provides for close tracking of the original price series, whereas an α closer to 0 provides more smoothing of the data. Figure 8–1 shows a comparison of a 10-day SMA and an EMA ($\alpha = .4$) on a series of IBM stock prices.

The relationship of α to the number of days in the period n is given by

Other Useful Techniques

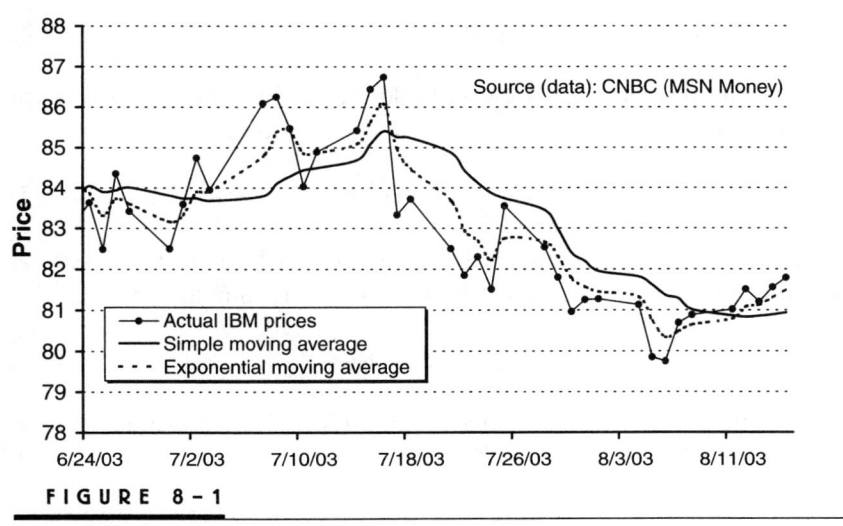

FIGURE 8-1

Daily IBM prices (6/24/03 to 8/15/03)

$$\alpha = \frac{2}{n+1} \qquad (8.4)$$

Therefore, the α for the EMA in Figure 8–1 is equivalent to four days.

FIRST-ORDER EQUATIONS: THE STRAIGHT LINE

Straight lines play an important role in analyzing options. In most cases, the geometry of option prices at expiration consists of two or more straight lines. Determining the slope of an option price curve at a given point involves constructing a straight line that is tangent to (touches) the curve at the specified point. Equation (8.5) represents the generalized formula for a straight line.

$$y = mx + b \qquad (8.5)$$

where m = the slope of the line (rise over run)
b = a constant representing the y intercept on a graph

Once m and one point x_1, y_1 on the line are known, the straight line is defined completely. Called the *point-slope form*, Equation (8.6) can be used to define the line.

$$y - y_1 = m(x - x_1) \tag{8.6}$$

For example, suppose we want to derive the formula for the straight line that is tangent to the point $x = 1$ and $y = 3$ on the curve

$$f(x) = 2x - 4x^2 + 5 \tag{8.7}$$

This equation has been numbered because it will be referenced several times in the following sections. The derivative of Equation (8.7) is

$$f'(x) = 2 - 8x$$

At $x = 1$, the slope m of the tangent line $[f'(x)]$ is -6. From Equation (8.6),

$$y - 3 = -6(x - 1)$$

Therefore, the formula for the tangent line is

$$y = 9 - 6x$$

Figure 8–2 shows the graph of Equation (8.7) together with the straight-line tangent.

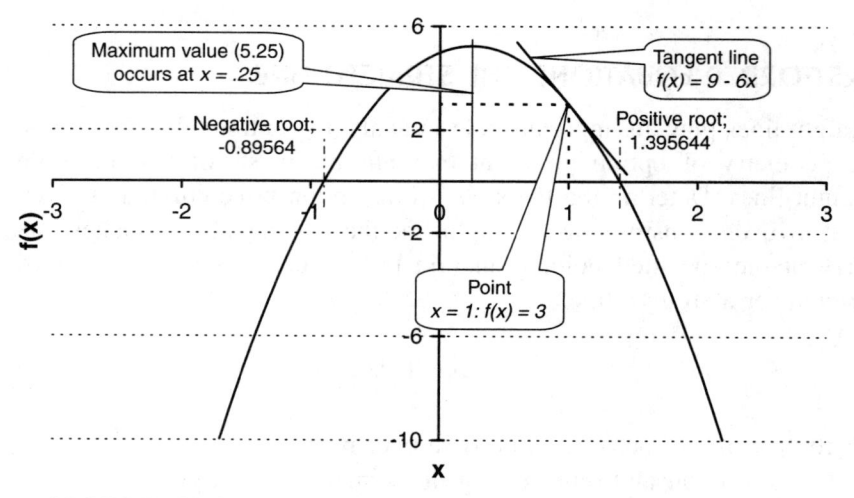

FIGURE 8-2

Graph of $f(x) = 2x - 4x^2 + 5$

Other Useful Techniques

If two points x_1, y_1 and x_2, y_2 on the line are known, the line is also defined completely. Called the *two-point form,* Equation (8.8) can be used to define the line.

$$y - y_1 = \frac{y_2 - y_1}{x_2 - x_1}(x - x_1) \tag{8.8}$$

Suppose, for example, that m in the preceding example is not known, but we do know that the point $x = 1.4$ and $y = .6$ also lie on the tangent line. From Equation (8.8), we have

$$y - 3 = \frac{.6 - 3}{1.4 - 1}(x - 1)$$

Therefore, the formula for the tangent line is

$$y = 9 - 6x \quad \text{as before}$$

Suppose we want to fit a linear trendline to a set of data. We would do so using the *method of least squares,* that is, finding the equation of a straight line that minimizes the sum of the squared deviations between the data points and the line itself. Called *linear regression,* this technique makes use of Equation (8.5) and its first-moment equation obtained by multiplying Equation (8.5) by x.

$$xy = mx^2 + bx \tag{8.9}$$

After completing a table of the data points and certain calculations performed on them (x, y, xy, x^2, and the sums thereof, including the number of data points n), we substitute the sums into Equations (8.5) and (8.9) and obtain the two equations necessary to find m and b of the regression line.

$$\sum y = \left(\sum x\right)m + nb \tag{8.10}$$

$$\sum xy = \left(\sum x^2\right)m + \left(\sum x\right)b \tag{8.11}$$

We now have two equations in two unknowns that can be solved algebraically (simultaneously) or directly by

$$m = \frac{n\sum xy - \sum x \sum y}{n\sum x^2 - \left(\sum x\right)^2} \qquad (8.12)$$

$$b = \frac{\sum y - m\sum x}{n} \qquad (8.13)$$

For example, suppose we had the following observations concerning a lawyer's annual salary and wanted to find the trend. Table 8–1 contains the year together with the annual salary expressed in thousands of dollars.

To make the numbers more manageable, we define

$$x = \frac{Y - 1975}{5} \quad \text{and} \quad y = \frac{S - 100}{5}$$

and complete Table 8–2.

From Equations (8.12) and (8.13), we have

$$m = \frac{6(289) - 15(78)}{6(55) - (15)^2} = 5.3714$$

$$b = \frac{78 - 5.3714(15)}{6} = -.4285$$

Therefore,

$$y = 5.3714x - .4285$$

Substituting S and Y for x and y, we get

TABLE 8–1

Salary data

Y year	S salary
1975	100
1980	120
1985	155
1990	175
1995	210
2000	230

Other Useful Techniques

TABLE 8-2

Data for fitting a straight line

Y year	S salary	x	y	x^2	xy
1975	100	0	0	0	0
1980	120	1	4	1	4
1985	155	2	11	4	22
1990	175	3	15	9	45
1995	210	4	22	16	88
2000	230	5	26	25	130
Totals		15	78	55	289

$$S = 5.37(Y - 1975) + 97.86$$

the regression equation.

Figure 8-3 shows the graph of the regression equation together with the data points.

A glance at Figure 8-3 tells us the trendline is a pretty good fit to the actual data. But how good a fit? The statistic R^2 measures how much of the variation in y is accounted for by the variation in x and takes on values from 0 to 1—with 1 being perfect correlation and 0 being no correlation at all. Using the "Add Trendline" feature in Excel, different

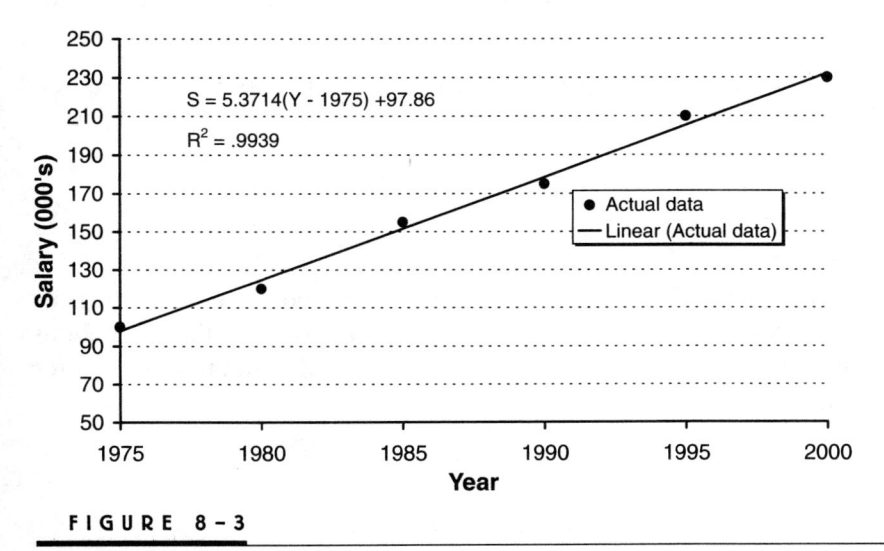

FIGURE 8-3

Salary (1975-2000)

types of curves can be fitted to almost any number of data points, including the calculation of R^2. R^2 for the trendline in Figure 8–3 is .9939—an extremely good fit.

SECOND-ORDER EQUATIONS: THE PARABOLA

Parabolas are important to the study of options because one of the more sophisticated techniques for determining optimal position size (how much to risk) depends on a parabolic approach. In addition, the relationship between the expected results of an option trade (covered in Chapter 6) and the volatility of the underlying instrument (covered in Chapter 5) is a nearly perfect parabolic function. A class of generalized second-order equations known as *quadratic equations* graphs as parabolas. Indeed, Equation (8.7) is a quadratic equation whose graph appears as Figure 8–2. The generalized form of a quadratic equation is

$$f(x) = ax^2 + bx + c = 0 \qquad (8.14)$$

There are several methods for finding the *roots* of a quadratic equation [solving the equation for $f(x) = 0$]. The generalized form is

$$\text{Roots} = \frac{-b \pm \sqrt{b^2 - 4ac}}{2a} \qquad (8.15)$$

For Equation (8.7), the two roots (shown on Figure 8–2) are determined by

$$\text{Root} = \frac{-b + \sqrt{b^2 - 4ac}}{2a} = \frac{-2 + \sqrt{4 - (4)(-4)(5)}}{-8} = -.89564$$

$$\text{Root} = \frac{-b - \sqrt{b^2 - 4ac}}{2a} = \frac{-2 - \sqrt{84}}{-8} = 1.39564$$

Three points are necessary to define a parabola. Letting $y = f(x)$, if we have x_1, x_2, and x_3 and y_1, y_2, and y_3, then we have three equations in three unknowns that can be solved algebraically (simultaneously) for a, b, and c as follows

$$y_1 = ax_1^2 + bx_1 + c$$

$$y_2 = ax_2^2 + bx_2 + c$$

$$y_3 = ax_3^2 + bx_3 + c$$

Other Useful Techniques

Most often it is desirable to solve for a, b, and c directly—particularly when repetitive solutions are needed in a computer program or spreadsheet. The coefficients may be calculated from

$$b = \frac{(x_1^2 - x_2^2)(y_1 - y_3) - (x_1^2 - x_3^2)(y_1 - y_2)}{(x_1^2 - x_2^2)(x_1 - x_3) - (x_1^2 - x_3^2)(x_1 - x_2)} \quad (8.16)$$

$$a = \frac{y_1 - y_3 - b(x_1 - x_3)}{x_1^2 - x_3^2} \quad (8.17)$$

$$c = y_1 - ax_1^2 - bx_1 \quad (8.18)$$

For example, suppose we want to find the equation of the parabola in Figure 8–2 from three known points. We know its roots and the point for which we derived the tangent line all lie on the parabola.

$$x_1 = 1, \quad y_1 = 3$$
$$x_2 = -.89564, \quad y_2 = 0$$
$$x_3 = 1.39564, \quad y_3 = 0$$

Substituting in Equations (8.16), (8.17), and (8.18), we have

$$b = \frac{(.19783)(3) - (-.94781)(3)}{(.19783)(-.39564) - (-.94781)(1.89564)} = 2$$

$$a = \frac{3 - 0 - 2(-.39564)}{-.94781} = -4$$

$$c = 3 - (-4)(1) - 2(1) = 5$$

which agrees with the coefficients in Equation (8.7).

Using a parabola's coefficients a and b, the *slope* m of the straight-line equation that is tangent to the parabola at any point (x_i, y_i) is given by

$$m = 2ax_i + b \quad (8.19)$$

The intercept (or constant) of the straight-line equation is

$$b = y_i - mx_i \quad (8.20)$$

For the tangent to the parabola in Figure 8–2 at $(x = 1, y = 3)$, the slope is calculated by

$$m = 2(-4)(1) + 2 = -6$$

And the intercept is

$$b = 3 - (-6)(1) = 9$$

Therefore, the full equation of the tangent is

$$y = 9 - 6x$$

which agrees with the previous result.

If a series of observations exhibits a nonlinear trend, fitting a parabola might just fill the bill. Just like linear functions, parabolas may be fitted to a series of data points. The moment equations for a parabola are

$$\sum y = \left(\sum x^2\right)a + \left(\sum x\right)b + nc \qquad (8.21)$$

$$\sum xy = \left(\sum x^3\right)a + \left(\sum x^2\right)b + \left(\sum x\right)c \qquad (8.22)$$

$$\sum x^2 y = \left(\sum x^4\right)a + \left(\sum x^3\right)b + \left(\sum x^2\right)c \qquad (8.23)$$

and these may be solved algebraically (simultaneously) or directly as provided below.

The table of data values must be expanded to include x^3, $x^2 y$, x^4 for n observations and the sums thereof. To solve for a, b, and c directly, we define three constants to keep the algebra manageable.

$$\alpha = n\sum x^3 - \sum x \sum x^2 \qquad (8.24)$$

$$\beta = n\sum x^4 - \left(\sum x^2\right)^2 \qquad (8.25)$$

$$\gamma = n\sum x^2 - \left(\sum x\right)^2 \qquad (8.26)$$

Then a, b, and c may be determined from

$$b = \frac{\beta\left(n\sum xy - \sum x\sum y\right) - \alpha\left(n\sum x^2 y - \sum x^2 \sum y\right)}{\beta\gamma - \alpha^2} \quad (8.27)$$

$$a = \frac{n\sum xy - \gamma b - \sum x \sum y}{\alpha} \quad (8.28)$$

$$c = \frac{\sum y - a\sum x^2 - b\sum x}{n} \quad (8.29)$$

Suppose we had five observations (x_i, y_i) and completed Table 8–3. To fit a parabola to these data, we begin by calculating the three constants.

$$\alpha = n\sum x^3 - \sum x \sum x^2 = 5(1438) - 28(190) = 1{,}870$$

$$\beta = n\sum x^4 - \left(\sum x^2\right)^2 = 5(11554) - (190)^2 = 21{,}670$$

$$\gamma = n\sum x^2 - \left(\sum x^2\right)^2 = 5(190) - (28)^2 = 166$$

Next, we solve for the parabolic coefficients.

$$b = \frac{21{,}670[5(259) - 28(35)] - 1870[5(2075) - 35(190)]}{21{,}670(166) - (1870)^2}$$

$$= \frac{-139{,}700}{100{,}320} = -1.39254$$

$$a = \frac{5(259) - 166(-1.39254) - 28(35)}{1870} = .29207$$

$$c = \frac{35 - .29207(190) - 28(-1.39254)}{5} = 3.69956$$

Thus the equation of the best-fitting parabola to these data is

$$y = .2921x^2 - 1.3925x + 3.6997$$

TABLE 8-3

Data for fitting a parabola

x	y	xy	x^2	x^2y	x^3	x^4
2	2	4	4	8	8	16
4	3	12	16	48	64	256
5	4	20	25	100	125	625
8	11	88	64	704	512	4,096
9	15	135	81	1,215	729	6,561
28	35	259	190	2,075	1,438	11,554

Plotting the data with Excel and using the "Add Trendline" feature, we get Figure 8–4. Again, we have an extremely close fit with an R^2 of .9989.

CURVE FITTING WITH OTHER NONLINEAR FORMS

Sometimes a set of observations does not exhibit either a linear trend or a trend that may be approximated by a parabola or higher-order polynomial. In such cases, an exponential, logarithmic, or power function might apply.

An *exponential* function takes the form

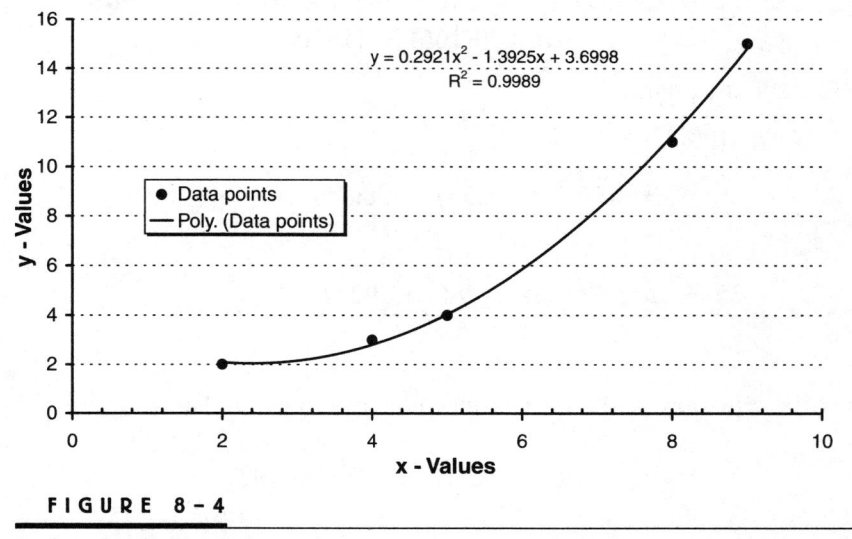

FIGURE 8-4

Curve fitting with a parabola

Other Useful Techniques

$$y = be^{mx}$$

Letting

$$Y = \ln(y) \quad \text{and} \quad B = \ln(b)$$

we have

$$Y = mx + B$$

which is a linear function. To fit an exponential function to the data in Table 8–4, use Equations (8.12) and (8.13) to find m and B.

$$m = \frac{5(16.036) - 10(5.481)}{5(30) - (10)^2} = .5074$$

$$B = \frac{5.481 - 10(.5074)}{5} = .0814$$

Since $B = \ln(b)$, $b = e^B$ and $b = 1.085$. Therefore, the equation of the regression curve is

$$y = 1.085e^{.5074x}$$

as shown in Figure 8–5.

A *logarithmic* function takes the form of

$$y = m \ln(x) + b$$

To fit a logarithmic function to the data in Table 8–5, use Equations (8.12) and (8.13) to find m and b.

TABLE 8-4
Data for an exponential function

x	y	Y	xY	x^2
0	1	0.000	0.000	0
1	2	0.693	0.693	1
2	3	1.099	2.197	4
3	5	1.609	4.828	9
4	8	2.079	8.318	16
10	19	5.481	16.036	30

FIGURE 8-5

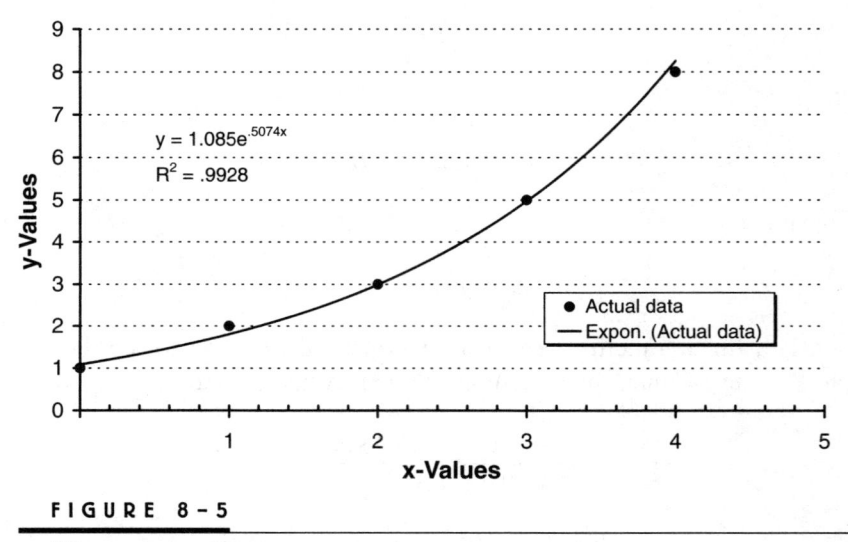

Fitting an exponential curve

$$m = \frac{5(181.873) - 6.579(136)}{5(9.41) - (6.579)^2} = 17.1556$$

$$b = \frac{136 - 17.1556(6.579)}{5} = 4.6267$$

Therefore, the regression curve is

$$y = 17.1556 \ln(x) + 4.6267$$

as shown in Figure 8-6.

A *power* function takes the form

TABLE 8-5

Data for a logarithmic function

x	y	ln(x)	y ln(x)	[ln(x)]²
2	20	0.693	13.863	0.480
3	25	1.099	27.465	1.207
4	30	1.386	41.589	1.922
5	35	1.609	56.330	2.590
6	40	1.792	71.670	3.210
20	150	6.579	210.918	9.410

Other Useful Techniques

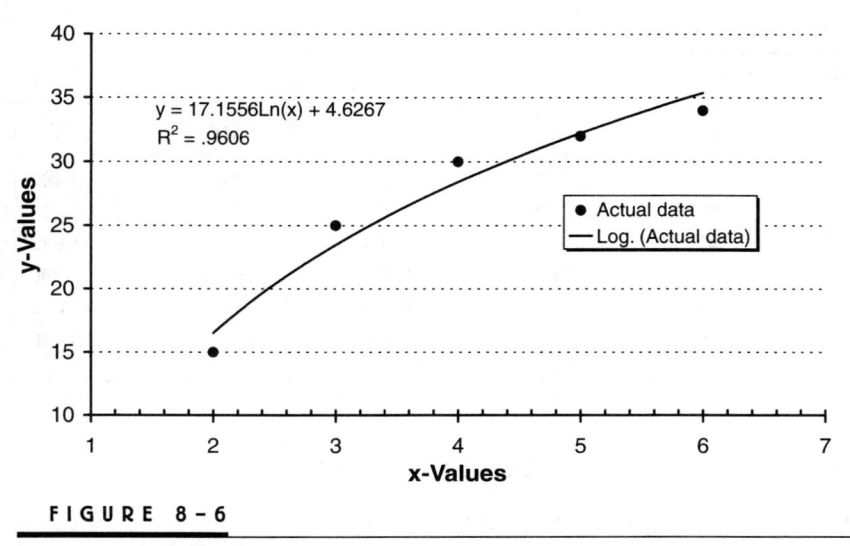

FIGURE 8-6

Fitting a logarithmic curve

$$y = bx^m$$

Taking the log of both sides gives

$$\ln(y) = m \ln(x) + \ln(b)$$

Letting

$$Y = \ln(y), \qquad B = \ln(b), \qquad \text{and} \qquad X = \ln(x)$$

we have

$$Y = mX + B$$

which is a linear function.

To fit a power function to the data in Table 8–6, use Equations (8.12) and (8.13) to find m and B.

$$m = \frac{5(25.168) - 6.579(18.38)}{5(9.41) - (6.579)^2} = 1.3056$$

$$B = \frac{18.38 - 1.3056(6.579)}{5} = 1.95806$$

Therefore,

TABLE 8-6

Data for a power function

x	y	X	Y	XY	X²
2	20	0.693	2.996	2.076	0.480
3	25	1.099	3.219	3.536	1.207
4	40	1.386	3.689	5.114	1.922
5	60	1.609	4.094	6.590	2.590
6	80	1.792	4.382	7.852	3.210
20	225	6.579	18.380	25.168	9.410

$$Y = 1.3056X + 1.95806$$

Taking the exponential of both sides, we get

$$y = 7.08554x^{1.3056}$$

The graph of the fitted power function is shown in Figure 8–7.

DETERMINING EXTREME VALUES

Instead of (or in addition to) finding the roots of an equation, sometimes we will want to find a value of a variable in an *objective* function that

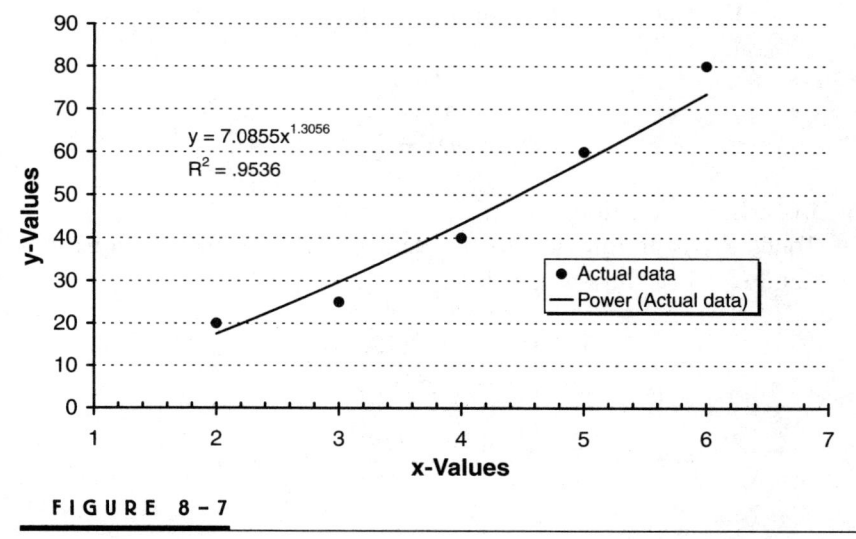

FIGURE 8-7

Fitting a power curve

maximizes that function. An example would be to maximize the return on investment. Other times we might want to find a value that *minimizes* an objective function, such as a function that describes risk.

Suppose we want to find the x value x^* that maximizes Equation (8.7) (see Figure 8–2). If it exists, a function's extreme value (maximum or minimum) occurs at the point where its first derivative = 0. Taking the first derivative of the generalized quadratic Equation (8.14), we have

$$f'(x) = 2ax + b$$

Setting $f'(x) = 0$, we get

$$x^* = \frac{-b}{2a}$$

Substituting the Equation (8.7) values, we get

$$\frac{-b}{2a} = \frac{-2}{2(-4)} = .25 \quad \text{and} \quad f(x) \text{ at } x^* = 5.25$$

We now know that an extreme value of $f(x) = 5.25$ will occur at $x^* = .25$. Is it a maximum or a minimum? If the second derivative of $f(x)$ is negative, we have a maximum; otherwise, we have a minimum.

$$f'(x) = 2 - 8x$$
$$f''(x) = -8$$

Therefore, Equation (8.7) is *maximized* at $x^* = .25$.

Rarely, if ever, will an objective function be a simple quadratic equation. Many times there is no closed-form solution to finding the extreme (maximum or minimum) values of an equation, and such values must be found by successive approximation. The methods for finding the extreme values of an equation by such successive approximations are called *search algorithms*.

SEARCH ALGORITHMS: BINARY SEARCH

By far the simplest search algorithm is the *binary search* (sometimes called the *dicotomic search*). First, we choose a tolerance level ε that defines how close we want the value of x^* to be to the real answer. Second, we choose an interval from a to c, that is, $[a, c]$, that includes x^*. Frequently, we choose $a = 0$ so that all positive values of x up to and including c are candidates for x^*. We then define an interior point b (the estimate of x^*) by

$$b = \frac{a + c}{2}$$

such that

$$a < b < c$$

Finally, we substitute $b - \varepsilon$ and $b + \varepsilon$ into our objective function to find $f(b - \varepsilon)$ and $f(b + \varepsilon)$. If $f(b - \varepsilon) > f(b + \varepsilon)$, we repeat the whole process with the new interval $[a, b]$; otherwise, we repeat with the new interval $[b, c]$. When the latest estimate b differs from the previous estimate by less than ε, we have converged on x^*.

For example, suppose we want to find the maximum of Equation (8.7) by the binary search method within a tolerance ε of .00001. We arbitrarily select $a = 0$ and $c = 100$. Table 8–7 shows the convergence on x^*.

The search required 23 iterations for an initial interval of 0 to 100 and a tolerance level of .00001. Lowering the tolerance level to .0001 and shortening the initial interval from 0 to 3 requires only 14 iterations.

Note that x^* has been found to be .2500 to four decimal places—which agrees with the known answer.

SEARCH ALGORITHMS: THE GOLDEN RATIO SEARCH

The *golden ratio* (sometimes called the *golden mean* or *golden section*) was known by the ancient Greeks and Egyptians and was employed frequently in their art and architecture. If a line of known length is divided into two unequal segments of lengths a and b with a being the larger segment and the ratio $a + b$ to a is equal to the ratio of a to b, then we have the golden ratio, which, to six decimal places, is 1.618034. The *golden rectangle* is a rectangle for which the longer side is 1.618034 times the shorter side—said to be the most pleasing proportion to the eye.

Although unknown to the ancients, the exact value of the golden ratio Φ is

$$\Phi = \frac{1 + \sqrt{5}}{2} = 1.618034 \qquad (8.30)$$

and its corollary ϕ (the reciprocal of Φ) is

TABLE 8-7

Binary search for maximum in Equation (8.7)
Tolerance level = .00001

Iteration	a	b	c	$f(b - \varepsilon)$	$f(b + \varepsilon)$
1	0.0000	50.000000	100.0000	−9,894.9960200	−9,895.0039800
2	0.0000	25.000000	50.0000	−2,444.9980200	−2,445.0019800
3	0.0000	12.500000	25.0000	−594.9990200	−595.0009800
4	0.0000	6.250000	12.5000	−138.7495200	−138.7504800
5	0.0000	3.125000	6.2500	−27.8122700	−27.8127300
6	0.0000	1.562500	3.1250	−1.6405200	−1.6407300
7	0.0000	0.781250	1.5625	4.1211362	4.1210512
8	0.0000	0.390625	0.7813	5.1709097	5.1708872
9	0.0000	0.195313	0.3906	5.2380327	5.2380415
10	0.1953	0.292690	0.3906	5.2426182	5.2426113
11	0.1953	0.244141	0.2930	5.2498622	5.2498631
12	0.2441	0.268555	0.2930	5.2486244	5.2486214
13	0.2441	0.256348	0.2686	5.2498393	5.2498383
14	0.2441	0.250244	0.2563	5.2499998	5.2499997
15	0.2441	0.247182	0.2502	5.2499682	5.2499687
16	0.2472	0.248718	0.2502	5.2499933	5.2499935
17	0.2487	0.249481	0.2502	5.2499989	5.2499990
18	0.2495	0.249863	0.2502	5.2499999	5.2499999
19	0.2499	0.250053	0.2502	5.2500000	5.2500000
20	0.2499	0.249958	0.2501	5.2500000	5.2500000
21	0.2500	0.250006	0.2501	5.2500000	5.2500000
22	0.2500	0.249982	0.2500	5.2500000	5.2500000
23	0.2500	0.249994	0.2500	5.2500000	5.2500000

$$\phi = \frac{\sqrt{5} - 1}{2} = .618034 \qquad (8.31)$$

Note that ϕ is also $\Phi - 1$.

The golden ratio is also present in the *Fibonacci series*. Leonardo de Pisa (1170–1250), whose pseudonym was Fibonacci, considered the problem of multiplying pairs of rabbits over one year's time and developed the famous Fibonacci series of numbers. Beginning with 0, 1, the next number in the series is the sum of the two previous numbers, that is,

$$0, 1, 1, 2, 3, 5, 8, 13, 21, 34, \ldots$$

Any Fibonacci number F_n can be found from

$$F_n = \frac{1}{\sqrt{5}}\left[\left(\frac{1+\sqrt{5}}{2}\right)^n - \left(\frac{1-\sqrt{5}}{2}\right)^n\right] \quad (8.32)$$

where n is the sequence number beginning with 0. Believe it or not, Equation (8.32) results in an *integer* solution. Try it on the computer.

The ratio of any Fibonacci number to its previous number in the sequence tends toward the golden ratio as the series expands. In mathematical terms,

$$\Phi = \lim_{n \to \infty} \frac{F_n}{F_{n-1}}$$

For example, from Equation (8.32), the twenty-fifth and twenty-fourth Fibonacci numbers are 75,025 and 46,368, respectively. Their ratio is 1.618034. The Fibonacci series is observable in nature (branching plants, petals on flowers, sunflower seed growth, etc.). Both Φ and ϕ are employed in many stock-trading systems—primarily as retracement functions after a price reversal. For the golden ratio search, only ϕ is used.

For the golden ratio search, we consider an interval [a, b] that includes x^*. If $f(x)$ has a single extreme value (maximum or minimum), it is possible to replace interval [a, b] with a subinterval in which $f(x)$ takes on its extreme value. The golden ratio search requires two interior points:

$$c = a + (\phi - 1)(b - a)$$

and

$$d = a + \phi(b - a)$$

such that

$$a < c < d < b$$

The values of $f(c)$ and $f(d)$ are then calculated.

For the case in which the extreme value is a *minimum,* if $f(c) \leq f(d)$, then the minimum must lie in the subinterval [a, d], and we replace b with d and continue the search in the new subinterval. If $f(c) > f(d)$, the minimum must lie in the subinterval [c, b], and we replace a with c and continue the search.

For the case in which the extreme value is a *maximum,* if $f(c) \geq f(d)$, then the maximum must lie in the subinterval [a, d], and we replace b with d and continue the search in the new subinterval. If $f(c) <$

$f(d)$, the maximum must lie in the subinterval $[c, b]$, and we replace a with c and continue the search.

The search for a maximum of Equation (8.7) continues until the value $(d - c)$ is less than the tolerance level ε. Assume the same values as used in the binary search example. This time, the interval values $[a, b]$ will be 0 and 100, respectively. Table 8–8 shows the first and last three lines of the convergence using an initial interval from 0 to 3 and a tolerance of .00001.

SEARCH ALGORITHMS: THE PARABOLIC INTERPOLATION METHOD

A more sophisticated search may be attempted based on the theory that a fitted *parabola* will have the same maximum as $f(x)$ for $f(x^*)$. Since three points uniquely define a parabola (as long as they do not lie on a straight line), we have the interval $[a, c]$ that includes x^* and a single interior point b such that

$$a < b < c$$

Beginning with an initial estimate for b that ensures the entire range from a to c will be considered,

$$b = c - \varepsilon$$

First, we calculate $f(a)$, $f(b)$, and $f(c)$. Second, we solve one of the following equations for $\hat{b}$ (the new estimate for b).

For a maximum:

$$\hat{b} = b - \frac{1}{2} \left\{ \frac{(b - a)^2[f(b) - f(c)] - (b - c)^2[f(b) - f(a)]}{(b - a)[f(b) - f(c)] - (b - c)[f(b) - f(a)]} \right\}$$

(8.33)

For a minimum:

$$\hat{b} = b + \frac{1}{2} \left\{ \frac{(b - a)^2[f(b) - f(c)] - (b - c)^2[f(b) - f(a)]}{(b - a)[f(b) - f(c)] - (b - c)[f(b) - f(a)]} \right\}$$

(8.34)

If $\hat{b} < b$, replace c with b. If $\hat{b} > b$, replace a with b. Replace b with $\hat{b}$, and calculate new values for $f(a)$, $f(b)$, and $f(c)$. Then solve

TABLE 8-8

Golden ratio search for maximum in Equation (8.7)

Tolerance level = .00001

Iteration	a	c	d	b	f(a)	f(c)	f(d)	f(b)
1	0.00	1.145898	1.854102	3.0000	5.00	2.0395	(5.0426)	(25.0000)
2	0.00	0.708204	1.145898	1.8541	5.00	4.4102	2.0395	(5.0426)
3	0.00	0.437694	0.708204	1.1459	5.00	5.1091	4.4102	2.0395
...								
23	0.25	0.249980	0.249998	0.2500	5.25	5.2500	5.2500	5.2500
24	0.25	0.249998	0.250009	0.2500	5.25	5.2500	5.2500	5.2500
25	0.25	0.249991	0.249998	0.2500	5.25	5.2500	5.2500	5.2500

either Equation (8.33) or Equation (8.34) for a new $\hat{b}$. Repeat the process until the difference between $\hat{b}$ and the previous b is less than or equal to the tolerance level ε.

As an example of the parabolic interpolation search, we choose not to use Equation (8.7) this time because it is itself a parabola, and the parabolic interpolation search simply will jump to the maximum in two iterations—the trivial case. Rather, assume we want to find the maximum of Equation (8.35) to a tolerance of .00001.

$$f(x) = x\sqrt{9 - x} \qquad (8.35)$$

The roots of Equation (8.35) are found by setting each of the factors x and $\sqrt{9 - x}$ equal to 0.

$$x = 0$$
$$\sqrt{9 - x} = 0$$

Squaring both sides,

$$9 - x = 0$$

Therefore,

$$x = 9$$

Since $f(x) = 0$ for $x = 0$ and $x = 9$, if $f(x)$ has a maximum, x^* will lie in the interval from 0 to 9. Letting $a = 0$ and $c = 9$, we calculate b. Since $b = c - \varepsilon$,

$$b = 9 - .00001 = 8.9999$$

After calculating $f(a)$, $f(b)$, and $f(c)$, we substitute the values into Equation (8.33) and solve for $\hat{b}$. Table 8–9 shows the first and last three lines of the convergence on $x^* = 6$ (to four decimal places). For $x^* = 6$, $f(x^*) = 10.3923$.

Figure 8–8 contains a graph of Equation (8.35) showing its roots and maximum value.

SEARCH ALGORITHMS: THE NEWTON-RAPHSON METHOD

Rather than searching for maxima and minima, sometimes we will want to find the roots of an equation when no simple algebraic solution exits. The Newton-Raphson search method makes use of the equation's deriv-

TABLE 8-9

Parabolic search for maximum in Equation (8.35)
Tolerance level = .00001

Iteration	a	b	c	f(a)	f(b)	f(c)
1	0.0000	8.999999	9.0000	0.0285	0.0285	0.0000
2	0.0000	4.500000	9.0000	0.0000	9.5459	0.0285
3	4.5000	4.503354	9.0000	9.5459	9.5495	0.0285
⋮						
34	5.9999	5.999936	8.9999	10.3923	10.3923	0.0285
35	5.9999	5.999953	8.9999	10.3923	10.3923	0.0285
36	6.0000	5.999965	8.9999	10.3923	10.3923	0.0285

ative—defining tangents at successive points on the curve until the solution is reached. Let x be a solution to (root of) $f(x)$ such that $f(x) = 0$. Beginning with a *guess* for x_1 (can be any number), successively better approximations of x are given by

$$x_{n+1} = x_n - \frac{f(x_n)}{f'(x_n)} \quad (8.36)$$

where $f(x_n)$ = the original function
$f'(x_n)$ = the function's first derivative

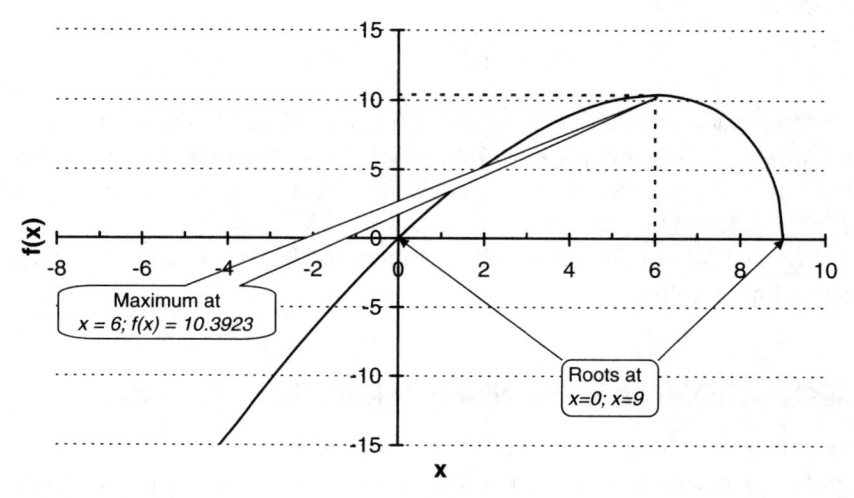

FIGURE 8-8

Graph of $f(x) = x(9 - x)^{1/2}$

x_n = an approximation of the root (the solution)
ε = tolerance level

The solution is found when

$$x_{n+1} - x_n \leq \varepsilon$$

This method converges rapidly on the correct solution. For example, suppose we want to find a solution to (positive root of) Equation (8.7). First, we define the zero of the function.

$$f(x) = 2x - 4x^2 + 5 = 0$$

Next, we take the derivative of $f(x)$.

$$f'(x) = 2 - 8x$$

Now we guess at the solution, say, $x_1 = 5$. The next approximation x_2 is found from Equation (8.36).

$$x_2 = x_1 - \frac{f(x_1)}{f'(x_1)} = 5 - \frac{10 - 100 + 5}{2 - 40} = 2.763158$$

Successive approximations are

$$x_3 = x_2 - \frac{f(x_2)}{f'(x_2)} = 2.763158 - \frac{-20.01385}{-20.10526} = 1.767705$$

$$x_4 = x_3 - \frac{f(x_3)}{f'(x_3)} = 1.767705 - \frac{-3.963709}{-12.14164} = 1.441249$$

$$x_5 = x_4 - \frac{f(x_4)}{f'(x_4)} = 1.441249 - \frac{-.0426294}{-9.52999} = 1.396517$$

$$x_6 = x_5 - \frac{f(x_5)}{f'(x_5)} = 1.396517 - \frac{-.008004}{-9.172135} = 1.395644$$

$$x_7 = x_6 - \frac{f(x_6)}{f'(x_6)} = 1.395644 - \frac{-.000003}{-9.165154} = 1.395644$$

To five decimal places, the positive root of Equation (8.7) obtained in an earlier section was 1.39564—precisely the same answer obtained by Newton-Raphson in six iterations.

FINDING IMPLIED VOLATILITY BY NEWTON-RAPHSON[1]

Recalling that vega measures the change in an option's price for a given change in implied volatility, it is actually the *derivative* of the curve relating price to implied volatility. As such, vega may be used in the Newton-Raphson search technique to find implied volatility. Because an option's vega is relatively linear, the method converges quite quickly—even with a poor first guess. Letting implied volatility be denoted by σ, we have

$$\sigma_{i+1} = \sigma_i - \frac{y_i - P}{\nu_i} \qquad (8.37)$$

where y_i = option's theoretical value at σ_i
P = market price of option
ν_i = option's vega at σ_i

We solve Equation (8.37) iteratively until the difference between P and y_i is less than some predetermined error level.

For example, from Table 6–2, the market price of the CSCO August 2003 17.5 Call on July 11, 2003, was $1.60. The Black-Scholes theoretical value was $1.53, the historical volatility was .398, and this option's vega was 1.928. What is the implied volatility for an error less than .00001?

Using historical volatility as our first guess, we have

$$\sigma_2 = .398 - \left(\frac{1.53227 - 1.6}{1.928}\right) = .43313$$

$$\sigma_3 = .43313 - \left(\frac{1.600689 - 1.6}{1.96571}\right) = .43278$$

Since the error of .000689 is more than our limit, we will try another iteration.

$$\sigma_4 = .43278 - \left(\frac{1.600001 - 1.6}{1.96538}\right) = .43278$$

The error is now .0000001. Thus, in only three iterations, we have found the implied volatility of .433.

---

[1] Sheldon Natenberg, *Option Volatility and Pricing* (New York: McGraw-Hill, 1994), p. 446.

PUT/CALL RATIO[2]

Believers in technical analysis employ *indicators* such as moving averages and Fibonacci numbers to aid in their forecasts of market direction and sentiment. The Put/Call ratio is a market sentiment indicator that shows the relationship between the number of Puts and Calls traded on the Chicago Board of Options Exchange (CBOE) each day. Generally speaking, the higher the level of the Put/Call ratio, the more bearish the investors are in the market. Conversely, lower readings suggest high Call volume and bullish sentiment.

The Put/Call ratio is a contrarian indicator; that is, when it reaches excessive levels, the market typically corrects and moves in the other direction. A single reading on a single day is virtually meaningless—the Put/Call ratio should be viewed as a process over time using moving averages. One suggested interpretation of the Put/Call ratio is given in Table 8–10.

The Put/Call ratio is calculated from

$$\text{Put/Call ratio} = \frac{\text{volume of Puts}}{\text{volume of Calls}}$$

for any given instrument on any given day. The ratios for index and equity options together with a total Put/Call ratio are posted daily at www.cboe.com/MktData/default.asp.

On December 12, 2003, the CBOE reported

Equity options   .5
Index options   1.49
Total options   .75

TABLE 8-10

Meaning of Put/Call ratio

	10-Day moving average	4-Week moving average
Excessively bearish (buy)	>0.8	>0.7
Excessively bullish (sell)	<.45	<.4

Source: equis.com.

---

[2] Steven B. Achilis, *Technical Analysis from A to Z* (New York: McGraw-Hill, 1995), pp. 248–250.

Since we want to discern the "herd instinct" of the majority of speculators and use a contrarian indicator, we do not want to be influenced by what the professionals are doing. Professional money managers use index options to hedge large stock portfolios, typically distorting the sentiment of the purely speculative crowd. On December 12, 2003, the Put/Call ratio stood at 1.49—regarded as excessively bearish from Table 8–4. However, it is likely that the professionals are buying a large number of protective Puts and the market is not bearish at all. A better measure of the speculative sentiment is given by the equity Put/Call ratio. At .5 on December 12, 2003, it suggests that speculators are becoming excessively bullish and it might be prudent to consider selling. Of course, the bullish indicator should be checked by looking at a moving average of the past Put/Call ratios.

As always, a single measure such as the Put/Call ratio should not be used in a vacuum but rather in conjunction with other indicators that tend to confirm or conflict with the single measure of interest.

A POLYNOMIAL APPROXIMATION TO THE NORMAL DENSITY FUNCTION

This polynomial approximates $N(z)$ for $-\infty < z < +\infty$, where z represents the number of standard deviations. In short, it finds the normal probability to the left of z. This polynomial returns the same answer as the NORMSDIST function in Excel and is used repeatedly in the programs supplied on the accompanying CD.

$$N(z) = 1 - \frac{1}{\sqrt{2\pi}} e^{-z^2/2}(a_1 x + a_2 x^2 + a_3 x^3 + a_4 x^4 + a_5 x^5) \quad (8.38)$$

where

$$x = \frac{1}{1 + .2316419z}$$

and

$a_1 = .31938153$
$a_2 = -.3565638$
$a_3 = 1.78147794$
$a_4 = -1.821256$
$a_5 = 1.33027443$

Sometimes it will be necessary to find the number of standard deviations z when the normal probability p is known. This polynomial is simply the inverse of Equation (8.38).

$$z = x - \frac{c_0 + c_1 x + c_2 x^2}{1 + d_1 x + d_2 x^2 + d_3 x^3} \qquad (8.39)$$

where

$$x = \sqrt{\ln\left(\frac{1}{p^2}\right)}$$

and

$c_0 = 2.515517$
$c_1 = .802853$
$c_2 = .010328$
$d_1 = 1.432788$
$d_2 = .189269$
$d_3 = .001308$

THE CENTRAL LIMIT THEOREM

The importance of the normal curve cannot be overstated. Not only does it represent an astounding number of elements in our everyday lives, but it also is the basis for a great many scientific inquiries and economic studies. Its widespread applicability stems from a concept known as the *central limit theorem*.

The central limit theorem states that the distribution of sample means taken from *any* distribution (normal or not) will approach a normal distribution as the size of the samples increases. Furthermore, the sampling distribution of the means will have the mean $\mu_{\bar{x}} = x$ and the standard deviation $\sigma_{\bar{x}} = s/\sqrt{n}$, where n is the sample size. This provides for sampling from distributions of unknown shapes and applying the properties of the normal curve.

If n is large, the binomial distribution can be approximated with a normal curve having $\mu = np$ and $\sigma = \sqrt{np(1-p)}$. The rule of thumb is that n should be large enough for $np \geq 5$ and $n(1-p) \geq 5$. For example, we can calculate the probability of getting 5 heads out of 12 tosses of a balanced coin from the binomial distribution using Equation (2.20).

$$P(5:12) = {}_{12}C_5 p^5(1-p)^7$$

$$= 792\left(\frac{1}{2}\right)^5\left(\frac{1}{2}\right)^7 = \frac{792}{4096} = .1934$$

The sample size is sufficient for a normal-curve approximation. To determine the normal-curve approximation to this binomial probability, we need to find the *area under the curve* between 4.5 and 5.5 because, on the normal curve, the probability of a single point is 0.

$$\mu = np = 12\left(\frac{1}{2}\right) = 6$$

and

$$\sigma = \sqrt{np(1-p)} = \sqrt{12\left(\frac{1}{2}\right)\left(\frac{1}{2}\right)} = 1.732$$

Conversion to the z scale results in

$$z_{4.5} = \frac{4.5 - 6}{1.732} = -.8661$$

$$z_{5.5} = \frac{5.5 - 6}{1.732} = -.2887$$

And the probability is

$$N(z_{5.5}) - N(z_{4.5}) = N(-.2887) - N(-.8661)$$

$$= .3864 - .1932 = .1932$$

Figure 8–9 is a graphic representation of the problem.

The difference between the result from the binomial distribution (19.34 percent) and the result from the normal distribution (19.32 percent) is negligible.

The approximation is quite accurate *unless p* is extremely close to 0 or 1. For cases in which n is very large and p very small, a better approximation to the binomial distribution is the *Poisson distribution*—sometimes referred to as the *distribution of rare events*. The formula for this distribution is

Other Useful Techniques   283

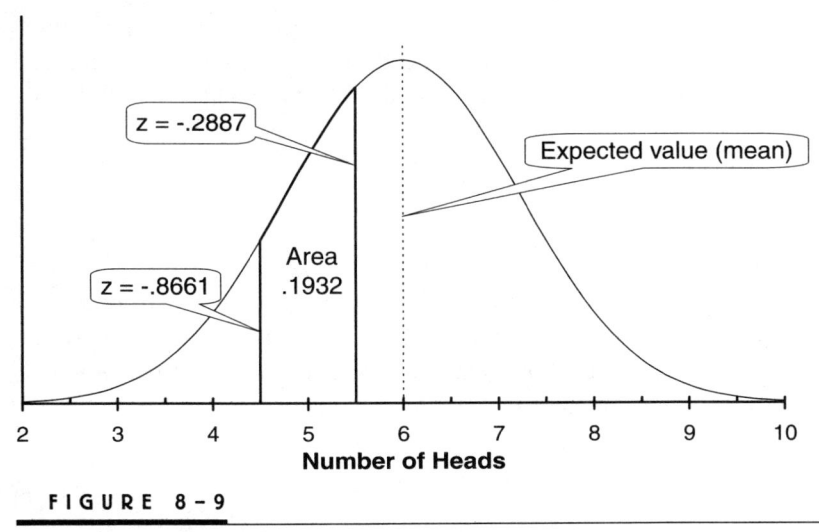

[Figure showing a normal distribution curve with callouts: "z = -.2887", "Expected value (mean)", "z = -.8661", "Area .1932". X-axis labeled "Number of Heads" with values 2, 3, 4, 5, 6, 7, 8, 9, 10.]

FIGURE 8-9

Normal distribution of heads in trials

$$P(x) = \frac{\mu^x e^{-\mu}}{x!} \qquad (8.40)$$

As with the binomial distribution, $\mu = np$. The standard deviation σ, however, is $\sqrt{np}$. Note that in Equation (8.40) $P(x)$ is not dependent on σ. The distribution was first derived in 1837 by S. D. Poisson. The most famous application of the Poisson distribution appeared in a book by von Bortkiewicz in 1898, wherein he calculated the probabilities of a Prussian cavalryman being killed by the kick of a horse. Since the Prussian army was extremely large and the number of deaths from horse kicks was extremely small, the author believed the number of horse-kick deaths in a given year should follow the Poisson distribution.

Von Bortkiewicz collected data from 10 army corps over a period of 20 years, giving him 200 readings. There were 122 actual deaths, so the average number of deaths per year per corps was .61, which was used as an estimate of μ. In no year were there more than 4 deaths; hence the problem is one of solving Equation (8.40) repeatedly for $P(0)$, $P(1)$, $P(2)$, $P(3)$, and $P(4)$. The probability of getting *no* deaths is

$$P(0) = \frac{.61^0 e^{-.61}}{0!} = \frac{(1).543}{1} = .543$$

In 200 readings, the expected number of no deaths would be 109. Table 8–11 shows a comparison between the expected number of deaths and the actual reported number of deaths from horse kicks. A remarkably good fit!

SKEWNESS AND KURTOSIS[3]

If we have approximated a group of data with a normal distribution, we might want to know how our approximation compares with a *true* normal distribution. Many distribution measures are derived from their *moments* about the mean. The jth moment about the mean is given by

$$\alpha_j = \frac{1}{n}\sum_{i=1}^{n}(x_i - \bar{x})^j \qquad (8.41)$$

where α = moment
x_i = individual observation
$\bar{x}$ = mean of the distribution
n = number of observations
j = moment designator

The first moment of a distribution α_1 is simply its mean $\bar{x}$. The second moment of a distribution is its variance s^2 (the standard deviation squared), given by

TABLE 8–11

Comparison of actual and expected horse-kick deaths

No. of deaths per year	Probability	Expected frequency	Actual
0	0.543	109	109
1	0.331	66	65
2	0.101	20	22
3	0.021	4	3
4	0.003	1	1

---

[3] Sheldon Natenberg, *op. cit.*, pp. 440–441.

$$\alpha_2 = \frac{1}{n}\sum_{i=1}^{n}(x_i - \bar{x})^2$$

Likewise, the third and fourth moments are given by

$$\alpha_3 = \frac{1}{n}\sum_{i=1}^{n}(x_i - \bar{x})^3 \qquad (8.42)$$

and

$$\alpha_4 = \frac{1}{n}\sum_{i=1}^{n}(x_i - \bar{x})^4 \qquad (8.43)$$

The *skewness* of a distribution indicates the degree of symmetry present (whether one tail is longer than the other). Positive skewness means the right tail is longer than the left tail. Negative skewness means the left tail is longer than the right tail. In a perfectly normal distribution, skewness equals 0. Skewness is calculated by

$$\text{Skewness} = \frac{\alpha_3}{\alpha_2\sqrt{\alpha_2}} \qquad (8.44)$$

The *kurtosis* of a distribution describes how fat or skinny (or short or tall) the distribution is. A perfectly normal distribution has a kurtosis of 0 (called *mesokurtic*). If a distribution has positive kurtosis, called *leptokurtic* or "narrow humped," it will be tall and skinny with long tails. If a distribution has a negative kurtosis, called *platykurtic* or "broad humped," it will be short and fat with short tails. Kurtosis is calculated by

$$\text{Kurtosis} = \frac{\alpha_4}{\alpha_2^2} - 3 \qquad (8.45)$$

For example, the normal distribution of the data in Table 2–3 has a mean of 70.275 and a variance of 4.9716. From Equation (8.41), the first four moments are

$$\alpha_1 = 70.275$$

$$\alpha_2 = 4.9716$$

$$\alpha_3 = 7.8719$$

$$\alpha_4 = 84.9012$$

From Equations (8.43) and (8.42), the skewness and kurtosis are

$$\text{Skewness} = \frac{\alpha_3}{\alpha_2\sqrt{\alpha_2}} = \frac{7.8719}{4.9716\sqrt{4.9716}} = .77$$

$$\text{Kurtosis} = \frac{\alpha_4}{\alpha_2^2} - 3 = \left(\frac{84.9012}{4.9716^2} - 3\right) = .43$$

This sample distribution will be slightly peaked and skewed to the right.

THE CONSEQUENCES OF TAKING SAMPLES

To begin with, whenever we take samples, we mean *random* samples. A random sample from a *finite* population is one in which all the elements of that population had an equal chance of being selected. Often, the elements of a finite population can be numbered and the sample taken on the basis of a table of random numbers. Starting at *x* and taking every *n*th item, where *x* and *n* are selected randomly, is also a viable selection method. Sometimes it is simply not practical to number each item or arrange them in some specific order. Take, for instance, a bin containing 500,000 ball bearings that needs the average diameter calculated on the basis of a sample. Here we can only proceed "haphazardly without definite aim or purpose."[4]

The preceding remarks about randomness do not apply to *infinite populations,* such as a sample of 100 flips of a balanced coin out of all possible flips. Here, once a sample has been observed, it must be subjected to a *test* to determine randomness. Also, on occasion, we have no choice but to rely on past data to make predictions about the future because the past data are all we have. Such samples may or may not contain a bias. Again, tests must be performed to see if any patterns emerge that would suggest bias or nonrandomness. Descriptions of such tests may be found in most college statistics texts. They are not included here because they are not particularly germane to the study of options.

The central limit theorem holds that the mean of the sampling distribution of all means of samples from a population $\mu_{\bar{x}}$ is equal to the mean μ of the population. Furthermore, the theorem states that the standard deviation of the means in the sampling distribution $\sigma_{\bar{x}}$ is given by the formula $\sigma/\sqrt{n}$. This statistic is called the *standard error of the mean.*

---

[4] Freund, John E., Benjamin M. Perles, Charles M. Sullivan, and Levine, *Modern Business Statistics,* Revised, 1st Edition, © 1969, p. 172. Reprinted by permission of Pearson Education, Inc., Upper Saddle River, NJ.

$$\sigma_{\bar{x}} = \frac{\sigma}{\sqrt{n}} \quad (8.46)$$

where σ is the standard deviation of the population, and n is the sample size.

It is apparent from Equation (8.46) that the standard error of the mean *decreases* when n increases, so the larger the sample size, the closer a sample mean $\bar{x}$ will be the population mean μ. In practice, n is said to be large if $n \geq 30$.

If n is large, we generally may approximate the sampling distribution of interest by a normal curve. Thus the z-scale conversion will be[5]

$$z = \frac{\bar{x} - \mu}{\sigma/\sqrt{n}} \quad (8.47)$$

where z will fall within 2 standard deviations of the mean 95.4 percent of the time (1.96 standard deviations if we want 95 percent probability).

Performing a bit of algebra and substituting s as an estimate of σ (since we cannot know σ), we may now claim with a probability of 95 percent that the population mean μ lies in the following interval:

$$\bar{x} - 1.96 \frac{s}{\sqrt{n}} \leq \mu \leq \bar{x} + 1.96 \frac{s}{\sqrt{n}} \quad (8.48)$$

This inequality is known as the *95 percent confidence interval*. If we wanted a 98 or 99 percent confidence interval, the 1.96 would have been replaced with 2.33 and 2.58, respectively. An alternative statement to Equation (8.46) is that if we take a sample whose mean is m and whose standard deviation is s, we may assert with a probability of 95 percent that m will be different from μ by *no more than* the quantity

$$1.96 \frac{s}{\sqrt{n}}$$

This quantity is useful in making *point estimates* such as μ in Equation (8.46).

---

[5] Ibid., pp. 188–193.

When n is small (less than 30), the data typically will not fit the normal curve, and a special distribution called the *Student t distribution* generally is used instead. It defines a statistic t that has a distribution close to the normal curve. Values of t are tabulated for different *degrees of freedom*. The degrees of freedom for any given problem are equal to $n - 1$. The t statistic is defined by

$$t = \frac{\bar{x} - \mu}{s} \sqrt{n} \tag{8.49}$$

This distribution was first investigated by W. S. Gosset in 1908. Precluded by his employers from publishing research papers, he chose the pen name *Student;* hence the name Student t distribution.[6]

---

[6] Ibid., p. 196.

CHAPTER 9

Putting It All Together

> *Long-run is a misleading guide to current affairs. In the long-run we are all dead.*
>
> —John Maynard Keynes (1883–1946)

Keynes had it right. Forecasts based on long-run expected results *are* misleading guides to current (short-run) trials. Flipping an unbiased coin 10 million times certainly will produce a ratio of heads extremely close to one-half. Almost any ratio is possible with only 10 flips. The long-run expectation of tossing a seven with a pair of dice is 16.7 percent, but in the short run, say, 100 tosses, anywhere from 9 to 24 sevens could be expected. Expected results for options trades are based on what should happen in the long run. How can we reconcile this with the short-run activities of most options traders? This chapter is devoted to applying the theory developed thus far to actual trading.

USING THE SOFTWARE

Before selecting and analyzing specific trades or strategies, it is useful to understand how the accompanying software that determines $E(R)$ and various other component values can be used. If you do not intend to use the software, this section may be skipped. As mentioned in Chapter 6, there are two programs on the accompanying "Reehl Option Trader" CD that make all the tedious calculations introduced in Chapters 6, 7, and elsewhere. *Expectation.exe* takes inputs for a *single* strategy involving one or more options and produces an on-screen report that also may be printed. The report shows all pertinent information about employing that particular strategy. *DailyCheck.exe* takes inputs for 11 strike prices on a single underlying asset or index (5 on either side of the closest to the at-the-money strike) for a particular day. Bid, ask, and last prices are entered for Calls and Puts for each strike. Reports may be printed showing the results of all single and combination strategies (covered in this book) for each applicable set of strike prices. When nonzero quotes are available for all 11 strike prices, typically there will be from 200 to 300 individual trades produced having a positive expectation. These trades then can be subjected to the selection criteria developed in the next section.

To select and run either of the two programs, place the "Reehl Option Trader" CD into the CD drive of your computer, and locate the two programs. For Windows XP operating systems, this is done by clicking on "Start" and then on "Run." In the "Run" dialog box, click on "Browse." A new dialog box will appear containing both programs. Select the desired program, and click on "Open." The "Run" dialog box will reappear. Click on "OK."

The two programs also may be copied from the CD drive to your computer's hard drive and run from there. This is the favored method if continuous use of the programs is intended.

Each program begins with the same input screen asking for certain basic information, including trade date and expiration date, as shown in Figure 9–1. Follow the five on-screen instructions.

1. *Enter risk-free interest rate.* The cursor automatically starts blinking at the correct entry point. The risk-free interest rate is usually considered to be the T-bill rate of comparable maturity. Enter the interest rate as a decimal; that is, 1.2 percent would be entered as .012.

2. *Check target price multiple.* To the right of the interest rate box is the target price multiple box with the default 1.0000 entered. If the target price is to be the *current* price, make no changes. If the target price is a price other than the current price, divide the target price by the current price, and enter the result up to five decimal places (1.0xxxx or .9xxxx).

3. *Answer dividend question* (*discrete dividends only*). The default answer is "No." If dividends are *not* to be considered, go to instruction 4. Otherwise, check the "Yes" option and go to instruction 4.

4. *Click on trade date.* On the calendar, click on the appropriate month and year from the pull-down menus located at the upper right. Click

Welcome To Expectational Analysis

1. Enter Risk-free Interest Rate
2. Check Target Price Multiple
3. Answer Dividend Question
4. Click on Trade Date
5. Click on Expiration Date

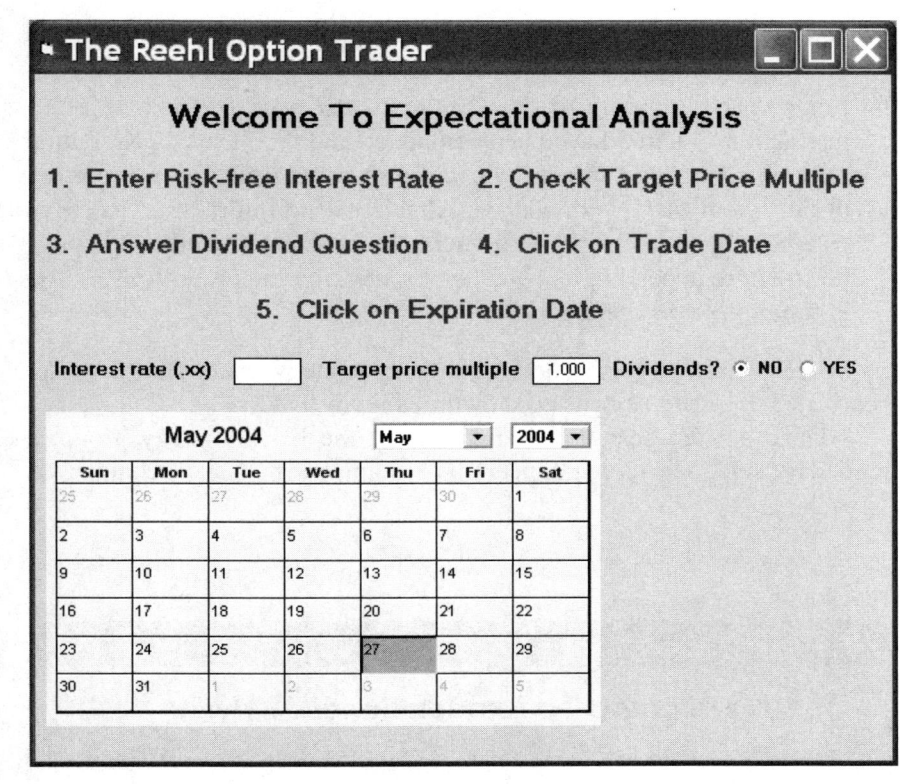

FIGURE 9-1

Opening input screen

on the specific trade date on the calendar. The trade date will appear to the right of the calendar.

5. *Click on expiration date.* In the same manner as in instruction 4, click on the appropriate month and year from the pull-down menus, and then click on the specific expiration date. The expiration date will appear to the right of the calendar together with the number of days until expiration. If the dates are correct, click on "Dates OK." If any part of the dates is incorrect, click on "Change Dates," and repeat instructions 4 and 5 until correct. After clicking on "Dates OK" and the "Yes" option has been selected for instruction 3, a dividend box will appear. Go to instruction 6. After clicking on "Dates OK" and the default "No" option has been accepted for instruction 3, a new screen will appear, its structure depending on whether *Expecta-*

tion.exe or *DailyCheck.exe* is running. Figure 9–2 shows a completed opening input screen without dividends.

6. *Enter dividends* (*only if "Yes" was checked in instruction 3*). After instructions 4 and 5 have been completed and the "Dates OK" button clicked, a dividend screen will appear automatically, allowing entry of up to four *discrete* dividends. After dividend information has been entered, click on "Done With Dividends." A new screen will appear, its structure depending on whether *Expectation.exe* or *DailyCheck.exe* is running. See Figure 9–3.

If *Expectation.exe* is running, a basic strategy selection screen appears after the date screen, as shown in Figure 9–4.

Once a main selection is made from the basic strategy group, a secondary selection screen appears. For example, if "Naked Options" is

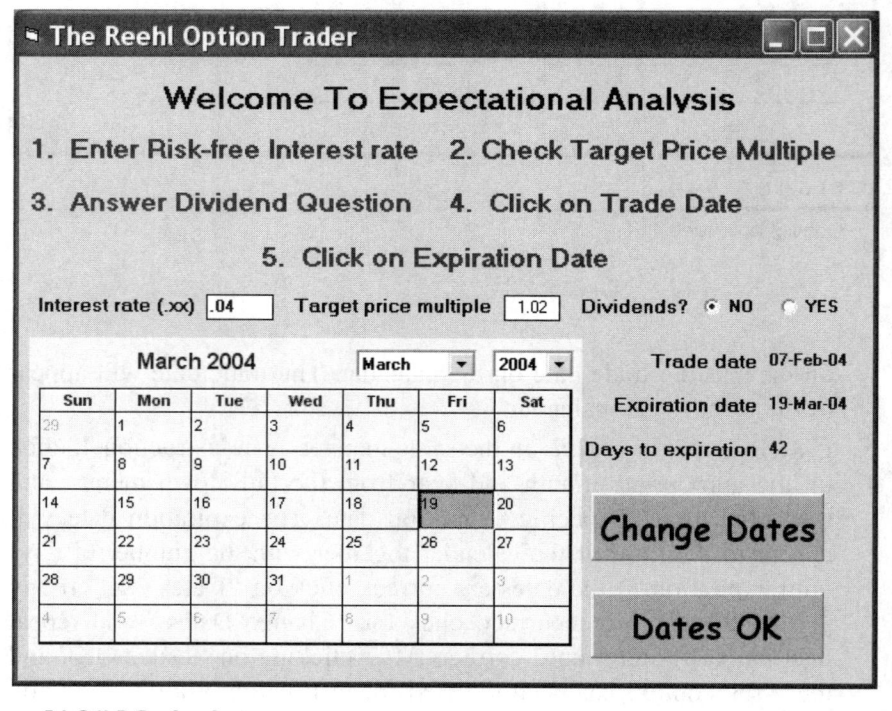

FIGURE 9–2

Completed opening input screen

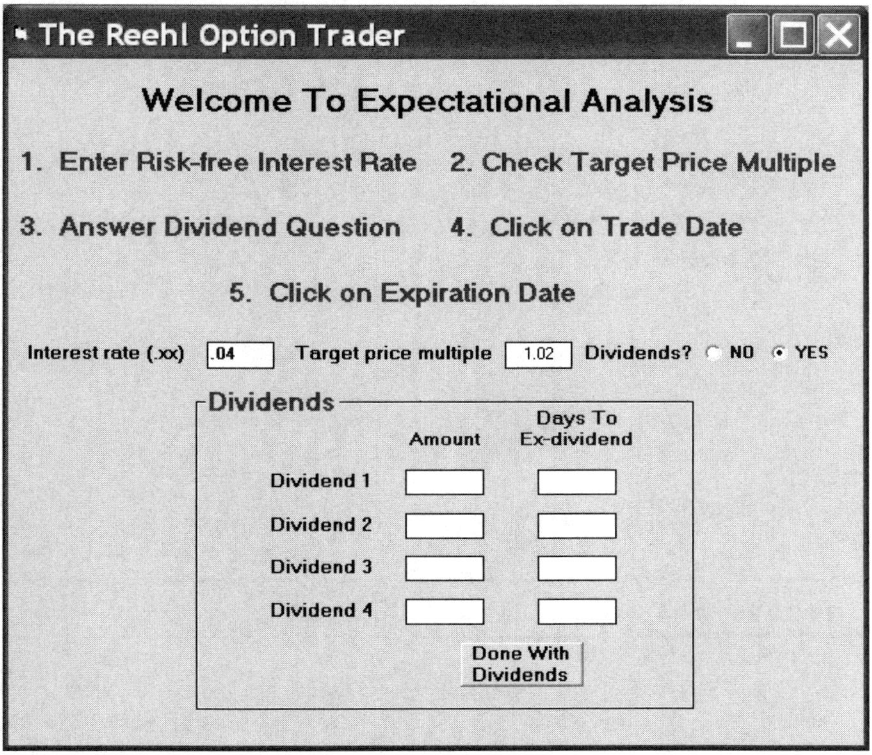

FIGURE 9-3

Opening screen with dividends

selected from the basic screen, the secondary screen offers choices among purchased Calls, written Calls, purchased Puts, and written Puts. When a choice is made and the "Select Option" button is clicked, a new screen appears to the right where only a solid-color blank existed previously. See Figure 9–5 for the sold Put screen.

The uppermost portion of this screen contains the basic information entered earlier on the date screen. This information should be checked for accuracy before proceeding. Entries should be made in the four boxes in the upper half of the screen—symbol, interest rate, value of underlying asset or index, and volatility. The last two items *must* be entered.

The bottom half of the screen will contain input frames for pricing and other information for the selected trade. Entries *must* be made for all items colored blue. When all information is complete, the "Get Re-

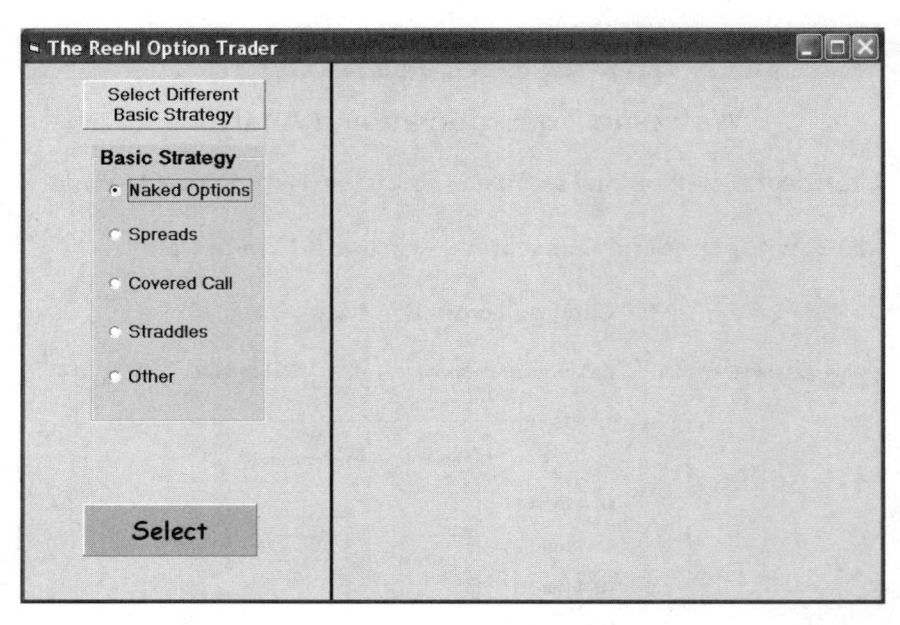

FIGURE 9-4

Basic strategy selection screen

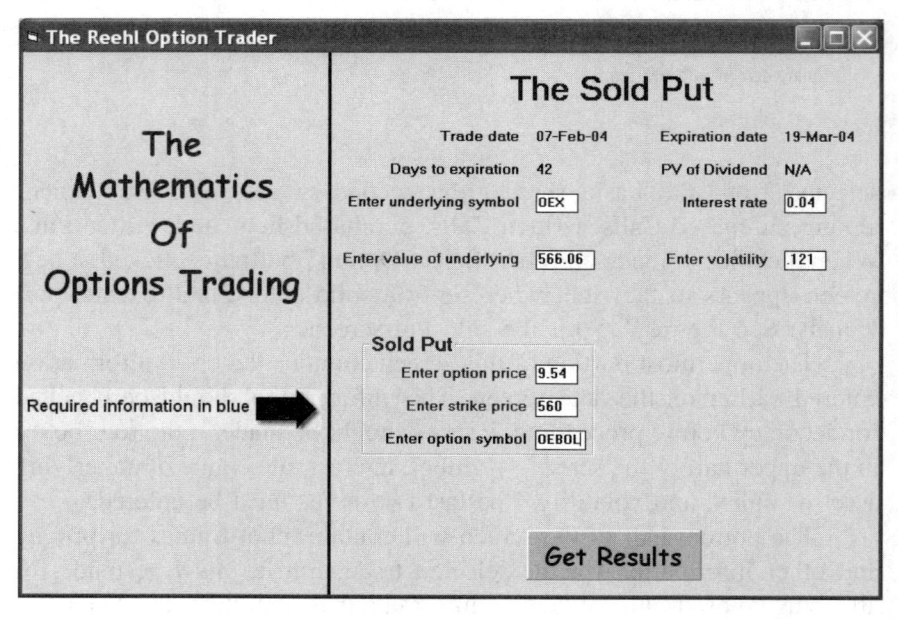

FIGURE 9-5

Sold Put screen

sults" button is clicked. A new screen containing a complete report on the selected trade will appear, as shown in Figure 9–6.

The *ER* tangent slope and intercept refer to the straight line that is tangent to the *ER* curve. The *a*, *b*, and *c* parabolic coefficients of the *ER* curve are also listed.

The report may be printed by clicking on the "Print Results" button. A new trade using the same trade and expiration dates may be analyzed by clicking the "New Strategy" button and then clicking the "Same Dates?" option. This procedure avoids having to reenter all the initial date screen information. Appendix A contains the printed reports for each of the Cisco Systems, Inc., options analyzed in Chapters 6 and 7.

The Reehl Option Trader

The Sold Put

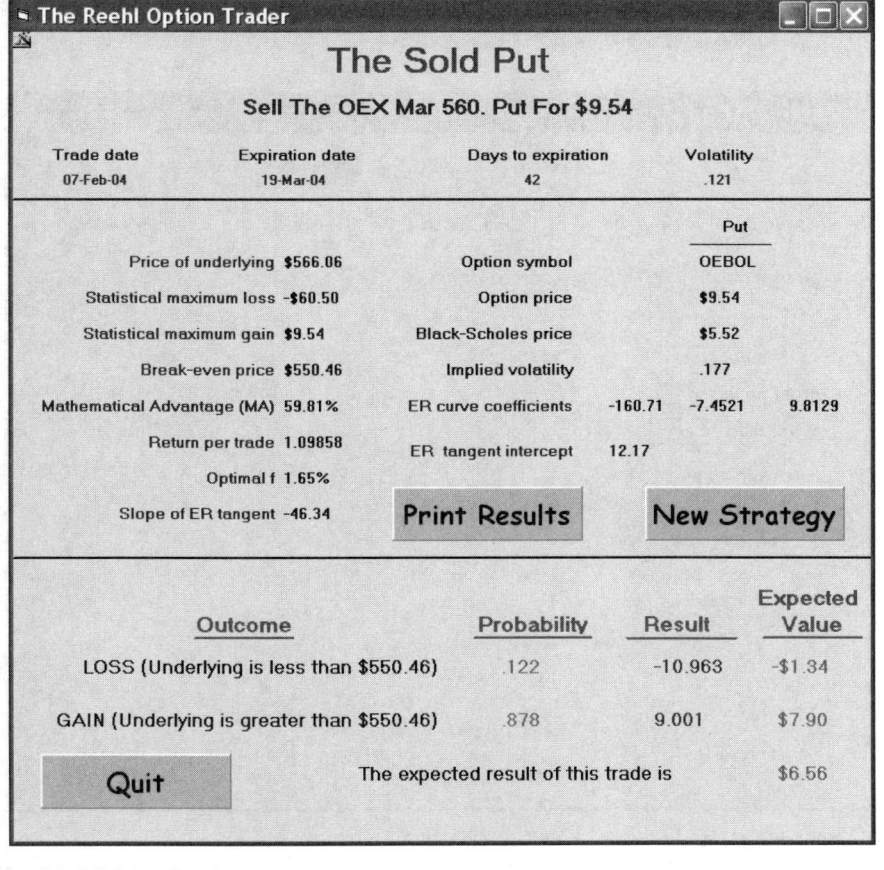

Sell The OEX Mar 560. Put For $9.54

Trade date	Expiration date	Days to expiration	Volatility
07-Feb-04	19-Mar-04	42	.121

		Put
Price of underlying $566.06	Option symbol	OEBOL
Statistical maximum loss -$60.50	Option price	$9.54
Statistical maximum gain $9.54	Black-Scholes price	$5.52
Break-even price $550.46	Implied volatility	.177
Mathematical Advantage (MA) 59.81%	ER curve coefficients	-160.71 -7.4521 9.8129
Return per trade 1.09858	ER tangent intercept	12.17
Optimal f 1.65%		
Slope of ER tangent -46.34	**Print Results**	**New Strategy**

Outcome	Probability	Result	Expected Value
LOSS (Underlying is less than $550.46)	.122	-10.963	-$1.34
GAIN (Underlying is greater than $550.46)	.878	9.001	$7.90
Quit	The expected result of this trade is		$6.56

FIGURE 9–6

Sold Put results screen

If *DailyCheck.exe* is running, after the date screen is complete, the "Daily Quote Sheet" will appear, as shown in Figure 9–7.

1. *Enter basic information.* The cursor will automatically start blinking in the "Symbol" box. Enter the appropriate *symbol* for the underlying asset or index. Press the "Tab" key. Enter *current price* for the underlying asset or index. Press the "Tab" key. Enter *volatility* of underlying asset or index as a decimal; that is, enter 39.8 percent as .398. Select the appropriate strike price increment from the "Strike Increment" option frame (the default is $5.00).
2. *Input quotes.* Click on "Get Strike Prices." An input frame appears containing boxes for entering bid, ask, and last quotes for both Calls and Puts for the first of 11 strike prices, as shown in Figure 9–8. Also, the target price is computed from the target price multiple and displayed on the screen.

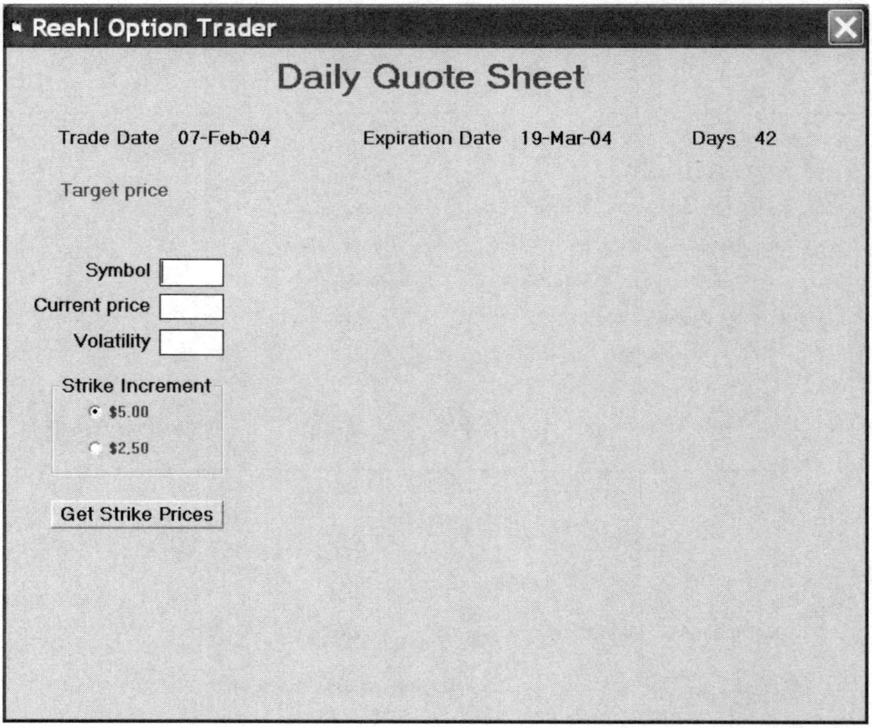

FIGURE 9–7

Daily quote sheet (initial screen)

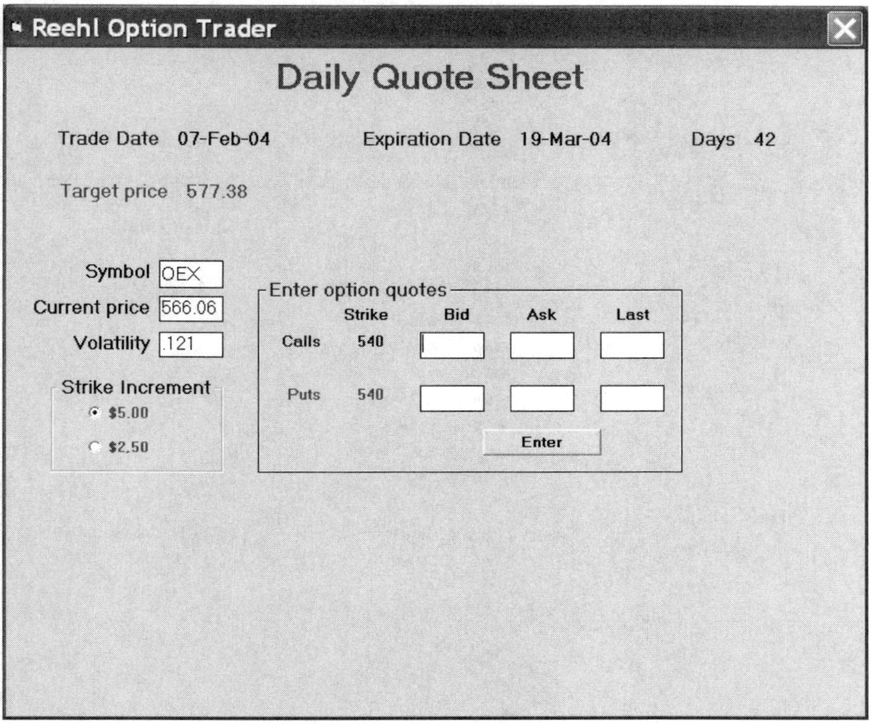

Daily Quote Sheet

Reehl Option Trader

Trade Date 07-Feb-04   Expiration Date 19-Mar-04   Days 42

Target price 577.38

Symbol: OEX
Current price: 566.06
Volatility: .121

Strike Increment:
- $5.00
- $2.50

Enter option quotes — Strike, Bid, Ask, Last
Calls 540
Puts 540

Enter

FIGURE 9-8

Daily quote sheet (quotes section)

Use the "Tab" key to navigate from the "Call bid" box to the "Put last" box. If an option's quotes do not exist for a particular strike price, enter six zeros or simply click on the "Enter" button (in the "Option Quote" frame). If one of the three boxes for either a Call or a Put contains a nonzero entry, all three boxes must contain a nonzero entry. For example, if there is no "Last" quote for a particular Put or Call, enter the "Ask" quote. After entering the six quotes for each strike price, click on the "Enter" button to get the next strike. After the information for the eleventh strike price has been entered, the "Option Quote" frame will disappear automatically and be replaced by a table, as shown in Figure 9-9. Check the table carefully making any necessary changes before proceeding.

3. *Get trade reports.* A "Print Strategies" option frame appears in the lower left section of the screen, with choices for either printing results for all strategies or just those with positive expectation. If all strate-

Reehl Option Trader

Daily Quote Sheet

Trade Date 27-Feb-04   Expiration Date 19-Mar-04   Days 22

Target price 576.80

Symbol OEX
Current price 565.49
Volatility .111

Strike Increment
- $5.00
- $2.50

Print Strategies
- Positive E(R)
- All strategies

Strike	Calls	Puts
540.0	26.90	1.28
545.0	22.24	1.80
550.0	18.21	2.50
555.0	13.65	3.70
560.0	10.21	5.06
565.0	7.00	7.15
570.0	4.50	9.80
575.0	2.82	13.12
580.0	1.58	17.08
585.0	.90	21.51
590.0	.52	26.24

Review quotes before submitting

Submit Quotes

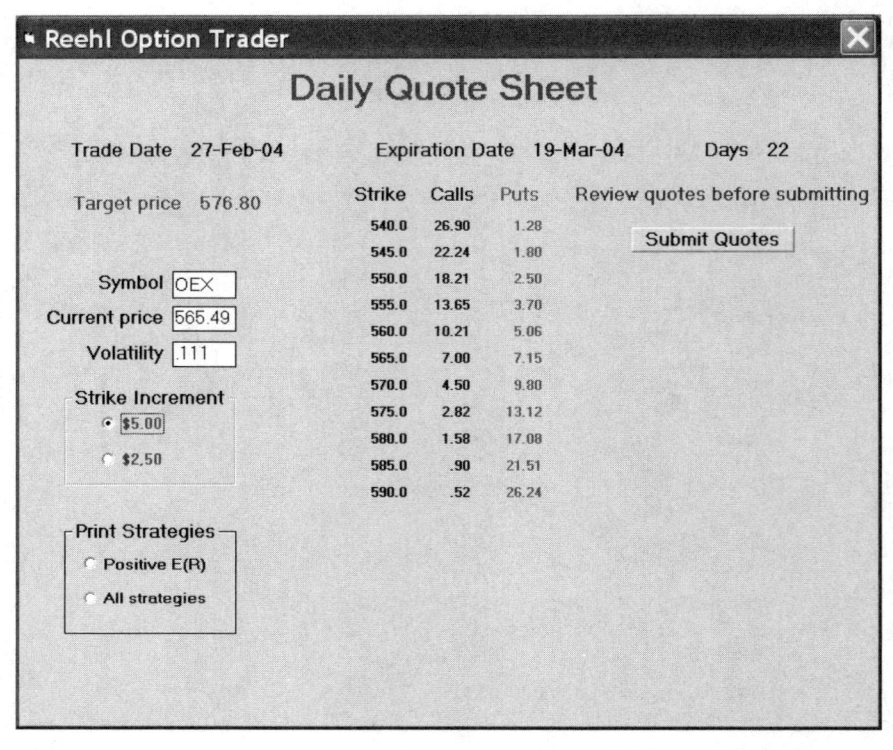

FIGURE 9-9

Daily quote sheet (completed table of quotes)

gies are desired, click on that option. Otherwise, the default choice is those with positive $E(R)$. Click on the "Submit Quotes" button. A new set of strategy buttons appears, as shown in Figure 9–10. Click on the "Option Matrix" button. A report is printed showing the basic price information on the selected asset or index together with Black-Scholes prices, implied volatility, the delta, and the vega for each strike price. Clicking on any of the other strategy buttons will produce a complete report on all possible trades for that particular group of strategies represented by that button. For example, the "Naked Options" button includes strategies for purchased Calls, written Calls, purchased Puts, and written Puts. For ratio spreads, backspreads, and butterfly spreads, a new dialog box will appear in the lower left corner of the "Daily Quote Sheet" that calls for entry of the number of Calls and/or Puts to be used. A red dot appears to the left of the "Strategy" button once the analysis is complete and printing has begun. See

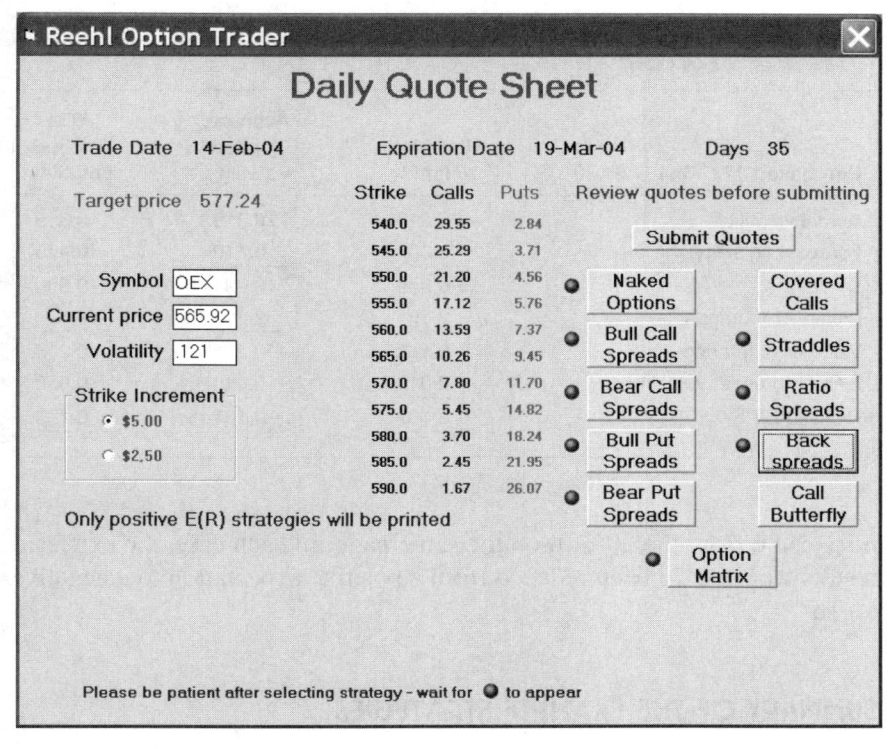

Putting It All Together

FIGURE 9-10
Completed daily quote sheet

Appendix B for examples of the option matrix and strategy reports for the Cisco Systems, Inc., options on July 11, 2003.

HOW OMEGA REFLECTS POTENTIAL INACCURACIES

Recall that omega measures the approximate change in expected results given a change in volatility. In the example strategies in Chapters 6 and 7, we used the historical volatility of .398 for the Cisco Systems, Inc., options. With hindsight, we find the *actual* volatility based on the 25 trading days (34 calendar days) between the trade date and the expiration date was .319. Table 9-1 shows how the expected results of the example purchased Call would have been affected using three different forecasts of volatility—historical, average implied, and at-the-money implied.

The average implied volatility was calculated from the 11 Calls listed on the first page of Appendix B. The at-the-money implied vola-

TABLE 9-1

Affect of omega on expected results

Purchased 17.5 Call @ $1.60	Historical volatility	Average implied volatility	ATM implied volatility
Actual volatility	0.319	0.319	0.319
Forecast volatility	0.398	0.410	0.415
Difference	−0.079	−0.091	−0.096
Multiply by omega	2.18	2.21	2.22
Value of difference	−0.172	−0.201	−0.213
E(R) at forecast volatility	0.010	0.040	0.050
Revised E(R)	−0.162	−0.161	−0.163

tility came from the 20 Call on the same page. In each case, the expected results would have been reduced from a positive expectation to a negative $0.16.

SUMMARY OF THE EXAMPLE STRATEGIES

The stock of Cisco Systems, Inc., wound up at $17.79 on the expiration date. In these examples, the target price was equal to the current price. A summary of expected results from the example strategies as calculated in Chapter 6 and 7 (one contract for each option) is presented in Table 9–2 together with the expected results if the volatility had been .319 (actual) instead of .398 (historical). The last column in Table 9–2 contains the *actual* results of implementing the given strategy using historical volatility.

As expected, overestimating volatility for the purchased Call is undesirable. A purchased Call needs *increasing* volatility to become more and more profitable. On the other hand, overestimating volatility for the bull Call spread underestimates just how good a trade this would have been.

SHORT RUN VERSUS LONG RUN

The answer to reconciling short-run trading with long-run profitability estimates lies in first eliminating trades not likely to produce a profit in the long run. We saw in Chapter 6 that only 144 of 306 options trades

TABLE 9-2

Expected versus actual results

Example strategy	Expected results (historical volatility)			Expected results (actual volatility)			Actual results
	E(R)	MA	p(gain)	E(R)	MA	p(gain)	
Purchased Call	0.01	0.7%	0.408	−0.17	−15.0%	0.386	−1.31
Sold Call	−0.01	−0.5%	0.592	0.17	12.5%	0.614	1.31
Purchased Put	−0.10	−20.7%	0.234	−0.23	−48.7%	0.182	−0.79
Sold Put	0.10	8.6%	0.766	0.23	26.8%	0.818	0.79
Bull Call spread	0.14	12.3%	0.772	0.27	31.9%	0.824	0.54
Bear Call spread	−0.01	−1.0%	0.518	0.00	−0.5%	0.522	0.88
Bull Put spread	0.08	5.1%	0.486	0.02	1.1%	0.482	−0.86
Bear Put spread	0.04	3.5%	0.947	0.08	9.9%	0.978	0.10
Covered Call	0.13	11.4%	0.771	0.26	30.7%	0.823	0.53
Long straddle	−0.13	−11.0%	0.417	−0.41	−35.0%	0.346	−0.07
Short straddle	0.19	11.8%	0.532	0.24	18.4%	0.542	−0.59
Long strangle	−0.10	−13.0%	0.336	−0.40	−50.9%	0.230	−0.93
Short strangle	0.15	13.4%	0.748	0.33	39.8%	0.824	0.62
Call ratio spread	0.02	1.1%	0.588	0.31	26.0%	0.660	1.71
Put ratio spread	0.12	9.9%	0.566	0.35	35.1%	0.635	−0.01
Call backspread	−0.04	−2.3%	0.460	−0.13	−9.0%	0.450	−1.01
Put backspread	−0.12	−10.5%	0.434	−0.35	−31.1%	0.365	0.01
Butterfly spread	0.04	2.8%	0.583	0.30	26.2%	0.656	1.69

on the stock of Cisco Systems, Inc., had long-run positive expectation (limited to those strategies presented in this book). Obviously, the first cut is to eliminate the 162 negative-expectation trades. From there it becomes a winnowing process much like the handicapper who methodically eliminates unlikely horses from the field or the stock picker who screens out stocks based on fundamentals such as earnings and certain financial ratios.

For example, suppose we had set the following arbitrary selection criteria:

- There must be a 75 percent or better gain probability.
- There must be a 10 percent or greater mathematical advantage.
- There must be expected results of $0.10 or greater.
- If for any given strategy there is more than one trade meeting the preceding criteria, pick the one with the highest expected result.

Why a 75 percent long-run gain probability? By choosing a high probability of a long-run gain, we hope to wind up with at least a better than even chance of a short-run gain. This is especially important if trading with optimal f, where we want a high percentage of gains and fewer devastating drawdowns. The same logic holds for choosing an *MA* of at least 10 percent.

Although the strategies listed in Table 9–2 were selected randomly and only for the purpose of explaining the related math, as a first exercise, we can check out our arbitrary selection scheme. Remember, this was only one trial, and its result is statistically meaningless. Still, it is human nature to want to see the results after so much work. Only three strategies from Table 9–2 met our criteria; the bull Call spread, the covered Call, and the short strangle. All three strategies were winners, with a total gain of $169. With hindsight, the four actual *best* trades (those with over a $1.00 actual gain) were never in contention using our scheme.

For a more realistic (but still statistically meaningless) check, we look at Appendix B, which contains all 144 positive-expectation strategies for the August expiration of options on the stock of Cisco Systems, Inc., priced on July 11, 2003. Again, there are only three strategies meeting the criteria. Although they are the same three winning *strategies* from Table 9–2, different option series were selected based on the selection criteria. The gain on these three trades was $158. If an asterisk appears to the left of a listed strategy, the $f*$ for that strategy should be ignored.

USING TARGET PRICES

For all the explanatory calculations, the current price was used as the target price (the forecast price on which the probability distribution was centered). When an identifiable trend is evident, it might be preferable to use a target price above or below the current price. Consider the OEX closing price on November 19, 2003, of 514.96. Is there a trend? What is the most likely price for the OEX at the December expiration? What strategies should we employ for the next day? First, we can check the trend of OEX prices between August 20, 2003, and November 20, 2003 (roughly 90 calendar days). Because most historical quote services are based on trading days, we look at the 66 trading days between the two dates. Labeling the trading days between 1 and 66, we plot the time series and overlay a linear regression line, as in Figure 9–11.

The December expiration is 30 calendar days away on December 19, 2003. Since we are using trading days in the equation, we multiply 30 by .69 to arrive at 20.7—the approximate number of trading days

Putting It All Together

FIGURE 9-11

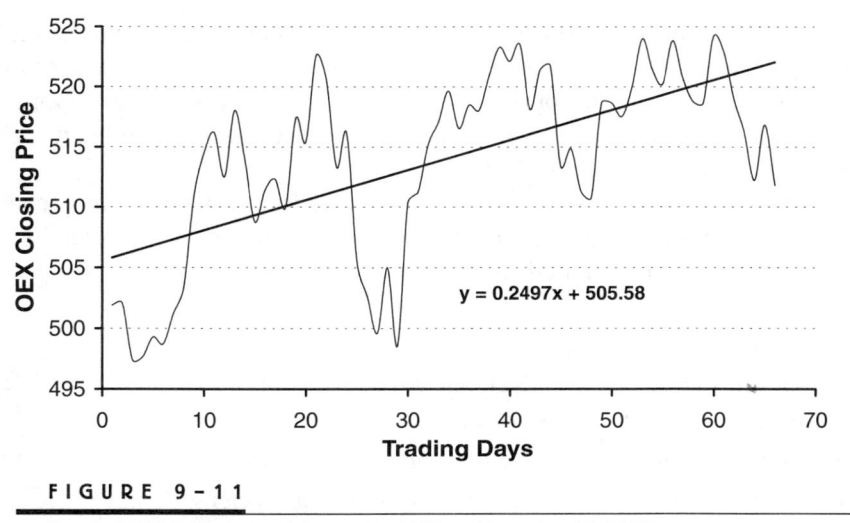

Trend of OEX closing prices (August 20, 2003, to November 20, 2003)

between November 20 and December 19, 2003. Adding 20.7 to the 66 trading days in the sample, we get 86.7, which is the number we plug into the formula for x. Solving the formula for y, we get a target price of 527.23. Dividing 527.23 by the current price of 514.96, we obtain a *target price multiple* of 1.0238 (for use in the opening screen of *DailyCheck.exe*).

There are various methods of calculating a target price. More sophisticated techniques, such as exponential moving averages or GARCH, may be employed. Traders skilled in technical analysis no doubt will have their favorite techniques for determining a target price. The effect of the final calculated target price may be modified. For example, because a 90-day linear regression of closing prices during a sharp trend has a long "memory" (continues to show a trend long after an actual trend reversal), the trader may wish to limit the target price multiple to a certain percentage above and below the current price. Also, a one-half trend might be employed by adding one-half the difference between the calculated target price and the current price to the current price to come up with a lower target.

THE SELECTION CRITERIA

It must be emphasized again that this book is concerned with the mathematics of option trading—not the development of a supersystem to produce instant riches. That said, however, there should be a significant correlation between expected results and actual results in the long run. The main question is, of course, can long-run expectation predict short-term results? One way to test this theory is to select trades with the most promising attributes and check the results.

Certain selection basic criteria were introduced in the previous sections for the Cisco options. The following is a typology of selection criteria that might be applied to a set of trades:

- Minimum gain probability
- Minimum mathematical advantage MA
- Minimum expected results $E(R)$
- Minimum distances between BEP and current price
- Limiting differences between current and target prices
- Handling multiple qualifying trades

Depending on which criteria are chosen and how they are used, the overall strategy will become more conservative or more aggressive. The screening process is necessarily subjective. There is always a tradeoff between rejecting good trades and selecting bad ones.

DEVELOPING AND TESTING SOME CRITERIA

The tests below were conducted on randomly selected days beginning on October 14, 2003, for options on the S&P 100 Index (OEX). The last day for sampling the OEX was February 27, 2004. Therefore, trades with November and December 2003 expirations together with January, February, and March 2004 expirations are included. The days were chosen without any definite aim or purpose by the author based on time available. Gains and losses were calculated as of the expiration date, and the results do not include any gains or losses from early covering sales or purchases.

Target prices calculated based on a 90-calendar-day linear regression were used for each new trade date but limited to plus or minus 2 percent from the current price. The basic screening criteria were

- There must be a minimum 75 percent gain probability and a minimum MA of 10 percent.

- For 1 to 30 days prior to expiration, the minimum requirement for expected results $E(R)$ was $1.50.
- For 31 to 60 days prior to expiration, the minimum requirement for expected results $E(R)$ was $2.50.
- For more than 61 days prior to expiration, the minimum requirement for expected results $E(R)$ was $3.50.
- For single-option *long* strategies, the *BEP* must be *less than* 1 standard deviation from the current price, and for single-option *short* strategies, the *BEP* must be *greater than* 1 standard from the current price.
- For *long* straddles and strangles, the *BEP* values must be *less than* 1.5 standard deviations from the current price in either direction, and for *short* straddles and strangles, the *BEP* values must be *greater than* 1.5 standard deviations from the current price in either direction.
- For Put ratio spreads, the *downside BEP* must be *greater than* 1 standard deviation from the current price, and for Call ratio spreads, the *upside BEP* must be *greater than* 1 standard deviation from the current price.
- For Put backspreads, the *downside BEP* must be *less than* 1 standard deviation from the current price, and for Call backspreads, the *upside BEP* must be *less than* 1 standard deviation from the current price.
- If a bullish trend exists, the target price can be no *less than* the current price.
- If a bearish trend exists, the target price can be no *more than* the current price.
- No countertrend strategy will be selected.
- Ratio spreads and backspreads will be considered only if there is a guaranteed gain in one direction.
- No more than two option series will be employed.
- If there is more than one qualifying trade, select the highest $E(R)$.

These requirements were added to limit plays to worthwhile dollar amounts, to provide some room for the underlying index price to move about before triggering any stop losses a trader might impose, and to ensure that target prices and strategies were not counter to an identified trend. Again, any set of selection criteria may have been established. The preceding criteria were based on common sense and the desire to have expected results of at least $150 per contract, at least a 75 percent chance of profitability, and at least a 10 percent mathematical advantage. Other criteria may have produced superior (or inferior) results.

THE NOVEMBER AND DECEMBER 2003 EXPIRATIONS

Table 9–3 shows the 15 selected trades in six days for options having the November and December 2003 expirations. Losses occurred for only one of the 15 selected trades.

While such a small sample is by no means statistically significant, it does show a total six-day profit of $5,267 if all qualified strategies

TABLE 9–3

Trade results (November and December expirations)
(*November = 511.77; December = 540.26*)

Trade date	Expiration date	Strategy	Days	Contracts	E(R)	Gain (loss)	Gain max E(R)
15-Oct-03	17-Oct-03	No selection					
15-Oct-03	21-Nov-03	Sold Put	38	1	2.79	4.47	4.47
15-Oct-03	21-Nov-03	Put ratio spread	38	3	2.77	4.22	
						8.69	
20-Nov-03	19-Dec-03	Sold Put	30	1	5.89	6.77	
20-Nov-03	19-Dec-03	Bull Put spread	30	2	1.64	2.00	
20-Nov-03	19-Dec-03	Short strangle	30	2	3.83	5.71	
20-Nov-03	19-Dec-03	Put ratio spread	30	3	8.41	7.44	7.44
						21.92	
22-Nov-03	19-Dec-03	Sold Put	28	1	4.87	5.45	5.45
22-Nov-03	19-Dec-03	Short strangle	28	2	3.18	(3.56)	
22-Nov-03	19-Dec-03	Put ratio spread	28	3	4.78	5.00	
						6.89	
27-Nov-03	19-Dec-03	Sold Put	23	1	1.86	2.72	2.72
27-Nov-03	19-Dec-03	Put ratio spread	23	3	1.58	1.44	
						4.16	
2-Dec-03	19-Dec-03	Sold Put	18	1	2.00	3.16	3.16
2-Dec-03	19-Dec-03	Short strangle	18	2	1.76	2.40	
						5.56	
6-Dec-03	19-Dec-03	Sold Put	14	1	1.67	3.00	
6-Dec-03	19-Dec-03	Short strangle	14	2	1.73	2.45	2.45
						5.45	
Totals				28		52.67	25.69
Average gain per trade, all strategies						3.51	
Average gain per trade, single daily strategy							4.28

were played (minimum number of contracts each). Taking positions in 28 contracts (15 trades), the per-trade profit was $351. Only one of the 15 trades resulted in a loss. If only the largest $E(R)$ strategy were played each of the six days, the total profit would have been $2,569, or $428 per trade, with no losing trades.

THE JANUARY 2004 EXPIRATION

Tables 9–4 and 9–5 show the results of selecting trades with the January 2004 expiration. This time there are 29 qualifying trades in 13 days, yielding a total of $5,724, or $197.38 per trade, if all strategies were played. Five trades of 29 showed a loss. Selecting only the strategy with the highest $E(R)$ each day produces a total gain of $2,579 on 13 trades, or $198.38 per trade, with only one losing trade.

THE FEBRUARY 2004 EXPIRATION

Tables 9–6 and 9–7 show the 33 trades selected for the February expiration. For the February expiration, making each of the 33 trades in the 13 days would have resulted in a gain of $21,505, or $651.67 per trade. There were no losing trades. Trading only the contract with the highest $E(R)$ each day would have resulted in 13 trades for $7,520, or $578.46 per trade.

THE MARCH 2004 EXPIRATION

Tables 9–8 and 9–9 show the 24 selected trades for the March expiration. There were 24 selected trades for the March 2004 expiration covering 10 days. Playing each of these yielded a gain of $19,404, or $808.50 per trade. There were five losing trades out of 24. Trading only the strategy with the highest $E(R)$ each day would have resulted in $7,232, or $723.20 per trade, with 3 of 10 losing trades.

SUMMARY OF THE TEST PERIOD RESULTS

Figure 9-12 shows the OEX closing prices based on trading days for the test period. Note the presence of an easily identifiable upward trend for days 33 through 68. No trend is present for days 1 through 32 or for days 69 through 93. With hindsight, we know that prices flatten out and

TABLE 9-4

Trade results (January expiration, 564.72)

(*First 15 trades*)

Trade date	Expiration date	Strategy	Days	Contracts	E(R)	Gain (loss)	Gain max E(R)
22-Nov-03	16-Jan-04	Sold Put	56	1	6.24	6.94	
22-Nov-03	16-Jan-04	Put ratio spread	56	3	7.43	2.24	2.24
						9.18	
27-Nov-03	16-Jan-04	Sold Put	51	1	4.08	5.40	
27-Nov-03	16-Jan-04	Put ratio spread	51	3	4.16	5.20	5.20
						10.60	
2-Dec-03	16-Jan-04	Sold Put	46	1	3.77	5.94	
2-Dec-03	16-Jan-04	Put ratio spread	46	3	4.55	1.79	1.79
						7.73	
6-Dec-03	16-Jan-04	Sold Put	42	1	4.45	6.36	
6-Dec-03	16-Jan-04	Short strangle	42	2	3.89	(8.77)	
6-Dec-03	16-Jan-04	Put ratio spread	42	3	4.64	1.70	1.70
						(0.71)	
11-Dec-03	16-Jan-04	Sold Put	37	1	3.67	5.11	
11-Dec-03	16-Jan-04	Short strangle	37	2	3.17	(9.58)	
11-Dec-03	16-Jan-04	Put ratio spread	37	3	4.09	0.91	0.91
						(3.56)	
12-Dec-03	16-Jan-04	Sold Put	36	1	2.55	4.71	
12-Dec-03	16-Jan-04	Put ratio spread	36	3	3.25	0.17	0.17
						4.88	
13-Dec-03	16-Jan-04	Put ratio spread	35	3	2.89	2.70	2.70
						2.70	
Totals carried forward to Table 9–5				31		30.82	14.71

signify the beginning of a trend reversal in March 2004. These data are ideal for testing the selection criteria because both trending and nontrending patterns are present.

Not surprisingly, writing Puts and establishing Put ratio spreads (involving written Puts) represent the highest probability of success and the bulk of the strategies selected for our 42-day sample. Many others have come to the same conclusion for options trading in general. While these strategies have considerable downside risks in the event of a major adverse market move, they can be partially protected with trailing stops, early exits, or other safety measures discussed below.

TABLE 9-5

Trade results (January expiration, 564.72)

(*Second 14 trades*)

Trade date	Expiration date	Strategy	Days	Contracts	E(R)	Gain (loss)	Gain max E(R)
Totals carried forward from Table 9–4				31		30.82	14.71
16-Dec-03	16-Jan-03	Sold Put	32	1	2.88	4.60	
16-Dec-03	16-Jan-03	Short strangle	32	2	3.06	(5.41)	
16-Dec-03	16-Jan-03	Put ratio spread	32	3	3.26	2.86	2.86
						2.05	
17-Dec-03	16-Jan-04	Put ratio spread	31	3	3.10	2.26	2.26
						2.26	
25-Dec-03	16-Jan-04	Sold Put	23	1	2.59	3.76	
25-Dec-03	16-Jan-04	Short strangle	23	2	3.15	(0.52)	
25-Dec-03	16-Jan-04	Put ratio spread	23	3	3.77	2.02	2.02
						5.26	
30-Dec-03	16-Jan-04	Sold Put	18	1	2.90	3.95	
30-Dec-03	16-Jan-04	Short strangle	18	2	4.35	1.55	
30-Dec-03	16-Jan-04	Short strangle	18	3	2.56	2.30	1.55
						7.80	
3-Jan-04	16-Jan-04	Sold Put	14	1	2.94	4.56	
3-Jan-04	16-Jan-04	Short strangle	14	2	5.67	(0.76)	(0.76)
						3.80	
10-Jan-04	16-Jan-04	Sold Put	7	1	1.62	2.10	
10-Jan-04	16-Jan-04	Short strangle	7	2	2.40	3.15	3.15
						5.25	
Totals				58		57.24	25.79

Table 9–10 summarizes the results of the test period. Table 9–11 presents the per-day, per-strategy, and per-contract statistics. Of the 101 selected strategies, there were only 11 losses, for a gain ratio of 89 percent compared with the cutoff gain probability of 75 percent.

The calculated returns are quite impressive whether calculated per day, per strategy, or per contract. The *rates* of return are a little more tricky to calculate because the risks (amounts invested) are not fixed with written Puts, short straddles and strangles, or Put ratio spreads. We do know, however, the maximum statistical risk for each trade. If we average the L_{max} for the 101 selected strategies in Appendix C, we get $45.87. Assuming we would risk no more than 25 percent of the maximum statistical exposure (using trailing stops, exiting positions early, etc.), the

TABLE 9-6

Trade results (February expiration, 564.87)

(First 17 trades)

Opening date	Expiration date		Days	Contracts	E(R)	Gain (loss)	Gain max E(R)
27-Nov-03	20-Feb-04	Sold Put	86	1	7.09	9.33	
27-Nov-03	20-Feb-04	Put ratio spread	86	3	6.18	3.18	3.18
						12.51	
2-Dec-03	20-Feb-04	Sold Put	81	1	6.86	10.31	
2-Dec-03	20-Feb-04	Put ratio spread	81	3	7.28	3.49	3.49
						13.80	
6-Dec-03	20-Feb-04	Sold Put	77	1	5.52	8.01	
6-Dec-03	20-Feb-04	Put ratio spread	77	3	6.96	3.75	3.75
						11.76	
11-Dec-03	20-Feb-04	Sold Put	72	1	5.84	6.94	
11-Dec-03	20-Feb-04	Put ratio spread	72	3	6.63	2.67	2.67
						9.61	
16-Dec-03	20-Feb-04	Sold Put	67	1	8.85	7.86	7.86
16-Dec-03	20-Feb-04	Put ratio spread	67	3	6.19	6.91	
						14.77	
25-Dec-03	20-Feb-04	Sold Put	58	1	6.78	8.62	8.62
25-Dec-03	20-Feb-04	Short strangle	58	2	6.01	9.52	
25-Dec-03	20-Feb-04	Put ratio spread	58	3	6.75	4.04	
						22.18	
30-Dec-03	20-Feb-04	Sold Put	53	1	6.01	9.36	
30-Dec-03	20-Feb-04	Short strangle	53	2	8.70	12.78	12.78
30-Dec-03	20-Feb-04	Call ratio spread	53	3	3.24	4.93	
30-Dec-03	20-Feb-04	Put ratio spread	53	3	7.51	5.80	
						32.87	
Totals carried forward to Table 9–7				35		117.50	42.35

risk would be limited to $1,147 per trade, or $115,847 over the total 101 trades. Since the 101 trades yielded $51,890, the average rate of return for employing all selected strategies would be 44.8 percent.

The results obtained for the 42-day period represent results for a specific set of patterns, as shown in Figure 9–12. While it tempting to generalize these results to future periods (having different sets of patterns), no such generalization is yet possible. Before claiming a successful system has been born, further rigorous testing will be required.

Putting It All Together 311

TABLE 9-7

Trade results (February expiration, 564.87)

(*Second 16 trades*)

Opening date	Expiration date		Days	Contracts	E(R)	Gain (loss)	Gain max E(R)
Totals carried forward from Table 9-6				35		117.50	42.35
3-Jan-04	20-Feb-04	Sold Put	49	1	7.00	9.07	
3-Jan-04	20-Feb-04	Short strangle	49	2	10.86	12.03	12.03
3-Jan-04	20-Feb-04	Call ratio spread	49	3	5.07	2.81	
3-Jan-04	20-Feb-04	Put ratio spread	49	3	8.64	6.04	
						29.95	
10-Jan-04	20-Feb-04	Sold Put	42	1	7.46	8.84	8.84
10-Jan-04	20-Feb-04	Short strangle	42	2	6.96	11.76	
10-Jan-04	20-Feb-04	Put ratio spread	42	3	6.68	5.45	
						26.05	
22-Jan-04	20-Feb-04	Sold Put	30	1	3.71	4.05	4.05
22-Jan-04	20-Feb-04	Short strangle	30	2	1.72	4.30	
22-Jan-04	20-Feb-04	Put ratio spread	30	3	3.40	11.94	
						20.29	
27-Jan-04	20-Feb-04	Sold Put	25	1	2.92	3.45	3.45
27-Jan-04	20-Feb-04	Short strangle	25	2	2.28	3.17	
27-Jan-04	20-Feb-04	Put ratio spread	25	3	2.83	7.82	
						14.44	
1-Feb-04	20-Feb-04	Sold Put	21	1	2.43	2.80	2.80
1-Feb-04	20-Feb-04	Put ratio spread	21	3	2.23	2.34	
						5.14	
7-Feb-04	20-Feb-04	Sold Put	14	1	1.58	1.68	1.68
						1.68	
Totals				67		215.05	75.20

However, without claiming statistical significance, I have experienced favorable results subsequent to the 42-day test period.

In contrast to strategies involving written options, limited-loss strategies (long Calls and Puts, bull and bear spreads, long straddles and strangles, etc.) will only be selected when the trader *lowers* his probability and/or *MA* horizons. For example, assume the selection criterion were limited to selecting only long Calls with the highest gain probability over 50 percent for each of the 42 days in the test period. One might think that buying Calls would be a profitable strategy, especially when

TABLE 9-8

Trade results (March expiration, 543.68)

(First 12 trades)

Opening date	Expiration date		Days	Contracts	E(R)	Gain (loss)	Gain max E(R)
25-Dec-03	19-Mar-04	Sold Put	86	1	8.07	9.08	
25-Dec-03	19-Mar-04	Put ratio spread	86	3	12.02	18.89	18.89
						27.97	
30-Dec-03	19-Mar-04	Sold Put	81	1	10.34	13.09	
30-Dec-03	19-Mar-04	Short strangle	81	2	10.58	15.87	
30-Dec-03	19-Mar-04	Put ratio spread	81	3	10.73	19.11	19.11
						48.07	
3-Jan-04	19-Mar-04	Sold Put	77	1	10.85	12.59	
3-Jan-04	19-Mar-04	Short straddle	77	2	13.20	26.35	26.35
3-Jan-04	19-Mar-04	Short strangle	77	2	12.65	23.74	
3-Jan-04	19-Mar-04	Put ratio spread	77	3	10.60	18.67	
						81.35	
10-Jan-04	19-Mar-04	Sold Put	70	1	8.12	8.83	
10-Jan-04	19-Mar-04	Short strangle	70	2	8.98	13.28	
10-Jan-04	19-Mar-04	Put ratio spread	70	3	10.19	7.70	7.70
						29.81	
Totals carried forward to Table 9–9				24		187.20	72.05

there is a pronounced 36-day upward trend in the data in the test period. Such is not the case. Table 9–12 shows the results of employing this limited-risk strategy.

Only 23 trades during the test period meet the selection criterion of a 50 percent or better gain probability, and 13 of those are losses, making the actual gain ratio only 43 percent. Although there are profits in the beginning of the sequence, once the trend reverses, the earlier gains are nearly wiped out. The Calls simply were too expensive over this 42-day period for there to be any significant profit opportunities.

SAFETY MEASURES

The best strategies in terms of profit potential appear to be those with the greatest exposure to downside risk. Selling Puts and establishing short straddles or strangles makes the trader quite vulnerable to adverse market moves. While a trader might be able to keep her finger on the

TABLE 9-9

Trade results (March expiration, 543.68)

(Second 12 trades)

Opening date	Expiration date		Days	Contracts	E(R)	Gain (loss)	Gain max E(R)
Totals carried forward from Table 9-8				24		187.20	72.05
22-Jan-04	19-Mar-04	Sold Put	58	1	7.07	(3.05)	(3.05)
22-Jan-04	19-Mar-04	Put ratio spread	58	3	4.72	7.15	
						14.10	
27-Jan-04	19-Mar-04	Sold Put	53	1	6.56	(8.56)	(8.56)
27-Jan-04	19-Mar-04	Put ratio spread	53	3	6.54	(8.89)	
						(17.45)	
31-Jan-04	19-Mar-04	Sold Put	49	1	5.08	6.30	
31-Jan-04	19-Mar-04	Put ratio spread	49	3	5.21	9.88	9.88
						16.18	
7-Feb-04	19-Mar-04	Sold Put	42	1	4.31	3.79	
7-Feb-04	19-Mar-04	Put ratio spread	42	3	4.33	3.59	3.59
						7.38	
14-Feb-04	19-Mar-04	Sold Put	35	1	3.16	2.39	2.39
14-Feb-04	19-Mar-04	Put ratio spread	35	3	3.03	2.04	
						4.43	
27-Feb-04	19-Mar-04	Sold Put	22	1	2.26	(3.82)	
27-Feb-04	19-Mar-04	Put ratio spread	22	3	2.34	(3.98)	(3.98)
						(7.80)	
Totals				48		194.04	72.32

pulse of the market, it is sometimes difficult to get decent fills in a rapidly moving market and possible to get no execution at all in a market crash. Other than watching the market continuously and exiting positions when there is an adverse move, there are two basic safety measures—insurance and stop loss orders.

INSURANCE

Insurance is provided by giving up some of a trade's potential gain by purchasing options that fare well when the market moves against the trader's original position. A simple example of insuring a sold Put would be to purchase a Put with a higher strike price, thus converting the naked

FIGURE 9-12

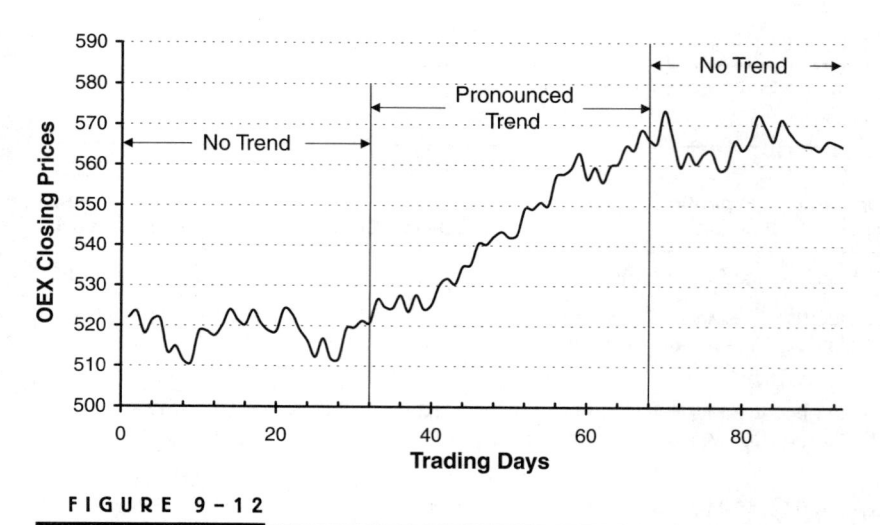

Test period: OEX closing prices (October 15, 2003, to February 27, 2004)

TABLE 9-10

Summary of test period results

Expiration	Days	Number of strategies	Number of All contracts	Number of Max $E(R)$ contracts	Gain All contracts	Gain Max $E(R)$ contracts
Nov–Dec 2003	6	15	28	11	5,257	2,569
Jan 2004	13	29	58	37	5,724	2,579
Feb 2004	13	33	67	23	21,505	7,520
Mar 2004	10	24	48	23	19,404	7,232
	42	101	201	94	51,890	19,900

TABLE 9-11

Per-unit gain statistics

	Per Day	Per Strategy	Per Contract
All strategies	1,235	514	258
Max $E(R)$ strategies	474	474	212

TABLE 9-12

Summary of test period results for purchased Calls

Expiration	Days	Number of trades	Number of losses	Gains (losses)
Nov–Dec 2003	6	4	1	5,041
Jan 2004	13	2	0	8,482
Feb 2004	13	8	3	7,528
Mar 2004	10	9	9	(19,366)
	42	23	13	1,685

option strategy into a bear Put spread. A more complex situation is insuring a short straddle or strangle. For example, in the preceding test, on January 3, 2004, the best single strategy was a short straddle established by simultaneously selling the March OEX 550 Put for $16.38 and the 550 Call for $16.29. The OEX closed at 549.99 on January 2, 2004, and the break-even range for this short straddle was 517.33 to 582.67 (65.34 points). Since the March OEX wound up at 543.68 on March 19, 2004, this strategy would have made $26.35 per contract—a sizable gain (see Table 9–8). Such gain was, of course, due to the very small net change in the OEX (6.31 points, or 1 percent) between January 3 and March 19, 2004 (77 days).

What if there had been a significant adverse move? The estimated volatility (annual standard deviation) was 8.4 percent. If we consider the worst-case result being over plus or minus 3 standard deviations from the beginning OEX value of 549.99, we have

$$\ln\left(\frac{x}{s}\right) = 3(.084)\sqrt{\frac{77}{365}} = .1157$$

Lower limit = $549.99 e^{-.1157}$ = 489.90

Upper limit = $549.99 e^{.1157}$ = 617.45

Outside the 3σ probability envelope, the *potential loss* would range from $27.43 to $517.33 on the downside and from $34.78 to infinity on the upside.

Assume an OEX March 505 Put can be purchased for $5.40 and an OEX March 600 Call can be purchased for $1.75. This represents an *insurance premium* of $7.15 ($5.40 + $1.75)—it will reduce the gains and increase the losses of the original straddle by $7.15. Purchasing these two additional options converts the original straddle to the form of the butterfly spread shown in Figure 9–13.

The new spread has a break-even range from 524.48 to 575.52 (51.04 points, compared with the 65.34 points in the original straddle)—a reduced difference of twice the insurance premium. The maximum downside risk is now limited to $19.48 (was $517.33 for the original straddle)—it would have been $27.43 for minus 3 standard deviations in the original straddle. The maximum upside risk is now limited to $24.48 (was unlimited in the original straddle)—it would have been $34.78 for plus 3 standard deviations in the original straddle.

The adjusted result for the new spread for the March expiration is a gain of $19.20 (543.68 − 524.48). *Note:* The revised gain is $7.15 less than the reported gain of $26.35. The relevant mathematics for this butterfly spread are

$$G_{max} = P_{SP} + P_{SC} - P_{PP} - P_{PC} \quad (9.1)$$

$$BEP_{up} = K_{SC} + G_{max} \quad (9.2)$$

$$BEP_{dn} = K_{SP} - G_{max} \quad (9.3)$$

$$R = \begin{cases} K_{PP} - K_{SP} + P_{SP} + P_{SC} - P_{PP} - P_{PC} & \text{for } x \leq K_{PP} \\ x - BEP_{dn} & \text{for } K_{PP} < x < K_{SP} \\ BEP_{up} - x & \text{for } K_{SC} < x < K_{PC} \\ K_{SC} - K_{PC} + P_{SP} - P_{PP} + P_{SC} - P_{PC} & \text{for } x \geq K_{PC} \end{cases}$$
$$(9.4)$$

Just as insurance options convert a short straddle to a butterfly spread, they likewise could convert a short strangle to a condor spread.

STOP LOSS ORDERS

Setting stops on the underlying asset or index is a little less safe than insurance because there can be no assurance that a stop loss order will be executed at the designated price. Remember, the stop order becomes a market order when the stop price is hit. If the market is extremely fast moving, the fill may be very different from the trader's intended price. Nevertheless, stop loss orders are an important safety measure and should

Putting It All Together 317

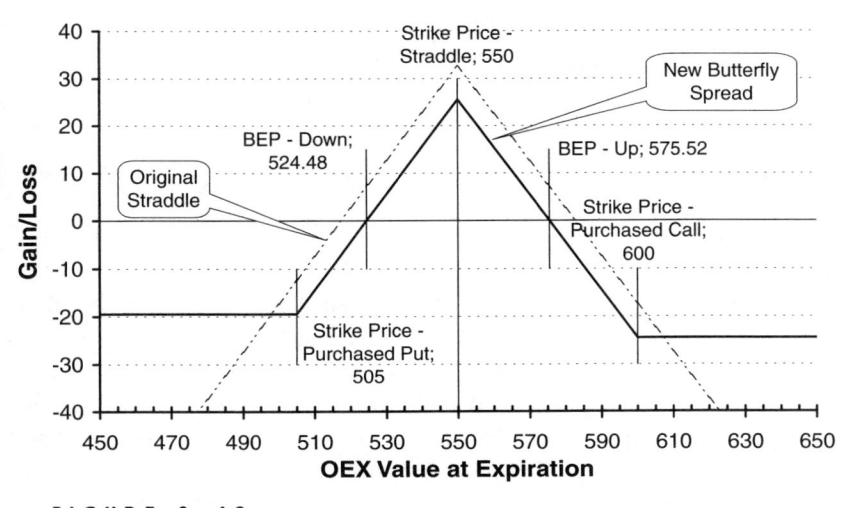

FIGURE 9-13

Butterfly spread from straddle

be used any time a naked option is sold or short strategies without insurance are undertaken.

A stop price for a sold put may be based on the *current* price. However, without solving the Black-Scholes model for constantly changing prices over time, a trader cannot know the potential option gain or loss for any given change in the underlying price. Calculating the option's delta will be necessary. For example, assume a trader is willing to risk no more than an amount equal to the price received for a written option. In Chapter 3 we looked at selling an 80 Put for $2.57 (see Figure 3-9). The current price of the underlying stock was $83, the volatility was 30 percent, there were 90 days until expiration, and the risk-free interest rate was 1.2 percent. Our trader is only willing to risk $2.57. Where should he place his original stop at the inception of the trade?

In Chapter 5 we learned that the delta of a Call (Δ_{Call}) was equal to $N(d)$, where d is defined by

$$d = \frac{\ln\left(\frac{S}{K}\right) + t\left(r + \frac{\sigma^2}{2}\right)}{\sigma\sqrt{t}}$$

Calculating d for the preceding example, we have

$$d = \frac{\ln\left(\frac{83}{80}\right) + .2466\left(.012 + \frac{.09}{2}\right)}{.3(.4966)} = .3414$$

$$\Delta_{\text{Call}} = N(d) = N(.3414) = .6336$$

$$\Delta_{\text{Put}} = 1 - \Delta_{\text{Call}} = .3664$$

Therefore, at inception, the price of this Put will fall $0.37 for each dollar reduction in the underlying stock price. Since the trader is willing to lose $2.57, the stock price may fall $6.95 from $83.00 to $76.05 before such loss will occur. The stop loss order should be entered at $76.05 at inception. Bear in mind this calculation is only good for the inception date. As time passes, the values of the variables used in the calculation of d change, which means the appropriate stop price also will change.

The stop price also may be based on the expiration price. In this case, the trader is not concerned with the loss exceeding $2.57 *prior* to expiration but only that the final loss *at* expiration is no more than $2.57. Here we use Equation (3.23) for the case in which the expiration price is less than the strike price.

$$R = x - BEP \quad \text{where } BEP = K_{SP} - P_{SP}$$

$$R = x - 80 + 2.57 = x - 77.43$$

Since R is limited to -2.57,

$$x - 77.43 = -2.57 \quad \text{and} \quad x = 74.86$$

The stop would be entered at $74.86 and designated "good until canceled" for the duration of the trade. Using stops based on expiration prices requires the trader to keep careful watch during the life of the trade. The entire position could, of course, be canceled in the event of a catastrophic adverse move prior to expiration.

POSITION SIZING

In the preceding analyses, only the minimum number of contracts were used to keep the explanations simple. To make use of optimal f (which values are included for each trade in Appendix C), it is necessary to make some assumptions. First, of course, is the size of the trader's capital account and whether there will be subamounts devoted to each strategy type or just one amount for all strategies. For the restricted-loss trades, the calculations are easy. Assume a $50,000 single capital account exits and a long Call costing $2.50 has been selected. With an f^* of 1.5 percent, $750 of capital would be committed to this trade. Therefore, three contracts of the Call would be purchased ($750/$250).

The problem of position sizing for written options is similar to the problem of determining the rate of return discussed earlier. The trader will have to choose for herself how much she is willing to commit on trades with significant downside risk. This could be a certain percentage of the maximum statistical loss, as explained earlier, or this simply could be the amount initial margin deposited. For example, assume a trader will risk only 25 percent of the maximum statistical loss on any one trade. He has a $50,000 single capital account. He has selected a written Put to trade whose maximum statistical loss is $25, and the trade's f^* is 2.5 percent. With $1,250 of capital available (.025 × $50,000) and a maximum loss of $6.25 (.25 × $25), two contracts of this Put would be sold ($1,250/$625).

WHAT'S NEXT?

This book has been about developing the mathematics of options trading. These mathematics can be used to produce certain useful information about potential options trades based on actual long-run probabilities. Finally, we have seen the results of using this information together with certain arbitrarily selected criteria on actual options trades that also have been selected arbitrarily (hopefully somewhat randomly) for examination. While by no means statistically significant, the small sample results are impressive and suggest further research that is beyond the scope of this book.

Such research could be conducted by using continuous live data feeds with historical and current options prices as a "front end" to *DailyCheck.exe,* eliminating the need for inputting data for each option by hand. The program also could be modified to accept certain selection criteria and produce reports such as those contained in Appendix C directly. Finally, provisions in the program could be made to actually *optimize* the selection criteria based on historical data for testing on future expirations.

APPENDIX A
Sample Output from *Expectation.exe*

Sample Output from *Expectation.exe*

The Purchased Call

Purchase The CSCO Aug 17.5 Call For $1.60

Trade date	13-Jul-03	Expiration date	15-Aug-03
Days to expiration	34	Volatility	.398
Price of underlying	$18.57	Underlying symbol	CSCO
Statistical maximum loss	-$1.60	Mathematical Advantage (MA)	.73%
Break-even price	$19.10	Statistical maximum gain	11.09
Return per trade	1.00001	Optimal f	.25%
Slope of ER tangent	2.18	ER tangent intercept	-.86

	Call
Option symbol	CYQHW
Option price	$1.60
Black-Scholes price	$1.53
Implied volatility	.433
Number of contracts	1

Outcome	Probability	Result	Expected Value
LOSS (Underlying is less than $19.10)	.592	-1.222	-$.72
GAIN (Underlying is greater than $19.10)	.408	1.793	$.73
The expected result of this trade is			$.01

ER-Volatilty curve coefficients   a = 1.5789   b = .9185   c = -.6067

The Sold Call

Sell The CSCO Aug 17.5 Call For $1.60

Trade date	13-Jul-03	Expiration date	15-Aug-03
Days to expiration	34	Volatility	.398
Price of underlying	$18.57	Underlying symbol	CSCO
Statistical maximum loss	-$11.09	Mathematical Advantage (MA)	-.51%
Break-even price	$19.10	Statistical maximum gain	$1.60
Return per trade	N/A	Optimal f	N/A
Slope of ER tangent	-2.18	ER tangent intercept	.86

	Call
Option symbol	CYQHW
Option price	$1.60
Black-Scholes price	$1.53
Implied volatility	.433
Number of contracts	1

Outcome	Probability	Result	Expected Value
GAIN (Underlying is less than $19.10)	.592	1.222	$.72
LOSS (Underlying is greater than $19.10)	.408	-1.793	-$.73
The expected result of this trade is			-$.01

ER-Volatilty curve coefficients   a = -1.5789   b = -.9185   c = .6067

Sample Output from *Expectation.exe*

The Purchased Put

Purchase The CSCO Aug 17.5 Put For $.50

Trade date	13-Jul-03	Expiration date	15-Aug-03
Days to expiration	34	Volatility	.398
Price of underlying	$18.57	Underlying symbol	CSCO
Statistical maximum loss	-$.50	Mathematical Advantage (MA)	-20.71%
Break-even price	$17.00	Statistical maximum gain	5.58
Return per trade	N/A	Optimal f	N/A
Slope of ER tangent	1.48	ER tangent intercept	-.69

	Put
Option symbol	CYQTW
Option price	$.50
Black-Scholes price	$.43
Implied volatility	.434
Number of contracts	1

Outcome	Probability	Result	Expected Value
LOSS (Underlying is greater than $17.00)	.766	-.475	-$.36
GAIN (Underlying is less than $17.00)	.234	1.137	$.27
The expected result of this trade is			-$.10

ER-Volatilty curve coefficients a = .6937   b = .9270   c = -.5771

The Sold Put

Sell The CSCO Aug 17.5 Put For $.50

Trade date	13-Jul-03	Expiration date	15-Aug-03
Days to expiration	34	Volatility	.398
Price of underlying	$18.57	Underlying symbol	CSCO
Statistical maximum loss	-$5.58	Mathematical Advantage (MA)	8.64%
Break-even price	$17.00	Statistical maximum gain	$.50
Return per trade	1.00615	Optimal f	11.42%
Slope of ER tangent	-1.48	ER tangent intercept	.69

	Put
Option symbol	CYQTW
Option price	$.50
Black-Scholes price	$.43
Implied volatility	.434
Number of contracts	1

Outcome	Probability	Result	Expected Value
LOSS (Underlying is less than $17.00)	.234	-1.137	-$.27
GAIN (Underlying is greater than $17.00)	.766	.475	$.36
The expected result of this trade is			$.10

ER-Volatilty curve coefficients   a = -.6937   b = -.9270   c = .5771

The Bull Put Spread

Sell The CSCO Aug 30. Put & Buy The 15. Put: Net Credit = $11.35

Trade date	13-Jul-03	Expiration date	15-Aug-03
Days to expiration	34	Volatility	.398
Price of underlying	$18.57	Underlying symbol	CSCO
Statistical maximum loss	-$3.65	Mathematical Advantage (MA)	5.14%
Break-even price	$18.65	Statistical maximum gain	$11.35
Return per trade	1.00074	Optimal f	1.75%
Slope of ER tangent	1.05	ER tangent intercept	-.33

	15.0 Put	30.0 Put
Option symbol	CYQTF	CYQTC
Option price	$.10	$11.45
Black-Scholes price	$.03	$11.37
Implied volatility	.512	.846
Number of contracts	1	1

Outcome	Probability	Result	Expected Value
LOSS (Underlying is less than $18.65)	.514	-1.650	-$.85
GAIN (Underlying is greater than $18.65)	.486	1.921	$.93
The expected result of this trade is			$.08

ER-Volatilty curve coefficients   a = 1.7207   b = -.3203   c = -.0602

The Bull Call Spread

Sell The CSCO Aug 17.5 Call & Buy The 5.0 Call: Net Debit = $11.96

Trade date	13-Jul-03	Expiration date	15-Aug-03
Days to expiration	34	Volatility	.398
Price of underlying	$18.57	Underlying symbol	CSCO
Statistical maximum loss	-$11.96	Mathematical Advantage (MA)	12.30%
Break-even price	$16.96	Statistical maximum gain	$.54
Return per trade	1.00899	Optimal f	8.35%
Slope of ER tangent	-1.48	ER tangent intercept	.73

	5.0 Call	17.5 Call
Option symbol	CYQHA	CYQHW
Option price	$13.56	$1.60
Black-Scholes price	$13.58	$1.53
Implied volatility	.398	.433
Number of contracts	1	1

Outcome	Probability	Result	Expected Value
LOSS (Underlying is less than $16.96)	.228	-1.125	-$.26
GAIN (Underlying is greater than $16.96)	.772	.511	$.39
The expected result of this trade is			$.14

ER-Volatilty curve coefficients   a = -.6934   b = -.9277   c = .6176

Sample Output from *Expectation.exe*

The Bear Put Spread

Sell The CSCO Aug 22.5 Put & Buy The 25. Put: Net Debit = $2.40

Trade date	13-Jul-03	Expiration date	15-Aug-03
Days to expiration	34	Volatility	.398
Price of underlying	$18.57	Underlying symbol	CSCO
Statistical maximum loss	-$2.40	Mathematical Advantage (MA)	3.51%
Break-even price	$22.60	Statistical maximum gain	$.10
Return per trade	1.00479	Optimal f	21.38%
Slope of ER tangent	-.52	ER tangent intercept	.25

	22.5 Put	25.0 Put
Option symbol	CYQTE	CYQTX
Option price	$4.00	$6.40
Black-Scholes price	$3.95	$6.39
Implied volatility	.456	.450
Number of contracts	1	1

Outcome	Probability	Result	Expected Value
GAIN (Underlying is less than $22.60)	.947	.100	$.09
LOSS (Underlying is greater than $22.60)	.053	-1.072	-$.06
The expected result of this trade is			$.04

ER-Volatilty curve coefficients   a = -1.0250   b = .2938   c = .0832

The Bear Call Spread

Sell The CSCO Aug 17.5 Call & Buy The 20. Call: Net Credit = $1.17

Trade date	13-Jul-03	Expiration date	15-Aug-03
Days to expiration	34	Volatility	.398
Price of underlying	$18.57	Underlying symbol	CSCO
Statistical maximum loss	-$1.33	Mathematical Advantage (MA)	-1.00%
Break-even price	$18.67	Statistical maximum gain	$1.17
Return per trade	N/A	Optimal f	N/A
Slope of ER tangent	-.21	ER tangent intercept	.07

	17.5 Call	20.0 Call
Option symbol	CYQHD	CYQHW
Option price	$1.60	$.43
Black-Scholes price	$1.53	$.40
Implied volatility	.433	.415
Number of contracts	1	1

Outcome	Probability	Result	Expected Value
GAIN (Underlying is less than $18.67)	.518	.936	$.48
LOSS (Underlying is greater than $18.67)	.482	-1.026	-$.49
The expected result of this trade is			-$.01

ER-Volatilty curve coefficients   a = .3657   b = -.5010   c = .1312

The Covered Call

Sell The CSCO Aug 17.5 Call & Buy The Underlying Stock

Trade date	13-Jul-03	Expiration date	15-Aug-03
Days to expiration	34	Volatility	.398
Price of underlying	$18.57	Underlying symbol	CSCO
Statistical maximum loss	-$5.55	Mathematical Advantage (MA)	11.41%
Break-even price	$16.97	Statistical maximum gain	$.53
Return per trade	1.00998	Optimal f	13.81%
Slope of ER tangent	-1.48	ER tangent intercept	.72

	Call
Option symbol	CYQHW
Option price	$1.60
Black-Scholes price	$1.53
Implied volatility	.433
Number of contracts	1

Outcome	Probability	Result	Expected Value
LOSS(Underlying is less than $16.97)	.229	-1.127	-$.26
GAIN (Underlying is greater than $16.97)	.771	.502	$.39
The expected result of this trade is			$.13

ER-Volatilty curve coefficients   a = -.6935   b = -.9277   c = .6077

The Long Straddle

Buy The CSCO Aug 20. Call & Buy The 20. Put: Net Debit = $2.28

Trade date	13-Jul-03	Expiration date	15-Aug-03
Days to expiration	34	Volatility	.398
Price of underlying	$18.57	Underlying symbol	CSCO
Statistical maximum loss	-$2.28	Mathematical Advantage (MA)	-11.02%
Break-even price	$17.72 $22.28	Statistical maximum gain	$7.91
Return per trade	N/A	Optimal f	N/A
Slope of ER tangent	3.23	ER tangent intercept	-1.42

	20.0 Call	20.0 Put
Option symbol	CYQHD	CYQTD
Option price	$.43	$1.85
Black-Scholes price	$.40	$1.79
Implied volatility	.415	.428
Number of contracts	1	1

Outcome	Probability	Result	Expected Value
GAIN (Underlying < $17.72 or > $22.28)	.417	1.338	$.56
LOSS (Underlying between $17.72 and $22.28)	.583	-1.178	-$.69
The expected result of this trade is			-$.13

ER-Volatilty curve coefficients   a = 3.0041   b = .8435   c = -.9413

Sample Output from *Expectation.exe*

The Short Straddle

Sell The CSCO Aug 22.5 Call & Sell The 22.5 Put: Net Credit = $4.12

Trade date	13-Jul-03	Expiration date	15-Aug-03
Days to expiration	34	Volatility	.398
Price of underlying	$18.57	Underlying symbol	CSCO
Statistical maximum loss	-$6.96	Mathematical Advantage (MA)	11.83%
Break-even price	$18.38 $26.62	Statistical maximum gain	$4.12
Return per trade	1.00428	Optimal f	4.51%
Slope of ER tangent	-1.1	ER tangent intercept	.63

	22.5 Call	22.5 Put
Option symbol	CYQHX	CYQTE
Option price	$.12	$4.00
Black-Scholes price	$.06	$3.95
Implied volatility	.464	.456
Number of contracts	1	1

Outcome	Probability	Result	Expected Value
LOSS (Underlying < $18.38 or > $26.62)	.468	-1.593	-$.74
GAIN (Underlying between $18.38 and $26.62)	.532	1.754	$.93
The expected result of this trade is			$.19

ER-Volatilty curve coefficients   a = -3.3836   b = 1.5942   c = .0899

The Long Strangle

Buy The CSCO Aug 20. Call & Buy The 17.5 Put: Net Debit = $.93

Trade date	13-Jul-03	Expiration date	15-Aug-03
Days to expiration	34	Volatility	.398
Price of underlying	$18.57	Underlying symbol	CSCO
Statistical maximum loss	-$.93	Mathematical Advantage (MA)	-13.01%
Break-even price	$16.57 $20.93	Statistical maximum gain	$9.26
Return per trade	N/A	Optimal f	N/A
Slope of ER tangent	3.44	ER tangent intercept	-1.47

	20.0 Call	17.5 Put
Option symbol	CYQHD	CYQTW
Option price	$.43	$.50
Black-Scholes price	$.40	$.43
Implied volatility	.415	.434
Number of contracts	1	1

Outcome	Probability	Result	Expected Value
GAIN (Underlying < $16.57 or > $20.93)	.336	1.214	$.41
LOSS (Underlying between $16.57 and $20.93)	.664	-.766	-$.51
The expected result of this trade is			-$.10

ER-Volatilty curve coefficients   a = 2.6384   b = 1.3445   c = -1.0526

Sample Output from *Expectation.exe*

The Short Strangle

Sell The CSCO Aug 22.5 Call & Sell The 17.5 Put: Net Credit = $.62

Trade date	13-Jul-03	Expiration date	15-Aug-03
Days to expiration	34	Volatility	.398
Price of underlying	$18.57	Underlying symbol	CSCO
Statistical maximum loss	-$7.07	Mathematical Advantage (MA)	13.38%
Break-even price	$16.88 $23.12	Statistical maximum gain	$.62
Return per trade	1.01164	Optimal f	13.68%
Slope of ER tangent	-2.38	ER tangent intercept	1.09

	22.5 Call	17.5 Put
Option symbol	CYQHX	CYQTW
Option price	$.12	$.50
Black-Scholes price	$.06	$.43
Implied volatility	.464	.434
Number of contracts	1	1

Outcome	Probability	Result	Expected Value
LOSS (Underlying < $16.88 or > $23.12)	.252	-1.112	-$.28
GAIN (Underlying between $16.88 and $23.12)	.748	.573	$.43
The expected result of this trade is			$.15

ER-Volatilty curve coefficients   a = -2.8281   b = -.1256   c = .6468

The Call Ratio Spread

Buy 1 CSCO Aug 15. Call & Sell 2 17.5 Call: Debit = $.50

Trade date	13-Jul-03	Expiration date	15-Aug-03
Days to expiration	34	Volatility	.398
Price of underlying	$18.57	Underlying symbol	CSCO
Statistical maximum loss	-$10.69	Mathematical Advantage (MA)	1.14%
Break-even price	$15.50 $19.50	Statistical maximum gain	$2.00
Return per trade	1.00006	Optimal f	.65%
Slope of ER tangent	-3.25	ER tangent intercept	1.31

	15.0 Call	17.5 Call
Option symbol	CYQHC	CYQHW
Option price	$3.70	$1.60
Black-Scholes price	$3.63	$1.53
Implied volatility	.515	.433
Number of contracts	1	2

Outcome	Probability	Result	Expected Value
LOSS (Underlying < $15.50 and > $19.50)	.412	-1.476	-$.61
GAIN (Underlying between $15.50 and $19.50)	.588	1.064	$.63
The expected result of this trade is			$.02

ER-Volatilty curve coefficients   a = -1.2651   b = -2.2403   c = 1.1089

Sample Output from *Expectation.exe*

The Put Ratio Spread

Buy 1 CSCO Aug 22.5 Put & Sell 2 20.0 Put: Debit = $.30

Trade date	13-Jul-03	Expiration date	15-Aug-03
Days to expiration	34	Volatility	.398
Price of underlying	$18.57	Underlying symbol	CSCO
Statistical maximum loss	-$6.38	Mathematical Advantage (MA)	9.91%
Break-even price	$17.80 $22.20	Statistical maximum gain	$2.20
Return per trade	1.00335	Optimal f	5.49%
Slope of ER tangent	-2.34	ER tangent intercept	1.05

	22.5 Put	20.0 Put
Option symbol	CYQTX	CYQTD
Option price	$4.00	$1.85
Black-Scholes price	$3.95	$1.79
Implied volatility	.456	.428
Number of contracts	1	2

Outcome	Probability	Result	Expected Value
LOSS (Underlying < $17.80 and > $22.20)	.434	-1.202	-$.52
GAIN (Underlying between $17.80 and $22.20)	.566	1.134	$.64
The expected result of this trade is			$.12

ER-Volatilty curve coefficients   a = -.8697   b = -1.6449   c = .9116

The Call Backspread

Buy 2 CSCO Aug 15. Call & Sell 1 10.0 Call: Credit = $1.20

Trade date	13-Jul-03	Expiration date	15-Aug-03
Days to expiration	34	Volatility	.398
Price of underlying	$18.57	Underlying symbol	CSCO
Statistical maximum loss	-$3.80	Mathematical Advantage (MA)	-2.26%
Break-even price	$11.20 $18.80	Statistical maximum gain	$11.39
Return per trade	N/A	Optimal f	N/A
Slope of ER tangent	1.51	ER tangent intercept	-.64

	15.0 Call	10.0 Call
Option symbol	CYQHC	CYQHB
Option price	$3.70	$8.60
Black-Scholes price	$3.63	$8.59
Implied volatility	.515	.398
Number of contracts	2	1

Outcome	Probability	Result	Expected Value
GAIN (Underlying < $11.20 and > $18.80)	.46	1.876	$.86
LOSS (Underlying between $11.20 and $18.80)	.54	-1.665	-$.90
The expected result of this trade is			-$.04

ER-Volatilty curve coefficients   a = 2.8930   b = -.7941   c = -.1798

Sample Output from *Expectation.exe*

The Put Backspread

Buy 2 CSCO Aug 20. Put & Sell 1 22.5 Put: Credit = $.30

Trade date	13-Jul-03	Expiration date	15-Aug-03
Days to expiration	34	Volatility	.398
Price of underlying	$18.57	Underlying symbol	CSCO
Statistical maximum loss	-$2.20	Mathematical Advantage (MA)	-10.52%
Break-even price	$17.80 $22.20	Statistical maximum gain	$6.38
Return per trade	N/A	Optimal f	N/A
Slope of ER tangent	2.34	ER tangent intercept	-1.05

	20.0 Put	22.5 Put
Option symbol	CYQTD	CYQTX
Option price	$1.85	$4.00
Black-Scholes price	$1.79	$3.95
Implied volatility	.428	.456
Number of contracts	2	1

Outcome	Probability	Result	Expected Value
LOSS (Underlying < $17.80 and > $22.20)	.566	-1.134	-$.64
GAIN (Underlying between $17.80 and $22.20)	.434	1.202	$.52
The expected result of this trade is			-$.12

ER-Volatilty curve coefficients   a = .8697   b = 1.6449   c = -.9116

The Long Call Butterfly Spread

Buy 1 CSCO Aug 12.5 Call & 1 22.5 Call: Sell 2 17.5 Calls: Debit = -$3.02

Trade date	13-Jul-03	Expiration date	15-Aug-03
Days to expiration	34	Volatility	.398
Price of underlying	$18.57	Underlying symbol	CSCO
Statistical maximum loss	-$3.02	Mathematical Advantage (MA)	2.82%
Break-even price	$15.52 $19.48	Statistical maximum gain	$1.98
Return per trade	1.00037	Optimal f	1.89%
Slope of ER tangent	-2.7	ER tangent intercept	1.11

	12.5 Call	17.5 Call	22.5 Call
Option symbol	CYQHV	CYQHX	CYQHW
Option price	$6.10	$1.60	$.12
Black-Scholes price	$6.09	$1.53	$.06
Implied volatility	.542	.433	.464
Number of contracts	1	1	2

Outcome	Probability	Result	Expected Value
LOSS (Underlying < $15.52 and > $19.48)	.417	-1.379	-$.57
GAIN (Underlying between $15.52 and $19.48)	.583	1.052	$.61
The expected result of this trade is			$.04

ER-Volatilty curve coefficients   a = .0337   b = -2.7289   c = 1.1197

APPENDIX B
Sample Output from *DailyCheck.exe*

Sample Output from *DailyCheck.exe*

CSCO 13-Jul-03 Naked Options - Aug Expiration (34 Days)
CSCO Stock Price = $18.57: Target Price = $18.57: Volatility = 0.398

Calls:

Strike	Bid	Ask	Last	Market	Black Scholes	Implied Volatility	Delta	Vega
5.0	13.50	13.70	12.80	13.56	13.58	.398	1.000	.000
7.5	11.00	11.20	10.40	11.07	11.08	.398	1.000	.000
10.0	8.50	8.70	8.70	8.60	8.59	.398	1.000	.000
12.5	6.00	6.20	6.10	6.10	6.09	.542	1.000	.009
15.0	3.60	3.80	3.60	3.70	3.63	.515	.967	.421
17.5	1.55	1.65	1.60	1.60	1.53	.433	.714	1.928
20.0	.40	.45	.45	.43	.40	.415	.296	1.960
22.5	.10	.15	.10	.12	.06	.464	.066	.729
25.0	.00	.00	.00	.00	.01	.252	.009	.136
27.5	.00	.00	.00	.00	.00	.322	.001	.016
30.0	.00	.00	.00	.00	.00	.376	.000	.001

Puts:

Strike	Bid	Ask	Last	Market	Black Scholes	Implied Volatility	Delta	Vega
5.0	.00	.00	.00	.00	.00	.398	.000	.000
7.5	.00	.00	.00	.00	.00	.398	.000	.000
10.0	.00	.00	.00	.00	.00	.398	.000	.000
12.5	.00	.10	.10	.00	.00	.344	.000	.009
15.0	.05	.15	.10	.10	.03	.512	-.033	.421
17.5	.45	.55	.55	.50	.43	.434	-.286	1.928
20.0	1.80	1.90	1.85	1.85	1.79	.428	-.704	1.960
22.5	3.90	4.10	4.00	4.00	3.95	.456	-.934	.729
25.0	6.30	6.50	6.50	6.40	6.39	.450	-.991	.136
27.5	8.80	9.00	10.00	8.95	8.88	.714	-.999	.016
30.0	11.30	11.50	12.50	11.45	11.37	.846	-1.000	.001

CSCO 13-Jul-03 Naked Options - Aug Expiration (34 Days)
CSCO Current Price = $18.57: Target Price = $18.57: Volatility = 0.398

Purchased Calls:

Strike Price	Strike	Price	E(Gain)	E(Loss)	E(R)	BEPdn	BEPup	P(Gain)	MA	Gmax	Lmax	Omega	Opt. f	RTN
5.0	13.56		.9777	-.8302	.1475	18.56		.5017	8.84%	11.63	-13.56	.70	2.89%	1.00212
7.5	11.07		.9727	-.8353	.1374	18.57		.5000	8.22%	11.62	-11.07	.70	2.69%	1.00184
10.0	8.60		.9578	-.8504	.1073	18.60		.4947	6.37%	11.59	-8.60	.70	2.09%	1.00112
12.5	6.10		.9578	-.8503	.1075	18.60		.4947	6.38%	11.59	-6.10	.75	2.10%	1.00113
15.0	3.70		.9092	-.8743	.0349	18.70		.4771	2.08%	11.49	-3.70	1.10	0.70%	1.00012
17.5	1.60		.7322	-.7232	.0090	19.10		.4084	0.73%	11.09	-1.60	2.18	0.25%	1.00001

Sold Calls:

Strike Price	Strike	Price	E(Gain)	E(Loss)	E(R)	BEPdn	BEPup	P(Gain)	MA	Gmax	Lmax	Omega	Opt. f	RTN
20.0	.43		.3256	-.3244	.0012		20.43	.7840	0.08%	.43	-9.76	-1.97	0.12%	1.00000
* 22.5	.12		.1134	-.0629	.0506		22.62	.9478	4.19%	.12	-7.57	-.90	13.20%	1.00471

Purchased Puts:

Strike Price	Strike	Price	E(Gain)	E(Loss)	E(R)	BEPdn	BEPup	P(Gain)	MA	Gmax	Lmax	Omega	Opt. f	RTN

Sold Puts:

Strike Price	Strike	Price	E(Gain)	E(Loss)	E(R)	BEPdn	BEPup	P(Gain)	MA	Gmax	Lmax	Omega	Opt. f	RTN
* 15.0	.10		.0963	-.0239	.0724	14.90		.9650	10.57%	.10	-3.48	-.41	28.73%	1.01870
17.5	.50		.3638	-.2655	.0983	17.00		.7664	8.64%	.50	-5.58	-1.48	11.42%	1.00615
20.0	1.85		.7696	-.6411	.1285	18.15		.5747	8.52%	1.85	-6.73	-1.27	4.46%	1.00293
22.5	4.00		.9387	-.8008	.1379	18.50		.5124	8.39%	4.00	-7.08	-.20	3.05%	1.00211
25.0	6.40		.9506	-.8505	.1001	18.60		.4947	5.94%	6.40	-7.18	.32	1.99%	1.00099
27.5	8.95		.9823	-.8254	.1569	18.55		.5035	9.43%	8.95	-7.13	.55	3.09%	1.00241
30.0	11.45		.9828	-.8254	.1573	18.55		.5035	9.46%	11.45	-7.13	.64	3.09%	1.00242

CSCO 13-Jul-03 Spreads - Aug Expiration (34 Days)
CSCO Current Price = $18.57: Target Price = $18.57: Volatility = 0.398

Bull Call Spreads:

	Purch. Call Strike Price	Purch. Call Price	Sold Call Strike	Sold Call Price	E(Gain)	E(Loss)	E(R)	BEPdn	BEPup	P(Gain)	MA	Gmax	Lmax	Omega	Opt. f	RTN
*	5.0	13.56	12.5	6.10	.0400	.0000	.0400	12.46		.9995	73.59%	.04	-7.46	-.06	13.39%	1.00533
*	5.0	13.56	15.0	3.70	.1349	-.0223	.1126	14.86		.9667	16.76%	.14	-9.86	-.41	10.13%	1.01120
*	5.0	13.56	17.5	1.60	.3946	-.2561	.1385	16.96		.7723	12.30%	.54	-11.96	-1.48	8.35%	1.00899
	5.0	13.56	20.0	.43	.7811	-.6324	.1487	18.13		.5782	9.91%	1.87	-13.13	-1.27	5.12%	1.00389
	5.0	13.56	22.5	.12	.9697	-.7717	.1981	18.44		.5230	12.23%	4.06	-13.44	-.20	4.38%	1.00434
*	7.5	11.07	12.5	6.10	.0300	-.0001	.0299	12.47		.9994	27.38%	.03	-4.97	-.06	20.10%	1.00599
*	7.5	11.07	15.0	3.70	.1253	-.0227	.1025	14.87		.9663	15.17%	.13	-7.37	-.41	13.55%	1.01353
*	7.5	11.07	17.5	1.60	.3869	-.2585	.1284	16.97		.7708	11.38%	.53	-9.47	-1.48	10.55%	1.00929
	7.5	11.07	20.0	.43	.7753	-.6367	.1386	18.14		.5764	9.22%	1.86	-10.64	-1.27	4.79%	1.00339
	7.5	11.07	22.5	.12	.9645	-.7765	.1880	18.45		.5213	11.58%	4.05	-10.95	-.20	4.16%	1.00392
*	10.0	8.60	15.0	3.70	.0963	-.0238	.0724	14.90		.9650	10.61%	.10	-4.90	-.41	20.39%	1.01389
	10.0	8.60	17.5	1.60	.3638	-.2655	.0983	17.00		.7664	8.64%	.50	-7.00	-1.48	11.43%	1.00615
	10.0	8.60	20.0	.43	.7581	-.6496	.1086	18.17		.5711	7.16%	1.83	-8.17	-1.27	3.81%	1.00210
	10.0	8.60	22.5	.12	.9490	-.7911	.1579	18.48		.5159	9.66%	4.02	-8.48	-.20	3.49%	1.00276
	12.5	6.10	15.0	3.70	.0963	-.0237	.0726	14.90		.9650	10.69%	.10	-2.40	-.35	40.21%	1.02371
	12.5	6.10	17.5	1.60	.3638	-.2653	.0985	17.00		.7664	8.66%	.50	-4.50	-1.42	11.49%	1.00619
	12.5	6.10	20.0	.43	.7581	-.6494	.1087	18.17		.5711	7.17%	1.83	-5.67	-1.21	3.81%	1.00211
	12.5	6.10	22.5	.12	.9490	-.7909	.1580	18.48		.5159	9.67%	4.02	-5.98	-.15	3.49%	1.00277
	15.0	3.70	17.5	1.60	.2879	-.2620	.0259	17.10		.7514	2.45%	.40	-2.10	-1.07	4.76%	1.00063
	15.0	3.70	20.0	.43	.7019	-.6658	.0361	18.27		.5533	2.42%	1.73	-3.27	-.86	1.44%	1.00026
	15.0	3.70	22.5	.12	.8983	-.8128	.0855	18.58		.4982	5.27%	3.92	-3.58	.21	2.01%	1.00086
	17.5	1.60	20.0	.43	.4948	-.4846	.0102	18.67		.4823	1.09%	1.33	-1.17	.21	0.94%	1.00005
	17.5	1.60	22.5	.12	.7130	-.6534	.0596	18.98		.4286	5.20%	3.52	-1.48	1.28	2.36%	1.00069
	20.0	.43	22.5	.12	.2817	-.2324	.0493	20.31		.2304	16.33%	2.19	-0.31	1.07	10.32%	1.00244

345

CSCO 13-Jul-03 Spreads - Aug Expiration (34 Days)

CSCO Current Price = $18.57: Target Price = $18.57: Volatility = 0.398

Bear Call Spreads:

Purch. Call Strike Price	Sold Call Strike Price	E(Gain)	E(Loss)	E(R)	BEPdn	BEPup	P(Gain)	MA	Gmax	Lmax	Omega	Opt. f	RTN

CSCO 13-Jul-03 Spreads - Aug Expiration (34 Days)
CSCO Current Price = $18.57: Target Price = $18.57: Volatility = 0.398

Bull Put Spreads:

Purch.Put Strike	Price	Sold Put Strike	Price	E(Gain)	E(Loss)	E(R)	BEPdn	BEPup	P(Gain)	MA	Gmax	Lmax	Omega	Opt. f	RTN
15.0	.10	17.5	.50	.2879	-.2620	.0259	17.10		.7514	2.45%	.40	-2.10	-1.07	4.76%	1.00063
15.0	.10	20.0	1.85	.7130	-.6569	.0561	18.25		.5569	3.78%	1.75	-3.25	-.86	2.18%	1.00062
15.0	.10	22.5	4.00	.8883	-.8229	.0655	18.60		.4947	4.01%	3.90	-3.60	.21	1.53%	1.00050
15.0	.10	25.0	6.40	.9020	-.8743	.0277	18.70		.4771	1.65%	6.30	-3.70	.73	0.57%	1.00008
15.0	.10	27.5	8.95	.9328	-.8484	.0845	18.65		.4859	5.11%	8.85	-3.65	.96	1.73%	1.00073
15.0	.10	30.0	11.45	.9333	-.8484	.0849	18.65		.4859	5.14%	11.35	-3.65	1.05	1.75%	1.00074
17.5	.50	20.0	1.85	.5045	-.4743	.0302	18.65		.4859	3.27%	1.35	-1.15	.21	2.70%	1.00041
17.5	.50	22.5	4.00	.7044	-.6649	.0396	19.00		.4252	3.41%	3.50	-1.50	1.28	1.53%	1.00030
17.5	.50	25.0	6.40	.7250	-.7232	.0018	19.10		.4084	0.14%	5.90	-1.60	1.80	0.06%	1.00000
17.5	.50	27.5	8.95	.7524	-.6938	.0586	19.05		.4168	4.92%	8.45	-1.55	2.03	1.87%	1.00054
17.5	.50	30.0	11.45	.7529	-.6938	.0590	19.05		.4168	4.96%	10.95	-1.55	2.12	1.87%	1.00055
20.0	1.85	22.5	4.00	.2726	-.2633	.0093	20.35		.2255	2.74%	2.15	-0.35	1.07	1.71%	1.00008
20.0	1.85	27.5	8.95	.3305	-.3022	.0284	20.40		.2195	7.32%	7.10	-0.40	1.82	3.25%	1.00043
20.0	1.85	30.0	11.45	.3310	-.3022	.0288	20.40		.2195	7.44%	9.60	-0.40	1.91	3.25%	1.00044
22.5	4.00	27.5	8.95	.0662	-.0472	.0190	22.55		.0549	38.09%	4.95	-0.05	.75	20.00%	1.00164
22.5	4.00	30.0	11.45	.0667	-.0472	.0195	22.55		.0549	39.01%	7.45	-0.05	.84	20.00%	1.00168

347

CSCO 13-Jul-03 Spreads - Aug Expiration (34 Days)
CSCO Current Price = $18.57: Target Price = $18.57: Volatility = 0.398

Bear Put Spreads:

Purch. Put Strike Price	Purch. Put Price	Sold Put Strike	Sold Put Price	E(Gain)	E(Loss)	E(R)	BEPdn	BEPup	P(Gain)	MA	Gmax	Lmax	Omega	Opt. f	RTN
25.0	6.40	20.0	1.85	.3413	-.3129	.0284		20.45	.7863	1.93%	.45	-4.55	-1.59	2.86%	1.00042
25.0	6.40	22.5	4.00	.0945	-.0568	.0377		22.60	.9470	3.51%	.10	-2.40	-.52	21.38%	1.00479

CSCO 13-Jul-03 Covered Calls - Aug Expiration (34 Days)
CSCO Current Price = $18.57: Target Price = $18.57: Volatility = 0.398

Covered Calls:

	Strike Price	Price	E(Gain)	E(Loss)	E(R)	BEPdn	BEPup	P(Gain)	MA	Gmax	Lmax	Omega	Opt. f	RTN
*	12.5	6.10	.0300	-.0002	.0298		12.47	.9994	8.09%	.03	-1.05	-.05	95.45%	1.02837
*	15.0	3.70	.1253	-.0229	.1024		14.87	.9663	15.07%	.13	-3.45	-.41	28.98%	1.02756
	17.5	1.60	.3869	-.2586	.1283		16.97	.7708	11.36%	.53	-5.55	-1.48	13.81%	1.00998
	20.0	.43	.7753	-.6368	.1385		18.14	.5764	9.21%	1.86	-6.72	-1.27	4.79%	1.00339
	22.5	.12	.9645	-.7767	.1878		18.45	.5213	11.57%	4.05	-7.03	-.20	4.16%	1.00392

349

CSCO 13-Jul-03 Straddles - Aug Expiration (34 Days)
CSCO Current Price = $18.57: Target Price = $18.57: Volatility = 0.398

Long Straddles:

Purch. Put Strike Price	Purch Call Strike Price	E(Gain)	E(Loss)	E(R)	BEPdn	BEPup	P(Gain)	MA	Gmax	Lmax	Omega	Opt. f	RTN
15.0 .10	15.0 3.70	.8999	-.8624	.0375	11.20	18.80	.5403	1.99%	3.80	-11.39	-1.51	0.77%	1.00015

Short Straddles:

Sold Put Strike Price	Sold Call Strike Price	E(Gain)	E(Loss)	E(R)	BEPdn	BEPup	P(Gain)	MA	Gmax	Lmax	Omega	Opt. f	RTN
17.5 .50	17.5 1.60	.6852	-.5959	.0893	15.40	19.60	.6100	5.84%	2.10	-10.59	-3.65	3.18%	1.00146
20.0 1.85	20.0 .43	.6873	-.5575	.1298	17.72	22.28	.5833	9.69%	2.28	-7.91	-3.23	5.43%	1.00360
22.5 4.00	22.5 .12	.9333	-.7449	.1884	18.38	26.62	.5322	11.83%	4.12	-6.96	-1.10	4.51%	1.00428

Long Strangles:

Purch. Put Strike Price	Purch Call Strike Price	E(Gain)	E(Loss)	E(R)	BEPdn	BEPup	P(Gain)	MA	Gmax	Lmax	Omega	Opt. f	RTN

Short Strangles:

Sold Put Strike Price	Sold Call Strike Price	E(Gain)	E(Loss)	E(R)	BEPdn	BEPup	P(Gain)	MA	Gmax	Lmax	Omega	Opt. f	RTN
15.0 .10	17.5 1.60	.7569	-.6936	.0634	13.30	19.20	.6052	3.60%	1.70	-10.99	-2.58	1.90%	1.00061
15.0 .10	20.0 .43	.3893	-.3157	.0736	14.47	20.53	.7756	5.23%	.53	-9.66	-2.37	5.93%	1.00235
* 15.0 .10	22.5 .12	.2008	-.0779	.1230	14.78	22.72	.9215	12.38%	.22	-7.47	-1.30	13.38%	1.01417
17.5 .50	20.0 .43	.5080	-.4085	.0995	16.57	20.93	.6636	8.19%	.93	-9.26	-3.44	6.47%	1.00341
17.5 .50	22.5 .12	.4286	-.2798	.1489	16.88	23.12	.7483	13.38%	.62	-7.07	-2.38	13.68%	1.01164
20.0 1.85	22.5 .12	.7825	-.6034	.1791	18.03	24.47	.5844	12.33%	1.97	-6.61	-2.17	6.30%	1.00580

CSCO 13-Jul-03 Ratio Spreads - Aug Expiration (34 Days)

CSCO Current Price = $18.57; Target Price = $18.57; Volatility = 0.398

Call Ratio Spread (buy 1 Call and sell 2 Calls at higher strike):

Purch. Call Strike	Call Price	Sold Call Strike	Price	E(Gain)	E(Loss)	E(R)	BEPdn	BEPup	P(Gain)	MA	Gmax	Lmax	Omega	Opt. f	RTN
5.0	13.56	15.0	3.70	.9216	-.8439	.0777	11.16	18.84	.5473	4.16%	3.84	-11.35	-1.51	1.59%	1.00062
5.0	13.56	17.5	1.60	.7098	-.5803	.1295	15.36	19.64	.6186	8.51%	2.14	-10.55	-3.65	4.47%	1.00299
5.0	13.56	20.0	.43	.6990	-.5491	.1500	17.70	22.30	.5877	11.25%	2.30	-12.70	-3.24	6.20%	1.00477
5.0	13.56	22.5	.12	.9655	-.7169	.2486	18.32	26.68	.5430	15.84%	4.18	-13.32	-1.10	5.91%	1.00742
7.5	11.07	15.0	3.70	.9161	-.8485	.0676	11.17	18.83	.5456	3.62%	3.83	-11.36	-1.51	1.38%	1.00047
7.5	11.07	17.5	1.60	.7036	-.5842	.1194	15.37	19.63	.6164	7.83%	2.13	-10.56	-3.65	4.15%	1.00256
7.5	11.07	20.0	.43	.6931	-.5533	.1399	17.71	22.29	.5855	10.47%	2.29	-10.21	-3.24	5.81%	1.00417
7.5	11.07	22.5	.12	.9601	-.7216	.2385	18.33	26.67	.5412	15.16%	4.17	-10.83	-1.10	5.67%	1.00684
10.0	8.60	15.0	3.70	.8999	-.8623	.0376	11.20	18.80	.5403	2.00%	3.80	-11.39	-1.51	0.77%	1.00015
10.0	8.60	17.5	1.60	.6852	-.5958	.0894	15.40	19.60	.6100	5.84%	2.10	-10.59	-3.65	3.18%	1.00146
10.0	8.60	20.0	.43	.6757	-.5659	.1098	17.74	22.26	.5789	8.17%	2.26	-7.93	-3.23	4.64%	1.00259
10.0	8.60	22.5	.12	.9439	-.7355	.2085	18.36	26.64	.5358	13.15%	4.14	-8.36	-1.10	4.98%	1.00523
12.5	6.10	15.0	3.70	.9000	-.8623	.0377	11.20	18.80	.5403	2.00%	3.80	-11.39	-1.46	0.78%	1.00015
12.5	6.10	17.5	1.60	.6852	-.5957	.0895	15.40	19.60	.6100	5.85%	2.10	-10.59	-3.60	3.19%	1.00146
12.5	6.10	20.0	.43	.6757	-.5657	.1100	17.74	22.26	.5789	8.18%	2.26	-7.93	-3.18	4.65%	1.00261
12.5	6.10	22.5	.12	.9439	-.7353	.2086	18.36	26.64	.5358	13.16%	4.14	-5.86	-1.04	4.98%	1.00524
15.0	3.70	17.5	1.60	.6253	-.6084	.0169	15.50	19.50	.5878	1.14%	2.00	-10.69	-3.25	0.65%	1.00006
15.0	3.70	20.0	.43	.6189	-.5815	.0374	17.84	22.16	.5565	2.84%	2.16	-8.03	-2.83	1.79%	1.00034
15.0	3.70	22.5	.12	.8913	-.7552	.1360	18.46	26.54	.5179	8.68%	4.04	-3.65	-.69	3.51%	1.00238
17.5	1.60	20.0	.43	.4148	-.4034	.0115	18.24	21.76	.4627	1.52%	1.76	-8.43	-1.76	1.16%	1.00007
17.5	1.60	22.5	.12	.6984	-.5883	.1101	18.86	26.14	.4468	10.35%	3.64	-4.05	.38	5.09%	1.00275
* 20.0	.43	22.5	.12	.2495	-.1496	.0999	20.19	24.81	.2370	50.92%	2.31	-5.38	.17	18.58%	1.01237

Put Ratio Spread (buy 1 Put and sell 2 Puts at lower strike):

Purch. Put Strike	Put Price	Sold Put Strike	Price	E(Gain)	E(Loss)	E(R)	BEPdn	BEPup	P(Gain)	MA	Gmax	Lmax	Omega	Opt. f	RTN

351

Put Ratio Spread (buy 1 Put and sell 2 Puts at lower strike):

Purch. Put Strike Price	Sold Put Strike Price	E(Gain)	E(Loss)	E(R)	BEPdn	BEPup	P(Gain)	MA	Gmax	Lmax	Omega	Opt. f	RTN
17.5 .50	15.0 .10	.2605	-.2140	.0465	12.80	17.20	.2630	16.01%	2.20	-1.38	.66	12.64%	1.00280
20.0 1.85	15.0 .10	.6745	-.6582	.0163	11.65	18.35	.4609	1.33%	3.35	-1.65	.45	0.67%	1.00006
22.5 4.00	15.0 .10	.8467	-.8398	.0069	11.30	18.70	.5229	0.39%	3.70	-3.80	-.61	0.16%	1.00001
25.0 6.40	15.0 .10	.8999	-.8552	.0447	11.20	18.80	.5403	2.40%	3.80	-6.20	-1.13	0.95%	1.00021
20.0 1.85	17.5 .50	.4340	-.3659	.0681	15.85	19.15	.5038	9.22%	1.65	-4.43	-1.69	8.25%	1.00281
22.5 4.00	17.5 .50	.6253	-.5666	.0587	15.50	19.50	.5878	4.27%	2.00	-4.08	-2.76	2.82%	1.00083
25.0 6.40	17.5 .50	.6852	-.5887	.0965	15.40	19.60	.6100	6.39%	2.10	-5.40	-3.28	3.57%	1.00177
27.5 8.95	17.5 .50	.6550	-.6153	.0397	15.45	19.55	.5990	2.58%	2.05	-7.95	-3.51	1.48%	1.00030
30.0 11.45	17.5 .50	.6550	-.6157	.0393	15.45	19.55	.5990	2.55%	2.05	-10.45	-3.60	1.46%	1.00029
22.5 4.00	20.0 1.85	.6413	-.5222	.1192	17.80	22.20	.5655	9.91%	2.20	-6.38	-2.34	5.49%	1.00335
25.0 6.40	20.0 1.85	.6990	-.5421	.1569	17.70	22.30	.5877	11.93%	2.30	-6.28	-2.86	6.68%	1.00538
27.5 8.95	20.0 1.85	.6699	-.5697	.1002	17.75	22.25	.5766	7.44%	2.25	-6.33	-3.09	4.27%	1.00218
30.0 11.45	20.0 1.85	.6699	-.5702	.0997	17.75	22.25	.5766	7.40%	2.25	-7.75	-3.18	4.23%	1.00215
25.0 6.40	22.5 4.00	.9286	-.7530	.1756	18.40	26.60	.5301	10.95%	4.10	-6.98	-.72	4.20%	1.00371
27.5 8.95	22.5 4.00	.8965	-.7776	.1188	18.45	26.55	.5197	7.33%	4.05	-7.03	-.95	2.86%	1.00171
30.0 11.45	22.5 4.00	.8965	-.7781	.1184	18.45	26.55	.5197	7.30%	4.05	-7.03	-1.05	2.85%	1.00169
27.5 8.95	25.0 6.40	.9193	-.8760	.0433	18.65	31.35	.4859	2.54%	6.35	-7.23	.09	0.87%	1.00019
30.0 11.45	25.0 6.40	.9188	-.8760	.0429	18.65	31.35	.4859	2.51%	6.35	-7.23	.00	0.86%	1.00018
30.0 11.45	27.5 8.95	.9818	-.8254	.1564	18.55	36.45	.5035	9.40%	8.95	-7.13	.46	3.07%	1.00240

352

CSCO 13-Jul-03 Backspreads - Aug Expiration (34 Days)

CSCO Current Price = $18.57: Target Price = $18.57: Volatility = 0.398

Call backspreads (buy 2 Calls and sell 1 Call at lower strike):

Purch. Call Strike	Purch. Call Price	Sold Call Strike	Sold Call Price	E(Gain)	E(Loss)	E(R)	BEPdn	BEPup	P(Gain)	MA	Gmax	Lmax	Omega	Opt. f	RTN
7.5	11.07	5.0	13.56	.9677	-.8403	.1273	-3.58	18.58	.4982	7.60%	11.61	-11.08	.70	2.49%	1.00158
10.0	8.60	5.0	13.56	.9381	-.8709	.0672	1.36	18.64	.4876	3.95%	11.55	-8.64	.70	1.31%	1.00044
12.5	6.10	5.0	13.56	.9381	-.8706	.0675	6.36	18.64	.4876	3.97%	11.55	-6.14	.81	1.32%	1.00044
10.0	8.60	7.5	11.07	.9430	-.8657	.0773	1.37	18.63	.4894	4.55%	11.56	-8.63	.70	1.51%	1.00058
12.5	6.10	7.5	11.07	.9430	-.8654	.0776	6.37	18.63	.4894	4.57%	11.56	-6.13	.81	1.52%	1.00059
12.5	6.10	10.0	8.60	.9578	-.8501	.1076	6.40	18.60	.4947	6.39%	11.59	-6.10	.80	2.10%	1.00113

Put backspreads (buy 2 Puts and sell 1 Put at higher strike):

Purch. Put Strike	Purch. Put Price	Sold Put Strike	Sold Put Price	E(Gain)	E(Loss)	E(R)	BEPdn	BEPup	P(Gain)	MA	Gmax	Lmax	Omega	Opt. f	RTN
15.0	.10	27.5	8.95	.8852	-.8731	.0121	11.25	18.75	.4683	0.73%	8.75	-3.75	1.36	0.24%	1.00002
15.0	.10	30.0	11.45	.8856	-.8731	.0125	11.25	18.75	.4683	0.76%	11.25	-3.75	1.46	0.27%	1.00002

CSCO 13-Jul-03 Long Call Butterfly Spreads - Aug Expiration (34 Days)
CSCO Current Price = $18.57: Target Price = $18.57: Volatility = 0.398

Long Call Butterfly spreads (buy 1 low-strike Call and 1 high-strike Call and sell 2 mid-strike Calls):

Purch. Call Strike	Price	Sold Calls Strike	Price	Purch. Call Strike	Price	E(R)	BEPdn	BEPup	P(Gain)	MA	Gmax	Lmax	Omega	Opt. f	RTN
5.0	13.56	15.0	3.70	17.5	1.60	.0867	12.76	17.24	.2693	34.33%	2.24	-1.34	.66	27.01%	1.01063
5.0	13.56	17.5	1.60	20.0	.43	.1283	15.79	19.21	.5189	18.34%	1.71	-4.37	-1.69	15.41%	1.00996
5.0	13.56	20.0	.43	22.5	.12	.0994	17.82	22.18	.5610	8.21%	2.18	-6.40	-2.34	4.63%	1.00234
7.5	11.07	15.0	3.70	17.5	1.60	.0766	12.77	17.23	.2677	29.24%	2.23	-1.35	.66	23.02%	1.00811
7.5	11.07	17.5	1.60	20.0	.43	.1182	15.80	19.20	.5164	16.74%	1.70	-4.38	-1.69	14.23%	1.00847
7.5	11.07	20.0	.43	22.5	.12	.0893	17.83	22.17	.5588	7.36%	2.17	-6.41	-2.34	4.18%	1.00190
10.0	8.60	15.0	3.70	17.5	1.60	.0465	12.80	17.20	.2630	16.03%	2.20	-1.38	.67	12.64%	1.00280
10.0	8.60	17.5	1.60	20.0	.43	.0881	15.83	19.17	.5089	12.15%	1.67	-4.41	-1.69	10.64%	1.00471
10.0	8.60	20.0	.43	22.5	.12	.0592	17.86	22.14	.5520	4.83%	2.14	-6.44	-2.34	2.83%	1.00084
12.5	6.10	15.0	3.70	17.5	1.60	.0467	12.80	17.20	.2630	16.09%	2.20	-0.30	.72	12.67%	1.00282
12.5	6.10	17.5	1.60	20.0	.43	.0883	15.83	19.17	.5089	12.18%	1.67	-3.33	-1.63	10.72%	1.00474
12.5	6.10	20.0	.43	22.5	.12	.0594	17.86	22.14	.5520	4.84%	2.14	-5.36	-2.28	2.84%	1.00085
15.0	3.70	17.5	1.60	20.0	.43	.0157	15.93	19.07	.4832	2.13%	1.57	-0.93	-1.28	2.15%	1.00017
5.0	13.56	15.0	3.70	20.0	.43	.0765	11.59	18.41	.4716	6.45%	3.41	-1.59	.45	3.33%	1.00126
5.0	13.56	17.5	1.60	22.5	.12	.0789	15.48	19.52	.5923	5.76%	2.02	-4.06	-2.76	3.72%	1.00149
7.5	11.07	15.0	3.70	20.0	.43	.0664	11.60	18.40	.4698	5.57%	3.40	-1.60	.45	2.88%	1.00095
7.5	11.07	17.5	1.60	22.5	.12	.0689	15.49	19.51	.5901	5.01%	2.01	-4.07	-2.76	3.27%	1.00114
10.0	8.60	15.0	3.70	20.0	.43	.0363	11.63	18.37	.4644	3.00%	3.37	-1.63	.46	1.53%	1.00028
10.0	8.60	17.5	1.60	22.5	.12	.0388	15.52	19.48	.5833	2.81%	1.98	-4.10	-2.76	1.88%	1.00036
12.5	6.10	15.0	3.70	20.0	.43	.0365	11.63	18.37	.4645	3.01%	3.37	-1.63	.51	1.53%	1.00028
12.5	6.10	17.5	1.60	22.5	.12	.0389	15.52	19.48	.5833	2.82%	1.98	-3.02	-2.70	1.89%	1.00037
5.0	13.56	15.0	3.70	22.5	.12	.0271	11.28	18.72	.5264	1.54%	3.72	-3.78	-.61	0.66%	1.00009
7.5	11.07	15.0	3.70	22.5	.12	.0171	11.29	18.71	.5246	0.97%	3.71	-3.79	-.61	0.42%	1.00003

APPENDIX C
Details of Test Period Trades

Trade results (October, November, and December expirations)
(Detailed support for Table 9–3)

Opening trade			Expiration		Option 1						Option 2					Gain (loss)	BEP_{dn}	BEP_{up}	ER	L_{max}	f^*
Date	OEX		Date	Days	B/S	N	C/P	Strike	Price		B/S	N	C/P	Strike	Price						

Slope .3635: Target 519.56: Actual 518.12
No selection 15-Oct-03 519.56 17-Oct-03 3

Slope .3638: Target 526.63: Actual 511.77
Sold Put   15-Oct-03 519.56 21-Nov-03 38 S 1 P 495 4.47   4.47 490.53   2.79 67.11 1.49%
Put ratio spread 15-Oct-03 519.56 21-Nov-03 38 B 1 P 505 6.66 S 2 P 500 5.44 4.22 490.78 509.22 2.77 67.36 1.48%
                                                                        8.69

Slope .2497: Target 525.26: Actual 540.26
Sold Put   20-Nov-03 514.96 19-Dec-03 30 S 1 P 505 6.77   6.77 508.81   5.89 36.81 2.71%
Bull Put spread 20-Nov-03 514.96 19-Dec-03 30 B 1 P 490 3.50 S 1 P 500 5.50 2.00 498.00   1.64 8.00 11.18%
Short strangle   20-Nov-03 514.96 19-Dec-03 30 S 1 P 495 4.35 S 1 C 540 1.62 5.71 489.03 545.97 3.83 51.96 1.92%
Put ratio spread 20-Nov-03 514.96 19-Dec-03 30 B 1 P 515 6.10 S 2 P 505 6.77 7.44 487.56 522.44 8.41 26.34 3.82%
                                                                        21.92

Slope .2233: Target 522.01: Actual 540.26
Sold Put   22-Nov-03 511.77 19-Dec-03 28 S 1 P 500 5.45   5.45 494.55   4.87 33.46 2.99%
Short strangle   22-Nov-03 511.77 19-Dec-03 28 S 1 P 495 4.35 S 1 C 530 2.45 -3.56 488.20 536.80 3.18 54.17 1.84%
Put ratio spread 22-Nov-03 511.77 19-Dec-03 28 B 1 P 510 8.70 S 2 P 505 6.85 5.00 495.00 515 4.78 33.91 2.95%
                                                                        6.89

Slope .175: Target 523.66: Actual 540.26
Sold Put   27-Nov-03 521.21 19-Dec-03 23 S 1 P 505 2.72   2.72 502.28   1.86 38.53 2.59%
Put ratio spread 27-Nov-03 521.21 19-Dec-03 23 B 1 P 515 3.16 S 2 P 510 2.30 1.44 503.56 516.44 1.58 25.13 3.98%
                                                                        4.16

Slope .1468: Target 526.60: Actual 540.26
Sold Put   2-Dec-03 526.60 19-Dec-03 18 S 1 P 515 3.16   3.16 511.84   2.00 33.41 2.99%
Short strangle 2-Dec-03 526.60 19-Dec-03 18 S 1 P 505 1.65 S 1 C 545 0.75 2.40 502.60 547.4 1.76 32.22 3.10%
                                                                       5.56

Slope .1729: Target 524.05: Actual 540.26
Sold Put   6-Dec-03 523.51 19-Dec-03 14 S 1 P 520 3.00   3.00 515.55   1.67 31.60 3.16%
Short strangle 6-Dec-03 523.51 19-Dec-03 14 S 1 P 510 2.05 S 1 C 545 0.40 2.45 507.55 547.45 1.73 27.15 3.68%
                                                                       5.45
Total   52.67

Trade results (January expiration, 564.72)
(Detailed support for Tables 9–4 and 9–5)

	Opening trade		Expiration		Option 1						Option 2					Gain					
	Date	OEX	Date	Days	B/S	N	C/P	Strike	Price	B/S	N	C/P	Strike	Price	(loss)	BEP_{dn}	BEP_{up}	ER	L_{max}	f^*

Slope .1746: Target 522.01
Sold Put	22-Nov-03	511.77	16-Jan-04	56	S	1	P	490	6.94						6.94	483.06		6.24	45.07	2.22%
Put ratio spread	22-Nov-03	511.77	16-Jan-04	56	B	1	P	530	24.28	S	2	P	510	13.26	2.24	487.76	532.24	7.43	49.77	2.01%
															9.18					

Slope .1746: Target 527.02
Sold Put	27-Nov-03	521.21	16-Jan-04	51	S	1	P	500	5.40						5.40	494.60		4.08	54.65	1.83%
Put ratio spread	27-Nov-03	521.21	16-Jan-04	51	B	1	P	510	8.00	S	2	P	505	6.60	5.20	494.80	515.20	4.16	30.23	1.82%
															10.60					

Slope .1468: Target 526.60
Sold Put	2-Dec-03	526.60	16-Jan-04	46	S	1	P	510	5.94						5.94	504.06		3.77	52.33	1.91%
Put ratio spread	2-Dec-03	526.60	16-Jan-04	46	B	1	P	535	16.29	S	2	P	520	9.04	1.79	503.21	536.79	4.55	51.48	1.94%
															7.73					

Slope .1729: Target 527.40
Sold Put	6-Dec-03	523.61	16-Jan-04	42	S	1	P	510	6.36						6.36	503.64		4.45	49.89	2.00%
Short strangle	6-Dec-03	523.61	16-Jan-04	42	S	1	P	500	4.15	S	1	C	550	1.80	−8.77	494.05	555.95	3.89	57.29	1.74%
Put ratio spread	6-Dec-03	523.61	16-Jan-04	42	B	1	P	535	17.50	S	2	P	520	9.60	1.70	503.30	536.70	4.64	49.55	2.02%
															−0.71					

Slope .2033: Target 529.39
Sold Put	11-Dec-03	525.33	16-Jan-04	37	S	1	P	510	5.11						5.11	504.89		3.67	47.04	2.12%
Short strangle	11-Dec-03	525.33	16-Jan-04	37	S	1	P	500	3.32	S	1	C	550	1.82	−9.58	494.86	555.14	3.17	56.97	1.75%
Put ratio spread	11-Dec-03	525.33	16-Jan-04	37	B	1	P	535	15.29	S	2	P	520	8.10	0.91	506.31	533.69	4.09	48.46	2.06%
															−3.56					

Slope .2036: Target 530.16
Sold Put	12-Dec-03	530.16	16-Jan-04	36	S	1	P	515	4.71						4.71	510.29		2.55	51.09	1.96%
Put ratio spread	12-Dec-03	530.16	16-Jan-04	36	B	1	P	540	15.25	S	2	P	525	7.71	0.17	509.83	540.17	3.25	50.63	1.97%
															4.88					

Slope .2156: Target 531.78
| Put ratio spread | 13-Dec-03 | 531.78 | 16-Jan-04 | 35 | B | 1 | P | 535 | 11.30 | S | 2 | P | 525 | 7.00 | 2.70 | 512.30 | 537.70 | 2.89 | 50.74 | 1.97% |
| | | | | | | | | | | | | | | | 2.70 | | | | | |

358

(Continued)

Trade results (January expiration, 564.72)

(Detailed support for Tables 9–4 and 9–5)

Opening trade		Expiration			Option 1						Option 2					Gain (loss)	BEP_{dn}	BEP_{up}	ER	L_{max}	f^*
Date	OEX	Date	Days	B/S	N	C/P	Strike	Price	B/S	N	C/P	Strike	Price								

Slope .22.13: Target 530.47
Sold Put	16-Dec-03	530.47	16-Jan-03	32	S	1	P	515	4.60							4.60	510.40		2.88	45.94	2.17%
Short strangle	16-Dec-03	530.47	16-Jan-03	32	S	1	P	505	3.08	S	1	C	555	1.23		−5.41	500.69	559.31	3.06	46.55	2.15%
Put ratio spread	16-Dec-03	530.47	16-Jan-03		B	1	P	535	12.04	S	2	P	525	7.45		2.86	512.14	537.86	3.26	47.68	2.10%
																2.05					

Slope .2432: Target 534.75
Put ratio spread	17-Dec-03	534.75	16-Jan-03	31	B	1	P	535	9.14	S	2	P	525	5.70		2.26	512.74	537.26	3.10	44.53	2.24%
																2.26					

Slope .3947: Target 542.01
Sold Put	25-Dec-03	542.01	16-Jan-04	23	S	1	P	530	3.76							3.76	526.24		2.59	33.54	2.98%
Short strangle	25-Dec-03	542.01	16-Jan-04	23	S	1	P	525	2.85	S	1	C	560	1.35		−0.52	520.80	564.20	3.15	32.06	3.12%
Put ratio spread	25-Dec-03	542.01	16-Jan-04	23	B	1	P	550	12.10	S	2	P	540	7.06		2.02	527.98	552.02	3.77	35.28	2.83%
																5.26					

Slope .3942: Target 549.23
Sold Put	30-Dec-03	549.23	16-Jan-04	18	S	1	P	540	3.95							3.95	536.05		2.90	27.21	3.67%
Short strangle	30-Dec-03	549.23	16-Jan-04	18	S	1	P	540	3.95	S	1	C	560	2.32		1.55	533.73	566.27	4.35	26.56	3.76%
Put ratio spread	30-Dec-03	549.23	16-Jan-04	18	B	1	P	545	5.60	S	2	P	540	3.95		2.30	532.70	547.30	2.56	23.86	4.19%
																7.80					

Slope .4346: Target 549
Sold Put	3-Jan-04	549.99	16-Jan-04	14	S	1	P	545	4.56							4.56	540.44		2.94	25.48	3.92%
Short strangle	3-Jan-04	549.99	16-Jan-04	14	S	1	P	545	4.56	S	1	C	555	4.40		−0.76	536.04	563.96	5.67	23.44	4.26%
																3.80					

Slope .5966: Target 556.65
Sold Put	10-Jan-04	556.65	16-Jan-04	7	S	1	P	550	2.10							2.10	547.90		1.62	16.06	6.22%
Short strangle	10-Jan-04	556.65	16-Jan-04	7	S	1	P	550	2.10	S	1	C	565	1.05		3.15	546.85	568.15	2.40	15.01	6.65%
																5.25					

Total 57.24

Trade results (February expiration, 564.87)
(Detailed support for Tables 9–6 and 9–7)

	Opening trade		Expiration		Option 1						Option 2					Gain (loss)	BEP_{dn}	BEP_{up}	ER	L_{max}	f^*
	Date	OEX	Date	Days	B/S	N	C/P	Strike	Price	B/S	N	C/P	Strike	Price							
Slope .1746: Target 531.24																					
Sold Put	27-Nov-03	521.21	20-Feb-04	86	S	1	P	500	9.33						9.33	490.67		7.09	70.66	1.48%
Put ratio spread	27-Nov-03	521.21	20-Feb-04	86	B	1	P	530	21.54	S	2	P	510	12.36	3.18	486.82	533.18	6.18	66.91	1.50%
															12.51					
Slope .1468: Target 529.25																					
Sold Put	2-Dec-03	526.60	20-Feb-04	81	S	1	P	510	10.31						10.31	499.69		6.86	67.89	1.47%
Put ratio spread	2-Dec-03	526.60	20-Feb-04	81	B	1	P	540	23.79	S	2	P	520	13.64	3.49	496.51	543.49	7.28	64.71	1.54%
															13.80					
Slope .1729: Target 531.24																					
Sold Put	6-Dec-03	523.51	20-Feb-04	77	S	1	P	500	8.01						8.01	491.99		5.52	65.06	1.54%
Put ratio spread	6-Dec-03	523.51	20-Feb-04	77	B	1	P	540	25.09	S	2	P	520	14.42	3.75	496.25	543.75	6.96	69.32	1.44%
															11.76					
Slope .2033: Target 534.30																					
Sold Put	11-Dec-03	525.33	20-Feb-04	72	S	1	P	500	6.94						6.94	493.06		5.84	56.72	1.76%
Put ratio spread	11-Dec-03	525.33	20-Feb-04	72	B	1	P	540	22.99	S	2	P	520	12.83	2.67	497.33	542.67	6.63	60.99	1.64%
															9.61					
Slope .2213: Target 535.63																					
Sold Put	16-Dec-03	530.47	20-Feb-04	67	S	1	P	510	7.86						7.86	502.14		5.85	61.57	1.62%
Put ratio spread	16-Dec-03	530.47	20-Feb-04	67	B	1	P	530	14.67	S	2	P	520	10.79	6.91	503.09	536.91	6.19	62.52	1.60%
															14.77					

(Continued)

Trade results (February expiration, 564.87)
(Detailed support for Tables 9–6 and 9–7)

Opening trade			Expiration		Option 1						Option 2					Gain					
Date	OEX		Date	Days	B/S	N	C/P	Strike	Price	B/S	N	C/P	Strike	Price	(loss)	BEP_{dn}	BEP_{up}	ER	L_{max}	f^*

Slope .3947: Target 549.23
Sold Put	25-Dec-03	542.01	20-Feb-04	58	S	1	P	530	8.62						8.62	521.38		6.78	49.35	2.02%
Short strangle	25-Dec-03	542.01	20-Feb-04	58	S	1	P	520	6.07	S	1	C	565	3.45	9.52	510.48	574.52	6.01	64.54	1.55%
Put ratio spread	25-Dec-03	542.01	20-Feb-04	58	B	1	P	555	20.32	S	2	P	540	12.18	4.04	520.96	559.04	6.75	48.93	2.04%
															22.18					

Slope .3942: Target 549.23
Sold Put	30-Dec-03	549.23	20-Feb-04	53	S	1	P	540	9.36						9.36	530.64		6.01	48.89	2.04%
Short strangle	30-Dec-03	549.23	20-Feb-04	53	S	1	P	535	7.83	S	1	C	565	4.95	12.78	522.22	577.78	8.70	48.38	2.07%
Call ratio spread	30-Dec-03	549.23	20-Feb-04	53	B	1	C	555	8.72	S	2	C	560	6.76	4.93	550.20	569.80	3.24	56.36	1.77%
Put ratio spread	30-Dec-03	549.23	20-Feb-04	53	B	1	P	570	26.31	S	2	P	550	13.49	5.80	529.23	570.67	7.51	47.58	2.10%
															32.87					

Slope .4346: Target 552.96
Sold Put	3-Jan-04	549.99	20-Feb-04	49	S	1	P	540	9.07						9.07	530.93		7.00	42.02	2.38%
Short strangle	3-Jan-04	549.99	20-Feb-04	49	S	1	P	540	9.07	S	1	C	560	7.83	12.03	523.10	576.90	10.86	48.50	2.06%
Call ratio spread	3-Jan-04	549.99	20-Feb-04	49	B	1	C	535	22.92	S	2	C	550	12.80	2.81	532.32	567.68	5.07	57.72	1.73%
Put ratio spread	3-Jan-04	549.99	20-Feb-04	49	B	1	P	570	24.53	S	2	P	550	12.72	6.04	529.09	570.91	8.64	40.18	2.49%
															29.95					

Slope .611: Target 564.72
Sold Put	10-Jan-04	556.55	20-Feb-04	42	S	1	P	550	8.84						8.84	541.16		7.46	35.90	2.78%
Short strangle	10-Jan-04	556.55	20-Feb-04	42	S	1	P	545	7.06	S	1	C	570	4.70	11.76	533.24	581.76	6.96	49.42	2.02%
Put ratio spread	10-Jan-04	556.55	20-Feb-04	42	B	1	P	565	16.30	S	2	P	555	10.81	5.45	539.68	570.32	6.68	34.42	2.90%
															26.05					

361

(Continued)

Trade results (February expiration, 564.87)

(Detailed support for Tables 9–6 and 9–7)

	Opening trade		Expiration		Option 1					Option 2				Gain						
	Date	OEX	Date	Days	B/S	N	C/P	Strike	Price	B/S	N	C/P	Strike	Price	(loss)	BEP_{dn}	BEP_{up}	ER	L_{max}	f^*
Slope .8815: Target 578.87																				
Sold Put	22-Jan-04	568.64	20-Feb-04	30	S	1	P	555	4.05						4.05	550.95		3.71	30.69	3.26%
Short strangle	22-Jan-04	568.64	20-Feb-04	30	S	1	P	550	3.00	S	1	C	590	1.30	4.30	545.70	594.30	1.72	51.14	1.95%
Put ratio spread	22-Jan-04	568.64	20-Feb-04	30	B	1	P	575	12.71	S	2	P	565	7.39	11.94	552.93	577.07	3.40	32.67	3.06%
														20.29						
Slope .9355: Target 580.11																				
Sold Put	27-Jun-04	573.44	20-Feb-04	25	S	1	P	560	3.45						3.45	556.55		2.92	32.45	3.08%
Short strangle	27-Jan-04	573.44	20-Feb-04	25	S	1	P	555	2.52	S	1	C	600	0.65	3.17	551.83	603.17	2.28	38.94	2.57%
Put ratio spread	27-Jan-04	573.44	20-Feb-04	25	B	1	P	570	6.55	S	2	P	565	4.75	7.82	557.05	572.95	2.83	32.95	3.03%
														14.44						
Slope .9662: Target 571.52																				
Sold Put	1-Feb-04	560.31	20-Feb-04	21	S	1	P	545	2.80						2.80	542.20		2.43	34.79	2.87%
Put ratio spread	1-Feb-04	560.31	20-Feb-04	21	B	1	P	555	5.46	S	2	P	550	3.90	2.34	542.66	557.34	2.23	35.25	2.83%
														5.14						
Slope .9971: Target 577.38																				
Sold Put	7-Feb-04	566.06	20-Feb-04	14	S	1	P	550	1.68						1.68	548.32		1.58	23.15	4.31%
														1.68						
Total														215.05						

Trade results (March expiration, 543.68)
(Detailed support for Tables 9-8 and 9-9)

Opening trade		Expiration			Option 1						Option 2				Gain					
Date	OEX	Date	Days	B/S	N	C/P	Strike	Price	B/S	N	C/P	Strike	Price	(loss)	BEP_{dn}	BEP_{up}	ER	L_{max}	f^*

Slope .3947: Target 552.85
Sold Put	25-Dec-03	542.01	19-Mar-04	86	S	1	P	520	9.08						9.08	510.92		8.07	51.19	1.95%
Put ratio spread	25-Dec-03	542.01	19-Mar-04	86	B	1	P	560	26.89	S	2	P	550	21.05	18.89	524.79	575.21	12.02	65.06	1.54%
														27.97					

Slope .3942: Target 556.98
Sold Put	30-Dec-03	549.23	19-Mar-04	81	S	1	P	540	13.09						13.09	526.91		10.34	53.26	1.88%
Short strangle	30-Dec-03	549.23	19-Mar-04	81	S	1	P	530	9.70	S	1	C	570	6.17	15.87	514.13	585.87	10.58	69.09	1.45%
Put ratio spread	30-Dec-03	549.23	19-Mar-04	81	B	1	P	570	28.95	S	2	P	550	17.19	19.11	524.57	575.43	10.73	50.92	1.96%
														48.07					

Slope .4346: Target 560.99
Sold Put	3-Jan-04	549.99	19-Mar-04	77	S	1	P	540	12.59						12.59	527.41		10.85	46.65	2.14%
Short straddle	3-Jan-04	549.99	19-Mar-04	77	S	1	P	550	16.38	S	1	C	550	16.29	26.35	517.33	582.67	13.20	71.93	1.39%
Short strangle	3-Jan-04	549.99	19-Mar-04	77	S	1	P	540	12.59	S	1	C	560	11.15	23.74	516.26	583.74	12.65	70.86	1.41%
Put ratio spread	3-Jan-04	549.99	19-Mar-04	77	B	1	P	570	27.77	S	2	P	550	16.38	18.67	525.01	574.99	10.60	44.25	2.26%
														81.35					

Slope .5966: Target 567.68
Sold Put	10-Jan-04	556.55	19-Mar-04	70	S	1	P	540	8.83						8.83	531.17		8.12	39.45	2.53%
Short strangle	10-Jan-04	556.55	19-Mar-04	70	S	1	P	540	8.83	S	1	C	580	4.45	13.28	526.72	593.28	8.98	62.09	1.61%
Put ratio spread	10-Jan-04	556.55	19-Mar-04	70	B	1	P	580	29.64	S	2	P	560	16.83	7.70	535.98	584.02	10.19	44.26	2.26%
														29.81					

Slope .8481: Target 580.01
Sold Put	22-Jan-04	568.64	19-Mar-04	58	S	1	P	555	8.27						-3.05	546.73		7.07	47.45	2.11%
Short strangle	22-Jan-04	568.64	19-Mar-04	58	S	1	P	545	5.74	S	1	C	595	2.73	7.15	536.53	603.47	4.72	70.33	1.42%
														4.10					

363

(Continued)

Trade results (March expiration, 543.68)

(Detailed support for Tables 9–8 and 9–9)

Opening trade		Expiration			Option 1					Option 2					Gain					
Date	OEX	Date	Days	B/S	N	C/P	Strike	Price	B/S	N	C/P	Strike	Price	(loss)	BEP_{dn}	BEP_{up}	ER	L_{max}	f^*

Slope .9355: Target 584.90
Sold Put	27-Jan-04	573.44	19-Mar-04	53	S	1	P	560	7.76						−8.56	552.24		6.56	47.72	2.09%
Put ratio spread	27-Jan-04	573.44	19-Mar-04	53	B	1	P	570	11.41	S	2	P	565	9.42	−8.89	552.57	577.43	6.54	48.05	2.08%
														−17.45					

Slope : Target 571.52
Sold Put	31-Jan-04	560.31	19-Mar-04	49	S	1	P	540	6.30						6.30	533.70		5.08	57.16	1.75%
Put ratio spread	31-Jan-04	560.31	19-Mar-04	49	B	1	P	550	9.14	S	2	P	545	7.67	9.88	533.80	556.20	5.21	57.26	1.74%
														16.18					

Slope : Target 577.38
Sold Put	7-Feb-04	566.06	19-Mar-04	42	S	1	P	545	5.11						3.79	539.89		4.31	49.93	2.00%
Put ratio spread	7-Feb-04	566.06	19-Mar-04	42	B	1	P	555	7.77	S	2	P	550	6.34	3.59	540.09	559.91	4.33	50.13	1.99%
														7.38					

Slope : Target 577.24
Sold Put	14-Feb-04	565.92	19-Mar-04	35	S	1	P	545	3.71						2.39	541.29		3.16	44.39	2.25%
Put ratio spread	14-Feb-04	565.92	19-Mar-04	35	B	1	P	555	5.76	S	2	P	550	4.56	2.04	541.64	558.36	3.03	44.74	2.23%
														4.43					

Slope : Target 576.80
Sold Put	27-Feb-04	565.49	19-Mar-04	22	S	1	P	550	5.06						−3.82	547.50		2.26	30.27	3.30%
Put ratio spread	27-Feb-04	565.49	19-Mar-04	22	B	1	P	560		S	2	P	550	3.70	−3.98	547.66	562.34	2.34	30.43	3.28%
														−7.80					

Total 194.04

INDEX

Addition, probability rules for, 46–48
Advantage, mathematical, 128–129
Agency securities, 5–6, 13
Algebra overview, 30–34
Algorithms (*See* Search algorithms)
American-style options, 24–25, 73–74, 76–77, 88
Appraisal, real estate, 12–13
Arbitrage, 74
Area under the curve, 39, 57–62, 187, 190, 282
Arithmetic mean, 34–36
Assets, wasting, 70, 90–91, 156
At-the-money Call deltas, 163–165
Averages, moving, 253–255
(*See also* Mean)

Backspreads
 Calls, 112–114, 242–245, 305, 338, 353
 Puts, 114–116, 245–248, 305, 339
Bear Call spreads, 94–97, 214, 216–217, 330, 346
Bear Put spreads, 97–99, 220, 222–223, 329, 348
Bearish strategies, 83, 84
Bell-shaped curve, 61
BEP (break-even stock price), 80
 (*See also* Expected results; Spreads)
Bernoulli equivalents, 199–200
 (*See also* Expected results)
Bernoulli trials, 50–51, 132, 133
Binary search algorithm, 269–270
Binomial distribution, 49–50, 52–53
Binomial options pricing model, 72
Black-Scholes options pricing model, 72–74, 155, 183, 317
 (*See also* Expected results)
Bonds, 4–5, 6–7
Break-even stock price (BEP), 80
 (*See also* Expected results; Spreads)
Bull Call spreads, 92–94, 212–215, 328, 345

Bull Put spreads
 expected results, 217–221, 327
 sample output, 347
 strategy overview, 96–97
 strategy testing, 306, 308–313
Bullish strategies, 81, 88
Butterfly spreads, 110–118, 248–252, 340, 354

Calendar spreads, 107, 122
Call backspreads, 112–114, 242–245, 305, 338, 353
Call ratio spreads, 107–109, 235–239, 310, 311, 335, 351
Calls
 at-the-money Call deltas, 163–165
 backspreads, 112–114, 242–245, 305, 338, 353
 bear Call spreads, 94–97, 214, 216–217, 330, 346
 bull Call spreads, 92–94, 212–215, 328, 345
 defined, 16, 17, 70, 74
 long Call butterfly spreads, 110–118, 248–252, 340, 354
 prices of, 70–78, 302–303
 purchasing, 79, 80–83, 191–199, 323
 Put/Call parity, 74, 76, 121
 Put/Call ratio, 279–280
 ratio spreads, 107–109, 235–239, 310, 311, 336, 351
 (*See also* Covered Calls; Writing calls)
CD software (*See* Software)
Central limit theorem, 281–284
Central tendency (*See* Statistical measures)
Cisco (*See* Expected results)
Classes of data, 35–36
Closed-form solutions, 187–192
Codes, ticket symbols, 21–23
Collar spreads, 121–122
Commissions, 78–79

365

Commodity futures and options, 13–16, 25–28
 (*See also specific topics*)
Commodity futures contracts, 13–17
Compound interest rate, 130, 154
Compounding, 130
COMPX (Nasdaq Composite Index), 10, 24
Contingent orders, 79
Continuous method for dividends, 73–76
Continuous probability distribution, 60–64, 124, 147
Contracts, futures, 13–17, 25–28
 (*See also specific topics*)
Conversion position, 121
Corporate bonds, 6–7
Covered Calls
 defined, 20
 expected results, 208, 210–212, 331
 sample output, 331, 349
 strategy overview, 89–91
Covered Puts, 91
Curves
 area under, 39, 57–62, 187, 190, 282
 bell-shaped, 61
 fitted to nonlinear data, 264–268
 normal, 60–64, 147–151, 282–283
 parabolas, 256, 260–264
 volatility of, expected results, 198–199

DailyCheck.exe software
 and *Expectation.exe*, 185, 290–295, 321–340
 input, 290–292, 296–299
 overview, 289–290
 results of trades, 185, 186
 sample output, 341–354
 strategy selection, 300–302
 target prices, 302–303
Data sources, options, 70–72
de Mere, Chevalier (Antoine Gomband), 44–45, 51
Delta Δ (mathematical notation), 34, 57–58
Delta Δ (volatility), 163–165, 317
Delta-neutral hedging, 174–177
Density functions, 60–62
Derivatives (investment), 16
Derivatives (math), 53–57, 58, 149, 187–191
Dice games (*See* Probability distributions)

Differentials, 53–57, 58, 149, 187–191
Discrete method for dividends, 75
Discrete probability distribution, 48–52, 124–128, 147
Distribution, statistical, 36–38, 48–53, 60–67
 (*See also* Probability distributions)
Dividends, 74–76, 290, 292
Division, rules for, 31, 32
Drawdowns, 146

Elasticity of volatility, lambda λ, 174
Equations
 first-order, straight line, 255–260
 quadratic equation, 260–261
 second-order, for parabolas, 260–264
Equities, 7–10, 16–23
Equity options, 17
$E(R)$ (*See* Expected results)
Error function erf(x), 190
Euler number, 32–33
European-style options, 24–25, 73–74, 76–77
Excel software, 29, 33, 62, 190, 259, 264, 280
Exchange-traded funds (ETFs), 10–11
Exchanges, 2–4, 14–16, 17
Expectation.exe software, 185, 290–295, 321–340
Expected results $E(R)$, 185–252
 bear Call spreads, 214, 216–217, 330
 bear Put spreads, 220, 222–223, 329
 Bernoulli equivalents, 199–200
 bull Call spreads, 212–215, 328
 bull Put spreads, 217–221, 327
 Call backspreads, 242–245, 305, 338
 Call ratio spreads, 235–239, 336
 closed-form solutions, 187–192
 covered Calls, 208, 210–212, 331
 and expiration, 304–313, 314
 long Call butterfly spreads, 248–252, 340, 354
 long straddle spreads, 225–228, 305, 332, 350
 long strangle spreads, 230–233, 305, 334
 maximum gains and losses, 191–192
 naked options, closed-form, 187–192
 purchasing Calls, 191–199, 323
 purchasing Puts, 200–202, 325
 Put backspreads, 245–248, 305, 339
 Put ratio spreads, 239–242, 305, 337

Expected results $E(R)$ (cont.)
  short straddle spreads, 228–230, 305, 333
  short strangle spreads, 233–235, 305–306, 308–313, 335
  simulation, and optimal position size, 143–147, 151–153
  strategy testing, 304–314
  test criteria, 304–305
  volatility curve, 198–199
  writing Calls, 202, 204–205, 206, 324
  writing Puts, 205, 207–208, 209, 326
  (See also Position size, optimal)
Expiration
  codes for, 21
  dates for, 16, 20–21, 291–292
  expected results, 304–313, 314
  options expire worthless, 20
Exponential function, curve fitting, 264–265
Exponents, 30–32
Extreme value determination, 268–269

Factorials, 33
Federal agency securities, 5–6, 13
de Fermat, Pierre, 44
Fibonacci series, 271–273
Financial products, 1–28
  agency securities, 5–6, 13
  bonds, 4–5, 6–7
  commodity futures, 13–16, 25–28
  defined, 1–2
  equities, 7–10, 16–23
  exchange-traded funds (ETFs), 10–11
  exchanges, 2–4
  federal agency securities, 5–6, 13
  fixed-income (debt) securities, 4–5
  futures contracts and options, 13–17, 25–28
  index options, 23–25
  investment companies, 8
  mutual funds, 8–9
  options overview, 16–25, 69–70
  real estate investments, 11–13
  selection criteria, 2
  stock, 7–10, 16–23
  treasury securities, 5
  unit investment trust (UIT), 9, 10
  (See also Options, strategy and structure)
First-order equations for straight line, 255–260

Forecasting, volatility, 180–183
Functional notation $f(x)$, 55, 57, 60
Futures contracts and options, 13–17, 25–28
  (See also specific topics)

Gains, 191–192
  (See also Expected results)
Gamma Γ, volatility, 165–169
Gaussian distribution, 61
Geometric mean G, 37–38, 151–152
Geometric mean return per event (RTN), 132–134, 138–139
Golden ratio search algorithm, 270–273, 274
"The Greeks" (See Volatility and price sensitivity)

Harmonic mean H, 38
Hedging, 14, 70, 91, 174–177
Histograms, 36–37, 57
Historical volatility, 154–162
  calculating, 155–156, 160–162
  defined, 154–155
  probability distribution, 159–160
  sources for, 160
  time effects on, 156–159
Horizontal spreads, 122

Implied volatility (omega Ω), 162–163, 198–199, 278, 299–300
In-the-money options, 70, 82, 83
Index options, 23–25
Indexes, equity, 9–10
Indicators, 279
"Insurance," trade, 313, 314–316
Integration and integrals, 57–60, 148–148
Interest rates, 130, 154, 290
Investment companies and funds, 8–9
  (See also Financial products)
Investment return, 129–130

Kelly criteria, 132, 138, 140
Kurtosis, 285–286

Lambda λ, elasticity of volatility, 174
LEAPS (long-term equity options), 21–23
Lenders, real estate investments, 11–13

Leptokurtic returns, 178, 285–286
Limits, mathematical, 33
Linear regression, 257–260
Linear results function (*See* Options, strategy and structure; Probability distributions)
Lines, straight, 255–260
LN (natural logs), 33–34
Log-normal distribution, 63–67, 150, 154, 187
Logarithmic function, curve fitting, 265–266
Logarithms, 31–34
Long Call butterfly spreads, 110–118, 248–252, 340, 354
Long straddle spreads, 100, 225–228, 305, 332, 350
Long strangle spreads, 103–104, 230–233, 305, 334, 350
Long-term equity options (LEAPS), 21–23
Losses, 191–192
(*See also* Expected results)

MA (mathematical advantage), 128–129, 150–151
(*See also* Expected results)
Margin requirements, 78–79, 90–91
(*See also* Naked options; Spreads)
Margins, 8, 15–16, 78–79
Market price, 122
Math basics, 30–67
addition, probability rules for, 46–48
algebra overview, 30–34
area under the curve, 39, 57–62, 187, 190, 282
central limit theorem, 281–284
central tendency, 34–44
derivatives and differentials, 53–57, 58, 149, 187–191
distribution, 36–38, 48–53, 60–67
division, rules for, 31, 32
exponents, 30–32
kurtosis, 285–286
log-normal distribution, 63–67, 150, 154, 187
logarithms, 31–34
median, 39–40
moments about mean, 284–285
multiplication, rules for, 30, 31, 45–46
parabolas, 256, 260–264

Math basics (*cont.*)
polynomial approximation to normal probability, 280–281
Put/Call ratio, 279–280
quadratic equation, 260–261
random sampling, 286–288
skewness, 285–286
standard deviation σ, 40–43, 52, 191–192, 280–281, 284
straight lines, 255–260
variability, 40–43
variance, 41–42
(*See also* Curves; Mean; Probability distributions; Search algorithms)
Mathematical advantage (*MA*), 128–129, 150–151
(*See also* Expected results)
Mathematical expectation, 123–124
Maximum gains and losses, 191–192
(*See also* Expected results)
Mean (average)
binomial distributions, 52
defined, 34
formula, 30
historical volatility, 155–156
moment about mean, 284–285
moving averages, 253–255
standard error of, 286–287
as statistical measure, 34–39
and volatility, 163
Median, 39–40
Method of least squares, 257
Microsoft Excel, 29, 33, 62, 190, 259, 264, 280
Mode, 39, 40
Moments about mean, 284–285
Mortgages, 11–13
Moving averages, 253–255
(*See also* Mean [average])
Multiple outcomes, optimal position size, 137–143
Multiplication, rules for, 30, 31, 45–46
Municipal bonds, 6
Mutual funds, 8–9

Naked options, 79–88
closed-form expected results, 187–192
defined, 20, 70, 79–81
purchasing Calls, 80–83
purchasing Puts, 83–84
sample output, 343–344

Index

Naked options (*cont.*)
   writing Calls, 84–86
   writing Puts, 86–88
   (*See also* Spreads)
Nasdaq-100 Tracking Stock (QQQ), 10, 24
Nasdaq Composite Index (COMPX), 10, 24
Natural logs (ln), 33–34
Newton-Raphson search algorithm, 275–278
95 percent confidence interval, 287
Normal curves, 60–64, 147–151, 282–283
Normal distribution, 60–63, 148, 154–155

OEX (Standard & Poor's 100), 10, 24, 314, 315–318
Omega Ω implied volatility, 162–163, 198–199, 278, 299–300
Optimal f^*, 132–135
   (*See also* Expected results; Position size, optimal)
Optimal position size (*See* Position size, optimal)
Options, defined, 16, 69
Options, strategy and structure, 69–122
   American vs. European-style options, 24–25, 73–74, 76–77, 88
   Call price-stock price relationship, 78
   combination strategies, 89–106
   commissions and margin requirements, 78–79
   contingent orders, 79
   contracts, 13–17, 25–26
   data sources, 70–72
   dividends, 74–76, 290, 292
   equities, 16–23
   futures, 25–28
   index, 23–25
   insurance, 313, 315–316
   naked, 79–88
   pricing models, 72–74, 122
   purchasing a Call, 79, 80–83
   purchasing a Put, 79, 83–84
   risk, and safe approaches, 312–313
   spreads, 107–122
   stop loss orders, 316–318
   strategy selection, 300–302, 303–305, 341–354

Options, strategy and structure (*cont.*)
   strategy testing, 304–312
   synthetic positions, 119–121
   (*See also under* Purchasing; Spreads; Writing)
Out-of-the-money options, 70, 83
Outcomes, optimal position size
   multiple, 137–143
   single, 130–137

Parabolas, 256, 260–264
Parabolic interpolation search algorithm, 273–275, 275
Partial derivatives, 56–57
Pascal, Blaise, 44–45, 50
Point-slope form, 255–256
Poisson distribution, 282–283
Polynomial approximation to normal probability, 280–281
Position, open or closed, 19–20
Position size, optimal, 130–152
   expected results, 130–152
   multiple outcomes, 137–143
   normal probability distribution approximation, 147–151
   results simulation and comparison, 143–147, 151–153
   single outcome, 130–137
   test strategies, 318–319, 355–358
Power (exponents), 30–32
Power function, curve fitting, 266–268
Premiums, 16–18, 20, 69, 76–77, 315–316
Prices
   pricing models, 72–74, 122
   Puts, 70–78
   spot price, 26
   strike prices, 16–18, 21–22, 24, 70, 296
   target prices, 290, 302–303
   (*See also* Volatility and price sensitivity)
Probability density function, 60, 61, 124–125
Probability distributions, 48–67, 123–130
   binomial, 52–53
   concept and theory of, 43–45
   continuous, and normal curve, 60–64
   derivatives and differentials, 53–57
   discrete distributions, 48–52, 75, 124–128

Probability distributions (*cont.*)
  historical volatility, 159–160
  integration and integrals, 57–60
  investment return, 129–130
  log-normal distribution, 63–67, 150, 187
  mathematical advantage, 128–129
  mathematical expectation, 123–124
  normal probability distribution, 147–148
  polynomial approximation to normal, 280–281
  rules of, 45–48
  symbolic expression of, 44
  (*See also* Position size, optimal)
Protective Puts, 91–92
Purchasing options
  Calls, 79, 80–83, 191–19, 323
  Puts, 79, 83–84, 200–202, 323, 325
Put/Call parity, 74, 76, 121
Put/Call ratio, 279–280
Put ratio spreads
  expected results, 239–242, 305, 337
  sample output, 352
  strategy overview, 109–112
  strategy testing, 308–313
Puts
  backspreads, 114–116, 245–248, 305, 339
  bear Put spreads, 97–99, 220, 222–223, 329, 348
  covered, 91
  defined, 16, 17, 70, 74
  prices of, 70–78
  protective, 91–92
  purchasing, 79, 83–84, 200–202, 323, 325
  Put/Call parity, 74, 76, 121
  Put/Call ratio, 279–280
  ratio spreads, 239–242, 305, 337
  sold Put screen, *Expectation.exe*, 293–295
  (*See also* Bull Put spreads; Put ratio spreads; Writing Puts)

QQQ (Nasdaq-100 Tracking Stock), 10, 24
Quadratic equation, 260–261

Random sampling, 286–288
Range, 41, 161

Ratios, 239–242, 305, 337
  Call ratio spreads, 107–109, 235–239, 310, 311, 336, 351
  golden ratio search algorithm, 270–273, 274
  Put/Call ratio, 279–280
  (*See also* Put ratio spreads)
Real estate investments, 11–13
Regression, linear, 257–260
Results from trades (*See* Expected results)
Results function
  defined, 123
  discrete model, 124–125, 127
  normal probability distribution, 147–148
  purchasing Calls, 80–81
  purchasing Puts, 84
  writing Calls, 85
  writing Puts, 87
  (*See also* Expected results; Spreads)
Returns
  geometric mean return per event (RTN), 132–134, 138–139
  investment return, 129–130
  leptokurtic, 178, 285–286
  (*See also* Expected results)
Rho ρ volatility, 172–174
Risk, and safe approaches, 13–14, 312–313
RTN (geometric mean return per event), 132–134, 138–139

Sampling, random, 286–288
Search algorithms
  binary, 269–270
  defined, 269
  golden ratio, 270–273, 274
  Newton-Raphson, 275–278
  parabolic interpolation, 273, 275
Second-order equations for parabolas, 260–264
Selling options (*See under* Writing)
Sensitivity (*See* Volatility and price sensitivity)
Short straddle spreads, 100–101, 228–230, 305, 333
Short strangle spreads
  expected results, 233–235, 305, 306, 308–313, 335
  strategy overview, 105–106

Index

Sigma
    standard deviation σ, 40–43, 52, 191–192, 280–281, 284
    summation Σ, 30
Simulation of results, optimal position size, 143–147, 151–153
Single outcome optimal position size, 130–137
Skewness, 285–286
Slope, 191, 255
Software
    Expectation.exe on CD, 185, 290–295, 321–340
    Microsoft Excel, 29, 33, 62, 190, 259, 264, 280
    (*See also DailyCheck.exe* software)
Sold Put screen, *Expectation.exe*, 293–295
Spot price, 26
Spreads, 107–122, 233–235, 305, 335
    bear Call, 94–97, 214, 216–217, 330, 346
    bear Put, 97–99, 220, 222–223, 329, 348
    bull Call, 92–94, 212–215, 328, 345
    butterfly, 116–118, 248–252, 340, 354
    calendar, 107, 122
    Call backspreads, 112–114, 338, 353
    Call ratio, 107–109, 310, 311, 336, 351
    collar, 121–122
    conversion position, 121
    expected results, 185, 192–224
    insurance, 313, 315–316
    long Call butterfly, 248–252, 340, 354
    Put backspreads, 114–116, 339
    Put ratio, 109–112, 306, 308–313, 337, 352
    straddle, 99–102, 225–230, 332, 333, 350
    synthetic position, 119–121
    (*See also* Bull Put spreads; Strangle spreads)
Standard & Poor's 100 (OEX), 10, 24, 314, 315–318
Standard deviation σ, 40–43, 52, 191–192, 280–281, 284
    (*See also* Historical volatility)
Standard error of the mean, 286–287
Standard normal curve, 61–62
Statistical measures, 34–44
    classes of data, 35–36

Statistical measures (*cont.*)
    defined, 34
    distribution, 36–38, 48–53, 60–67
    frequency distributions, 36–38
    median, 39, 40
    mode, 39–40
    standard deviation, 40–43, 52, 191–192, 280–281, 284
    variability, 40–43
    (*See also* Mean; Probability distributions)
Statistics and central tendency, 34–44
    (*See also* Probability distributions)
Stock, 7–10, 16–23
Stock equities, 7–10, 16–23
Stock equity options, 17
Stop loss orders, 316–318
Straddle spreads, 99–102, 225–230, 332, 333, 350
Straight lines, 255–260
Strangle spreads
    long, 103–104, 230–233, 334, 350
    short, 105–106, 233–235, 306, 308–313, 335
    strategy overview, 103–106
    (*See also* Short strangle spreads)
Strategy testing, 304–314
    (*See also* Options, strategy and structure)
Strike price codes, 21–22
Strike prices, 16–18, 21–22, 24, 70, 78, 296
Student t distribution, 288

Tangent lines, 256–257
Target prices, 290, 302–303
Test criteria, expected results, 304–305
Theta Θ volatility, 170–172
Time factors
    compound interest rate, 130, 154
    expiration date, 16, 20–21
    historical volatility, 156–159
    options, 69–70
    returns, 129–130
    (*See also* Historical volatility)
Trade date, *Expectation.exe*, 290–291
Trade reports, *DailyCheck.exe*, 297–299
Trades (*See specific topics*)
Treasury securities, 5
Trends, 253
Two-point form, 257

Unit investment trust (UIT), 9, 10

Variability, 40–43
Variables, notations for, 72, 107, 116, 130, 131, 132
Variance, 41–42, 183
Vega (or kappa) volatility, 169–170
Vertical spreads, 92
Vince, Ralph, 137–139
Visualization (*See* Options, strategy and structure)
Volatility and price sensitivity, 153–183
   defined, 153, 154
   delta Δ, 163–165
   delta-neutral hedging, 174–177
   elasticity, 174
   forecasting of, 180–183
   gamma Γ, 165–169
   "the Greeks," 163–177, 198
   historical, 154–162, 300, 301
   implied, 162–163, 198–199, 278, 299–300
   lambda λ elasticity, 174
   omega Ω, 198–199

Volatility and price sensitivity (*cont.*)
   rho ρ, 172–174
   theta Θ, 170–172
   vega (or kappa), 169–170
   volatility skew, 177–180
Volatility curve, 198–199

Wasting assets, 70, 90–91, 156
Weighted average, 157
Writing Calls
   benefits, 19–20
   expected results, 202, 204–205, 206, 324
   sample output, 323
   strategy overview, 79, 84–86
Writing Puts
   benefits, 19–20
   expected results, 205, 207–208, 209, 326
   sample output, 326
   strategy overview, 86–88
   strategy testing, 306, 308–313

Z scale, 61–62, 187–189

ABOUT THE AUTHOR

Mr. Reehl has been trading options for over 15 years. His undergraduate degree is in business administration, with a minor in mathematics. After receiving an MBA in finance and economics from the University of California at Berkeley, he spent the next 10 years with Price Waterhouse & Co. (now PriceWaterhouseCoopers), earning his CPA license along the way. While there, he specialized in financial consulting.

Mr. Reehl served as the president of a division of a Fortune 500 NYSE-listed manufacturing company and has held several senior executive positions with other companies, both public and private.

For the 10 years prior to his recent retirement, he served as a financial and economic advisor in bankruptcy matters, testifying as an expert witness in over 250 cases, becoming a court-appointed mediator, and publishing several articles in the *California Bankruptcy Journal*. During that period, he served as Managing Partner of Squar, Milner & Reehl (now Squar, Milner, Reehl & Williamson, LLP), an accounting and business consulting firm in Newport Beach, California.

Mr. Reehl lives in southern California with his wife, Kathryn.

CD-ROM WARRANTY

This software is protected by both United States copyright law and international copyright treaty provision. You must treat this software just like a book. By saying "just like a book," McGraw-Hill means, for example, that this software may be used by any number of people and may be freely moved from one computer location to another, so long as there is no possibility of its being used at one location or on one computer while it also is being used at another. Just as a book cannot be read by two different people in two different places at the same time, neither can the software be used by two different people in two different places at the same time (unless, of course, McGraw-Hill's copyright is being violated).

LIMITED WARRANTY

Customers who have problems installing or running a McGraw-Hill CD should consult our online technical support site at http://books.mcgraw-hill.com/techsupport. McGraw-Hill takes great care to provide you with top-quality software, thoroughly checked to prevent virus infections. McGraw-Hill warrants the physical CD-ROM contained herein to be free of defects in materials and workmanship for a period of sixty days from the purchase date. If McGraw-Hill receives written notification within the warranty period of defects in materials or workmanship, and such notification is determined by McGraw-Hill to be correct, McGraw-Hill will replace the defective CD-ROM. Send requests to:

McGraw-Hill
Customer Services
P.O. Box 545
Blacklick, OH 43004-0545

The entire and exclusive liability and remedy for breach of this Limited Warranty shall be limited to replacement of a defective CD-ROM and shall not include or extend to any claim for or right to cover any other damages, including, but not limited to, loss of profit, data, or use of the software, or special, incidental, or consequential damages or other similar claims, even if McGraw-Hill has been specifically advised of the possibility of such damages. In no event will McGraw-Hill's liability for any damages to you or any other person even exceed the lower of suggested list price or actual price paid for the license to use the software, regardless of any form of the claim.

McGRAW-HILL SPECIFICALLY DISCLAIMS ALL OTHER WARRANTIES, EXPRESS OR IMPLIED, INCLUDING, BUT NOT LIMITED TO, ANY IMPLIED WARRANTY OF MERCHANTABILITY, OR FITNESS FOR A PARTICULAR PURPOSE.

Specifically, McGraw-Hill makes no representation or warranty that the software is fit for any particular purpose and any implied warranty of merchantability is limited to the sixty-day duration of the Limited Warranty covering the physical CD-ROM only (and not the software) and is otherwise expressly and specifically disclaimed.

This limited warranty gives you specific legal rights; you may have others which may vary from state to state. Some states do not allow the exclusion of incidental or consequential damages, or the limitation on how long an implied warranty lasts, so some of the above may not apply to you.